Causation and Explanation

Topics in Contemporary Philosophy

Causation and Explanation

edited by Joseph Keim Campbell, Michael O'Rourke, and Harry Silverstein

A Bradford Book

The MIT Press

Cambridge, Massachusetts

London, England

#73926881
¡12818938

MIT Press books may be purchased at special quantity discounts for business or sales promotional use. For information, please email special_sales@mitpress.mit.edu or write to Special Sales Department, The MIT Press, 55 Hayward Street, Cambridge, MA 02142.

This book was set in Stone Serif and Stone Sans on 3B2 by Asco Typesetters, Hong Kong, and was printed and bound in the United States of America.

Library of Congress Cataloging-in-Publication Data

Causation and explanation / edited by Joseph Keim Campbell, Michael O'Rourke, and Harry S. Silverstein.
     p.   cm.—(Topics in contemporary philosophy; v. 4)
"A Bradford Book."
Includes bibliographical references and index.
ISBN 978-0-262-03363-3 (hardcover : alk. paper)—ISBN 978-0-262-53290-7 (pbk. : alk. paper)
1. Causation. 2. Explanation. I. Campbell, Joseph Keim, 1958–. II. O'Rourke, Michael, 1963–. III. Silverstein, Harry S.
BD541.C193   2007
122—dc22   2006033531

10 9 8 7 6 5 4 3 2 1

Contents

Acknowledgments   vii

Introduction   ix
Raymond Dacey

1 Explaining Four Psychological Asymmetries in Causal Reasoning: Implications of Causal Assumptions for Coherence   1
Patricia W. Cheng, Laura R. Novick, Mimi Liljeholm, and Christina Ford

2 Causality and Computation   33
Patrick Suppes

3 Actual Causes and Thought Experiments   43
Clark Glymour and Frank Wimberly

4 What's Wrong with Neuron Diagrams?   69
Christopher Hitchcock

5 Mackie Remixed   93
Michael Strevens

6 Occasional Causes   119
Russell Wahl

7 In Defense of Explanatory Deductivism   133
Bruce Glymour

8 Goal-Directed Action and Teleological Explanation   155
Scott R. Sehon

9 Van Fraassen's Dutch Book Argument against Explanationism   171
Dorit Ganson

10   Counterfactuals in Economics: A Commentary   191
Nancy Cartwright

11   Why Don't You Want to Be Rich? Preference Explanation on the Basis
of Causal Structure   217
Till Grüne-Yanoff

12   Decisions, Intentions, Urges, and Free Will: Why Libet Has Not Shown
What He Says He Has   241
Alfred R. Mele

13   Constitutive Overdetermination   265
L. A. Paul

14   *Ex nihilo nihil fit*: Arguments New and Old for the Principle of
Sufficient Reason   291
Alexander Pruss

Index   311

Acknowledgments

This volume contains papers that were presented in their original form at the sixth annual Inland Northwest Philosophy Conference (INPC) in Moscow, Idaho and Pullman, Washington in April 2003. Hosted by the philosophy departments of Washington State University and the University of Idaho, the INPC brings about a hundred outstanding philosophers and other scholars to the hills of the Palouse region each spring. Presenters are encouraged to submit written versions of their work for the associated volume and, after a process of peer evaluation, a few of these are selected for inclusion in the volume. There are many fine submissions that could not be included owing simply to space limitations, and we regret that we could not publish more of these papers.

Many people contributed to the production of this volume, and we would like to acknowledge and thank them. We owe special thanks to Raymond Dacey for writing the opening chapter of this volume. Ray Dacey, Bruce Glymour, Clark Glymour, Ned Hall, Gary Hardcastle, Elizabeth Harman, Dan Hausman, Ken Himma, Christopher Hitchcock, Charlie Huenemann, Anne Jacobson, Elisabeth Lloyd, Sarah McGrath, Peter Murphy, L. A. Paul, Marcelo Sabates, Carolina Sartorio, Michael Strevens, and Jim Woodward refereed submissions. We would also like to thank the members of the editorial board of this series, Topics in Contemporary Philosophy, who are listed separately in this volume.

Administrators and chairs from both universities, including Robert Bates, Barbara Couture, Charles Hatch, Robert Hoover, Douglas Lind, James Peterson, Brian Pitcher, Lane Rawlins, David Shier, and Joseph Zeller, provided support to the conference and thus indirectly to this volume. The conference also received generous financial support through a grant from the Idaho Humanities Council to fund the Public Forum, a public event associated with the INPC in which panelists and audience members discuss an issue of significant public interest related to the conference theme. Both the conference and this volume have benefited enormously from the efforts of departmental administrative managers Dee Dee Torgeson and Vilyen Pidgornyy.

Finally, we would like to thank Delphine Keim Campbell, Lorinda Knight, and Rebecca O'Rourke, without whose support, efforts, and understanding this volume could not exist.

Introduction

Raymond Dacey

The Inland Northwest Philosophy Conference (INPC) is held annually and hosted jointly by the philosophy departments at Washington State University and the University of Idaho. The papers included here are extensions of presentations made at the sixth INPC, held in the spring of 2003. The topic of the conference was Causation and Explanation. The conference, by design, treated the topic widely, and the papers presented at the conference examined many issues in, and approaches to, explanation and causation.

On the face of it, we can conclude that all is well in the philosophical analyses of explanation and causation. We learn from Pearl (2000) that the theory of causation has been completed and mathematized. We learn from Salmon that the theory of explanation is completed when we put "cause" back into "because" (1998, p. 93), in particular, by establishing that explanations are not simply arguments (as per Salmon 1977). Thus, if we take the completed theory of causation to provide the explication of cause, and employ the resulting notion of cause as the foundation of explanation—then both causation and explanation are resolved as philosophical issues. Needless to say, not everyone agrees with this position.

In fact, explanation and causation present particularly difficult philosophical problems. As such, they have attracted the attention of remarkably talented philosophers. This volume contains recent contributions from leading scholars in the field and brings together treatments of various themes in causality and explanation that stand to profit relative newcomers as well as specialists.

The papers are grouped into two large and loosely specified groups. The papers in the first group concern the development of theories; those in the second concern the application of theories. The first group is composed of the papers by Patricia Cheng and her associates, Patrick Suppes, Clark

Glymour and Frank Wimberly, Christopher Hitchcock, Michael Strevens, and Russell Wahl; the second group consists of papers by Bruce Glymour, Scott Sehon, Dorit Ganson, Nancy Cartwright, Till Grüne-Yanoff, Alfred Mele, Laurie Paul, and Alexander Pruss.

In "Explaining Four Psychological Asymmetries in Causal Reasoning: Implications of Causal Assumptions for Coherence," Patricia Cheng and her coauthors examine "how untutored people infer causal relations" (p. 1). In particular, the paper examines four psychological phenomena via two psychological approaches—an associationist approach and a causal approach. The paper shows that the associationist approach fails, whereas the causal approach succeeds.

The associationist model is the ΔP model, wherein the strength of the causal relation between proffered cause i and effect e is measured by $\Delta P_i = P(e \mid i) - P(e \mid \bar{i})$, where $\bar{i}$ denotes not-i. The ΔP model holds that if ΔP_i is "noticeably positive," then i is taken to cause e; if noticeably negative, then i is taken to prevent e; and if not noticeably different from 0, i is taken to have no influence on e. The ΔP model, "the dominant associationist model of causal learning," is advanced to "illustrate the pitfall of associationism" (p. 2). The causal theory employs causal power—the probability with which a cause influences an effect—to arrive at a coherent explanation of the effect on the basis of the cause. The details of the causal model are richer than those of the associationist model, and are well developed in the paper.

In "Causality and Computation," Patrick Suppes raises a series of questions so as to address the causal issues surrounding intentional activities such as computation and decision making. In particular, Suppes addresses the isolation of intentional activities from causal influences with negative effects. Suppes notes that such isolation can never be absolute. He closes by suggesting that the confusions emanating from the usual distinction between mental processes and bodily processes can be clarified by examining computations made by biological processes. In doing so Suppes, in relatively few pages, examines the philosophical aspects of many of the fairly disparate issues treated in neuroeconomics (Glimcher 2003) and computer science (Baum 2004).

In "Actual Causes and Thought Experiments," Clark Glymour and Frank Wimberly provide a particularly useful discussion of the marvelously technical issues one encounters in formulating an account of actual causation.

They begin with Lewis's specification that C causes E if and only if C and E both occur, and if C had not occurred, then E would not have occurred (Lewis 1973). Glymour and Wimberly then provide four accounts of the concept of actual causation, each based on experiments conducted within Boolean networks. The four accounts display an "extensional inclusion structure" whereby the concept of actual cause captured by a given account is captured by each higher account.

The essay brings together elements of the conversation involving, among others, Cheng and Hitchcock (this volume), the earlier work of Glymour and his Carnegie Mellon colleagues, and the work of Pearl (2000). The chapter ends with a brief discussion of the connection, or lack thereof, between the concept of actual causation, as captured in the four accounts, and actual human reasoning about causation. This discussion points to numerous interesting open issues, including the issues surrounding the precision of psychological experiments, and the asymmetric treatment, by humans, of occurrences and nonoccurrences.

In "What's Wrong with Neuron Diagrams?," Christopher Hitchcock develops "the general complaint that neuron diagrams do not serve as all-purpose representational devices for causal systems" (p. 70), and provides an alternative mode of representation. There are numerous contributions here, two of which are immediate: first, the discussion is sufficiently concise so as to provide an introduction of value to readers not familiar with neuron diagrams, and it is sufficiently technical so as not to bore those who are. Second, the critique pertains to the use of neuron diagrams, and thereby benefits both "fans and foes" of the diagrams.

Hitchcock makes three basic points. First, "neuron diagrams fail ... to suggest new kinds of structures against which theories can be tested" (section 6). Second, "neuron diagrams can bias our intuitions about the neural structures they represent" (section 7). Third, "there are cases where neuron diagrams actually misrepresent the causal structure of the neural systems they are meant to depict" (section 8). Hitchcock argues for the superiority of causal graphs and structural equations. The exposition, while only a "quick introduction," is particularly helpful to readers new to the subject.

Michael Strevens, in "Mackie Remixed," provides a revised version of Mackie's 1974 INUS account of causation to treat cases of preemption. Mackie's account is called the INUS account, since the claim that C is a cause of E is true if and only if C is an Insufficient but Nonredundant part of an Unnecessary but Sufficient condition for the occurrence of E.

Strevens presents a two-part refinement of Mackie's INUS account of causation. The result, Strevens contends, is the best available account of causal claims. This contention alone makes the essay well worth the reader's serious attention. The analysis presented in the paper is straightforward. Strevens agrees with the Mackie-Lewis position that "causal claims are about difference-making," but disagrees with the usual supposition "that this difference-making is itself the fundamental causal relation" (p. 112). By refining the concept of difference-making, via the concept of causal entailment, Strevens's adaptation of Mackie's account is designed to treat cases of preemption.

Occasionalism is "the view that there is only one genuine cause, God; and that all other apparent, or secondary causes are merely occasions for the exercise of God's power and have, by themselves, no causal efficacy" (p. 120). Russell Wahl, in "Occasional Causes," examines "some of the issues surrounding occasionalism" and points out that "occasionalism is not quite as silly as it has been thought" (p. 119).

Wahl notes that Malebranche, as the primary spokesman for occasionalism, argues that God is the primary cause, and that God causes the laws of motion (general cause) but does not cause particular events (occasional cause). Furthermore, Malebranche, and thereby occasionalism, holds that "explanation should make reference to the occasional cause, not to God" (p. 127). Finally, "Malebranche's notion of occasional cause [is more] than constant conjunction: there is an element of necessity to it, a necessity which would support counterfactuals" (p. 128). Thereby, occasionalism, as per Malebranche, is not as silly as has been thought in that occasionalism engenders a theory of explanation not unlike the modern counterfactual accounts of causation.

This is a most unusual topic for a volume such as this. Occasionalism is quite easy to dismiss. In making the case that "occasionalism is not quite as silly as it has been thought," Wahl partially makes the case for not dismissing occasionalism out of hand; it remains to be determined if occasionalism should be dismissed for cause. I invite the reader to pursue Wahl's case for occasionalism.

Bruce Glymour, in "In Defense of Explanatory Deductivism," examines three classes of explanation—explanations that reduce surprise, Humean explanations that convey understanding, and conspiracy explanations that convey understanding—and their roles in accounting for chancy phenomena. The examination involves four theses taken from the "orthodox" view of inductive explanation:

1. Inductive explanations are understanding-conveying explanations.

2. Unlikely events can be explained equally as well as likely events.

3. Explanations of neither probable nor improbable chancy events can be contrastive (i.e., specifying why an event rather than a contrary event occurred).

4. The specified cause of an explanandum given by a contrastive explanation cannot be the specified cause of a contrary of the explanandum.

Glymour argues to an interesting claim: if these four theses hold, then "understanding-conveying explanations of chancy events have, either explicitly or implicitly, a deductive structure" (p. 152). Beyond this claim and its supporting argument, Glymour's essay also provides the reader with a greater understanding of the core themes of the conversation, involving, among others, Hitchcock and Strevens, whose essays also appear in this volume.

Scott Sehon's purpose in "Goal-Directed Action and Teleological Explanation" is to defend the view that, contra Davidson (1963/1980), explanations of human behavior are not causal but are rather irreducibly teleological. Specifically, Sehon defends teleological realism—the view that "when we explain an agent's behavior by citing her *reason*, we explain the behavior by specifying the state of affairs towards which the behavior was directed" (p. 156). In particular, Sehon's essay is a response to Mele 2000.

Sehon argues that under either of two interpretations of Mele's primary example, "teleological realism gives an intuitively acceptable diagnosis of the [example]" (p. 168). In particular, Sehon counters Mele's claim that the teleological realist's account is too liberal and accepts as action that which we would not intuitively regard as action.

In "Van Fraassen's Dutch Book Argument against Explanationism," Dorit Ganson addresses van Fraassen's claim, made in *Laws and Symmetry* (1989), that "anyone who allows explanatoriness to enhance her degree of credence is susceptible to a Dutch book" (p. 172). Ganson reviews the primary arguments advanced to counter van Fraassen's claim. This review is particularly helpful to those readers who have not immersed themselves in the "fairly extensive literature which aims to confront [van Fraassen's] criticisms of inference to the best explanation and scientific realism" (p. 173). The arguments under review, and Ganson's own argument lead to the counterclaim: "Neither van Fraassen's argument, nor more general probabilistic considerations, show that commitments to explanationism results in probabilistic incoherence" (p. 184).

In addition to the author's own arguments, this essay, as noted, is valuable for its review of the literature and the extant arguments advanced to counter van Fraassen's position. It is also valuable for the discussion, presented as an extended note (n. 4), of the Dutch book used in van Fraassen's argument.

Nancy Cartwright, in "Counterfactuals in Economics: A Commentary," examines the application of counterfactuals in economics. This topic is not new to economics. When raised in the late 1950s and developed through the mid-1970s, the primary concern was the use of counterfactual arguments in economic history (Dacey 1975). Cartwright addresses the use of counterfactuals in the development and evaluation of economic policies. Her primary claim is that the contemporary analysis of economic counterfactuals is misdirected toward what she calls "impostor counterfactuals," with the result that the analysis is not fruitful. The paper presents the argument that warrants the claim.

Cartwright focuses on the work of economists James Heckman and Stephen LeRoy, and methodologists Kevin Hoover and Daniel Hausman. Cartwright employs aspects of the work of Judea Pearl and an account of her own to conduct the critical assessment of counterfactuals as employed in economic policy analysis. She concludes that "the imposter counterfactuals of current interest in economics … play at best a very indirect role in helping" to provide the causal models needed for the development and evaluation of an economic policy (p. 213).

Till Grüne-Yanoff, in "Why Don't You Want to Be Rich? Preference Explanation on the Basis of Causal Structure," addresses the problem of explaining people's observed choice behavior on the basis of unobservable preferences. In particular, Grüne-Yanoff constructs a system of abstract preferences over worlds that, together with a principle of abstraction, define preferences over propositions. Grüne-Yanoff argues that "such a principle of abstraction is necessary for the explanation and prediction of behavior with preferences" (p. 235). The analysis is causal in that it incorporates the agent's beliefs as a causal model.

Grüne-Yanoff's analysis is technically interesting. The formalities are developed in detail and in a format that is easy to follow. The analysis contributes to the conversation on explaining behavior via preferences involving Joyce, Pettit, Spohn, Trapp, von Wright, and others. The analysis also incorporates the formal account of causality advanced by Pearl, so that the agent's beliefs, as a causal model, can be represented by an acyclical directed graph. Thus, Grüne-Yanoff's analysis connects the explanation of choice behavior to analyses presented elsewhere in this volume.

Alfred Mele's chapter, "Decisions, Intentions, Urges, and Free Will: Why Libet Has Not Shown What He Says He Has," is interesting on several counts. First, it reveals various aspects of a confrontation between scientists and philosophers. Second, it provides insight into the applicability of experimental results in psychology to the philosophical analysis of free will and self-control. Third, it leaves open the attribution of causal clout vis-à-vis desires and intentions, on the one hand, and the physical realizations of desires and intentions, on the other.

Mele's essay treats the work of physiologist Benjamin Libet and his colleagues on the difference between the time the brain decides to act and the time the decision maker is aware of the decision to act. Mele takes Libet's analysis to task for the imprecision of, and thereby the confounding of, the distinctions between and among deciding to act, intending to act, and having the urge to act. Libet notes that most of the criticism of his work comes from "philosophers and others with no significant experience in experimental neuroscience of the brain" (p. 257). Mele counters that one needs no such experience "to realize that there is a difference between deciding and intending, on the one hand, and wanting—including having an urge—on the other" (p. 257).

Mele's essay is also interesting for the applicability of his refined analysis of Libet's concepts to free will and self-control. Since Mele develops these analyses in greater detail elsewhere, he devotes but one section of the paper to free will. Nonetheless, this section is of immediate interest to readers.

In "Constitutive Overdetermination," Laurie Paul, after reviewing many of the difficulties faced by the nonreductionist regarding the layered world model of Oppenheim and Putnam, provides an account of how the layered world model can be made to work according to nonreductionist views. Specifically, Paul proposes to view objects as sums of properties (i.e., so that objects have properties as parts). This provides the nonreductionist with the basic tool for constructing a partial interpretation of the layered world model. While sums of objects at lower levels constitute objects at higher levels, "when objects constitute other objects, they are partly identical in that they partly overlap by sharing many of their property instances" (p. 280). Thus, "the nonreductionist's interpretation [of the layered world model] shows how the world is not extra-dense with respect to shared property instances in a constitutional hierarchy" (p. 280).

Paul employs the resulting "nonreductionist interpretation of objects related by constitution" (p. 280) to address constitutive overdetermination. She employs this tool to argue that "once we realize that it is the involvement of certain property instances that determine whether one thing causes another, and that in the cases of constitutive overdetermination we have considered, the causally important or relevant property instances are shared, we can see why causal responsibility is shared, not overdetermined" (pp. 284–285).

In *"Ex nihilo nihil fit:* Arguments New and Old for the Principle of Sufficient Reason," Alexander Pruss addresses the Causal Principle—every contingent event has a cause; and the Principle of Sufficient Reason—every contingent proposition has an explanation for why it is true. Pruss advances three arguments for the Causal Principle and the Principle of Sufficient Reason—an argument from the predictability of things in the world; a technical modal argument based on the nature of causality; and an argument based on the nature of modality.

The argument from predictability is straightforward and is an instance of inference to the best explanation. The technical modal argument is first sketched, and then presented in detail. While Pruss invites the uninterested reader to skip the technical details and go to the next section of the paper, the technicalities are very interesting and well-presented: I invite the reader to not skip to the next section, but to engage this argument. The argument based on the nature of modality is remarkably concise.

Before presenting the three arguments, Pruss responds to the objection advanced by van Inwagen (1983) that no contingent proposition can explain itself, and no necessary proposition can explain a contingent proposition. Pruss argues that either horn of the dilemma raised by van Inwagen can be embraced by the defender of the Principle of Sufficient Reason.

The papers collected here provide a broad overview of the contemporary account of explanation and causation, and specific papers provide in-depth treatments of important issues in explanation and causation. As such, the book provides an introduction to the field for newcomers and important contributions to the field for specialists. It is rare that a collection of papers from a professional meeting serves two audiences. The organizers are to be congratulated.

References

Baum, E. 2004. *What Is Thought?* Cambridge, Mass.: MIT Press.

Dacey, R. 1975. "The Role of Economic Theory in Supporting Counterfactual Arguments." *Philosophy and Phenomenological Research* 35: 402–410.

Davidson, D. 1963/1980. "Actions, Reasons, and Causes." Reprinted in *Essays on Actions and Events*. Oxford: Clarendon Press.

Glimcher, P. 2003. *Decisions, Uncertainty, and the Brain*. Cambridge, Mass.: MIT Press.

Hausman, D. 1998. *Causal Asymmetries*. Cambridge: Cambridge University Press.

Hausman, D., and J. Woodward. 1999. "Independence, Invariance, and the Causal Markov Condition." *British Journal for the Philosophy of Science* 50: 521–583.

Heckman, J. 2001. "Econometrics, Counterfactuals, and Causal Models." Keynote address, International Statistical Institute, Seoul, Korea.

Hoover, K. 2001. *Causality in Macroeconomics*. Cambridge: Cambridge University Press.

LeRoy, S. 2003. "Causality in Economics." Unpublished manuscript, University of California, Santa Barbara. (Available at http://www.econ.ucsb.edu/~sleroy/webpage/recent.html/.)

Lewis, D. 1973. "Causation." *Journal of Philosophy* 70: 556–567.

Mackie, J. 1974. *The Cement of the Universe*. Oxford: Oxford University Press.

Mele, A. 2000. "Goal-Directed Action: Teleological Explanations, Causal Theories, and Deviance." *Philosophical Perspectives* 14: 279–300.

Pearl, J. 2000. *Causality: Models, Reasoning, and Inference.* Cambridge: Cambridge University Press.

Salmon, W. 1977. "A Third Dogma of Empiricism." In *Basic Problems in Methodology and Linguistics,* edited by R. Butts and J. Hintikka. Dordrecht: D. Reidel.

Salmon, W. 1998. *Causality and Explanation.* Oxford: Oxford University Press.

van Fraassen, B. 1989. *Laws and Symmetry.* Oxford: Oxford University Press.

van Inwagen, P. 1983. *An Essay on Free Will.* Oxford: Oxford University Press.

1 Explaining Four Psychological Asymmetries in Causal Reasoning: Implications of Causal Assumptions for Coherence

Patricia W. Cheng, Laura R. Novick, Mimi Liljeholm, and Christina Ford

In this chapter, we describe four psychological phenomena that offer clues to how untutored people infer causal relations. We contrast the predictions for these phenomena, all involving asymmetries in causal inferences, according to two psychological approaches—an associationist approach (e.g., Cheng and Novick 1992; Jenkins and Ward 1965; Pearce 1987; Rescorla and Wagner 1972; Van Hamme and Wasserman 1994), and a causal approach (e.g., Cheng 1997, 2000; Novick and Cheng 2004). Our analysis reveals that each phenomenon is inexplicable by associationist models but follows coherently from a causal theory. What distinguishes these approaches is that the causal theory has the goal of explaining the occurrence of a target event by the potentially independent influences of candidate causes and other (background) causes. This goal has no analogue in associationist models. To arrive at a coherent explanation, the causal account creates a theoretical construct of causal power (Cartwright 1989)—the probability with which a cause influences an effect. According to this account, reasoners search for, or define, candidate causes with the goal of arriving at causes that influence a target effect independently of the background causes. In other words, they seek causes whose powers are (ideally) invariant regardless of how frequently the background causes occur (see Woodward 2003, for a discussion of the degree of invariance and depth of explanation; also see Haavelmo 1944, for a discussion of causes varying on degree of autonomy).

By "cause," we mean both *simple* causes that consist of a single element and *conjunctive* causes that consist of a combination of two or more elements acting in concert; we also mean a direct cause in the sense that, for the purpose of analysis, intermediate causes that lie on the path between the candidate cause and the effect are ignored or treated as part of the candidate. In our view, causal explanation occurs within a hypothesis-testing framework in which predictions based on various sets of assumptions are evaluated to reach the goal of a satisfactory explanation. This testing begins with simpler hypotheses unless there is evidence refuting them. Any processing system that cannot simultaneously evaluate all possible hypotheses needs an ordering bias; two reasons supporting a simplicity bias are: (1) simple causes are an inherent part of the definition of conjunctive causes (Novick and Cheng 2004), and (2) they are the elements in more complex networks. We restrict our discussion to causes and effects that are represented by binary variables with a present value and an absent value; this type of cause and effect, compared with the type represented by continuous variables, more clearly reveals the function of causal constructs. As will become clear, for situations that are well represented by binary variables of this type, associationist accounts do not allow for the possibility that the occurrence of the effect is the result of the independent influences of causes.

Psychology is not the only discipline that has inherited associationism. Some commonly used normative statistical measures—for example, the chi-square test and the cross-product ratio—are also associationist. Given that the asymmetry phenomena are manifestations of a coherent explanation of the occurrence of a target effect when causal assumptions are made, but only when such assumptions are made, a question arises: do these phenomena point to a basic problem that permeates both psychological and normative associationist models? When applied to test causal hypotheses, are associationist measures coherent? Before presenting the four phenomena, we first give a brief account of the two psychological approaches.

Alternative Psychological Accounts of Causal Learning

An Associationist Model

For brevity, we illustrate the pitfall of associationism primarily using only one such model, the ΔP model, which was independently proposed in philosophy (Salmon 1965) and in psychology (e.g., Jenkins and Wards 1965; Cheng and Novick 1992). It is the dominant associationist model of causal learning in the psychological literature; it makes the same predictions as Rescorla and Wagner's (1972) model—the dominant connectionist model of conditioning and causal learning—at equilibria if the two parameter values of the effect in question in the latter model are assumed to be equally salient (e.g., Danks 2003). Other associationist models (e.g., Pearce 1987; Rescorla and Wagner 1972; Van Hamme and Wasserman 1994), despite their greater flexibility due to added parameters, are nonetheless unable to account for some robust psychological findings, including those to be discussed here (for more extended evaluations of these models, see Buehner, Cheng, and Clifford 2003; Cheng, Park, Yarlas, and Holyoak 1996; and Novick and Cheng 2004). The only exception is if Rescorla and Wagner's model is modified to become consistent with the explanatory causal construct just mentioned (see the noisy-OR and noisy-AND-NOT modifications in Danks, Griffiths, and Tenenbaum 2003).

According to the ΔP model, the *strength* of a causal relation between candidate cause i and effect e is estimated by the difference in the probability of e given i and given not-i:

$$\Delta P_i = P(e \mid i) - P(e \mid \bar{i}). \tag{1}$$

If ΔP_i is noticeably positive, reasoners are predicted to conclude that i causes e; if ΔP_i is noticeably negative, they are predicted to conclude that i prevents e; and if ΔP_i is not noticeably different from 0, they are predicted to conclude that i has no influence on e. We interpret equation 1 under the assumption that alternative causes are "controlled" (i.e., held constant); this interpretation is sometimes called the *probabilistic contrast* model (Cheng and Novick 1992).

The Causal Power Theory of the Probabilistic Contrast Model

The causal power theory of the probabilistic contrast model (Cheng 1997, 2000; Novick and Cheng 2004) instantiates an approach to causal learning that adds an explanatory layer to associationist models. *Causal power* is the theoretical probability with which a cause influences an effect e when the cause is present (Cartwright 1989); this influence can be *generative* (i.e., the cause produces e with a certain probability) or *preventive* (i.e., the cause prevents e with a certain probability). According to this causal power theory (Cheng 1997), to evaluate the power of a candidate cause i to influence e, reasoners partition all causes of e into candidate i and the composite of (known and unknown) causes of e alternative to i, labeled a here, and they explain covariation defined in terms of observable frequencies by the unobservable hypothetical causal powers of i and a. The partitioning of all causes of e into i and a is the simplest possible conception of the causes of e that would still explain covariation between i and e.

The assumptions underlying the derivation of simple causal power are:

1. i and a influence e independently,

2. causes in a could produce e but not prevent it,

3. the causal powers of i and a are independent of their occurrences (e.g., the probability of a both occurring and producing e is the product of the probability of a occurring and the power of a), and

4. e does not occur unless it is caused.

Assumptions 1 and 2 are merely "working hypotheses" for the reasoner; they are adopted until the reasoner perceives evidence against them. If they are dropped, they are replaced by weaker assumptions, and alternative models apply (e.g., Cheng 2000; Novick and Cheng 2004).

With respect to assumption 1, *independent causal influence* is defined as follows: let us consider a simple case in which i and j, two causes of an effect e, are both present (j is different from a in that a, which includes unknown or unobserved causes, typically cannot be constrained to be present). If the *generative causal power* of i with respect to e is q_i (i.e., i produces e with probability q_i when i is present), and the generative causal power of j with respect to e is q_j, then if i and j influence e independently, the probability that e is produced both by i and by j would be $q_i \cdot q_j$. Under the same assumptions, the probability that e is produced by i *or* by j would be $q_i + q_j - q_i \cdot q_j$. This function relating the probability of e occurring (in the presence of i and j in this simple case) to the theoretical probabilities of e due to each constituent cause, is sometimes referred to as a noisy-OR gate (Glymour 2001).

When $\Delta P_i \geq 0$, reasoners evaluate the hypothesis that i produces e and estimate q_i. To do so, they allow the possibility that i produces e, and explain $P(e\,|\,i)$ by the probability of the *union* of two events: (1) e produced by i, and (2) e produced by a if a occurs in the presence of i. That is, they reason that when i is present, e can be produced by i or by a if a occurs in the presence of i. Likewise, they explain $P(e\,|\,\bar{i})$ by how often e is produced by a alone when a occurs in the absence of i.

Figure 1.1 illustrates these explanations of the two conditional probabilities by Euler circles. The dashed and undashed circles in the figure, respec-

Explaining Covariation by Generative Simple Causal Power (When $\Delta P_i \geq 0$)

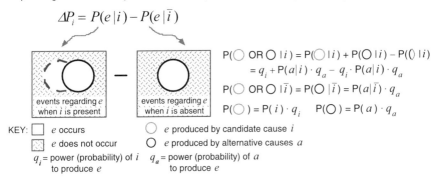

$$\Delta P_i = P(e\,|\,i) - P(e\,|\,\bar{i})$$

$P(\bigcirc \text{ OR } \bigcirc | i) = P(\bigcirc | i) + P(\bigcirc | i) - P(\bigcirc | i)$
$\qquad = q_i + P(a | i) \cdot q_a - q_i \cdot P(a | i) \cdot q_a$

$P(\bigcirc \text{ OR } \bigcirc | \bar{i}) = P(\bigcirc | \bar{i}) = P(a | \bar{i}) \cdot q_a$

$P(\bigcirc) = P(i) \cdot q_i \qquad P(\bigcirc) = P(a) \cdot q_a$

KEY: ☐ e occurs   ○ e produced by candidate cause i
▨ e does not occur   ○ e produced by alternative causes a
q_i = power (probability) of i q_a = power (probability) of a
to produce e   to produce e

events regarding e when i is present
events regarding e when i is absent

Figure 1.1
Euler diagrams illustrating the explanation of covariation in Cheng's (1997) theory of simple causal power (from Novick and Cheng 2004).

tively representing *e produced by i* and *e produced by a*, are both *unobservable*; they are theoretical constructs. What can be observed is the shading—the white and shaded areas respectively representing *e occurring* and *e not occurring*; and the two boxes—respectively representing *exposure to i* and *no exposure to i*. Now, *e occurring* in the presence of *i*—the white area in the left box representing the *union* of the dashed and undashed circles—can be decomposed theoretically into the sum of the area of the dashed circle and that of the undashed circle, minus their overlap (see top equation in the figure). The relative size of the dashed circle in the left box (i.e., how often *e* is produced by *i* when *i* is present) depends on how often *i* occurs (always in this situation) and its causal power, q_i (i.e., how often *i* produces *e* when *i* is present). The undashed circle can be similarly explained. (See bottom two equations in the figure.) Likewise, the white area in the right box (when *i* is absent) can be analogously explained, in this case by how often *e* is produced by *a* in the absence of *i* (see middle equation). These explanations of *e* set up equations relating the observable quantities to the various theoretical variables.

For situations in which $\Delta P_i \leq 0$, there are analogous explanations for evaluating preventive causal power. The only difference in the preventive case is that reasoners evaluate the hypothesis that *i prevents e* rather than produces it. This difference implies that when reasoners evaluate whether *i* prevents *e*, they explain $P(e\,|\,i)$ by the probability of the *intersection* of two events: (1) e produced by a if a occurs in the presence of i, and (2) e not stopped by i. That is, they reason that when i is present, e occurs only if it is both produced by a *and* not prevented by i. This function is sometimes referred to as a noisy-AND-NOT gate (Danks et al. 2003). The explanation of $P(e \mid \bar{i})$ remains as before.

The goal of these explanations of $P(e \mid i)$ and $P(e \mid \bar{i})$ is to yield an estimate of the (generative or preventive) power of i from observable frequencies alone, even though it may be impossible to observe the influence of i in isolation. For figure 1.1, this goal corresponds to estimating the size of the whole of the (invisible) dashed circle relative to the size of the left box (when i is present). These explanations show that, under some conditions but not others, covariation implies causation. One of the necessary conditions is "no confounding"—the independent occurrence of a and i. This condition is necessary when causal inference makes use of a probabilistic contrast, as we explain later.[1] In the figure, this condition corresponds to requiring that the undashed circles in the two boxes have the same size relative to their respective boxes. Whether one assumes that this condition is satisfied depends on perceived evidence for or against it.

When a and i do *not* occur independently (i.e., when there is confounding), one equation with four unknowns results, and there is no unique solution for q_i. But, in the special case in which a occurs independently of i (i.e., when there is no confounding), these explanations yield equations with only one unknown, the causal power of the candidate. Equation 2 gives an estimate of q_i when $\Delta P_i \geq 0$:

$$q_i = \frac{\Delta P_i}{1 - P(e \mid \bar{i})};$$ (2)

and equation 3 gives an estimate of p_i, the *preventive* simple power of i, when $\Delta P_i \leq 0$:

$$p_i = \frac{-\Delta P_i}{P(e \mid \bar{i})}.$$ (3)

The two equations are logically related in that replacing e with not-e in one equation will yield the right-hand-side (RHS) of the other equation. That is, generating e is equivalent to preventing not-e.

Note that the RHS's of equations 2 and 3 require observations regarding i and e only (intermediate terms involving a drop out under no-confounding), implying that q_i and p_i can be estimated *without* observing *a*. Also note that when $\Delta P_i = 0$, both generative and preventive powers can be evaluated; otherwise, the type of power to evaluate depends on the observed sign of ΔP_i. Finally, note that causal power has a well-defined meaning in terms of frequencies of events in the world (see Novick and Cheng 2004, for a contrast with associationist models in this regard). For example, $q_i = 1$ means that i is estimated to produce e in every entity, and $q_i = 0$ means that i is estimated to never produce e in any entity (i.e., to be noncausal). The values of p_i have analogous interpretations in terms of preventing e.

Myriad findings on psychological causal judgments that are inexplicable by associationist accounts are explained by this causal theory (see Buehner, Cheng, and Clifford 2003; Cheng 1997; Lien and Cheng 2000; Novick and Cheng 2004; White 2004; Wu and Cheng 1999). We discuss four such findings in the following sections.

Phenomenon 1: An Asymmetry between Cause and Effect

Empirical Finding

This asymmetry is revealed in a comparison across three figures, all taken from a psychological experiment on judgments of causal strength conducted on college students (Buehner, Cheng, and Clifford 2003). First, consider the pattern of information in figure 1.2. For this and similar figures, the subjects were told that the figure depicts the outcome of a fictitious experiment testing a medicine on allergy patients. The medicine was said to be effective for relieving the symptoms of allergies, but its unintended effects were undocumented; the study was conducted to evaluate one such possible side effect—headache. To encourage the no-confounding assumption, the patients were said to be randomly assigned to two groups—a group that did not receive the medicine (the top panel, the *control* group), and a group that did (the bottom panel, the *experimental* group). Each face in the figure represents a patient. A frowning face represents that the patient has a headache; a smiling face represents that the patient does not have a headache.

The subjects were asked to judge, based on the data in the figure, whether each medicine causes, prevents, or has no influence on headaches. If the medicine was judged to have an influence, a follow-up question asked them to rate the strength of the influence. For example, if subjects indicated that

Results for side effect of Medicine D:

Legend:

🙁 This patient has a headache

🙂 This patient does not have a headache

🥛 These patients did not receive medicine D:

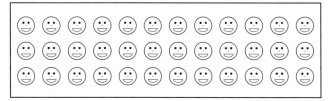

🥛 These patients received medicine D:

Figure 1.2
Stimulus material for Condition D from Buehner, Cheng, and Clifford (2003, Experiment 2) depicting the results of an experiment testing the side effect of a medicine.

a medicine causes headaches, they were asked to estimate, out of 100 allergy patients (selected from the same pool) who do not have headaches, the number who would get a headache if the medicine were given to them. Likewise, if subjects indicated that a medicine prevents headaches, they were asked to estimate, out of 100 allergy patients (from the same pool) all of whom have headaches, the number who would no longer have a headache if the medicine were given to them. A presentation of the information about individual patients in verbal, instead of pictorial form; patient-by-patient, in a sequence, instead of simultaneously as in our figures; produced the same pattern of psychological findings that we illustrate here.

For figure 1.2, most subjects indicated that medicine D causes headaches. They further estimated that if the medicine had been given to 100 allergy

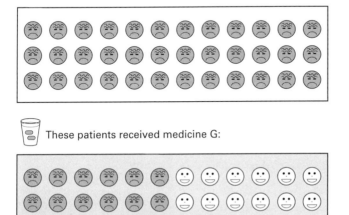

Figure 1.3
Stimulus material for Condition G from Buehner, Cheng, and Clifford (2003, Experiment 2).

patients who did not have headaches, 50 would get a headache from the medicine.

Next, consider the evaluation of the medicine in figure 1.3. The outcome pattern depicted in this figure results from changing each frowning patient in figure 1.2 into a smiling one, and vice versa (and grouping the resulting frowning patients and shifting them to the left). In other words, figure 1.3 transposes the two values of the outcome in figure 1.2. For this figure, most subjects answered that medicine G *prevents* headaches and estimated that about 50 out of 100 patients with headaches would no longer have headaches if given the medicine. Thus, from figure 1.2 to figure 1.3, there is a change in *causal direction*—from producing to preventing headaches—but no change in the magnitude of the strength of the causal relation.

Figure 1.4
Stimulus material for Condition J from Buehner, Cheng, and Clifford (2003, Experiment 2).

Finally, consider figure 1.4. The outcome pattern in this figure is identical to that in figure 1.2 except that now, for every patient, the two values of the candidate cause are transposed; in effect, the top and bottom panels are switched. For this figure, most subjects responded that medicine J prevents headaches and estimated that it would do so in *all* 100 of the patients given the medicine. Note that in contrast to figure 1.3, the transposition of values doubled the estimated causal strength, from 0.5 to 1. These three figures illustrate that transposing the values of the effect (figure 1.3 vs. figure 1.2) has a consequence different from that of transposing the values of the candidate cause (figure 1.4 vs. figure 1.2).

Associationist models are unable to explain the different consequences of the two transpositions. Although the ΔP model correctly predicts a change in causal direction for each transposition, it gives the same absolute magnitude of strength, namely, 0.5, for all three figures. As an examination of equation 1 will show, the two variables in the equation (*i and e*) behave the same way when their values are transposed: for both variables, the two values are symmetrical in the sense that transposing them yields a ΔP that has the opposite sign but the same absolute value. Similarly, the commonly used chi-square test (e.g., Feinberg 1980) would yield the same χ^2 value when given data sets that are transformations of each other in the two ways just described. This test neither distinguishes between cause and effect variables, nor between the values of each variable; the values of each variable therefore have an identical status, as do the variables themselves, resulting in the symmetric treatment of all three figures.

Let us briefly illustrate how an associationist model with added parameters still fails to explain the pattern of results. For example, one could generalize equation 1 by adding weights to the conditional probabilities (e.g., Lober and Shanks 2000), so that weighted-$\Delta P = w_i \cdot P(e \mid i) - w_2 \cdot P(e \mid \bar{i})$. To fit the modal judgments for figures 1.2 and 1.4 (corresponding to an estimated weighted-ΔP of 0.5 for figure 1.2, and -1 for figure 1.4), the only solution is to set $w_1 = 1$ and $w_2 = 2$. This pair of weights, however, would predict a strength of -1.5 for figure 1.3, thus failing to explain the observed constant magnitude of causal strength across figures 1.2 and 1.3. As should be clear, post-hoc values for w_1 and w_2 that can explain the judgments for any two of the three figures will inevitably fail to explain the judgment for the third.

In contrast, the observed difference between the two transformations of figure 1.2 is explained by the causal power theory of the probabilistic contrast model (Cheng 1997, 2000). Recall that by the definition of causal power, a cause exerts its influence when it is present; it does nothing when it is absent. It therefore should be not be surprising that transposing the present and absent values of the candidate cause would yield different estimated causal strengths. For figure 1.2, instantiating equation 2 yields $q_i = 0.5$; for figures 1.3 and 1.4, instantiating equation 3 yields $p_i = 0.5$ and $p_i = 1$, respectively. These predictions are parameter-free.

An Incoherent Definition of Independent Causal Influence under the Associationist Approach

Our three "medicine" figures illustrate a basic problem with the associationist approach when applied to causal situations: it does not allow a coherent definition of independent causal influence. Consider figures 1.3 and

1.4 again, but now treat medicines G and J as the same medicine. Under the ΔP model, the outcome patterns in the two figures are consistent with the medicine having no interaction with the background causes: the strength of the medicine according to the model remains invariant (-0.5 for both figures) across different levels of the background causes (as indicated by different proportions of patients having a headache in the control groups).

Concluding independent causal influence based on the invariant ΔP value in the two figures, however, results in a contradiction in the concept of independent causal influence: the probability with which a cause changes an effect *varies* depending on the how often other causes of the effect occur, even as the causes are supposedly independent causes of the effect. As mentioned, the two figures show different contexts in which the medicine acted. In figure 1.3, as can be inferred from the control group (top panel) under the "no confounding" condition, generative causes of headaches occurred and produced headaches in every patient. In figure 1.4, it can be analogously inferred that generative causes of headache occurred and produced headaches in only half of the patients. Now, consider the probability with which the medicine prevented or relieved headache for an individual patient in the experimental group (bottom panel). Note that this group would have been like its control counterpart before the medicine was administered. In figure 1.3, a medicine that relieves headache with a probability of 0.5 for an individual patient would be expected to yield the bottom panel of the figure. But, in figure 1.4, to yield its bottom panel, the analogous probability for the medicine would have to be 1; individual patients are the units to consider because the pill that went into each patient cannot "look" across patients to obtain a desired overall outcome. Thus, the *same* medicine that relieved headache with a probability of 0.5 in figure 1.3 now relieved headache with a probability of 1, contradicting the ΔP assumption that the medicine acts independently of the background causes. It is as if the medicine, to maintain the same ΔP value, "knew" in figure 1.4 that it should bypass the patients who did not have a headache, and "concentrate" its influence on the half who did so as to arrive at a constant ΔP value of -0.5.

In summary, our analysis reveals that no model that treats figures 1.3 and 1.4 as symmetric patterns is coherent, given the asymmetry between the two values of a candidate cause. Adopting associationist models amounts to assuming a specific form of interaction between the medicine and the background causes—the stronger the background generative causes, the weaker the preventive effect of the medicine—*even while* the medicine and the background causes are assumed to exert independent influences on headache. Such models violate the principle of invariance with respect to the basic concept of independent influence (Woodward 2003). The causal approach circumvents this problem by adopting the only coherent definition of independent causal influence.

Phenomenon 2: Causal-Reasoning Analogues of the Necker Cube

This section concerns an asymmetry between generative and preventive causes in situations in which $\Delta P = 0$ and there is no confounding. Recall that for such situations, both generative and preventive power may be evaluated. The general rule is to infer that the candidate is noncausal, regardless of whether generative or preventive power is evaluated. There are two exceptions, however, both of which are causal-reasoning analogues of the Necker Cube. Just as the Necker Cube, which results in a single visual input, can be interpreted in two ways perceptually, the exact same data set can yield two inferential interpretations. In the first analogue, if e always occurs, with or without i (see figure 1.5a), someone evaluating whether i prevents e would indeed infer that i is noncausal, but someone evaluating whether i produces e would allow the possibility that i produces e. Under the latter interpretation, even if i is a strong producer of e, there would be no room to show its influence on e because of the constant presence of e due to alternative causes; no conclusion, therefore, regarding whether i produces e can be drawn. This situation is referred to as the "ceiling effect" in experimental design.

A second analogue of the Necker Cube appears at the other extreme probability, when e never occurs, with or without i (see figure 1.5b). In that case, one would infer that i does not produce e; at the same time, i's preventive power cannot be evaluated—there would be no room to show the preventive influence of i on e, no matter how strongly i prevents e. This situation is the preventive analogue of the ceiling effect; it is so exceedingly intuitive that it is, as far as we know, never discussed in textbooks on experimental design. Thus, each of two clear-cut cases of statistical independence is interpreted differently depending on the direction of

(a) Ceiling Effect

	e	not-e
i	1	0
not-i	1	0

(b) Preventive Analogue of the Ceiling Effect

	e	not-e
i	0	1
not-i	0	1

Figure 1.5
Two inferential Necker cubes: Data patterns indicating the ceiling effect and its preventive analogue. Each cell entry is the P(column value | row value).

causality to be evaluated, and the interpretations for the two causal directions are reversed from one case to the other (for experimental evidence of this pattern of inference in college students, see Wu and Cheng 1999).

The differences in interpretation and the reversal in interpretation across the two cases are easy to overlook as crucial tests between associationist and causal accounts: being psychologically compelling rather than counterintuitive, the phenomena may suggest to some researchers that there is nothing interesting to explain. In fact, these phenomena pose unmet challenges to all associationist models, psychological or normative, and to some causal models as well; the compelling rationality of the pattern of judgments should render the gap in these accounts all the more conspicuous.

Associationist measures, such as the ΔP model and the chi-square test, always yield a single value for a data set; they therefore cannot yield two values for a ceiling situation. Some Bayesian network models make inferences regarding causal structure based on qualitative patterns of statistical independence and dependence (e.g., Spirtes, Glymour, and Scheines 1993/2000; Pearl 2000); these models would therefore also make the same inference, or set of inferences, for the same independence pattern. Some Bayesian network models and a version of the chi-square test exclude from analysis data sets with extreme probability values; these models would be unable to explain why it is actually fine to infer at $P(e) = 1$ that $p_i = 0$ and at $P(e) = 0$ that $q_i = 0$.

In contrast, these inferential Necker cubes are readily explained by equations 2 and 3 from the causal theory. If e occurs all the time, with or without i, q_i cannot be assessed (i.e., has the undefined value of 0/0 according to equation 2), as there are no remaining entities in which i can possibly manifest its generative power. But in this case, p_i would have a value of 0 according to equation 3—i never prevents e on the occasions when there is an opportunity to do so. Conversely, if e never occurs, p_i cannot be assessed (has the undefined value of 0/0 according to equation 3), because there are no entities in which i can possibly manifest its preventive power. But in that case, q_i would have a value of 0 according to equation 2.

Phenomenon 3: An Asymmetry between the "Present" and "Absent" Values of a Candidate Cause in Conjunctive Causal Inference

Implications for Inferring a Simple Cause versus Inferring a Conjunctive Cause

Recall that under our causal approach, a cause exerts its influence when it is present and does nothing when it is absent. At first glance, intuition may seem to blatantly contradict this assumption. There is no doubt that under some conditions people do speak of, and probably think of, the absence of factors as causes. For example, someone who is trying to quit smoking cigarettes might say, "The absence of nicotine is causing my withdrawal symptoms;" and someone who is separated from a loved one might say, "Absence makes the heart grow fonder." But presence and absence are complementary concepts—what is expressible in terms of one can be similarly expressed in terms of the other. For example, "The absence of nicotine causes withdrawal symptoms," is formally equivalent to, "The presence of nicotine prevents withdrawal symptoms," although the two expressions may have different connotations. The choice of representation in the case of a simple cause does not affect whether one infers a causal relation.

In contrast, for conjunctive causes, whether someone forms the category of a conjunctive cause (i.e., whether one judges that the component causes interact) does depend on which value (presence or absence) of the component simple candidates is believed to be causal (Novick and Cheng 2004).

People's intuitions regarding conjunctive causes differ from the predictions of normative associationist models such as the chi-square test or the cross-product ratio, which would not yield different output values if the two values of each candidate factor are transposed (Novick and Cheng 2004). Neither would our associationist extension of the ΔP model to describe conjunctive causation (Cheng and Novick 1992). For both causal and associationist accounts, the respective symmetry properties of simple causes carry over to conjunctive causes because the latter are estimated on the basis of deviation from the independent influences of simple causes.

Let us illustrate the dependence of conjunctive causation on the causal value of a component factor. We will consider judgments on causal interaction in four patterns of outcomes, treating presence as a cause and absence as a cause in turn. For the next three figures, assume the following cover story:

Scientists working for a company that raises a particular type of lizard for sale as pets are investigating factors that may influence the skin color of these lizards. In their natural habitats, lizards of this type have been found to have skin that is either yellow or black. These scientists have conducted an experiment to test the influence of two minerals, mineral i and mineral j, on the lizards' skin color. For each of four months, twelve lizards were exposed to mineral i, mineral j, neither mineral, or both minerals. At the beginning of each month, the lizards were given time to recover to their natural color before the relevant experimental manipulation began. All other influences on skin color were held constant throughout. The states of the lizards at the end of each month are depicted in the figure (with yellow represented by the lighter shade and black represented by black). Assume that the results are accurate and reliable, and suspend whatever prior knowledge you may have about lizards' skin colors.

Consider outcome pattern 1 (see figure 1.6). The four panels in this figure show the colors of the twelve lizards when the lizards were—respectively, from the top—exposed to neither mineral, exposed to mineral i alone, exposed to mineral j alone, and exposed to both minerals. A dominant interpretation of this pattern of outcomes is that the presence of the minerals independently causes some lizards to turn black (Liljeholm and Cheng 2005). Mineral i turned two lizards black; mineral j turned three other lizards black; and when exposed to both minerals, a lizard that was turned black by either mineral stayed black. This interpretation follows the principle of superimposition that is consistent with Novick and Cheng's (2004) theory of conjunctive causes: when two unlike values of an outcome are

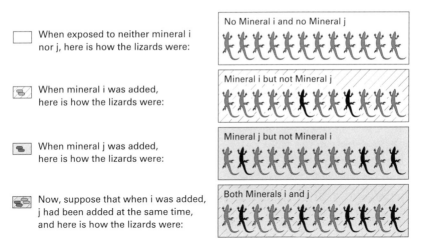

When exposed to neither mineral i nor j, here is how the lizards were:

No Mineral i and no Mineral j

When mineral i was added, here is how the lizards were:

Mineral i but not Mineral j

When mineral j was added, here is how the lizards were:

Mineral j but not Mineral i

Now, suppose that when i was added, j had been added at the same time, and here is how the lizards were:

Both Minerals i and j

Figure 1.6
Outcome Pattern 1: An illustration of outcomes that show the independent influence of minerals I and J on the color of the lizards.

superimposed in an entity (e.g., when the varied outcomes in the second and sixth lizards from the top three panels are combined in the bottom panel), the value that wins (blackness) is the one that the entity newly adopted when a cause was introduced (i.e., when a mineral changed from being absent to being present).[2]

Pattern 2 (see figure 1.7) is identical to pattern 1 except that all twelve lizards are black in the bottom panel. For this pattern, the minerals each individually cause blackness as before, but they also interact to cause more blackness than would be expected if the minerals had operated independently.

Now, let us consider patterns that are "absence" analogues of patterns 1 and 2. Imagine two patterns, patterns 3 and 4, that are respectively identical to patterns 1 and 2 except that the exposure-condition labels (but not the lizards) for the top and bottom panels are reversed, so that the progression through the panels by convention specifies the removal rather than the addition of the individual minerals. Because the reversal focuses attention on the removal of the minerals, it should encourage the representation of the absence of a mineral as causal. It should be clear that pattern 3, being an absence analogue of pattern 1, should convey no causal interaction if absence is the causal value. This pattern should still indicate no interaction,

When exposed to neither mineral i
nor j, here is how the lizards were:

When mineral i was added,
here is how the lizards were:

When mineral j was added,
here is how the lizards were:

Now, suppose that when i was added,
j had been added at the same time,
and here is how the lizards were:

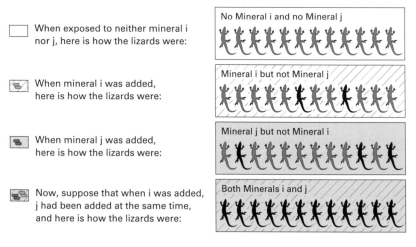

Figure 1.7
Outcome Pattern 2: An illustration of outcomes that show an interaction between
Minerals I and J on the color of the lizards.

however, if presence is the causal value. In that case, mineral *j* turned two
lizards yellow, mineral *i* turned three other lizards yellow, and when both
minerals were present, their influences superimposed, turning five lizards
yellow. Figure 1.8 shows pattern 4, the absence analogue of figure 1.7 (the
background shadings that redundantly represent the exposure conditions
are correspondingly shifted). If the *absence* of a mineral is perceived to
cause blackness, pattern 4 should show an interaction of the absence of
the two minerals to cause blackness, as does pattern 2 in terms of the *presence* of these minerals. Do reasoners spontaneously infer that the absence
of the minerals interact in this case? In a similar vein, do reasoners infer
that drugs that one is not taking interact with each other? We think not.

Our lizard figures were constructed to show that if only the "present"
value of a candidate factor can be causal, pattern 4 would convey no causal
interaction. Under this representation, the minerals each cause "yellow-
ness." Considering the panels in figure 1.8 from the bottom up, the presence of mineral *j* turned nine lizards "yellow," the presence of mineral *i*
turned ten lizards "yellow." When both minerals were present, every lizard
that was turned yellow by one or the other mineral, remained yellow (thus,
all twelve lizards in the top panel were yellow). In other words, following

When exposed to both minerals i and j, here is how the lizards were:

When mineral j was removed, here is how the lizards were:

When mineral i was removed, here is how the lizards were:

Now, suppose that when i was removed, j had been removed at the same time, and here is how the lizards were:

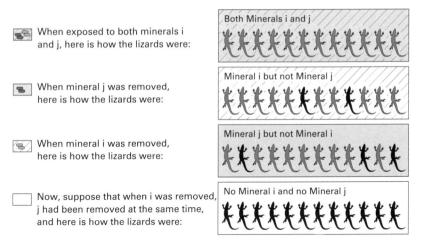

Both Minerals i and j

Mineral i but not Mineral j

Mineral j but not Mineral i

No Mineral i and no Mineral j

Figure 1.8
Outcome Pattern 4, the "absence" analogue of Pattern 2.

the same principle of superimposition as before—the value that wins is one that an entity newly adopted when a cause was introduced—the lighter shade now wins, and the pattern of superimposition (from the bottom up) conveys independence. Thus, the present and absent values of a causal factor are asymmetric, and judgments on causal interaction depend on this asymmetry.[3] Recall that, in contrast, predictions regarding causal interaction in associationist models are not dependent on the labeling of the two values of a candidate factor (Novick and Cheng 2004).

Empirical Evidence

To test whether only one value is causal and to measure untutored reasoners' default assumptions on the causal value, Liljeholm and Cheng (2005) conducted an experiment on college students. One practical difficulty to be overcome is that one cannot directly ask subjects about causal interactions without first essentially defining the concept for them, and potentially biasing their responses. To solve this problem, Liljeholm and Cheng showed subjects the four patterns and asked them to rate the complexity of the influences of the minerals; an interaction is more complex than independent influence. Because the ordering of the exposure conditions may contribute to complexity (e.g., the backwards ordering may feel more complex), the critical comparison is between two differences in subjects' complexity ratings:

1. that between patterns 1 and 2 (the latter should be more complex if presence is considered causal); and

2. that between patterns 3 and 4 (the latter should be more complex if absence is considered causal).

The two differences should be comparable if presence is not marked as causal.

College student volunteers were randomly assigned to receive one of the four outcome patterns along with the cover story. Each subject was asked two related questions about the stimuli: "What explains the changes in the lizards' skin color across the four panels?"; and, "Given your understanding of the minerals' influences on the lizards, how complex do you think are those influences?" Complexity, the dependent measure of actual concern, was specified as follows: "If one panel—either the top or the bottom one in particular—is different from what you would expect given the influences of the minerals in the other three panels, the pattern would be complex."

The subjects rated complexity on a numeric scale. If reasoners represent the presence of a factor as the causal value, the critical prediction is that the difference in complexity between patterns 3 and 4 would be smaller than that between patterns 1 and 2. A pattern of complexity ratings consistent with this prediction was observed: pattern 2 was (on average) rated considerably more complex than pattern 1 (more than 30 points higher on the 100-point scale); but patterns 3 and 4 were (on average) rated about equally complex (within 3 points of each other). The difference between the two differences was highly reliable. Recall that associationist models such as the ΔP and the chi-square predict no difference between the two differences.

In summary, at least in some situations, such as those in which the prevalence of the causal factors are unknown, the present value of a candidate factor is the one that exerts an influence despite the focus on the removal of the factor. The absent value does nothing, and the asymmetry between the two values is critical to whether two component factors form a conjunctive cause.

Phenomenon 4: An Asymmetry Around $P(e) = 0.5$ in Judgments of Whether a Causal Relation Exists

Overview

Another asymmetry occurs for answers to the basic qualitative question of whether a causal relation exists. When people are presented with data sets that have the same positive ΔP and are asked to judge whether a candidate cause produces an effect, and to rate their confidence in their judgment, their responses differ for data sets that are equidistant in opposite directions (i.e., symmetrical) around a 50/50 chance of the effect occurring. Consider two such data sets for which ΔP is 0.33: for one data set, on eighteen occasions on which c occurs, e occurs fifteen times; and on eighteen occasions on which c does not occur, e occurs nine times. For the other data set, on eighteen occasions on which c occurs, e occurs nine times; and on eighteen occasions on which c does not occur, e occurs three times. People are more confident that c causes e in the first data set than in the second (Liljeholm, Cheng, and Ford 2005). The chi-square test, in contrast, gives the same χ^2 value of 4.5 for both data sets, with the associated p-value of 0.03.

This asymmetry is interesting because it brings into focus the relations among structure learning, parameter estimation, and causal assumptions. Tenenbaum and Griffiths and others have drawn a distinction between structure learning and parameter estimation, and have characterized psychological work previous to their "causal support" model as concerning parameter estimation (Danks 2003; Griffiths and Tenenbaum 2005; Tenenbaum and Griffiths 2001). They write,

The ΔP and [causal] power models correspond to maximum likelihood parameter estimates on a fixed graph (Graph₁), while the support model corresponds to a (Bayesian) inference about which graph is the true causal structure. (Tenenbaum and Griffiths 2001, caption for figure 1)

(See figure 1.9, below, for the graphs under consideration.) Griffiths and Tenenbaum (2005, p. 347) further explain,

Structure learning refers to identification of the topology of the causal graph, while parameter estimation involves determining the parameters of the functional relationships between causes and effects for a given causal structure. Structure learning is arguably more fundamental than parameter estimation, since the parameters can only be estimated once the structure is known.

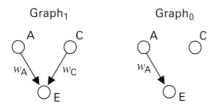

Figure 1.9
Two candidate causal structures representing, respectively, that C is, and is not, a cause of E.

In focusing on the topics of structure learning and parameter estimation, Tenenbaum and Griffiths have overlooked the causal assumptions that are at the heart of the debate between the associationist and causal approaches in the work on parameter estimation.

In fact, the causal assumptions that are critical to parameter estimation are just as critical to structure learning. To make this argument, it is necessary to begin with a description of Tenenbaum and Griffiths' (2001; Griffiths and Tenenbaum, in press) causal support model. (We limit our argument here to Bayesian inference, but a similar argument regarding causal asymmetry applies to null hypothesis testing.) As we will show, a causal variant of their model, which is consistent with the causal power theory, correctly predicts the asymmetry just described; in contrast, the other variant, an associationist one that is consistent with the ΔP model, incorrectly predicts symmetry. Ignoring the role of causal assumptions, Tenenbaum and Griffiths allow both variants in their model.

The Causal Support Model

The causal support model addresses the question of whether a causal relation exists (Griffiths and Tenenbaum 2005; Tenenbaum and Griffiths 2001); specifically, it evaluates which of the two causal structures in figure 1.9, $Graph_1$ or $Graph_0$, receives more support from the data. In the figure, C represents the candidate cause, and A represents alternative causes in the background. The parameters w_C and w_A are respectively the causal strength of C and of A to produce effect E. $Graph_1$ receiving greater support means that the evidence (the data) favors the existence of a causal relation between C and E. This model involves a comparison of the posterior probabilities of the two structures given the data—specifically, it takes the log of the ratio of those probabilities—assuming that the structures have an equal prior probability and that all values of causal strength are equally probable prior to the consideration of the data, both for C and for A. Thus, in this model, the assessment of whether a relation is causal involves assumptions and computations regarding causal strength. The relevant data consist of information on event frequencies such as that illustrated in our earlier figures on the side-effects of medicines.

Tenenbaum and Griffiths (2001) show that the ΔP and causal power measures are each a maximum likelihood estimate of w_C in Graph_1 (see figure 1.9). These measures are consistent with two alternative functional relationships in the calculation of the likelihoods of the data given Graph_1 in the causal support model. The ΔP measure corresponds to a linear relationship between the probability of e in the control group and the strength of the C, with ΔP estimating w_C; the probability of e in the control group estimating w_A; and the probability of e in the experimental group estimating $w_A + w_C$. In contrast, causal power corresponds to a noisy-OR relationship (as explained earlier), with w_C corresponding to generative power, q_C; and w_A corresponding to $P(A) \cdot q_A$, the probability of e produced by alternative causes. In this case, the probability of e in the experimental group estimates $w_C + w_A - w_C \cdot w_A$. There is nothing in the Bayesian approach adopted by the causal support model that inherently restricts it to either functional relationship, provided that for the linear function values of $w_A + w_C$ outside the $[0, 1]$ interval are omitted.

The Role of Causal Assumptions

Tenenbaum and Griffiths' (2001; Griffiths and Tenenbaum 2005) characterization of the psychological debate as confined to different estimates of parameters under a fixed graph, and their suggestion that issues concerning parameter estimation are less fundamental than those concerning structure learning, are misleading. It might be tempting to assume that structure learning models such as Tenenbaum and Griffiths', making use of graphs such as those in figure 1.9 with their arrows so intuitively interpreted to depict causal relations, necessarily provide a causal analysis. A more accurate characterization of the debate and of the relations among the various proposed models (e.g., ΔP, causal power, and causal support), however, is that both structure learning and parameter estimation models are critically dependent on whether causal assumptions (such as those underlying simple causal power) or associationist assumptions (such as those underlying ΔP) are made.

Even though the specific topic has been parameter estimation, the larger psychological debate has centered on whether causal assumptions are required, and the issues apply equally to structure learning. Like parameter estimation, structure learning can be causal or associationist. This distinction between causal versus associationist assumptions is critical because adopting the associationist linearity assumption implies that the structure learning model inherits the incoherent concept of independent causal influences discussed in the section on phenomenon 1.

The Asymmetry Revisited: Causal versus Associationist Predictions

As mentioned earlier, the assessment of whether a relation is causal in Tenenbaum and Griffiths' model (2001; Griffiths and Tenenbaum 2005), involves computations regarding the causal strengths of the candidate and background causes. When their model adopts the noisy-OR function (and corresponding causal assumptions) to combine causal strengths, it is able to explain the asymmetry in observed confidence judgments regarding whether a relation is causal mentioned at the beginning of this section; when their model adopts the linear function (and hence no causal assumptions), it is incapable of explaining these asymmetries. Let us return to the data sets that are symmetrical around the probability of 0.5, for which the chi-square test yields the same value of association. When the causal support model adopts the linear function, with values of $w_A + w_C$ restricted to the [0, 1] interval, the model gives the same support value, namely 1.85, for both sets. In contrast, when this model adopts the noisy-OR function, it gives support values of 1.89 and 1.38 respectively, in qualitative agreement with observed human causal judgments (Liljeholm, Cheng, and Ford 2005).

Summary

The observed asymmetry around the probability of 0.5 of causal judgments on whether a causal relation exists is consistent with the asymmetries in judgments of causal strength discussed earlier; the various asymmetries all stem from the causal assumptions underlying the judgments. An associationist process, by definition, does not make causal distinctions—such as the distinction between cause and effect, or the two values of a binary candidate cause—and thus gives rise to the various symmetric predictions,

predictions that reflect contradictory assumptions regarding independent causal influence. Thus, contrary to the view that assumptions about causal strength become relevant only after causal structure has been determined, these assumptions are in fact critical to a Bayesian evaluation of causal structure. Without the causal assumptions that underlie both parameter estimation and structure learning, neither the use of graphs nor Bayesian inference could constrain structure learning to be causal, or coherent.

The Appeal of Causal Representation: Coherence

The causal power theory (Cheng 1997, 2000; Novick and Cheng 2004) shows that there is coherence underlying people's intuitive causal judgments across multiple tasks. Current associationist models fail to capture this coherence in three related ways:

1. They do not allow for the possibility of independent causal influence.

2. They do not provide a parsimonious explanation of the four asymmetries; even with post-hoc settings of their current parameters, these models are still unable to account for the asymmetries.

3. They do not support the coherent derivation of other causal measures; in that sense, they fail to be *compositional*.

In contrast, the causal power theory (Cheng 1997, 2000; Novick and Cheng 2004) provides a parameter-free explanation of all four asymmetries. This unified explanation is a manifestation of the logical consistency and compositionality made possible by the causal assumptions under this approach.

A strong appeal of representing causal powers is that it allows the derivation of a variety of causal measures to answer different causal questions. We illustrated this capability in passing in our earlier sections. For example: (1) conjunctive causal power (Novick and Cheng 2004) is defined with respect to simple causal powers, making use of deviation from simple-power predictions; (2) generative simple power (equation 2) is logically related to preventive simple power (equation 3); and (3) the coherent variant of causal support (Tenenbaum and Griffiths 2001) incorporates the assumptions underlying simple causal power. Similarly, this approach allows one to derive answers to causal *attribution* questions; for example, what is the probability, given that an event has occurred, that the event is due to a particular candidate cause? Variants of attribution measures have appeared in the literatures in psychology, law, epidemiology, philosophy, and artificial intelligence (e.g., Cheng and Novick 2005; Pearl 2000; Salmon 1965; Stott, Stone, and Allen 2004). The causal-power framework allows one not only to see how and why causal strength and attribution measures are related; but also to understand the conditions under which the measures hold, for example, why the estimation of all of these measures requires no-confounding. (For derivations of several attribution measures using causal power, including the probability of the necessity of a candidate cause to produce an effect, see Cheng and Novick 2005.) No-confounding, after all, is not always a requirement for causal inference (e.g., Haavelmo 1943). In this section, we give an intuitive illustration of these aspects of coherence with three measures—causal power; a causal attribution measure; and an interpretation of ΔP not as causal strength, as we have argued against, but as the probability with which an effect is produced by a candidate cause i alone when i is present.

We mentioned earlier the role of no-confounding in the derivation of equation 2, the estimate of generative causal power (Cheng 1997). For an intuitive translation of this role, consider the data illustrated in figure 1.10, from which one might wish to estimate the causal power of medicine B. Recall that causal power is the probability that a candidate cause i produces an effect e when i is present. If one could wear lenses that allow one to see the causes of an outcome, one would "see," out of the patients in the experimental group (when medicine B is present), how many had headache caused by the medicine and arrive at the probability in question. Given the unavailability of causation lenses, some convoluted detective work is required: one first estimates the proportion of patients in the experimental group (the bottom panel) who would not have had a headache if they had not taken the medicine; then one observes the proportion out of this subgroup of patients who indeed have a headache, yielding the desired estimate. These patients' headaches must have come about as a result of medicine B and no other causes. One can estimate the first proportion by making use of the proportion of patients in the control group (the top panel) who do not have a headache (this is the denominator in equation 2; in the figure, this proportion is 2/3). But it should be clear from the nature of this estimate—in particular, from the use of the control group to make an inference regarding a quantity in the experimental group—that the estimate would be valid only if causes of headache other than the

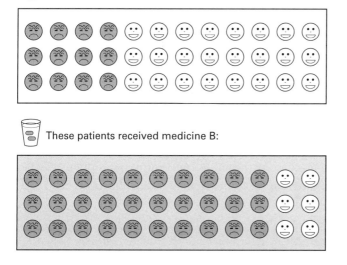

Figure 1.10
Stimulus material for Condition B from Buehner, Cheng, and Clifford (2003, Experiment 2).

medicine occur equally frequently in the two groups. This explains the no-confounding requirement for causal inference involving probabilistic contrast. In the figure, the second proportion—the proportion in the bottom panel who have a headache, out of those who would not have had a headache without the medicine—is 3/4. This is the generative causal power of medicine B.

Now, consider the probability that an effect e can be attributed to a candidate cause i, given that e has occurred, but not knowing whether i has occurred. (For psychological evidence for the use of this measure, see Johnson, Boyd, and Magnani 1994; and White 2004. For a more detailed explanation of the derivation of this measure, see Cheng and Novick 2005.) Let us denote this measure by $P(i \rightarrow e \mid e)$, where "$i \rightarrow e$" denotes that e is produced by i. It is easy to see how causal power can serve as a building block for constructing this measure. Because e is caused by i with probability $P(i) \cdot q_i$, the measure is simply

$$P(i \rightarrow e \,|\, e) = \frac{P(i) \cdot q_i}{P(e)}, \tag{4}$$

with q_i as given by equation 2. Thus, the no-confounding condition required for estimating q_i is also required for $P(i \rightarrow e \,|\, e)$.

Although ΔP is incoherent as a measure of causal strength, it can be interpreted instead as $P(i\text{-alone} \rightarrow e \,|\, i)$, the probability with which an effect e is due to a particular cause i alone, knowing that i is present (but other causes of e may be present as well). This interpretation is different from causal strength in that it restricts attribution of e to i alone. The value of the estimate is therefore dependent on how often alternative causes of e occur in the context in question. Pearl (2000) refers to this as the probability that a cause is both necessary and sufficient to produce an effect. Our more explicit expression of the multiple relevant causal relations clarifies the apparent contradiction that arises from speaking of necessity and sufficiency in probabilistic terms.

As an estimate of $P(i\text{-alone} \rightarrow e \,|\, i)$, the ΔP expression can be derived using causal power. Let us return to figure 1.1. In the left box (when i is present), e is produced by i (as represented by the dashed circle) with probability q_i. On some of these occasions, e is also produced by alternative causes (as represented by the overlap of the two circles). The crescent part of the dashed circle (the complete dashed circle minus the overlap area) therefore represents the set of events in which e is produced by i alone. Recall that when there is no confounding, the undashed circle in this box, representing $P(a \,|\, i) \cdot q_a$, is estimated by $P(e \,|\, \bar{i})$. Thus, the desired probability is:

$$P(i\text{-alone} \rightarrow e \,|\, i) = q_i - q_i \cdot P(e \,|\, \bar{i}) = q_i \cdot [1 - P(e \,|\, \bar{i})] = \Delta P. \tag{5}$$

The simplification in the last step makes use of equation 2. Thus, the no-confounding condition that is required for estimating q_i is also required for $P(i\text{-alone} \rightarrow e \,|\, i)$. It should be clear that, under this interpretation, the ΔP value of a given candidate cause should vary depending on how large the undashed circle (and hence the overlap) is; in other words, it is not an invariant property of the candidate, as strength ideally should be. Other measures of attribution can be similarly derived using the causal powers of candidate and alternative causes as elemental building blocks (Cheng and Novick 2005).

Summary and Conclusion

The four compellingly intuitive psychological asymmetries, which may appear unrelated at first glance, are in fact coherent under an approach that explains observable events by unobservable causal powers. Moreover, the theoretical construct of causal power—the ideally invariant probability with which a cause produces or prevents an effect—provides the building blocks that support the derivation of a variety of causal measures in answer to different causal questions, including:

1. measures for estimating the strength of simple causes and of conjunctive causes,
2. measures for evaluating the existence of causal relations, and
3. measures for estimating various causal attributions.

The coherence underlying the asymmetries, as well as the compositionality of causal power, reveals the incoherence of both psychological and normative associationist accounts. A central problem with the associationist approach is that, unlike the causal power approach, it does not allow the possibility of independent causal influence. The comparable problems that beset common statistical procedures have practical implications. Statistical inference is a cornerstone of science—and science distinguishes itself from quackery by its rationality. If some widely used associationist statistical measures suffer from a similar problem as their psychological counterparts —namely, the lack of causal representation—it would seem that science could benefit from a radical reassessment of associationist statistics when applied to test causal hypotheses.

Acknowledgments

The preparation of this paper was supported by NIH Grant MH64810. We thank Deborah Clifford for the graphic design of all of our figures, other than figures 1.5 and 1.9; Eric Ford for help with setting up integrals in our calculations; and Clark Glymour and Keith Holyoak for clarifying our arguments. Correspondence concerning this article may be addressed to: Patricia W. Cheng, Mimi Liljeholm, or Christina Ford, Department of Psychology, Franz Hall, University of California, Los Angeles, California 90095-1563; or to Laura R. Novick, Department of Psychology and Human Development, Peabody no. 512, 230 Appleton Place, Vanderbilt University, Nashville, Tennessee 37203-5721. Electronic mail may be sent to: cheng@lifesci.ucla.edu, laura.novick@vanderbilt.edu, mlil@ucla.edu, or christis@ucla.edu.

Notes

1. No-confounding is not a necessary condition when there is information on more than two variables. (See the literature on instrumental variables, e.g., Glymour 2001; Haavelmo 1943; Pearl 2000; Spirtes, Glymour, and Scheines 1993/2000).

2. Note that the causal relations in pattern 1 do not satisfy the assumptions in Novick and Cheng's (2004) theory of conjunctive causes: specifically, the influences of the two component causes, minerals i and j, are not independent of the background causes, but instead are mutually exclusive (if mineral i changes the color of a certain lizard, mineral j does not, and vice versa). The pattern was so constructed as to allow both it and its absence analogue, pattern 3, to indisputably convey the independent influences of the two minerals. To explain the intuitive judgments, an extension of Novick and Cheng's theory that allows for an interaction between each candidate cause and the background causes would be needed.

3. Although we have focused our discussion on presence as the causal value, the absent value being causal would simply be the other side of the same coin. As long as only one value of a binary candidate factor is causal, the designation of the causal value would make a difference to whether a given situation involves conjunctive causation.

References

Buehner, M., P. Cheng, and D. Clifford. 2003. "From Covariation to Causation: A Test of the Assumption of Causal Power." *Journal of Experimental Psychology: Learning, Memory, and Cognition* 29: 1119–1140.

Cartwright, N. 1989. *Nature's Capacities and Their Measurement.* Oxford: Clarendon Press.

Cheng, P. 1997. "From Covariation to Causation: A Causal Power Theory." *Psychological Review* 104: 367–405.

Cheng, P. 2000. "Causality in the Mind: Estimating Contextual and Conjunctive Causal Power." In *Explanation and Cognition*, edited by F. Keil and R. Wilson. Cambridge, Mass.: MIT Press.

Cheng, P., and L. Novick. 1992. "Covariation in Natural Causal Induction." *Psychological Review* 99: 365–382.

Cheng, P., and L. Novick. 2005. "Constraints and Nonconstraints in Causal Learning: Reply to White (2005) and to Luhmann and Ahn (2005)." *Psychological Review* 112: 694–707.

Cheng, P., J. Park, A. Yarlas, and K. Holyoak. 1996. "A Causal-Power Theory of Focal Sets." In *The Psychology of Learning and Motivation*, vol. 34: *Causal Learning*, edited by D. Shanks, K. Holyoak, and D. Medin. New York: Academic Press.

Danks, D. 2003. "Equilibria of the Rescorla-Wagner Model." *Journal of Mathematical Psychology* 47: 109–121.

Danks, D., T. Griffiths, and J. Tenenbaum. 2003. "Dynamical Causal Learning." In *Advances in Neural Information Processing Systems 15*, edited by S. Becker, S. Thrun, and K. Obermayer. Cambridge, Mass.: MIT Press.

Feinberg, S. 1980. *The Analysis of Cross-Classified Categorical Data*, 2d ed. Cambridge, Mass.: MIT Press.

Glymour, C. 2001. *The Mind's Arrows: Bayes Nets and Graphical Models in Psychology*. Cambridge, Mass.: MIT Press.

Griffiths, T., and J. Tenenbaum. 2005. "Elemental Causal Induction." *Cognitive Psychology* 51: 334–384.

Haavelmo, T. 1943. "The Statistical Implications of a System of Simultaneous Equations." *Econometrica* 11: 1–12.

Haavelmo, T. 1944. "The Probability Approach in Econometrics." *Econometrica* 12 (supplement): 1–118.

Jenkins, H., and W. Ward. 1965. "Judgment of Contingency between Responses and Outcomes." *Psychological Monographs* 7: 1–17.

Johnson, J., K. Boyd, and P. Magnani. 1994. "Causal Reasoning in the Attribution of Rare and Common Events." *Journal of Personality and Social Psychology* 66: 229–242.

Lien, Y., and P. Cheng. 2000. "Distinguishing Genuine from Spurious Causes: A Coherence Hypothesis." *Cognitive Psychology* 40: 87–137.

Liljeholm, M., and P. Cheng. 2005. "Do the Absences of Things Interact?" Unpublished manuscript, University of California, Los Angeles.

Liljeholm, M., P. Cheng, and C. Ford. 2005. "Structure Learning, Parameter Estimation, and Causal Assumptions." Unpublished manuscript, University of California, Los Angeles.

Lober, K., and D. Shanks. 2000. "Is Causal Induction Based on Causal Power? Critique of Cheng (1997)." *Psychological Review* 107: 195–212.

Novick, L., and P. Cheng. 2004. "Assessing Interactive Causal Influence." *Psychological Review* 111: 455–485.

Pearce, J. 1987. "A Model for Stimulus Generalization in Pavlovian Conditioning." *Psychological Review* 94: 61–73.

Pearl, J. 2000. *Causality: Models, Reasoning, and Inference.* Cambridge: Cambridge University Press.

Rescorla, R., and A. Wagner. 1972. "A Theory of Pavlovian Conditioning: Variations in the Effectiveness of Reinforcement and Nonreinforcement." In *Classical Conditioning II: Current Theory and Research,* edited by A. Black and W. Prokasy. New York: Appleton-Century Crofts.

Salmon, W. 1965. "The Status of Prior Probabilities in Statistical Explanation." *Philosophy of Science* 32: 137–146.

Spirtes, P., C. Glymour, and R. Scheines. 1993/2000. *Causation, Prediction and Search,* 2d ed. Cambridge, Mass.: MIT Press.

Stott, P., D. Stone, and M. Allen. 2004. "Human Contribution to the European Heatwave of 2003." *Nature* 432: 610–614.

Tenenbaum, J., and T. Griffiths. 2001. "Structure Learning in Human Causal Induction." In *Advances in Neural Information Processing Systems 13,* edited by T. Leen, T. Dietterich, and V. Tresp. Cambridge, Mass.: MIT Press.

Van Hamme, L., and E. Wasserman. 1994. "Cue Competition in Causality Judgment: The Role of Nonrepresentation of Compound Stimulus Elements." *Learning and Motivation* 25: 127–151.

White, P. 2004. "Judgment of Two Causal Candidates from Contingency Information: Effects of Relative Prevalence of the Two Causes." *Quarterly Journal of Experimental Psychology* 57A: 961–991.

Woodward, J. 2003. *Making Things Happen: A Theory of Causal Explanation.* Oxford: Oxford University Press.

Wu, M., and Cheng, P. 1999. "Why Causation Need Not Follow from Statistical Association: Boundary Conditions for the Evaluation of Generative and Preventive Causal Powers." *Psychological Science* 10: 92–97.

2   Causality and Computation

Patrick Suppes

First question: How do intentional computations relate to the surrounding physical causes?

I begin the answer with two examples of computation.

Example 1. I am a hardworking experimental biologist. I have a surprising observation and a too-simple probabilistic theory about the phenomena. I use a standard program to compute the probability p of this observation under the null hypothesis of the theory. The computer says to me, "p is less than ten to the power minus 15." (My computer often talks to me.)

Do I believe it? Maybe. But is this because I have some grand theory of deterministic causality that will not treat my intentional request with proper respect? Certainly not. On the other hand, I may not trust the intentional effort of the programmer who coded an algorithm for the computation. Why? The problem of rounding errors in such "fine-structure" computations. (Moreover, although I know he is a clever programmer, I also know that his statistical background is not his strong point.)

Example 2. I am a computer designer of a new supercomputer. I want it to be very fast, but also accurate. Do I worry about physical causes of errors, or, rather, do I worry about their frequency under "standard" conditions? Certainly yes.

Here is what von Neumann had to say in a famous early paper: "Error is … not an extraneous and misdirected or misdirecting accident, but an essential part of the process … fully comparable to that of the intended and correct logical structure" (von Neumann 1956, p. 43). Von Neumann goes on to compute methods for building a reliable computer out of unreliable components. These are important matters to those responsible for designing and manufacturing real computers. Or just as serious for those writing software—which for most of us is, in the form of "bugs," the really troublesome aspect of modern computing.

But such errors, standing in the way of pure and wholly reliable intentional implementations of whatever computations are needed, do not seem to raise any doubts or fears about the kind of universe we live in.

Why not?

I do not think I have ever heard a philosopher or scientist expressing a serious worry about how there could, in fact, be the billions of intentional computations, natural (i.e., in brains) and artificial (i.e., in computers), every day in what must be a dreary world of determinate causes for every event, fully in the spirit of the Antithesis of Kant's Third Antinomy. "There is no freedom, but everything in the world happens solely in accordance with laws of nature" (Kant 1781/1997, A445). Or, in a dual version, in a too-lively world of endless random causes, generated spontaneously, in the absolute sense characteristic of Kant's Thesis in the Third Antinomy. "Causality in accordance with laws of nature is not the only one from which all the appearances of the world can be derived. It is also necessary to assume another causality through freedom in order to explain them" (Kant 1781/1997, A444).

To someone seriously interested in the details of natural or artificial computing, it is clear that focusing on the outworn horns of Kant's Third Antinomy is a nonstarter. Something more subtle and flexible that matches the empirical phenomena, especially of biology, is needed.

How can watery messes of matter acquire intentional properties? In my view of things, computations started early—billions of years ago, at the very beginning of life. Here, there may well be a place for spontaneity, or chance combinations of elements that formed the first larger prebiological molecules leading up, after some considerable time, to what we might think of as the first living cells. Getting to these first cells almost certainly took millions of years; but even then, the computational power of these first cells was limited. Yet in my conceptual view they already had primitive intentional characteristics—were able to adapt in very restricted ways. It took an enormous amount of time to take the next steps.

The two most important characteristics of living beings as we know them are being able to reproduce and being able to adapt. Adaptability comes in two flavors, one is from genetic modification and the other from learning. (Cf. Aristotle 1975, 412a15: "... by life, we mean the capacity for self-sustenance, growth, and decay.") I do not want to argue with those who do not agree with my conceptual view that primitive intentions are manifested in the first single cells; but I take a much stronger stand once learning and conditioning occur in the smallest animals.

Already in little worms like *aplysia*, with a nervous system of about 10,000 neurons, it is easy to demonstrate the ability to be conditioned to move toward some phenomena and avoid others. Moreover, we can trace, even if not in a complete way, the physical modifications in the neurons that result from such associations or conditioning.

Indeed, we can continue this story up to the rich perceptual computations performed by many species of mammals, and in the case of vision, for example, birds and other animals as well. Above all, there is, as far as I can see, no real air of paradox about these computational developments that are clearly intentional in character, serving as they do as important means for achieving some goal.

Let us go now to digital computers. What happens to our mathematical concept of correct computation when actual computations are performed? Do physical causes interfere and make any concept of correctness irrelevant? Yes, sometimes physical causes do interfere, power failure being one of the best examples. But, no, this does not mean the concept of correctness is not applicable. As in all real applications of concepts of correctness, the best we can hope for is "most of the time." Von Neumann's calculations about reliable computations, referred to earlier, are in this spirit.

So, the short answer to the first question is that just given: the billions, indeed trillions, of computations—biological (i.e., natural), and artificial—intentionally performed each day, are mostly correct. For we know something about our physical environment—unconsciously, in the case of most biological computations; and scientifically and consciously, at least on the part of some persons, in the case of digital computations. This knowledge, implicit or explicit, guides us to compute mainly in ways that work. There is nothing a priori about these endless computations. They could take place only in some environments, but not in others—certainly not in randomly chosen locations in the physical universe.

Thus, not surprisingly, we find our computations conserved, if you will, in the physical environment surrounding them, most of the time.

Second question: Does it matter for computation whether physical causes are deterministic or probabilistic?

No, it does not matter, for the theory of random errors has historically been developed without addressing the question of whether or not there is genuine objective randomness in nature. Moreover, a modern result is this: with realism about systems never being completely isolated and therefore subject to variable external influences or forces, and ditto for the measuring instruments, we cannot distinguish deterministic systems without complete isolation from stochastic systems. No matter how hard we try.

An easily visualized example is that of Sinai billiards (named after the Russian mathematician Y. G. Sinai). Such a billiard setup is realized by placing a convex obstacle in the middle of the table, from which a ball hitting it is reflected and satisfies the same physical laws as in hitting one of the sides. Start a ball in motion, with the usual idealized assumption of no loss of energy, so that it continues indefinitely. After a while, only probabilistic predictions of its position on the table can be made.

Here is a general theorem about such systems.

Theorem 4: *There are processes which can equally well be analyzed as deterministic systems of classical mechanics or as indeterministic Markov processes, no matter how many observations are made, if observations have only a bounded finite accuracy.* (Ornstein and Weiss 1991, p. 40)

Such bounded accuracy has two natural universal sources present in observation of physical systems. There is no complete physical isolation possible, and instruments of measurement produce results that are not exactly accurate when measuring any continuous quantity. So, from this viewpoint, a universal positive or negative answer to the second question is misguided. For many important physical phenomena, the right answer is: "It does not matter." (For a detailed elaboration, see Suppes 1993, 1999.)

When such a choice between different models has occurred previously in physics—and it has occurred repeatedly in a variety of examples, such as free choice of a frame of reference in Galilean relativity, or choice between the Heisenberg or Schrödinger representation in quantum mechanics—the natural move is toward a more abstract concept of invariance. What is especially interesting about the empirical indistinguishability and resulting abstract invariance, in the case of Sinai billiards and the like, is that at the mathematical level the different kinds of models are inconsistent—that is, the assumption of both a deterministic and a stochastic model leads, in many standard cases, to a contradiction when fully spelled out. On the other hand, it leads, in these standard cases, to no contradiction at the level of observations.

Third question: How does the normative concept of correct computation relate to the actual empirical process of computation?

Answer: just like other norms relate to other actual processes. The conceptual problem is that we tend to think of computation as a nonphysical, purely theoretical matter. But this is nonsense, and just a matter of loose thinking. The longer answer requires expanding on my general theory of norms, which are also, for me, empirical processes, but I will not do that here.

More important is to say something in greater detail about the relation between norms for correctness of computation and actual computations. The first, and in many ways most enlightening, remark is that there is an enormous difference of detail between the two. I mean that in the sense that we impose a norm about the correctness of computation; but, ordinarily, that norm does not fix in any unique way the many individual steps of the computation. The main focus of the norm is to request correctness, where it is understood that a correct computation can be done in many different ways. So there is, in one sense, a one-many relation between the norm and the actual computation.

The second remark is that satisfaction of the notion of correctness has to be conditioned on the absence of "irregular" events and, also, upon a nonexplicit reference to *ceteris paribus* conditions. The examples to illustrate the kind of exceptions that are permitted here, without violating the norm, are unlimited in any ordinary sense. I just mention a few. If, in the middle of an actual computation, there is a power interrupt, then we accept the gap in time in the computation and the unusual steps that may be taken in shutdown of the computer system. We return to continuation of the computation, and we judge it as being correct when the uncorrupted steps are satisfactory. Of course, in almost all cases, we will be wary of something unexpected happening. If the computation is at all complex, almost certainly we will consider the safe thing to be that of restarting the computation from the beginning. In taking these steps of restarting, we are not saying that the norm has been violated, because it is understood that, in actual computing, external causes will occasionally intervene in an unexpected way, and these are not to be judged as principled failures of the correctness of the computation. We could spell this out in still other ways. We could say that we may well be inclined to judge the computation correct when each step, qua computation, is correct, even if some of the computational steps have intervening steps of accidental interventions. I will not go further into this here, but note that the judgment of correctness is very much more complicated when the errors are frequent enough to require statistical analysis, as in the case originally considered by von Neumann.

Another consideration often enters in satisfying the norm of correctness when computations are of great importance. They may deliberately be done several times on different computers and, even in some cases, using programs that are written by different programmers, just to make sure that the important correct answer is indeed well established as correct. Notice, in these cases, that what is taken as evidence of correctness is multiple confirmation. Obviously, a more analytical and explicit approach can be taken, as in verification step-by-step of an algorithm by a person checking correctness, or by another computer program that is checking correctness. A good deal of effort has been spent on computer programs to automatically verify the correctness of proofs, and the even more important problem of verifying the correctness of programs. It has turned out that for complex programs, this is a difficult task, and only in relatively more simple cases do we still have adequate programs to make an analytical but automatic verification of the correctness of a computation. Notice, of course, that these programs are written without attention to any intervention by accidental, external causes. They assume that all of that will be fine, and the focus is entirely on an error in the program itself.

Still another point—to show the complexity of the topic—is that the verification program or the human individual checking the correctness of each step can also make an error, because that process is not *a priori* or metaphysical, but strictly empirical as well. When we think a much-used program is correct, this is because it has been examined for errors from many different standpoints. This examination for errors is not due to unexpected incursions in the ordinary way of thinking about things, but due to a mistake in the original coding. But, such accidental incursions can occur in programs that are used for some considerable time and, in fact, do occur much too often because of machine failures or other kinds of possible errors. A large program that is used for a very long period of time will accumulate errors that were not in the program originally, and these also, empirically, must be searched for and found.

I emphasize, finally, that in spite of my remarks about the many empirical errors that can occur, this does not at all disturb the fact that norms are important and central to computation. Without a goal—without a norm for what is correct—computations would be of little use.

Fourth question: At the normative level, does the concept of correct computation correspond to the morally correct thing to do in the context of personal conduct?

My answer is affirmative, even though distinctions can be drawn. One distinction to be kept in mind is that we have an explicit theory of computations or algorithms that is more definite and detailed in formulation than almost anything about personal moral conduct. Given a proposed computation, we can often prove it is correct, or, if too complex, provide elaborate empirical data. The answer for human conduct requires some more distinctions.

The excruciatingly detailed verification of correct computation, or the exactness of von Neumann's arguments about how to handle error-prone computers with faulty hardware, have no analog of any close nature in terms of personal conduct, in the sense of moral conduct. On the other hand, they do have analogs in terms of norms about human conduct in many other arenas. The range that immediately suggests itself involves those areas of human performance requiring well-skilled perception and motor control. One obvious example is the meticulous and extended training of airplane pilots. A further range of examples is to be found in the current level of training in highly competitive sports—from the Tour de France, where there is much concern with the proper use of aerodynamics to facilitate the lead rider of a team, to the careful attention to every aspect of movement in a sprinter for the 100- or 200-meter, and longer races as well.

My point is that these activities, requiring such refined perception and motor activity, all depend completely on well-defined norms. In many cases, the norms are so obvious and clear that they receive little explicit formulation. But the kind of detailed use of physics in many of them is testimony to the elaboration of procedures meant to satisfy a clear and definite norm. Something similar is to be said about the many physical processes of manufacture of standard physical objects, such as high-performance motors or even motors that perform at a level that is not necessarily the very top. Quality control of manufacturing processes is now one of the better applications of modern statistics, and it moves hand in glove with clearly set norms. Satisfying these norms requires superb human performance and judgment.

In talking about these different kinds of human cases, instead of "perception and judgment" I could just as well have talked about "human computation," as opposed to computer computation. Note that the apple cart of all these good human computations can also be easily upset by unexpected external causes. It is just that in a large number of cases, no such unexpected events occur, so the norms can function in a realistic empirical way. The performance being judged by the norm will not be perfect, but it can be extremely good.

Fifth question: On the basis of the answers to the first four questions, does there remain a conceptual problem about free will?

My answer is, "Certainly not." But there is much to be learned about how the will actually works. I join Aristotle, Aquinas, and William James in liking this old-fashioned term, "will," which is not much used by psychologists and is looked upon with suspicion by many philosophers.

The theory of the will is the theory of how we make choices and take actions; a central question being, when do we want to claim that the will is free, and a free choice or free action has been taken? But there is no paradox—exotic or banal—about such exercise of the will. There is no mysterious conundrum about causes and free will, just as there is none about causes and computation.

Intentional computations and free choices by smart humans may be looked upon as the stratosphere of biological activity, but they are still biological in character and a natural part of the physical world, as is the rest of biology. Indeed, the questions raised here could be easily transferred to a discussion of DNA as another form of natural computation.

There is of course a beautiful, long, and complicated story in all of this. It is the story of how these quintessentially human activities developed billions of years after the first beginnings of life. As I have already said—but it bears repeating—for me intentions were embodied in all kinds of animals long before there were any humans. It is this development, not the very recent questions about moral responsibility, that is a wonder to behold. The earliest animals that mothered their young are the true miracle. The distance between these animals and inert, lifeless matter is much greater than the distance between them and us, however you think about the comparison.

But my descriptions of the phenomena of computing and choosing too much resemble what one would expect from a Victorian novel. The important remark about causes, I have saved for now. My chapter, and much work on intentional activities such as computation, are in terms of their being isolated and protected from bad causal influences. From one angle this is true; but what is not true is that there is, or can be, any absolute isolation. Why? Because any physical activity such as computing, thinking, or choosing must be constantly using energy and often matter as well. The causal interaction between intentional process and physical world is continual and essential. The realization physically of any intentional action must be fully supported by physical causes, such as inward flows of energy, matched approximately over time by outward flows as well. As Aristotle and Aquinas so aptly put it, there can be no separation of mind and body, and so it is with intentions and physical causes.

In fact, there is something mistaken about the phrase "mind and body." This common idiom suggests that bodies are well-defined physical objects, fixed in space and time at any given point. But, in fact, when we look at the detailed activities of what we call bodies, really a better description is "mind and bodily processes," because the physical object we refer to as a human body is not at all static, but something that is continually changing with the inflow and outflow of energy and matter. A fantasy computation in probability theory, for example, is how many humans now alive have, somewhere in their bodies, at the current time, a molecule that once occupied Newton's body. Now, "mind" also can be misleading in suggesting something separate—as it often has, in the history of philosophy—and I am wary of the phrase "mental processes and bodily processes," because it suggests, somehow, an invocation of the dualisms of old. A description that moves away from these confusing, if not mistaken, past concepts could be something like, *computations made by biological processes*. The wording is awkward, but the meaning is clearer. Additional clarity can result from distinguishing, wherever possible, between perceptual and mental computations.

References

Aristotle. 1975. *De Anima (On the Soul)*, 4th ed. Translated by W. Hett. Cambridge, Mass.: Harvard University Press.

Kant, I. 1781/1997. *Critique of Pure Reason*. Translated by P. Guyer and A. Wood. New York: Cambridge University Press.

Ornstein, D., and B. Weiss. 1991. "Statistical Properties of Chaotic Systems." *Bulletin of the American Mathematical Society* 24: 11–116.

Suppes, P. 1993. "The Transcendental Character of Determinism." In *Midwest Studies in Philosophy*, vol. 18, edited by P. French, T. Uehling, and H. Wettstein. South Bend, Ind.: University of Notre Dame Press.

Suppes, P. 1999. "The Noninvariance of Deterministic Causal Models." *Synthese* 121: 181–198.

von Neumann, J. 1956. "Probabilistic Logics and the Synthesis of Reliable Organisms from Unreliable Components." In *Automata Studies*, edited by C. Shannon and J. McCarthy. Princeton: Princeton University Press.

3 Actual Causes and Thought Experiments

Clark Glymour and Frank Wimberly

1

One set of questions about causation concerns how to discover a correct causal mechanism to explain the distribution of events. Quite another set of questions concerns whether one particular event caused another, or prevented another. The latter are questions of actual causation. Generally, actual causation has little if any bearing on predictions of phenomena, but it does bear on issues of responsibility, and so of morality, law, and historical explanation.

Absent some detailed specification of the structures of situations in which causation and prevention are to be assessed, trying to say anything general and informative about the conditions under which one event actually causes or prevents another seems a fool's task. Event E may be potentially caused by events B or C, for example, and all three may occur, but unless we know details of the mechanism we should be reluctant to judge whether B, or C, or both, or something else, is the cause. The causal connection between events of type B and C and events of type E might be stochastic; B might interrupt the mechanism by which C would otherwise cause E, or C might do that for B. The mechanism by which B produces E might be faster than the mechanism by which C produces E, and so on. For judgments of actual causation, we need details.

Even details are not enough. Our judgments of what caused what in a specific situation, with well-understood potential causal relations and mechanisms, surely depend on factors of different kinds. Some of those factors are "structural" or "formal," and have nothing to do with the nature of the particular features involved, but only with how their presence or absence influences, or could influence, one another. Other factors have to do with the usual intentions motivating a kind of action, or with how normal or abnormal a condition is, or with combinations of causal and moral attributions. If we are told a causal story in which a poison or an antidote is administered, we infer intentions, and those inferences affect our judgments of actual causation. If an untoward event (a boulder falling) causes another (ducking the boulder) which causes a third (survival), we may be reluctant to call the first event a cause of the third, because the third is the normal case (what would have happened in the normal course of things).

The first principle in science is to separate the variables in a problem, to break it into solvable pieces. So let it be with philosophy. The causal judgments that are independent of context should be determinable from relationships of unnamed variables or events, without cover stories about assassins and antidotes and so on. It may be that without such cover stories some, perhaps many, judgments are equivocal—varying from person to person, or simply uncertain for any one of us. If so, we need to understand the varieties, and the possible consistent principles, no one of which may account for all of the varying intuitions. It may be, of course, that some structural principles largely covary with judgments that involve other features, such as ordinary intentions; but that is insufficient reason for lumping them together without first studying the possible structural principles. Despite the interest and enormous ingenuity of the stories fitted over structures, we should leave them aside until we have better understood the possible causal properties of anonymous structures. Of course, once the plausible structural possibilities and alternatives are clarified, one should want to know how they combine and interact with informal features of situations to yield causal judgments, and whether those interactions and combinations obey any clear principles.

David Lewis introduced a simple class of examples in which all variables are binary, one representing an occurrence and zero an absence of an event of some type; and the dependencies among variables are all of the form

$$E = (A_1 + \cdots + A_n) * (1 - B_1) * \cdots * (1 - B_k)$$

$$=_{df.} fe(A_1, \ldots, A_n; B_1, \ldots, B_k); \quad \cdot \tag{1}$$

where $A_1, \ldots, A_n$, $B_1, \ldots, B_k$ are all parents (respectively "positive" and "negative") of E, and the plus is (and will be throughout this paper) Boolean addition (Lewis 1973). Lewis discussed such systems as "neuron diagrams" which, though represented pictorially, are formally equivalent to

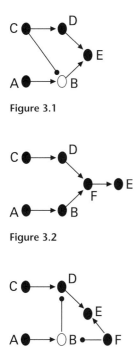

Figure 3.1

Figure 3.2

Figure 3.3

systems of equations of form (1) (above) with the intuitive caveat that the diagram and associated equations represent a complete description of the causal system. Circles are Boolean variables, whose values are one (dark) or zero (light); and each variable X is a function of its parents, with a parent in the role of an A in the formula above if the edge from it to X is marked $\rightarrow$, and in the role of a B above if the edge from it to X is marked $\bullet$. Completeness means this: only system values satisfying the equations are allowed unless there is an intervention setting values of variables; the only possible interventions are those setting values for represented varia- bles. We will later consider relaxations of the completeness assumption, but figures 3.1–3.8 are examples of such completeness.

Instead of restricting dependencies to form (1), following Halpern and Pearl (2000) we can allow that in networks of binary variables, a variable may be any Boolean function of its parents M,

$$E = \beta(X_1, \ldots, X_n),$$ (2)

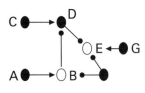

Figure 3.4

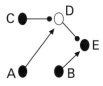

Figure 3.5

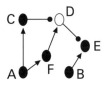

Figure 3.6

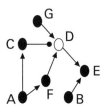

Figure 3.7

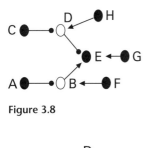

Figure 3.8

E = D * B; B = A; C = D

Figure 3.9

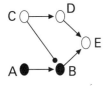

E = D * B; D = C; B = A

Figure 3.10

where $X_1, \ldots, X_n$ are the parents of E, and β is any Boolean function. Parent variables are no longer separated into positive and negative, because the distinction no longer makes sense except in a context of other causes: one and the same value can, in conjunction with a value of another variable, be a cause of an effect; and in conjunction with still another variable it can prevent that effect. There are just edges with arrowheads in these pictorial representations—and no edges with bullet endings. The nodes without any edges directed into them are zero-indegree variables. The values of the zero-indegree variables determine the values of all other variables. The nodes without any edges directed into them are zero-indegree variables.

48   C. Glymour and F. Wimberly

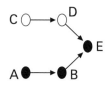

E = B(1−D); C=D; A=B

Figure 3.11

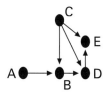

E=C+D; B=A*C; D=B*C

Figure 3.12

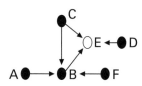

E=D(1−B)(1−C); B=A+F(1−C)

Figure 3.13

E=(C*B)+A

Figure 3.14

A minimal theory of actual causation should provide a decision procedure for all cases of these kinds answering the question: is the actual value X_a of X a cause of the actual value E_a of E? A more ambitious theory would provide a decision procedure when the variables may take on multiple values (not just present or absent); when dependencies are not 0/1 valued, but not Boolean functions; and when the dependencies are stochastic. All of these variations create special problems, and we will consider here only binary variables, Boolean functions, and a very limited form of stochastic dependency. It is not the least obvious how to decide the correctness of any such theory or decision procedure, since there is no independent standard of "actual causation" beyond reflective judgment, and judgments may differ considerably as the cases grow more intricate.

Although the problem is more or less embedded in the philosophical literature, and philosophers and computer scientists at least are apt to give quite firm answers to cases, there is something odd about it. Philosophers also commonly hold that causes and effects are events. Events are happenings, localized changes of circumstances. But in the the diagrams shown in figures 3.1–3.14 there are no changes—we are given only a system of potential dependencies, "equations of the system," and the actual *state* of the system. One can think of such diagrams as describing possible sequences of events: start with the system in some state; change the values of some of the zero-indegree variables; so long as the laws of the system are satisfied, values of other variables must change accordingly. Now a change in the values of some of the zero-indegree variables necessitates a cascade of changes in other variables. Imagine, for example, that the state in figure 3.2 had come about in the following way: all variables had value 0, then A changed to 1, so the state became $A = B = F = E = 1$; $C = D = 0$. Then C changed to 1, so the state became as in figure 3.2. Surely we would not say that $C = 1$ caused $E = 1$. The diagrams above do not say from what state the given state arose. Perhaps those who have clear judgments in these cases implicitly assume a standard alternative state from which the actual state was realized; most plausibly, that alternative state in which every zero-indegree variable with actual value 1 has alternative value 0, and every zero-indegree variable with actual value 0 has value 0. But when we consider arbitrary Boolean functions, even that alternative can yield unintuitive results; for example, if an event is actually absent and its absence is sufficient for the occurrence of an effect for which an actually occurring event is also sufficient.

Perhaps the question should be: did, or could, the state of the system come about in such a way that the X taking on its value caused E to take on its value? A little more precisely: given a state S_a, in which E has value E_a and variable X has value X_a; and another system state, S_{alt}, consistent with the laws of the system, in which the value of X is X_{alt} and the value of E is E_{alt}; if the system state changes from S_{alt} to S_a, is the change in the value of X a cause of the change in the value of E? Of course, if in changes from some alternative system states to the actual state, but not from others, the change in X causes the change in E, we can put probabilities over the alternative system states and judge the probability that a change in X caused a change in E. Conceivably, that is one source of our uncertainty about actual causation in practical circumstances. Whichever question we ask, we must still find criteria—an algorithm—for saying when a change in X from X_{alt} to X_a is a cause of a change in E from E_{alt} to E_a.[1]

2

Theories of actual causation can grow unattractively to fit around a trellis of intuitions about cases, all the more so if the cases are embedded in stories. Lewis (1973), for example, began with the thought that event A causes event B means, roughly, that A and B both occur and that if A had not occurred, B would not have occurred. Pulling the trigger caused the gun to fire, because if the trigger had not been pulled the gun would not have fired. His judgment—and that of most people—that there are cases in which there are multiple causes, each sufficient for the effect (e.g., figure 3.2 above), required him to modify the leading idea, and a series of revisions, ever vaguer, ensued. We do not think Lewis settled, even implicitly, on an algorithm for neuron-diagram cases or for Boolean diagrams more generally.

There are also theories of actual causation that, whatever the tacit considerations of their authors, appear to have few motivating principles other than to include various cases and to exclude others. Very technical proposals of Halpern and Pearl (2001) and of Pearl (2000) have this character;[2]

as, to appearances, does a much simpler and clearer proposal due to Hitch-cock (2001). Hitchcock's analysis yields the result, we believe, that the values of A, B, and D in figure 3.12 are not causes of $E = 1$. We will have more to say about that case later.

There is also, perhaps unsurprisingly, a literature that offers no definite proposals—certainly no algorithms—and that sometimes objects to more specific proposals for solving cases of Pearl's kind, by switching to cases with feedback or with multivalued variables.[3]

Some theories of actual causation impose constraints on any acceptable algorithm or analysis, while not actually providing an algorithm. For exam-ple, it may be required that actual causation be transitive; or that absences not be causes; or that complete absences of every event considered not be a cause of any of these absences; or that the prevention of the prevention of an occurring event is a cause of that occurrence; and so on. Various cases may give one doubts about some of these principles. In figure 3.6, for ex-ample, the occurrence of A seems undoubtedly an actual cause of the oc-currence of C. C in turn prevents the occurrence of an event D, which would otherwise occur and which, if it occurred, would prevent the occur-rence of E. We are inclined to say that the occurrence of C prevents the pre-vention of the occurrence of E, and so is an actual cause of the occurrence of E. But E's occurrence is indifferent to whether or not A occurs, and one is tempted, contrary to transitivity, to deny that the occurrence of A causes the occurrence of E. But the differing intuitions about transitivity need not stop progress: whatever analysis is proposed, champions of transitivity can always take the transitive closure of the proposed relation of actual causa-tion. A general refusal to allow absences as causes is more debilitating. It can be motivated by slippery slopes—a lot of stuff that would prevent some effect does not happen—but there is no slope evident in the simple Boolean mechanisms.

3

We suggest that the criteria we apply for judging actual causation in neu-ron diagrams and Boolean diagrams are loosely formed around require-ments for causal inference in experimental procedures, and our defensible judgments are limited by such requirements. First, in order for there to be

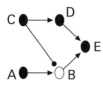

Figure 3.1
C, D.

an actual causal relation, there must be a possible causal relation; that is, there must be some experiment with the system in which variations in X vary the value of Y. What is an experiment with a system? We can think of it this way:

Experiment 1. An experiment to test whether X can influence Y in a system consists of an assignment of values to the zero-indegree variables and to all other variables, including X and Y, in accord with the equations of the system; and an intervention that changes the value of X in that assignment; and accordingly changes any variables whose values depend on the value of X for the assigned values to the zero-indegree variables. X can influence Y if and only if Y changes with the intervention.

An intervention that sets $X = x$ in a Boolean system in state S leaves the zero-indegree variables (save possibly X) at their values in S, alters the equations of the system by replacing the equation for X by $X = x$, and assigns all other variables the values determined by the modified equations and the values of the zero-indegree variables. Consider figure 3.1, for example, reprinted here for convenience.

Consider the state in which $C = 0$ and $A = 1$. It results by the equations of the system in $B = 1$, $D = 0$, $E = 1$; and changing that state by intervening to force $B = 0$, changes the value of E to $E = 0$. So in the sense above, B *can* influence E; although, intuitively, in the actual state shown in figure 3.1 it does not.

4

Suppose we take the possibility of an experiment of the kind of experiment 1, establishing potential causation as a necessary condition for actual causation. For actual causation we require then:

(4.1)   There is an assignment of values to the zero indegree variables and to all other variables, including X, and E, in accord with the equations of the system and an intervention on X that changes the value of E.

But of course more is required for the actual value of X, X_a, to cause the actual value of E, E_a. In particular, it seems necessary that in some such experiment X and E take their actual values, either before or after the intervention on X.

(4.2)   There is an experiment meeting the conditions of 4.1, in which $E = E_a$ and $X = X_a$ either before or after the intervention.

A still stronger requirement seems necessary: for an experiment to show that X_a could have actually caused E_a, the control settings of other variables must not destroy the process by which X_a could have caused E_a in the actual case. That is, the settings of the zero-indegree variables in the sort of experiment described in (4.1) and (4.2)—which may not be the actual values of those variables—must leave intact a replicate of some actual process through which X_a can have caused E_a. Hence,

(4.3)   The values of zero-indegree variables in 4.1 and 4.2 must be consistent with the actual values of all variables on some directed pathway p from X to E, hence in particular with the actual values of X and E.

But (4.3) only makes sense if the pathway p is a conduit of change from X to E, that is:

(4.4) An intervention that changes the value of X for the assigned values of the zero-indegree variables, must change the value of every variable on pathway p.

To avoid suggesting that this is a final analysis, we will call an actual value of any variable X meeting these conditions for actual causation of the actual value of E, a *candidate actual cause* of the value of E. More succinctly, the proposal is,

(D1) An event (or non-event) $C = c$ in a Boolean network in a state S, in which the value of C is c and the value of E is e, is an candidate actual cause of another event (or non-event) $E = e$ if and only if there is some setting of the zero-indegree variables such that, for that setting: (1) the value of E is e and the value of C is c, and for at least one directed pathway p from C to E, all nodes on that path have their actual values; and (2) an

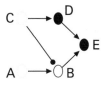

Figure 3.1
C, D.

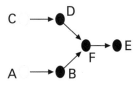

Figure 3.2
A, B, D, C, F.

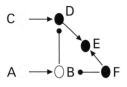

Figure 3.3
B, C, D, F.

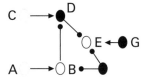

Figure 3.4
B, C, D, F.

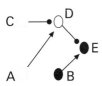

Figure 3.5
B, C, D.

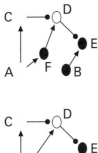

Figure 3.6
B, C, D.

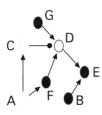

Figure 3.7
B.

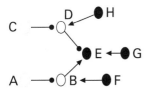

Figure 3.8
C, D, G.

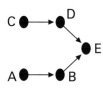

$E = D * B; B = A; C = D$

Figure 3.9
A, B, C, D.

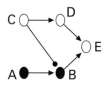

$E = D * B; D = C; B = A$

Figure 3.10
D, C.

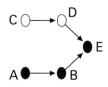

$E = B(1-D); C = D; A = B$

Figure 3.11
A, B, C, D.

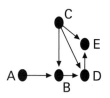

$E = C + D; B = A * C; D = B * C$

Figure 3.12
C.

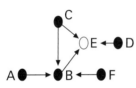

$E = D(1-B)(1-C); \; B = A + F(1-C)$

Figure 3.13
C, A, B, F.

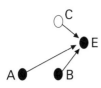

$E = (C * B) + A$

Figure 3.14
A, B.

intervention that changes the value of C changes the value of all nodes on p, and hence changes the value of E.

For most cases, the set of candidate actual causes is reasonable. We repeat figures 3.1–3.14 here and give the candidate actual causes of the value of E in the captions.[4]

5

The purpose of the idea of an experiment in (D1) is to permit the characterization of a mechanism or mechanisms connecting possible causes and effects. But in isolating a mechanism experimentally, we can do more than fix exogenous conditions as in experiment 1. When there are multiple possible mechanisms, we can control some of them by "clamping" their variables, fixing them so they do not vary in the experiment. So we might entertain a broader sense of experiment:

Experiment 2. An experiment to test whether X can influence Y in a system, consists of an assignment of values to the zero-indegree variables and to all other variables, including X, and Y, in accord with the equations of the system; and subsequent interventions that clamp some variables at their implied values while changing the value of X, and that accordingly change any variables whose values depend on the value of X (for the assigned values to the zero-indegree variables and to the clamped variables). X can influence Y if and only if Y changes with the intervention.

This suggests a variation on (D1):

(D2) An event (or non-event) $C = c$ in a Boolean network in a state S, in which the value of C is c and the value of E is e, is a candidate actual cause of another event (or non-event) $E = e$ if and only if there is some setting of the zero-indegree variables, and some set V of variables that are descendants of C in the graph, such that, for that setting: (1) the value of E is e and the value of C is c, and for at least one directed pathway p from C to E all nodes on that path have their actual values; (2) the values of variables in V for the setting are their values in S; and (3) an intervention that clamps the values of variables in V at their values in S and changes the value of C, changes the value of all nodes on p and hence changes the value of E.

Obviously, when there is only one directed pathway from C to E, (D1) and (D2) will agree as to whether the actual value of C is a candidate actual cause of the actual value of E. (D2) allows transitivities that (D1) prohibits, and admits ineffectual actual causes. Thus by (D2), in figure 3.6, $A = 1$ is a cause of $E = 1$—simply clamp $F = 1$. Again, in figure 3.15, with $D = (1 - A)$ and other relations as in neuron diagrams, $C = 1$ is a (candidate) actual cause of $E = 1$ by both (D1) and (D2); and similarly, $A = 1$ is a candidate actual cause of $C = 1$ by both proposals. $A = 1$ is not a candidate actual cause of $E = 1$ according to (D1), for no matter how we vary A, E does not vary. But according to (D2), $A = 1$ is a candidate actual cause of $E = 1$—simply clamp B at its actual value, 0.[5] (D2) is not, however, transitive in general.[6]

Figure 3.15

6

We have so far assumed that the diagram, Boolean equations, and actual values are the complete story. In many cases in which we must judge actual causation, however, we may have other beliefs about the system—beliefs which are not yet represented. We may, for example, believe there to be intervening variables which are not represented in the diagram. (D2) permits some of this. For example, consider again figure 3.6. All of the edges in figure 3.6 can be witnessed by experiments in accord with (D1). The $F \rightarrow D$ connection, for example, is established by setting $A = 0$, hence $C = F = D = 0$. Then, an intervention that changes F to 1 changes the value of D to 1. But suppose, in describing the system, F were omitted, as in figure 3.6a. There is no experiment in the sense of experiment 1 that witnesses the edge from A to D, and yet figure 3.6a is only a less informative description of the same mechanism in figure 3.6. Experiment 2 permits us to clamp C in figure 3.6a, and so demonstrate that A is a potential cause of D.

We could suppose that any edge $X \rightarrow Z$ in a diagram can be decomposed into a path $X \rightarrow Y \rightarrow Z$, where Y is a novel variable, allowing interventions on Y. The result must be either a theory of a restricted set of diagrams, or a theory that postulates equivalence relations for actual causation between different diagrams. In a sense, in experiment 2 and (D2) we have already allowed a different class of equivalencies between diagrams, since possible

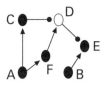

Figure 3.6

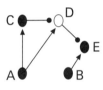

Figure 3.6a

interventions in positive-indegree variables can always be represented by additional variables having only a single edge directed into the manipulated variable, as in the policy variables in Spirtes, et al. 2001. With such a representation, experiment 2 reduces to experiment 1. That ambiguity is harmless, however, because of the provably general equivalence for acyclic systems of the representation of interventions by policy variables and the representation used here, following Pearl (2000), in which interventions are represented by replacing variables in an equation with constant values. The introduction of intervening variables may indeed represent our disposition towards certain situations—cover stories—and diagrams, but no such corresponding theorem is available for actual causation: we must legislate the equivalence of judgments of actual causation with and without novel intervening variables on which we can intervene, and try to justify the legislation by examining cases. And there are related disadvantages. The postulate excludes cases where we think there are no such variables, and it introduces a dependency of the analysis on unrepresented beliefs—a dependency that threatens to undermine the entire project: we can, after all, have diagrammatically unrepresented beliefs not only about intervening variables, but also about entire pathways.

There is, however, a more limited and less contextual way of modifying a given diagram and equations—namely, by assuming the Boolean equations are deterministic approximations of nondeterministic dependencies. We considered two senses of experiment, both of which had consequences for figure 3.12, excluding A and B as potential causes of E, and allowing only $C = 1$ as an actual cause of $E = 1$. But perhaps we should think of an experiment to test whether A *can* influence E as more disruptive of the structure: in figure 3.12, we can set the zero-indegree variable C to zero, but only *for* E. The value of C *for* B and D is left at 1. We are essentially changing the equations of the structure for the variables (except for E) on a pathway from A to E, so that each variable in the pathway depends only on the mechanism that descends from A. By doing so, we let that mechanism operate, and E varies as A, B, and D vary. That implies a different sense of experiment:

Experiment 3. An experiment to test whether X can influence Y in a system consists of an assignment of values to the zero-indegree variables and, in accord with the equations of the system, to all other variables—let

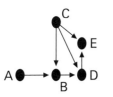

E = C + D; B = A * C; D = B * C

Figure 3.12

S be this state assignment—and an alternative state assignment, S^* constructed in the following way: S^* is the state assignment equal to S except for variables on one or more selected pathways from X to Y and their descendants. In the equations for the variables on the selected pathways, except for Y, each parent not on a selected pathway can be set to any value (the same value for each such parent variable in all equations in which it occurs, for variables on the selected pathways). Values in S^* of variables on the selected pathways, and their descendants (including Y), are determined by their equations, using the resulting values in S^* of their parents. In addition, the experiment requires an intervention that changes the value of X from its value in S^*, and accordingly changes any variables whose values depend on the value of X for S^*. X can influence Y if and only if the value of Y varies between the nonintervention on X and the intervention on X.

To illustrate, we return to figure 3.12. A can influence E in sense of experiment 3: set $C = 0$ for E, but leave C at its actual value, 1, in the equations for B and D on the path $A \to B \to D \to E$. We imagine, then, that in the experiment $C = 0$ did not have its normal or most probable effect on B and D in accord with the equations. Now, varying A will vary E.

This third sense of experiment may seem contrived, but it connects with a substantial body of work in computer science and in psychology. A common network in computer science involves "noisy gates" (Pearl 1987). A noisy-or gate, for example, is given by the Boolean equation $E = q_a A + q_b B$. The quantities q_a and q_b are parameters taking 0, 1 as values. A joint probability distribution is defined over the variables and parameters, generally requiring the parameters to be independent in probability of each other and of the values of A and of B. Thus, values of A and B need not determine a value of E, but only assign it a (conditional) probability. Cheng (1997) has used noisy gates as a model of human causal judgment (Glymour 2002). In essence, she treats the probability that $qa = 1$ in the above equation as the probability that, given that A occurs, A causes E to occur. On this model, such probabilities of parameter values, or "causal powers," can be estimated from observed frequencies of E, A, and B. She gives evidence that in appropriate circumstances adult judgments of causal strength accord qualitatively with such a model.

Conjecture for the moment that our judgments of actual causation are tacitly based on a model of causation like Cheng's, and even in cases we are told are deterministic, we merely set the causal powers to some value very close to, but not quite equal to, 1. If that were so, then something like the sense of experiment in experiment 2 would be appropriate for our judgments of whether X can possibly cause Y.

So we have this rather more complex alternative account of actual causation:

(D3) An event (or non-event) $C = c$ in a Boolean network in a state S in which $C = c$ and $E = e$ is an candidate actual cause of another event (or non-event) $E = e$ for system state S if and only if there is a set P of paths from C to E and some setting S_{alt} of all variables such that: (1) all variables that are not in members of P or descendants of members of P have their values determined by the equations of the system from the values in S_{alt} of zero-indegree variables; (2) the value of C in S_{alt} is c; (3) the values of variables in members of P, save for E, are determined by the actual values (i.e., the values in S) of their parents that are not in P and by the S_{alt} values of their parents that are members of P—hence in S_{alt} they equal their values in S; (4) the values of variables that are descendants of members of P (including Y) have their values determined by the values of their parents in S_{alt}; and (5) an intervention that changes the value of C from its value in S_{alt} changes the value of all variables on members of P from their values in S_{alt} and hence changes the value of E.

Clauses (3) and (4) are implicitly inductive and make use of the acyclicity of the diagrams. One worry is that (D3) is just too complex to be plausible; another is that it may be too liberal. This time in figure 3.12 the candidate actual causes of $E = 1$ are the actual values of A, B, C, and D. Setting $C = 0$ for E but leaving $C = 1$ for B and D, makes E a function of A, of B, and of D.

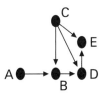

E=C+D; B=A*C; D=B*C

Figure 3.12

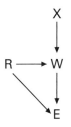

Figure 3.16

Figure 3.16 is a much simpler case with the same point: $W = R * X$; $E = W + R$. Actual values: $X = R = W = E = 1$. $X = 1$ is not a candidate actual cause by either (D1) or (D2). But setting $R = 0$ for E and leaving $R = 1$ for W, varying X varies E, so $X = 1$ is a candidate actual cause by (D3).

But, as with (D2), (D3) allows extra transitivity compared with (D1). For example, in figure 3.6 in the sense of (D3): $A = 1$ is a candidate actual cause of $F = 1$ and of $C = 1$; $C = 1$ is a candidate actual cause of $D = 0$; and $A = 1$ is an actual cause of $D = 0$ or of $E = 1$. (Let F have its actual value for D when A is changed to 0.) (D3) is not transitive. Every (D2) actual cause is obviously a (D3) actual cause.

(D3) could perhaps be made still more liberal by allowing clamping, in analogy with (D2); call that idea (D4). I will not go through the details, but the idea implies that $A = 1$ is a candidate actual cause of $D = 0$ and of $E = 1$ in figure 3.6. We do not know if the resulting definition implies transitivity in all cases.

The four accounts of actual causation have an extensional inclusion structure. Every actual cause according to a lower member of the graph in figure 3.17 is an actual cause according to any higher member.

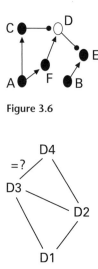

Figure 3.6

Figure 3.17

7

We should indicate some reasons why we have restricted the analysis to Boolean equations, or to noisy versions of them. Consider a simple and common non-Boolean function on binary variables—voting a proposition up or down. Suppose the proposition carries by a majority greater than one. Is the vote of a particular person in favor of the proposition a cause of its winning? We are uncertain, but on balance our inclination is to say not. According to (D1) or (D2), however, it most certainly is. One inclination (rather less than a conviction), is that sometimes groups or aggregates, rather than individuals, are causes of an effect; one can be a member of a group, or a component of an aggregate, and in some contexts thereby carry moral responsibility for group effects, without one's actions causing the group effects.

Multivalued variables immediately carry us outside of Boolean equations, with attendant complexities. Because transitivity fails for causal relations among multivalued *variables*, further ambiguities, or at least uncertainties, are created for actual causation. The actual value of B can depend on the actual value of A, and the actual value of C can depend on the actual value of B; but even with only a single pathway from A to C, variations in A can result in no changes in *C*. We do not preclude the development of plausible proposals for actual causation with non-Boolean dependencies, or for multivalued variables, but we have none to offer.

8

The disturbing thing about actual causation is that while in many practical matters judgments of actual causation may have important influence on human action and human fate, even in well-posed classes of problems there seems no clear fact of the matter, only intuitions that may vary considerably from person to person. Even if the principles of any of the four accounts sketched above were tacitly embraced, the complexity of the reasoning their application requires would in many cases prevent unaided human judgments from according with them. It is unfortunate that, so far as we know, with the single exception of a related paper by Sloman and Lagnado (2002), there is no psychological literature on how variable these judgments may be. The several caveats in this paper argue that unless the settings of psychological experiments are very carefully posed, variations in judgment can be expected because of ambiguities in the problem. But in view of the complexity considerations, and evidence that people do not treat occurrences and nonoccurrences at all symmetrically (Cheng 1997), we doubt that even in problems in which the mechanisms are unambiguously and thoroughly understood, human judgments will generally conform to any of these accounts. The apparently unanswerable question is whether they should.

Acknowledgments

One debt for this paper is to the late David Lewis, whose seminar on causation Clark Glymour attended in the early 1970s. The problem addressed in this paper, and Lewis's approach to it, were the focus of discussion in that seminar. We are indebted to Bruce Glymour for helping to fix drafts of this paper. Christopher Hitchcock provided many helpful exchanges and ideas. We thank Patricia Cheng for a correction, clarification, and much else; and Laurie Paul for providing a preprint of her work with Ned Hall. Any corrections would be gratefully accepted. Work for this paper was supported by grants NCC2-1295 and NCC2-1377 from the National Aeronautics and Space Administration to the Institute for Human and Machine Cognition at the University of West Florida.

Notes

1. In practical matters, actual causation may be still more complex, because the relevant change of state in which X_a causes E_a may not involve any change in X_a. This is particularly vivid when $E_a = 0$, when—because some preventive event, X_a, obtains—an event does not occur despite changes that would otherwise bring it about.

2. Pearl's proposal, in particular, does not seem well-formed to us because of quantifier ambiguities. We, at least, are am not able to parse it consistently.

3. See, for example, L. Paul and N. Hall, *Causation and Its Counterexamples: A Traveler's Guide* (forthcoming), which provides a very valuable compendium of ingenious cases.

4. Neither we, nor any of our helpful readers of drafts of this paper, were able accurately to apply (D1) to all of the cases. Whatever subconscious procedures we use for making intuitive judgments of actual causation, we have great difficulty explicitly following a rule with four quantifiers. Consequently, these cases have all been checked by a program implementing an algorithm for (D1). The program is available at http://www.phil.cmu.edu/projects/actual_causation/.

5. This is a slight variant of an example suggested by Bruce Glymour.

6. Our thanks to Chris Hitchcock.

References

Cheng, P. 1997. "From Covariation to Causation: A Causal Power Theory." *Psychological Review* 104: 367–405.

Glymour, C. 2002. *The Mind's Arrows: Bayes Nets and Graphical Causal Models in Psychology*. Cambridge, Mass.: MIT Press.

Halpern, J., and J. Pearl. 2000. "Causes and Explanations: A Structural-Model Approach—Part I: Causes." UCLA Cognitive Systems Laboratory, Technical Report (R-266-UAI).

Halpern, J., and J. Pearl. 2001. "Causes and Explanations: A Structural-Model Approach—Part I: Causes." In *Proceedings of the Seventeenth Conference on Uncertainty in Artificial Intelligence*. San Francisco: Morgan Kaufmann.

Hitchcock, C. 2001. "The Intransitivity of Causation Revealed in Equations and Graphs." *Journal of Philosophy* 98: 273–299.

Lewis, D. 1973. "Causation." *Journal of Philosophy* 70: 556–567.

Paul, L., and N. Hall. Forthcoming. *Causation and Its Counterexamples: A User's Guide.* Oxford: Oxford University Press.

Pearl, J. 1987. *Probabilistic Reasoning in Intelligent Systems.* San Francisco: Morgan Kaufmann.

Pearl, J. 2000. *Causality: Models, Reasoning, and Inference.* Oxford: Oxford University Press.

Sloman, S., and D. Lagnado. 2002. "Counterfactual Undoing in Deterministic Causal Reasoning." In *Proceedings of the Twenty-Fourth Annual Conference of the Cognitive Science Society.* Fairfax, Va.: George Mason University.

Spirtes, P., C. Glymour, and R. Scheines. 2001. *Causation, Prediction, and Search.* Cambridge, Mass.: MIT Press.

4   What's Wrong with Neuron Diagrams?

Christopher Hitchcock

1   Introduction

It is a familiar moral from the philosophy of science that the way in which we choose to *represent* some phenomenon can shape the way in which we think about that phenomenon. A mode of representation may allow for the simultaneous comprehension of numerous complex relationships, as when a chemical compound is represented with a three-dimensional "tinker-toy" model. A representational device may facilitate calculation: consider the representation of numbers by Arabic (as opposed, e.g., to Roman) numerals, or the representation of geometric objects by sets of points in a Cartesian coordinate system. A particular choice of representation may suggest previously unforeseen possibilities: the representation of multiple-particle systems using *product spaces* rather than *sum spaces* allows for the representation of entangled states, which are found in certain quantum phenomena. Sometimes a representation will mislead us. For example, the diagram accompanying Euclid's first problem tacitly smuggles in the assumption that a circle whose center lies on the circumference of a second circle will intersect that second circle. This assumption is essential to the solution of the problem, but it does not follow from Euclid's axioms and postulates.

In this essay, I examine a particular mode of representation that has become prevalent within philosophy—the use of "neuron diagrams" to represent systems of causal relations.[1] Neuron diagrams were first introduced by David Lewis in 1986 (Lewis 1986, pp. 196–210). They have spread, both through the direct influence of this work, and indirectly through the work of his many talented students, who learned of them in the classrooms and common rooms of Princeton. Neuron diagrams have now become a kind of lingua franca for discussion about causation, especially among those interested in Lewis's counterfactual theories of causation, and more recent refinements thereof. They appear not only in the published literature, but on blackboards and white boards; they are projected from slides and laptops, and are scribbled on napkins in bars and coffee shops. In short, they are bound to appear wherever causation is discussed.

I present the basic representational apparatus of neuron diagrams in section 2. In the following section, I develop the general complaint that neuron diagrams do not serve as all-purpose representational devices for causal systems. I give a brief sketch of an alternative mode of representation that I prefer, in section 4. In the following four sections, I will then present a number of specific difficulties for neuron diagrams. The difficulties do not arise from any in-principle limitations on the representational power of neuron diagrams, but rather from various infelicities in their actual use. These infelicities are, however, encouraged by certain features of the neuron diagrams themselves. It is not my intention to argue that neuron diagrams should *never* be used; nor do I condemn those who use them. Nonetheless, the *uncritical* use of neuron diagrams has impeded progress in the theory of causation, and may well continue to do so if some kind of warning call is not sounded. While users of neuron diagrams have occasionally admitted that they can sometimes be misleading,[2] there has been no extensive discussion of their shortcomings in the literature. Both fans and foes of neuron diagrams stand to benefit from such a critique.

2   Neuron Diagrams

In my exposition, I will distinguish *neuron diagrams* from what I will call *neural systems*. This distinction is never made in the literature, and this omission is one source of trouble in the use of neuron diagrams. Neuron diagrams are visual modes of representation consisting of circles and arrows. A neural system consists of *neurons* and *connections*. These neurons are not of the sort that can actually be found in our brains (although they do bear a superficial resemblance); rather, the neurons appearing in neural systems are hypothetical devices that follow very simple rules. Neurons are capable of *firing* briefly, and in so doing, they send signals to other neurons along connections. Neuron systems are often represented, or better, presented, using neuron diagrams. The relationship between the diagrams and the systems are governed by the following set of conventions: each circle in a neuron diagram corresponds to a neuron. In a diagram, some circles may be given labels, typically lower case Roman letters. A neuron that fires (at some particular time) is depicted as a shaded circle, while a neuron that does not fire is depicted as an unfilled circle. (There are variants on these conventions; I present only the most standard version.) The firing of a particular neuron is an *event*, while the non-firing of a neuron is the absence of a firing-event (or perhaps an event in its own right that is incompatible with firing, but we need not concern ourselves with this subtle issue here). Most writers are sufficiently careful to distinguish between a neuron and the event of that neuron's firing *in their written presentations* (the reason for the qualification will be revealed in section 8); a standard convention is to use **bold** letters to represent neurons, and *italic* letters to represent events.

In addition to circles, labels, and shading, neuron diagrams also contain *arrows*. Arrows come in two varieties: those with a triangular head represent *stimulatory connections* in a neural system, while those with circular heads represent *inhibitory connections*. If there is a stimulatory connection running from neuron **a** to **b**, and **a** fires, then **b** is said to be *stimulated by* **a**. If there is an inhibitory connection running from **a** to **b**, and **a** fires, then **b** is *inhibited by* **a**.

Neural systems obey the following rules: (1) a neuron will fire if it is stimulated by at least one other neuron, and inhibited by none; (2) a neuron will not fire if it is inhibited by any neuron. Both (1) and (2) state sufficient conditions only; in particular, an *initial* neuron, one that has no connections directed into it, may either fire or not. Figure 4.1 depicts a neural system compatible with these rules. There are three neurons: **a**, **b**, and **c**.

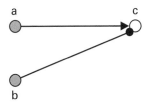

Figure 4.1
A typical neuron diagram. In the neural system depicted, neurons **a** and **b** both fire. **a** stimulates neuron **c**, while **b** inhibits **c**. **c** does not fire.

There is a stimulatory connection running from **a** to **c**, and an inhibitory connection running from **b** to **c**. Neurons **a** and **b** fire; equivalently, events *a* and *b* occur. By firing, neuron **a** stimulates **c**, while neuron **b** inhibits **c**. According to rule (2), then, **c** does not fire.

This presentation is sufficient to understand a large majority of the neuron diagrams that have appeared in the literature. There can be more complicated neural systems, which cannot be adequately represented using the two kinds of circles and two kinds of arrows described in this section. We will deal with this point in sections 5 and 6 below, but in the meantime, we have plenty to get us started.

3   The Role of Neuron Diagrams

The first neuron diagram in print appears in Lewis 1986 (pp. 195–196). The diagram is used to present a hypothetical example of a particular sort, a neural system. Lewis uses the example of the neural system to raise a particular concern about late preemption. The neural system is not the only example he uses—it stands beside more traditional examples involving murderers, firing squads, guns, poison, and so on. In this capacity, the role of neuron diagrams is similar to that of diagrams depicting colliding billiard balls: the diagram is intended to convey the structure of a particular example in a clear and simple manner.

But there is another, quite different, use of neuron diagrams—representing the abstract causal structure of examples that do not involve neural systems at all.[3] Schaffer presents the following example: "Pam throws a brick throw the window. Meanwhile, Bob … holds his throw on seeing Pam in action, though had Pam not thrown Bob would have" (2001, p. 79).[4] This description is accompanied the neuron diagram depicted in figure 4.2. What are the conventions for representing a causal system other than a neural system using a neuron diagram? Surprisingly, this issue has never been discussed. Indeed, there seems to be no recognition that a separate set of conventions is needed. For example, in a footnote accompanying the example just described,[5] Schaffer writes: "Diagram conventions: filled circles … represent neurons that fire …, arrows represent stimulatory connections …" (The ellipses will be filled out in section 8 below.) But the circles and arrows represent no such things: there *are* no neurons or connections under discussion, only vandals, windows, and bricks. A reader

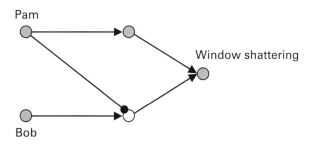

Figure 4.2
A neuron diagram used to represent a causal structure that does not involve neurons and connections.

who was unfamiliar with the use of neuron diagrams would find this exposition quite bewildering. Nor is it clear just how one *would* explain the conventions in terms of the elements of the diagram and the components of the example. For example, what do the circles represent? There are five objects in the story (Pam, Bob, the window, and the two bricks) and five circles; so do the circles represent objects? The top two arrows seem to represent a flying brick, while the bottom left arrow represents Bob just standing there at the ready, and the bottom right arrow corresponds to empty space. Why do these things, and no others, deserve an arrow? What do they all have in common?

Perhaps the most charitable interpretation is that the neuron diagram is to be interpreted in terms of a neural system, and the example discussed is isomorphic to, or analogous to, that neural system.[6] But even so, the rules for establishing isomorphism or analogy have never been articulated. Despite the desirability of having a general tool for representing causal systems of various types, the apparent suitability of neuron diagrams for this purpose, and actual attempts to use them for this purpose, no one has ever taken the time to explain the conventions for representing non–neural systems in terms of neuron diagrams.

This glaring lacuna has been obscured, no doubt, by the relative clarity of the conventions for representing neural systems using neuron diagrams. In neural systems, the spatial configuration of neurons and connections is isomorphic to the system of causal relations between neurons firing and failing to fire. In particular, connections between neurons are present regardless of whether any signal is being sent along those connections. These inert connections alert us to the presence of potential paths of causal influence, or something of the sort, that need to be represented diagrammatically. Perhaps in cases involving vandals, it is easy enough to think of non-actual brick trajectories as analogous inert connections in a neural system. In general, however, such spatial analogs will not be available. Consider the following example, discussed in Hitchcock 2001: "*Boulder*: A boulder is dislodged from the top of a hill, and starts rolling toward a passing hiker. The hiker sees the boulder, and ducks. The boulder bounces just over her head, and she survives." For clarity, let us stipulate that the hiker would not have survived had she not ducked, and that she would have survived had the boulder not fallen. This is a prima facie counterexample to the transitivity of causation: the fall of the boulder caused the hiker to duck; the hiker's duck caused her to survive; but it sounds at least a little odd to say that the boulder's fall caused her to survive. The events in this story all lie along a straight line (the path of the boulder). If we take this layout as a guide to causal structure, we will be inclined to represent the example with the neuron diagram depicted in figure 4.3. Here, b represents the boulder's fall, d the hiker's duck, and s the hiker's survival. Given what we've been told about neuron diagrams, it is not clear that there is anything wrong with this representation. The boulder's fall does indeed "stimulate" the hiker's duck, which in turn "stimulates" her survival, and it does not seem as though there is any other stimulation or inhibition going on. Yet this representation cannot be right, for if this diagram were used to present a neural system, we would unhesitatingly say that b causes s.

In light of these difficulties with the use of neuron diagrams as general purpose representational tools, a natural suggestion might be to scale back the use of neuron diagrams, to restrict them to their originally intended use. To the extent that we have clear intuitions about what causes what within neural systems, there can be little objection in using them as examples to test or motivate theories of causation. To the extent that neuron

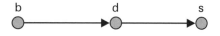

Figure 4.3
An attempt to model *Boulder* using a neuron diagram.

diagrams successfully convey the structures of the neural systems being used as examples, there can be little objection to using them in this capacity. While I mostly concur with this sensible line, some quibbles remain. In sections 5 and 6, I will raise the obvious point that as the neural systems used as examples get more complex, the diagrams used to present them become much less perspicuous. In section 7, I will argue that neuron diagrams can bias our intuitions about the neural structures they represent. Most importantly, I will argue in section 8 that there are cases where neuron diagrams actually misrepresent the causal structure of the neural systems they are meant to depict.

Even putting these quibbles aside momentarily, there is an additional reason for concern. Some papers on causation rely exclusively, or almost exclusively, on examples involving neural systems.[7] This usage conveys the impression that neural systems are broadly representative of causal structures. The literature on causation is heavily example-driven; one formulates theories, and then tests them against a battery of cases—early preemption, late preemption, symmetric overdetermination, trumping, and so on. To argue that a particular theory yields the right verdict in cases of late preemption (say), on the grounds that it yields the right verdict about a neural system in which there is late preemption, begs an important question: can all cases of late preemption be assimilated to the structure of that neural system? In section 6 I argue that neuron diagrams fail to serve an important heuristic role—that of suggesting new kinds of structures against which theories can be tested.

In any event, restricting the use of neuron diagrams in the way suggested leaves a vacuum: there is a genuine need for a general purpose representational tool. Consider, for example, Lewis's defense of the transitivity of causation in Lewis 2000. There, he claims that all putative counterexamples to transitivity have the same structure, which he describes as follows:

Imagine a conflict between Black and Red. . . . Black makes a move that, if not countered, would have advanced his cause. Red responds with an effective countermove, which gives Red the Victory. Black's move causes Red's countermove, Red's countermove causes Red's victory. (Lewis 2000, p. 194)

Is this true? I presented one potential counterexample to transitivity, *Boulder*, earlier in this section. Here is another, due to Michael McDermott (1995b):

Dog Bite: A right-handed terrorist is bitten on that hand by a dog, thus rendering that hand useless. As a result, he pushes a detonator button with his left hand, exploding a bomb.

The dog bite caused the terrorist to push the button with his left hand, which in turn caused the bomb to detonate; but (it seems) the dog bite did not cause the bomb to detonate. If all putative counterexamples to transitivity have the same structure, then these two surely do. How can we assess this claim? It would be nice to have more than a checkers metaphor to fall back on. This is just the sort of problem for which an effective mode of representation is an indispensable aid. If, following clearly stated rules, we were able to construct neuron diagrams exhibiting the underlying structures of the two cases, then we could assess Lewis's claim simply by inspecting the diagrams.

4   An Alternative Representation

The representational apparatus that I prefer uses *causal graphs* and *structural equations*. These devices are sometimes used to facilitate the comparison of statistical data with the predictions of various causal models (see, e.g., Pearl 2000; Spirtes, Glymour, and Scheines 2000). This work can get quite technical, and has, I suspect, scared away many philosophical readers. Divorced from these applications, however, the way in which equations and graphs can be used to represent causal structures is really quite simple.

I will only attempt a quick introduction here (see Hitchcock 2001, 2004; as well as Pearl 2000, chapter 7, for detailed exposition). Instead of beginning with a system of neurons, one starts with a system of variables, $X, Y, Z \ldots$ The values of a variable represent incompatible events, or states that an object or system can instantiate. For instance, if we are representing a system of neurons, we might have $X = 1$ representing that a certain neuron fires, $X = 0$ that it does not. In a different kind of hypothetical example, we might, for example, let $X = 1$ correspond to Pam's throwing a particular brick, and $X = 0$ to her not doing so. Variables need not be binary; we might, for example, let X represent the linear momentum that Pam imparted to her brick. Relations between variables are expressed as equations. In the causal structure depicted in figure 4.1, for example, the equation corresponding to neuron **c** would be:

$$C = A(1 - B).$$

We will take the liberty of rewriting arithmetic relations among binary variables using the corresponding logical connectives. Thus, the above equation can be rewritten as:

$C = A \ \& \sim B.$

These equations encode a set of counterfactuals,[8] one counterfactual for each combination of values of the variables on the right hand side. The counterfactuals result from replacing the equations with their instances, and are read from right to left. The equation above thus encodes the following counterfactuals:

1. If it were the case that $A = 1$, and $B = 1$, then C would equal 0.
2. If it were the case that $A = 1$, and $B = 0$, then C would equal 1.
3. If it were the case that $A = 0$, and $B = 1$, then C would equal 0.
4. If it were the case that $A = 0$, and $B = 0$, then C would equal 0.

For present purposes, it does not matter whether the relevant counterfactuals are to be understand in terms of similarity among possible worlds (à la Lewis 1973, 1979), in terms of idealized manipulations (Woodward 2003), in terms of minimally sufficient sets of events (as in McDermott 1995b; Hall 2004a), whether they are to be taken as primitive, or what have you. The important point is that the conditionals are not merely material conditionals, and have a directionality to them. Note that the counterfactual interpretation of an equation will be different from that of another equation that is equivalent from a purely algebraic point of view. The side on which the variables are placed makes an important difference.

The equations for some variables will simply stipulate the values of the variables; such variables are *exogenous*. To represent the neural system depicted in figure 4.1, we would add: $A = 1$, $B = 1$. We can represent the qualitative form of a system of equations in a causal graph by drawing an arrow from X to Y just in case X is a nonredundant argument in the structural equation for Y. The full representation for the structure shown in figure 4.1 is given in figure 4.4. Note that I have used slightly different arrowheads, to avoid confusing the arrows of causal graphs with the stimulatory connections of neuron diagrams.

While the value of C is not listed explicitly in figure 4.4, it can be computed algebraically from the equations listed. The equations can also be used to calculate the truth values of counterfactuals. For example, counterfactuals

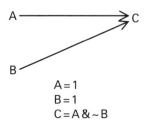

$$A = 1$$
$$B = 1$$
$$C = A \,\&\, {\sim} B$$

Figure 4.4
The neural system of figure 4.1 is represented by a causal graph and a system of structural equations.

with antecedents $A = 0$, or $B = 0$, are represented by replacing the equation for the appropriate variable with the equation stipulating the value specified in the antecedent. The values of the other variables in this counterfactual situation can then be computed algebraically. (Note that this procedure is consistent with giving the equations a direct counterfactual interpretation.) This demonstrates that there will be counterfactuals that are true of the system, that are not explicitly represented by equations (although they will be implied by the equations). The equations express the minimum set of counterfactuals sufficient to capture all true (non-backtracking) counterfactuals involving the variables used to represent the system. There is an effective procedure for generating this set of counterfactuals, described in Hitchcock 2001.

To illustrate the utility of representing causal systems using structural equations and causal graphs, I will provide the corresponding representations of the two (putative) counterexamples to transitivity introduced in the previous section. We represent *Boulder* using three variables: B takes the value 1 or 0 according to whether the boulder falls; D is 1 or 0 depending on whether the hiker ducks; and S is 1 or 0 depending upon the hiker's survival. The structural equations are as follows:

$$B = 1$$

$$D = B$$

$$S = D \vee {\sim} B$$

The corresponding graph is shown in figure 4.5. The last equation is particularly significant: it says (condensing four counterfactuals into one) that

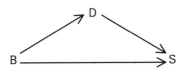

Figure 4.5
A causal graph representing *Boulder*. Compare with figure 4.3.

Figure 4.6
A causal graph representing *Dog Bite*. Compare with figure 4.5.

the hiker would survive just in case she were to duck or the boulder were not to fall. In particular, in the counterfactual situation where the hiker does not duck, her survival depends counterfactually upon whether or not the boulder falls. It is this very simple class of counterfactuals that tips us off to the need for an extra arrow from *B* to *S*. The construction of the graph is guided by very explicit rules connecting graphical structure with counterfactuals. When trying to represent this example using a neuron diagram, it is not at all clear what might tip us off to the need for an extra arrow between **b** and **s** in figure 4.3. Moreover, the reader may convince herself that neither a stimulatory or inhibitory connection between **b** and **s** will do the job.

To represent *Dog Bite*, we choose three variables: $D = 1$ or 0 depending upon whether the dog bites the terrorist's hand; $P = 2, 1$, or 0, depending upon whether the terrorist pushes the button with his left hand, with his right hand, or not at all; and $E = 1$ or 0 according to whether the bomb explodes. This gives us:

$D = 1$

$P = D + 1$

$E = \min\{P, 1\}$

The graph is shown in figure 4.6. Note that in this case there is no arrow directly from *D* to *E*. Given any specification of the value of *P*—of whether and with which hand the terrorist presses the button—there is no counterfactual dependence of the explosion on the dog bite. This shows that

Lewis's claim about the isomorphism of cases like *Boulder* and *Dog Bite* is false.[9]

5   Attacking a Straw Man

In the following three sections, I will present some more specific problems with neuron diagrams. In order to set up my first criticism, it will be useful to begin by attacking a straw man. This particular denizen of Oz believes that all causal structures can be represented using the conventions described in section 2.

This is quite obviously false. Consider, for example, a fire that was started when a match was lit and applied to spilt lighter fluid. If the match had not been lit, the fire would not have occurred; nor would the fire have occurred if the lighter fluid had not been spilt. If we draw three circles, we must ask: what kind of arrows should be drawn between the circles representing the spilling of the fluid and the fire, and between the lighting of the match and the fire? Circle-headed arrows are obviously wrong; neither event is in any way *inhibiting* the fire. But if we draw two stimulatory arrows it would indicate that either of these events alone would have sufficed for the fire. The representational apparatus described so far simply does not allow for the representation of this sort of case.

Note, by contrast, that this sort of case presents no difficulty for the structural equations mode of representation. The relevant equations would simply be:

$M = 1$

$S = 1$

$F = M \ \& \ F$

(Where $M = 1$ corresponds to the lighting of the match, $S = 1$ to the spilling of the lighter fluid, and $F = 1$ to the occurrence of the fire.) Indeed, it is simple to see that structural equations can be used to represent causal relationships of arbitrary complexity.

Of course, those who use neuron diagrams—unlike our straw man—do not claim that the conventions described above suffice to represent all causal structures. For example, Hall (2004a, 2004b) uses thick-walled circles to represent neurons that fire only when doubly stimulated. Thus the example described above would be represented as in figure 4.7.

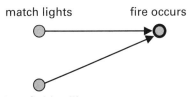

match lights   fire occurs

lighter fluid spills

Figure 4.7
A new convention to represent causes that are individually necessary, but only jointly sufficient.

6   Heuristic Value

With enough creativity, there is no limit to the patterns of causal dependence that can be represented with neuron diagrams. One can invent new ways of shading neurons—lighter and darker shades of gray, cross-hatching,[10] colors, polka dots, and so on. One can use different shapes for neurons,[11] and introduce new types of arrows—dashed or dotted, squiggly or zigzagging—and with all manner of heads. One of the supposed virtues of neuron diagrams is that they "can represent a complex situation clearly and forcefully, allowing the reader to take in its central causal characteristics at a glance" (Hall and Paul 2003, p. 102). It should be clear, however, that as one adds more and more modifications to the basic representational repertoire, the resulting diagrams become less perspicuous.

Moreover, the modifications that are introduced to represent new types of causal structures are completely ad hoc. This does not mean that the resulting diagrams can no longer serve their representational purpose; it does mean, however, that neuron diagrams fail to serve an important heuristic role. Since it is always possible to invent new conventions in order to accommodate new kinds of structures, neuron diagrams cannot delimit the logically possible structures *a* priori. One consequence is that neuron diagrams have little ability to suggest new possible structures that have not yet been discovered through the normal processes of counterexample-seeking.

Here is one trivial example. Consider a neural system with only two neurons, **a** and **b**, each of which is binary—that is, each can fire or not fire (no firing with different intensities, etc.). Let A and B be the corresponding variables. Then here is one very simple possibility expressed as a structural

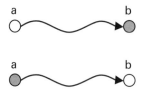

Figure 4.8
Two neuron diagrams that are never seen, even though the neural systems they represent are conceptually possible.

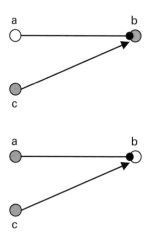

Figure 4.9
Two neuron diagrams commonly seen in place of those of figure 4.8.

equation:

$$B = \sim A$$

Indeed, it is trivial to show that this is one of only two ways in which the value of A can make a difference for the value of B in a model with two binary variables. Yet there is no way to express this relationship in terms of the standard triangle- or circle-headed arrows. One can, of course, introduce a new type of arrow to represent this relationship: I give one example in figure 4.8. (The wavy line evokes the tilde of negation.) Yet despite the apparent ease of representing this kind of two-neuron structure, no such structure has ever appeared in the literature. Rather, in every neural system in which two neurons stand in this relation, there is always a third neuron stimulating **b**, as shown in figure 4.9.

It might be argued that there is something funny about the neural systems depicted in figure 4.8. In the top figure, neuron **b** fires without being stimulated. This seems to violate some kind of metaphysical principle akin to the Principle of Sufficient Reason. I suspect that the absence of neuron diagrams like those in figure 4.8 is due to something like this line of thought. But there are at least three problems with this line of reasoning.

First, initial neurons such as **a** and **c** as depicted in figure 4.9 are allowed to fire without being stimulated.

Second, it is never stipulated that a neuron diagram is supposed to represent a *closed* causal system. Indeed, when a neuron diagram is used to present any realistic example, it will be impossible for *all* of the causes to be represented in the neuron diagram. Thus the patterns of dependence presented in a neuron diagram will typically hold only ceteris paribus, relative to specific circumstances that are not explicitly represented in the diagram. So even if the neural system is as depicted in figure 4.9, there seems to be no reason why we cannot relegate the firing of **c** to the fixed background, and represent the neural system by one of the diagrams shown in figure 4.8.

Third, and most significant, if there *are* metaphysical assumptions at work here, they should be stated *explicitly*, and not smuggled in via the representation. Indeed, I suspect that some version of the Principle of Sufficient Reason *does* play a role in our intuitive judgments of token causation, and that an adequate theory of causation will have to take account of this.[12] The role that this assumption plays has been masked by the use of neuron diagrams.

7   Causal Loading

Much of the language that is used to describe neuron diagrams is causally loaded: neurons are connected by stimulatory or inhibitory connections; they are said to stimulate or inhibit one another. "Stimulate" and "inhibit" certainly sound like causal terms, meaning "cause to fire" and "prevent from firing" respectively. If a neuron diagram is merely being used to present a causal structure in order to introduce a problem, or to motivate a modification, this causal loading is relatively harmless. However, if one is using a neuron diagram for purposes of *testing* a theory of causation—

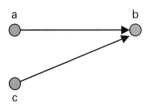

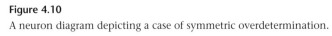

Figure 4.10
A neuron diagram depicting a case of symmetric overdetermination.

comparing the verdicts of one's theory against those of intuition—then it seems highly inappropriate for the mode of representation to be stipulating the presence of causal relationships. Consider, for example, a standard case of symmetric overdetermination, say, two gunmen firing bullets that simultaneously pierce a victim's heart. This structure is commonly represented abstractly by a neuron diagram such as that shown in figure 4.10. It seems a legitimate question to ask whether each shot, taken individually, is a cause of the death, or whether it is only the two shots somehow taken collectively that cause the death. (Note that the death does not counterfactually depend upon either shot taken singly.) Jonathan Schaffer (2003) refers to these positions as *individualism* and *collectivism*, respectively. Our intuitions can hardly help but be pushed toward individualism when we refer to the individual arrows in figure 4.10 as "stimulatory connections," and talk of "**a** stimulating **b**."

Contrast this situation with that of the structural equation models described in section 4 above. The equations and the graphs are interpreted in purely counterfactual terms; no causal language is used.[13] A system of equations precisely represents the set of true counterfactuals among the variables used to represent the system. If we use an example, real or hypothetical, to test a counterfactual theory of causation, it seems appropriate that the example be presented in such a way as to make clear exactly which counterfactuals are true. It is only in this form that the theory can be directly applied to the example; for if your intuitions are different from mine because you have misinterpreted the counterfactual structure of the case, then your intuitions do not count against the theory. Similar comments apply, mutatis mutandis, to other theories of causation, so long as they have the resources to interpret the equations in broadly counterfactual terms.

8 Neurons, Events, and Circles

In section 2 above, I wrote that most writers distinguish between a neuron and the event of that neuron's firing, *in their written presentations*. The qualifier is important, since these two things are not clearly distinguished in the neuron diagrams themselves. Let us now return to a quote introduced in section 3 above, and fill in the ellipses: "Diagram conventions: filled circles doubly represent neurons that fire and events that occur, unfilled circles doubly represent neurons that do not fire and events that do not occur …" (Schaffer 2001, p. 79, n. 14). If circles doubly represent neurons and events (or non-events), then we will be unable to represent neural systems where one neuron fires more than once, or where several neurons jointly participate in a single event (perhaps neurons can collide, sending out stimulatory or inhibitory signals). More generally, we will be unable to represent examples in which a physical object participates in multiple events, or vice versa. I believe that this limitation has led to particular problems in the treatment of late preemption (or late cutting, as Lewis 2000 prefers to call it).

The problem of late preemption is illustrated in the following example:

Suzy and Billy, expert rock-throwers, are engaged in a competition to see who can shatter a target bottle first. They both pick up rocks and throw them at the bottle, but Suzy throws hers a split second before Billy. Consequently, Suzy's rock gets there first, shattering the bottle. Since both throws are perfectly accurate, Billy's would have shattered the bottle if Suzy's had not occurred, so the shattering is overdetermined. (Hall 2004a, p. 235)

These cases are problematic because the effect does not counterfactually depend upon the cause, nor is there a chain of counterfactual dependence, as required in Lewis 1973.

Late preemption is also commonly presented using neuron diagrams. Figure 4.11 provides two examples. In the neural system represented by figure 4.11a, neurons **a** and **c** both fire. The process initiated by **c** leads to the stimulation of **e** before **d** can fire. As a result, **e** fires and prevents **d** from firing. A version of this diagram appears in Lewis 1986 (p. 204), and has been widely reproduced in the literature. Figure 4.11b shows **a** and **c** both firing, with the stimulatory signal from **c** triggering the firing of **e** before the signal from **a** arrives. This example appears in Hall and Paul 2003 (p. 111, fig. 6), and in Collins, Hall, and Paul 2004a (fig. 3).

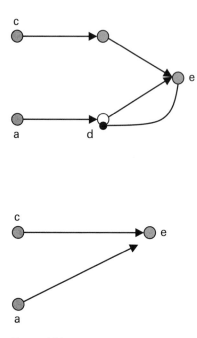

Figure 4.11
Two neuron diagrams representing cases of late preemption.

Unfortunately, neither of the diagrams in figure 4.11 is really satisfactory. Figure 4.11a shows a causal loop. Suppose for example that **a** fires and **c** does not. Then, according to the layout portrayed in the diagram, we become mired in paradox. If **e** fires, then **d** does not; but what, then, causes **e** to fire? If **e** does not fire, then **d** does fire, and **e** fires after all. In other words, figure 4.11a portrays a grandfather paradox waiting to happen. This is clearly not what is intended. Figure 4.11b, on the other hand, does not represent in any way the information that if **c** does not fire, then **a** will stimulate **e** and cause it to fire.

The problem is that we are using one circle to represent the possible firings of **e** at two different times. Following Maslen (2000, appendix), let us instead use two circles, labeled e and e'. If e is shaded, that represents the firing of **e** at time t, when it did in fact fire; if e' is shaded, that represents the firing of **e** at later time t', at which **e** would have fired if **c** had not fired. Expanding the diagram in figure 4.11a, for example, gives us the diagram in figure 4.12. Note that it is easy to represent this neural system in terms of structural equations:

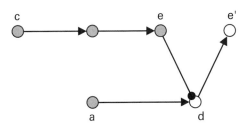

Figure 4.12
An alternative representation of late preemption.

$C = 1$

$A = 1$

$E = C$

$D = A \ \& \sim E$

$E' = D$

Since the structural equation framework never attempted to identify variables with individual objects such as neurons, there is no conceptual obstacle to identifying the correct model.

At this point, a refinement is in order. I said above that the problem for neuron diagrams was that the representation scheme did not allow for the same neuron to participate in more than one event. However, if e and e' are different events, then there *is* no problem of late preemption. In the neural system depicted in figure 4.12, e would not have occurred without c—end of story, no problem. In the bottle throwing example, if "the shattering" refers to an event that could not have occurred a fraction of a second later, then the shattering would not have occurred without Suzy's throw, and again a simple counterfactual account gets the case just right. The problem of late preemption only arises because we are willing to countenance firings (or shatterings, or …) at slightly different times as versions of the *same* event.

Lewis (2000) introduces the helpful concept of an event *alteration*. Consider the event e of neuron **e**'s firing at time t. Then we say that e', the (non-occurrent) firing of **e** at t', is an *alteration* of e. This implies that e' is different from e in some respects (in this case, time of occurrence), but says nothing about whether the events are numerically identical. We should not, *in general*, represent different alterations by different circles.

For example, if there is a neuron that can fire with different strengths, it would be misguided to represent these different possible firings with different circles. The alterations *e* and *e'*, however, stand in a very special relationship—the former *prevents* the latter from occurring. In Hall's example, the shattering of the bottle by Suzy's rock *prevents* Billy's rock from shattering the bottle. This extra bit of causal structure is, in fact, *the* defining feature of late preemption.[14] This extra structure is obscured in the diagrams of figure 4.11. I suspect that this obscurity has hindered efforts at formulating an adequate account of late preemption. Indeed, one promising account of late preemption, due to Halpern and Pearl (2005), makes use of a graphical representation (their figure 4) analogous to figure 4.12 above.

9 Conclusion

Although I have leveled a number of criticisms at the way in which neuron diagrams have been used, and more importantly, the way in which they *lend themselves* to being misused, I wish to conclude by reiterating my claim that these criticisms do not stem from any in-principle limitations on the representational power of neuron diagrams. Indeed, the superficial similarity between neuron diagrams and causal graphs might lead us to ask whether there is really any sharp boundary that separates them. For example, some of the difficulties with neuron diagrams could be eliminated by appending structural equations to them; this would be particularly helpful for representing cases where the pattern of dependence can not be assimilated to stimulatory and inhibitory connections. Glymour and Wimberly (this volume) adopts this strategy; and I have effectively done so in section 8, where I offered an improved neuron diagram and presented the accompanying structural equations. We may motivate the same hybrid form of representation from the other direction. Note that a causal graph, when divorced from its corresponding system of equations, conveys a lot less information than a neuron diagram; compare, for example, the neuron diagram in figure 4.1 with the causal graph in figure 4.4. The graph itself, unlike the accompanying equations, tells us nothing about what values the variables take, or about the form of the dependence of one variable upon another. It would be simple enough to develop conventions for including such information in the graph. We could, for example, display the variables in different fonts, sizes, or colors to indicate their values.

Such modifications would lend causal graphs the same visual perspicuity enjoyed by neuron diagrams; indeed, such causal graphs would simply be neuron diagrams with different representational conventions. The moral, then, is not that neuron diagrams should be abandoned. The moral, rather, is that neuron diagrams can be improved upon, and their use should always be accompanied with an awareness of the ways in which they influence our thinking about the causal structures they represent.

Acknowledgments

I would like to thank Clark Glymour, Cei Maslen, Laurie Paul, Jonathan Schaffer, and Jim Woodward for helpful comments and suggestions.

Notes

1. A list, no doubt partial, of papers where neuron diagrams are used includes: Barker 2004; Byrne and Hall 1998; Collins, Hall, and Paul 2004a; Dowe and Noordhof 2004a; Ehring 2004; Glymour and Wimberly, this volume; Hall 2004a, 2004b; Hall and Paul 2003; Lewis 2004; McDermott 1995a; Menzies 1989, 1996; Noordhof 1999, 2000; Ramachandran 1997, 1998, 2004a, 2004b; Rice 1999; Schaffer 2000a, 2000b, 2001, 2004.

2. See, e.g., Hall and Paul 2003, p. 102; Maslen 2000, appendix.

3. Of the papers mentioned above, in note 1, the following use neuron diagrams in this way: Ehring 2004; Hall 2004a, 2004b; Noordhof 2000; and Schaffer 2000a, 2000b, 2001, 2004. Collins, Hall, and Paul (2004a), and Hall and Paul (2003) *use* neuron diagrams in the same way that Lewis does, although they contain language *suggesting* that neuron diagrams can be used to represent the underlying causal structure of examples other than neural systems.

4. Schaffer's example is probabilistic, but that is irrelevant to the point made here.

5. The other papers by Schaffer, cited in previous notes, contain similar examples.

6. Maslen (2000, appendix), for example, is careful to talk this way.

7. See, e.g., Byrne and Hall 1998; Menzies 1989, 1996; and Ramachandran 1997, 1998, 2004a.

8. More specifically, they express *non-backtracking conditionals*, in the sense of Lewis 1979.

9. There are some complexities, particularly concerning the appropriate choice of variables, which I cannot address in this short exposition. For detailed discussion,

see Hitchcock 2001, 2004. These complexities do not in any way tell differentially against representations using directed graphs and structural equations: analogous complexities will arise for any attempt to represent such examples using neuron diagrams. Indeed, the complexities are made readily apparent by the explicit rules connecting equations and graphs to counterfactuals, rather than hidden because of the absence of rules. This is a further advantage of this mode of representation over neuron diagrams.

10. Hall and Paul (2003), for example, use different shades to represent different intensities of neural firing (p. 109, fig. 5) and cross-hatching to represent firing in a particular manner (p. 121, fig. 13).

11. Lewis (1986, pp. 208–209), for example, uses a bullet-shaped figure to represent a neuron that needs to be doubly stimulated, like the thick-walled neuron in figure 4.7.

12. I am currently working on a project to develop this suspicion into a positive proposal. See Hitchcock (forthcoming) and Hitchcock ms.

13. It may turn out that the non-backtracking counterfactuals are irreducibly causal. This does not especially concern me, since it is effectively everyone's problem, and not merely mine. Moreover, there is still a highly nontrivial problem about which patterns of these causal counterfactuals constitute cases of token causation.

14. Note that I do not say that the non-occurrence of some event in the backup process, such as the firing of neuron **d** in figure 4.12, is a defining feature of late preemption. We might have a case where *e directly* prevents *e'*, and does not do so by preventing an intermediary event such as *d*. It is this possibility that Collins, Hall, and Paul intend to capture by representing late preemption using figure 4.11b, instead of the more customary 4.11a. We could capture such a structure by modifying figure 4.11b in the following way: add an extra circle labeled *e'*; fill in circles *c*, *e*, and *a*; and draw triangle-headed arrows from *c* to *e* and *a* to *e'*, with a circle-headed arrow from *e* to *e'*.

References

Barker, S. 2004. "Analyzing Chancy Causation without Appeal to Chance-raising." In Dowe and Noordhof 2004b.

Byrne, A., and N. Hall. 1998. "Against the PCA-analysis." *Analysis* 58: 38–44.

Collins, J., N. Hall, and L. Paul. 2004a. "Counterfactuals and Causation: History, Problems, and Prospects." In Collins, Hall, and Paul 2004b.

Collins, J., N. Hall, and L. Paul. 2004b. *Causation and Counterfactuals*. Cambridge, Mass.: MIT Press.

Dowe, P., and P. Noordhof. 2004a. "Introduction." In Dowe and Noordhof 2004b.

Dowe, P., and P. Noordhof. 2004b. *Cause and Chance*. London and New York: Routledge.

Ehring, D. 2004. "Counterfactual Theories, Preemption, and Persistence." In Dowe and Noordhof 2004b.

Hall, N. 2004a. "Two Concepts of Causation." In Collins, Hall, and Paul 2004b.

Hall, N. 2004b. "The Intrinsic Character of Causation." In *Oxford Studies in Metaphysics*, vol. 1, edited by D. Zimmerman. Oxford: Oxford University Press.

Hall, N., and L. Paul. 2003. "Causation and Preemption." In *Philosophy of Science Today*, edited by P. Clark and K. Hawley. Oxford: Oxford University Press.

Halpern, J., and J. Pearl. 2005. "Causes and Explanations: A Structural-model Approach—Part I: Causes." *British Journal for the Philosophy of Science* 56: 843–887.

Hitchcock, C. 2001. "The Intransitivity of Causation Revealed in Equations and Graphs." *Journal of Philosophy* 98: 273–299.

Hitchcock, C. 2004. "Routes, Processes, and Chance-lowering Causes." In Dowe and Noordhof 2004b.

Hitchcock, C. MS. "Token Causal Structure."

Hitchcock, C. Forthcoming. "Prevention, Preemption, and the Principle of Sufficient Reason." *Philosophical Review*.

Lewis, D. 1973. "Causation." *Journal of Philosophy* 70: 556–567.

Lewis, D. 1979. "Counterfactual Dependence and Time's Arrow." *Noûs* 13: 455–476.

Lewis, D. 1986. "Postscripts to 'Causation.'" In Lewis, *Philosophical Papers*, vol. 2. Oxford: Oxford University Press.

Lewis, D. 2000. "Causation as Influence." *Journal of Philosophy* 97: 182–197.

Lewis, D. 2004. "Causation as Influence," expanded version. In Collins, Hall, and Paul 2004b.

Maslen, C. 2000. "Causes, Effects, and Contrasts." Ph.D. dissertation, Princeton University.

McDermott, M. 1995a. "Lewis on Causal Dependence." *Australasian Journal of Philosophy* 73: 129–139.

McDermott, M. 1995b. "Redundant Causation." *British Journal for the Philosophy of Science* 40: 523–544.

Menzies, P. 1989. "Probabilistic Causation and Causal Processes: A Critique of Lewis." *Philosophy of Science* 56: 642–663.

Menzies, P. 1996. "Probabilistic Causation and the Pre-emption Problem." *Mind* 105: 85–117.

Noordhof, P. 1999. "Probabilistic Causation, Preemption, and Counterfactuals." *Mind* 108: 95–126.

Noordhof, P. 2000. "Ramachandran's Four Counterexamples." *Mind* 109: 315–324.

Pearl, J. 2000. *Causality: Models, Reasoning, and Inference.* Cambridge: Cambridge University Press.

Ramachandran, M. 1997. "A Counterfactual Analysis of Causation." *Mind* 106: 263–277.

Ramachandran, M. 1998. "The M-set Analysis of Causation: Objections and Responses." *Mind* 107: 465–471.

Ramachandran, M. 2004a. "Indeterministic Causation and Varieties of Chance-raising." In Dowe and Noordhof 2004b.

Ramachandran, M. 2004b. "A Counterfactual Analysis of Indeterministic Causation." In Collins, Hall, and Paul 2004b.

Rice, H. 1999. "David Lewis's Awkward Cases of Redundant Causation." *Analysis* 59: 157–164.

Schaffer, J. 2000a. "Causation by Disconnection." *Philosophy of Science* 67: 285–300.

Schaffer, J. 2000b. "Overlappings: Probability-Raising without Causation." *Australasian Journal of Philosophy* 78: 40–46.

Schaffer, J. 2001. "Causes as Probability Raisers of Processes." *Journal of Philosophy* 98: 75–92.

Schaffer, J. 2003. "Overdetermining Causes." *Philosophical Studies* 114: 23–45.

Schaffer, J. 2004. "Causes Need Not Be Physically Connected to Their Effects: The Case for Negative Causation." In *Contemporary Debates in Philosophy of Science*, edited by C. Hitchcock. Oxford: Blackwell.

Spirtes, P., C. Glymour, and R. Scheines. 2000. *Causation, Prediction, and Search*, 2d ed. Cambridge, Mass.: MIT Press.

Woodward, J. 2003. *Making Things Happen: A Theory of Causal Explanation.* Oxford: Oxford University Press.

5 Mackie Remixed

Michael Strevens

1 Introduction

A *singular causal claim* is a claim of the form "*c* was a cause of *e*," where *c* and *e* are token events. Much of the literature on the interpretation of causal claims is motivated by the intuition that "*c* was a cause of *e*" asserts that *c* *made a difference* to whether or not *e* occurred, in the sense that taking *c* "out of the picture" would result in a situation where *e* no longer occurred. The most natural way to interpret this difference-making intuition is in terms of natural language counterfactuals: *c* made a difference to *e* just in case, had *c* not occurred, *e* would not have occurred. This leads immediately to a simple counterfactual account of causal claims, according to which *c* was a cause of *e* just in case, had *c* not occurred, *e* would not have occurred. The simple counterfactual account is most often associated with Lewis (1973a), although Lewis himself went far beyond the simple account in the course of his writings on causation.

The simple counterfactual account's most notorious difficulty is its handling of cases of preemption, that is, cases in which, had the actual cause *c* not caused *e*, some other "backup" cause would have done so. A well-known example is the case of the backup assassin; in the interest of reducing the level of violence in the causation literature, I present in its place the case of the backup Circassian:

The grand vizier, seeking to please the sultan, introduces a beautiful Circassian maiden into the harem. She acquits herself superbly, and the sultan is well satisfied. Her ministrations, then, are the cause of the sultan's good mood. But the grand vizier, ever mindful of the contingency of his position, has the sultan's old favorite, also, coincidentally, from Circassia, in reserve. The favorite is absolutely reliable:

had the new Circassian failed to please the sultan, the backup Circassian would have
been dispatched immediately, and would certainly have transported his epicurean
majesty to a higher plane of happiness.[1]

Had the new Circassian's endeavors failed to please the sultan, the sultan
would still have been pleased. On a simple counterfactual understanding
of causal claims, then, the new Circassian did not cause the sultan's good
mood—the wrong answer.

It is now standard to follow Lewis in calling such scenarios cases of *preemption*, since what is intuitively the actual cause preempts the backup
cause. (For an excellent and wide-ranging discussion of the significance
of preemption scenarios for the causal claims literature, see Hall and Paul
2003.) On the face of it, preemption seems not only to be a problem for a
simple counterfactual analysis of causal claims, but for any analysis that
takes the difference-making intuition seriously, since whenever there is a
backup cause, the action of the actual cause in a sense genuinely does
make no difference to the occurrence of the effect.

There is, nevertheless, another sense in which it does make a difference,
and this sense is captured by the corresponding causal claim, or so defenders of the difference-making intuition maintain. Attempts to make
good on the difference-making intuition have tended to use natural language counterfactuals in more subtle and sophisticated ways so as to manufacture an account of causal claims that delivers the same judgment as the
simple counterfactual account in the straightforward cases but that gives
the right answer in cases of preemption. Among the best known examples
are, of course, Lewis's various accounts of causation (1973a, 1986b, 2000).

An alternative to this strategy is to abandon natural language counterfactuals as the proper technical tool for assessing difference-making, and to
look for some other way to remove c from the picture and to assess whether
e still occurs. One promising removal technique is an approach based on
work in computer science and other disciplines on "causal Bayesian networks" (Pearl 2000; see Hitchcock 2001, and in a different vein Yablo
2002, for the application to preemption). Another sophisticated alternative
to the counterfactual approach is John Mackie's INUS account of causal
claims, in Mackie 1974. The purpose of this paper is to argue that Mackie's
account supplies, without any of the complex amendments now standard
in counterfactual theories, a completely satisfactory treatment of the standard cases of preemption.

This is not, I think, a well-publicized fact. Certainly, Mackie himself seems not to have noticed all of the virtues of his theory; his own account of preempting causes is, as I will explain below, far less satisfactory than the account I offer here on his behalf.[2]

The success of the INUS approach in vindicating the difference-making intuition while taking care of preemption shows, I think, that it is well worth revamping for the new century. To this end, I examine two serious problems with Mackie's account, unrelated to preemption, and, drawing inspiration from related work on causal explanation (Strevens 2004), I propose a radical reinterpretation of the INUS machinery that solves both problems and transforms Mackie's account into something rather new—too new, I would guess, for Mackie. The result, then, is a novel theory of the meaning of causal claims.

For the sake of truth in advertising, let me remark on two ways in which this new theory is limited. The first limitation, common to much of the preemption literature, is a restriction to causal claims about processes governed by deterministic laws.

The second is that the theory of causal claims on offer is not also a reductive metaphysics of causation. It does not translate causal claims into claims about something not intrinsically causal; rather, it takes for granted a world permeated by a certain kind of primitive physical causal connection, and offers an account of what causal claims are saying about such a world. This interpretation of the role of causal claims in our causal understanding of the world is developed in section 5; first, however, my appreciation of the virtues of Mackie.

2   Mackie's Theory of Causation

According to the theory presented in Mackie 1974, the causal claim "c was a cause of e" is true just in case c is an insufficient but nonredundant part of an unnecessary but sufficient condition for the occurrence of e. When this requirement is satisfied, c is said to be an INUS condition for e. The critical aspects of the analysis are the part's nonredundancy and the whole's sufficiency; for my present purposes, it is enough to say that c is a cause of e just in case c is a nonredundant part of a sufficient condition for e. Though it is not always made explicit, the set of sufficient conditions must be *veridical*, that is, each of the conditions must be true.

Consider an example. The mischievous imperial prince's throwing a cannonball at a fine Iznik jar was a cause, say, of the jar's breaking. On Mackie's analysis, the reason for this is as follows. There is a set of conditions that were jointly sufficient for the jar's breaking. These include the prince's throwing the cannonball, but also various other elements of the situation—the fact that the prince was close enough to the jar for his throw to connect, the fact that the grand vizier, protecting the jar with a steel-plated fez, failed to parry the cannonball, and the fact that the gravity on earth exerted just the right pull on the ball that the prince's shot was neither too high nor too low. These conditions, together with the relevant laws of nature, are sufficient for the jar's breaking; for Mackie, this means that they entail the breaking. Or at least, sufficiency means entailment in those cases where the putative effect is the result of a deterministic process. If the process is probabilistic, the story is more complex. As noted above, this paper will assume determinism.

A nonredundant part of a sufficient condition for an event e is a part that cannot be removed from the sufficient condition without invalidating the entailment of e. Removal here is not negation: if I remove the gravity from the sufficient condition I do not leave behind a condition that says there is no gravity; rather, what is left is a condition that says nothing about gravity at all, leaving open the possibility that the gravitational acceleration acting on the cannonball has any value that you like. Removing the gravity in this way invalidates the entailment of the jar's breaking—the condition no longer entails breaking, because it is consistent with the possibility that the gravity is so great that the cannonball crashes to the ground long before it reaches the jar. The gravity, then, is a nonredundant part of the sufficient condition; it is therefore a cause of the breaking. The same is true for each of the conditions listed above, so that each of them counts, on Mackie's view, as a cause of the breaking.

It is important for the Mackie approach, as it is for the Lewis approach and indeed for any difference-making approach, that the relata of causal claims are not what Hempel (and Mackie) called "concrete events," but are rather what are often called "states of affairs" (Hempel 1965, pp. 421–423). A concrete event is individuated by every intrinsic detail of its happening; the concrete event of the breaking of a jar, for example, is individuated by the precise trajectory of every shard of ceramic, so that if one such trajectory had been slightly different, a different concrete event would have occurred. A state of affairs has coarser individuation conditions. The state of affairs of the jar's breaking obtains no matter how, exactly, the shards fly. When Mackie talks of a condition sufficient for the jar's breaking, he means a condition sufficient for the state of affairs to obtain, not a condition sufficient for the underlying concrete event that actually realized the state of affairs to obtain. On the latter interpretation absolutely any physical influence on the breaking would, most likely, count as a nonredundant part of a sufficient condition for the breaking (as explained below, in section 3). In what follows, then, by an *event* I mean a high level event or state of affairs; when I need to talk about concrete events, I will always refer to them as such.[3]

Mackie's account can and should be understood as a difference-making account, using the following notion of difference-making: c makes a difference to whether or not e occurs just in case it plays an essential role in entailing e. Mackie himself saw the INUS machinery in this light, but he thought of it as providing an analysis of natural language counterfactuals, rather than as an alternative to the counterfactual characterization of difference-making. In fact, Mackie's machinery constitutes a way of "removing c from the picture," and checking whether e still occurs, that is quite different from the technique we use for evaluating natural language counterfactuals. (This was not, I think, generally appreciated until Stalnaker's and Lewis's work on counterfactuals—in Stalnaker 1968, and Lewis 1973b—had been fully digested.)

I will return to this topic below, in section 4, but let me point out two salient differences between Mackie's difference-making and difference-making as defined using natural language counterfactuals. On a counterfactual account, to see whether c made a difference to e, you move to a "nearby" possible world (or set of possible worlds) in which c did not occur, and you see whether e occurs in that world. Observe (1) that the "removal" of c on the natural language account corresponds to a *negation* of c, rather than, as on Mackie's account, a lack of an assertion as to whether c occurs or not; and (2), that on the natural language account, you try to remove c only from a single "sufficient condition" for e—namely, the state of the entire world at the appropriate time—whereas on Mackie's account, you may try to remove c from any number of different sufficient conditions (and there will always be many such conditions). The putative cause c need only be essential to one of these sufficient conditions in order to qualify as a cause. It is this second difference that accounts, as you will see, for the Mackie account's superior handling of cases of preemption.

3 Mackie's Account of Preemption

Although Mackie's theory of causation contains all of the apparatus necessary for a completely successful treatment of preemption cases, Mackie's own comments on preemption are far from satisfying.[4]

Mackie considers a case much like that of the backup Circassian:[5] "Smith and Jones commit a crime, but if they had not done so the head of the criminal organization would have sent other members to perform it in their stead, and so it would have been committed anyway" (1974, p. 44). Suppose that Smith and Jones, acting on orders from the grand vizier, poisoned the sultan's wine, killing the sultan. Mackie's view is that Smith and Jones's act of putting poison in the wine is not an INUS condition for the sultan's death, and so is not a cause of the death. That is, he bites the bullet: backup causes really do render the events that preempt them causally impotent, in the sense that the claim that "Smith and Jones's poisoning of the wine caused the sultan's death" is false. We are simply wrong to think otherwise (Mackie 1974, pp. 44–47).

As consolation, Mackie allows that the poisoning is what he calls a "producing cause" of the sultan's death. To characterize a producing cause, I will use the notion of the "concrete realizer" of a high level event e, which I define to be just what you would think—the concrete event that realizes e (concrete events having been defined in section 2). The concrete realizer of a particular jar's breaking, for example, is the concrete event of the breaking, that is, the low level event that is individuated by every physical detail of the breaking.

An event c is a producing cause for another event e if c's concrete realizer is an INUS condition for e's concrete realizer. This condition will normally be satisfied if c's realizer had any physical influence at all on e's realizer. Consider, for example, the gravitational influence of the bulky chief white eunuch. If the eunuch's influence had been slightly different, the paths traced by the molecules in the chemical reaction that killed the sultan would have been slightly different. But then the actual concrete realizer of e, the sultan's death, would not have occurred. Some other concrete event—also a realizer of the sultan's dying—would have occurred in its place. It follows that the removal of the chief white eunuch's gravitational influence from the totality of physical influences on the realizer will invalidate the entailment of that precise realizer. Thus the chief eunuch's mass is an INUS condition for the realizer.

To be a producing cause, then, is not very difficult; and to say that something is a producing cause is not very informative. In particular, to be told that the poisoning is, like the gravitational influence of the chief white eunuch, a producing cause for the sultan's death, does not provide much compensation for the poisoning's being stripped of its causehood.

In any case, our practice in evaluating causal claims such as these is to hold that the poisoning of the sultan's wine was just as much a cause of his death as the prince's throwing the cannonball was a cause of the jar's breaking; the fact of the grand vizier's backup plan does not diminish the causal status of the poisoning at all. Mackie's position fails to capture this practice.

Yet Mackie could have done much better. The poisoning is clearly an INUS condition for the sultan's death—it belongs to a set of conditions sufficient to entail the sultan's death, and it cannot be removed from that set without invalidating the entailment. The relevant set of conditions does *not* mention the backup plan, but it does not need to: Mackie's sets of sufficient conditions need only be sufficient; unlike Lewis's possible worlds, they need not be maximally detailed. This point will be explained at greater length in the next section, where I develop an INUS approach to the standard cases of preemption.

4   Preemption with the Mackie Account

4.1   Actual Causes Are Not Discounted

Solving the preemption problem using the Mackie account will involve a careful scrutiny of the form of the conditions sufficient for the occurrence of a given event. I will, therefore, consider a causal process that is simpler than a poisoning or a caress.

The imperial prince heaves a cannonball at the backup Circassian's favorite Iznik jar, breaking it. The sultan's mother was standing by in case the prince fumbled his throw; had the prince failed to break the jar, the sultan's mother would have thrown her cannonball and smashed it for sure. In this standard example of *early preemption*, the prince's throw fails the simple counterfactual test for difference-making: had he not thrown, the jar would have been broken anyway. What does Mackie's INUS account have to say about the throw?

The prince's throw is part of a set of conditions sufficient for the jar's breaking, namely, the same set of conditions that would have obtained had the sultan's mother, the backup thrower, not been present. The list perhaps looks something like this:

1. The prince threw his ball at time t from such and such a point with such and such a velocity.

2. Nothing interfered with the trajectory of the ball.

3. The jar was in such and such a position at time $t + 1$.

4. The laws of physics imply that a ball thrown in this fashion at time t will strike a jar in this position at time $t + 1$ hard enough to break the jar, provided that nothing interferes with its flight.

(I have suppressed reference to the necessary assumptions about the structure of the jar.)

Clearly, condition (1) is a nonredundant part of the sufficient conditions—if it is removed, the conditions no longer entail the jar's breaking. Thus, the prince's throwing the ball is a nonredundant part of a set of conditions sufficient for the breaking, and so is, on Mackie's account, a cause of the breaking. The fact of the backup at no stage enters into the calculation, which is, I think, as it should be: the presence of the Sultan's mother is irrelevant to the causal status of the prince's throw.

Is handling preemption really this easy? Suppose that you add to the list of sufficient conditions the following condition:

5. The sultan's mother was standing by ready to throw her cannonball; and if the prince had failed to break the jar with his ball, she would have launched hers from such and such a position with such and such a velocity and so on.

Then, if condition (1) is removed from the list, the breaking of the jar is not invalidated: the new condition (5) contributes just enough to make up for the absence of (1). Thus (1) is not a nonredundant part of this set of sufficient conditions.

It is more or less this fact—(1)'s redundancy in the presence of (5)—that is responsible for the failure of the simple counterfactual account to handle cases of preemption. But it is irrelevant to Mackie's account. For c to count as a cause of e, Mackie's account requires that there exist a veridical set of conditions sufficient for e of which c is a nonredundant part. This allows that there are other sets of veridical conditions sufficient for e in which c is redundant. Provided that there is at least one set that fulfills Mackie's requirements, c was a cause of e. In normal circumstances, no matter how many backups are in place there will always be one set featuring the actual cause nonredundantly, a set that mentions none of the backups. Thus backups will normally make no difference to an event's causal status.

Why the *normally*? Keen-eyed readers will have noted a potential difficulty for the Mackie account in a case where a single state of affairs both acts as a backup and plays an essential role in the actual causal production of the effect, so that any set of sufficient conditions mentioning the actual cause must also mention the backup cause.

Let me give an example from Strevens 2003. Suppose that the imperial prince and the sultan's mother both throw cannonballs at a jar. The prince's is off target, but the sultan's mother's is deadly accurate. The balls collide in midair, however, and the mother's is directed away from the jar, whereas the prince's is deflected towards the jar, which it was otherwise going to miss. The trajectories of the balls are shown in figure 5.1.

Observe that any set of sufficient conditions for the jar's breaking that contains the prince's throw nonredundantly will also have to contain the sultan's mother's throw, since without her throw, the prince's throw would not have been redirected towards the jar. But the mother's throw is a backup cause for the jar's breaking: had the prince not thrown, her throw would certainly have broken the jar. Thus, it seems that the backup cause

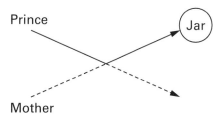

Figure 5.1
The sultan's mother's throw is a both a backup cause and an INUS condition for the jar's breaking.

must be mentioned in any set of sufficient conditions containing the prince's throw, making his throw a redundant part of all such sets of conditions, and so not a cause of the breaking.

Almost, but not quite. Look more closely at the claim that the prince's throw is redundant. Consider conditions (1) through (5) above, which are, I will suppose, sufficient for the breaking. The prince's throw is redundant if conditions (2) through (5) are sufficient in themselves to entail the breaking. But despite appearances, conditions (2) through (5) do not entail the breaking, and there is no way to tweak the conditions or the example to make them do so. The reason is this: in order for the conditions to entail the breaking, they must entail that the sultan's mother's throw hits the jar. In effect, they are describing what would have happened if the prince had not thrown. But for this entailment to go through, the conditions would have to include a condition of the form:

6. Nothing interfered with the trajectory of the sultan's mother's ball.

They do not include such a condition. More importantly, they could *never* contain this condition while satisfying the requirements of Mackie's account, for the account requires that the sufficient conditions be veridical— that is, true of the actual world—but (6) is false.

It follows that (1) is not, after all, redundant: it cannot be removed from the conditions without invalidating the entailment of the breaking. Thus it was a cause of the breaking, as desired.

This is not due to any peculiarity of the scenario. A backup cause is *merely* a backup cause because the conditions necessary for it to exert its characteristic effect (I mean the effect it would have if it were called on as backup) are not all present. The backup Circassian never cavorts with the sultan; Smith and Jones's boss, the grand vizier, never dispatches the B team; and the sultan's mother's cannonball never hits the jar. A set of conditions sufficient for the backup cause to have its characteristic effect would have to assert otherwise, but then it would assert falsely. The requirement of veridicality would not be met.[6]

For this reason, the Mackie account is sure to succeed where the simple counterfactual account does not—counting what are intuitively real causes as real in any case of preemption, including not only all the variants of early preemption discussed above but also what is called *late preemption*, an example of which will be given in the next section.

4.2 Backup and Other Ineffective Causes Are Discounted

The success of the Mackie account in coping with preemption where the simple counterfactual account fails might be explained as follows: the Mackie account is far more liberal than the counterfactual account. The Mackie account declares an event *c* a cause of *e* as long as *c* is a nonredundant part of just one out of the great number of sets of conditions sufficient for *e*, whereas the counterfactual account demands that *c*'s role be essential in a very particular set of sufficient conditions for *e*, namely, the set describing every aspect of the actual world. (The counterfactual test means something different by *essential* than the Mackie account means by *nonredundant*, of course—I am speaking rather loosely here.)

If the Mackie account works its magic in virtue of its liberality, you might worry that it is perhaps too liberal. Does it classify as causes events that are not causes at all? I will consider two cases that present prima facie problems for Mackie.

Consider jar-breaking again. This time, the sultan's mother throws her cannonball immediately after the prince throws his, with her usual deadly accuracy. The prince is on target this time, and his ball breaks the jar, but his grandmother's ball was close on its tail. Had he missed, her throw would have connected. This is what Lewis calls *late preemption*.

The question I want to ask is, not whether the prince's throw counts as a cause—which it does for the reasons given above—but whether the Mackie account erroneously counts the sultan's mother's throw, too, as a cause. Is there a set of conditions, sufficient for the jar's breaking, of which her throw is an essential part? At first, it may seem so. Her ball is thrown in the right direction with the right amount of heft, and—in contrast to the case of the colliding balls considered above—nothing interferes with its flight. Put together these conditions, saying nothing about the prince's throw, and do you not have what is needed to elevate the mother's throw to the status of a cause?

Not quite. One of the conditions that must be present for a throw to entail a jar's breaking is, recall from above,

3. The jar was in such and such a position at time $t + 1$,

where the relevant ball was thrown at time t and, given the relevant laws of nature and other physical parameters, the ball takes one unit of time to reach the jar. It is this condition that does not hold in the present scenario:

if time *t* is the time of the sultan's mother's throw, then at time $t + 1$ the jar is no longer at the required position; indeed, the jar is no longer anywhere at all, since it has been destroyed by the prince's throw. There is no set of veridical conditions, then, that entails that the mother's ball strikes the jar. The mother's ball is not a cause.

If there *were* a set of veridical conditions entailing that the mother's ball hits the jar, it would indeed have hit the jar. But then it would, intuitively, be a cause of the breaking, in which case Mackie's account would be correct in deeming it so.[7]

That takes care of putative causes of an event *e* that come too late to be real causes of *e*. What of putative causes that come early, but that fail to bring about *e* for some other reason? Suppose, for example, that the grand vizier poisons the sultan, but that the sultan survives. The next day, he slips on a jar shard and breaks his neck. Will the Mackie account correctly discount the grand vizier's poisoning the sultan as a cause of the sultan's death? It will: since the poison did not kill the sultan, and all underlying processes are by working assumption deterministic, some condition must have failed to hold that was required in the circumstances for the poison to have its effect. Perhaps the sultan had just taken an antidote; perhaps he had an iron constitution; perhaps he drank the poison on a full stomach. Whatever this condition, its negation, or something that entails its negation, would have to be a part of any set of conditions in which the poisoning played an essential part in entailing the sultan's death. But this negation would be nonveridical: it would assert that some condition—the actual condition responsible for the sultan's survival—did not obtain, when in fact it did. The poisoning, then, cannot be a cause of death.

One further case of preemption that can cause trouble for the Mackie approach will be discussed in section 5.4.

4.3   Symmetric Overdetermination

In order to bolster the INUS account's claim to handle difficult cases better than any other account of causal claims, let me consider another kind of scenario that has interested philosophers of causation: symmetric overdetermination.

The chief white eunuch and the chief black eunuch simultaneously hurl their scimitars at an intruder in the palace. One scimitar impales the left lobe of the intruder's heart, the other the right lobe. Are both throws—or either, or neither—causes of the intruder's death? This is the question raised by overdetermination.

On the Mackie approach, it appears that both throws are causes. Each belongs to a set of conditions sufficient for the sultan's death, and plays an essential part in the entailment. The relevant set of conditions is, of course, the usual set of conditions that you would use to establish the causal status of such a throw, with the fact of the other throw excluded.

Is this the right answer to the question about overdetermining causes? Some writers believe so (see Schaffer 2003). Yet there is something a little odd about these cases: you feel, for each throw, that the existence of the other throw somehow does detract a little, though far from completely and in a very hard-to-define way, from its causal status. Compare and contrast with cases of preemption, where a backup cause in no way compromises the status of the actual cause.

The Mackie account can explain what is going on, if it is extended in a certain way. I will briefly sketch the extension I have in mind; it will not be developed or defended, however, nor will the extension play any further role in this paper. (For the necessary development and defense, see Strevens 2004.)

The Mackie account uncovers causes of an event e by removing from a set of sufficient conditions for e all those conditions not essential to the entailment of e. I propose the following extension: you can remove not only conditions, but also *parts* of conditions. More exactly, you can remove particular details from a condition, leaving behind something strictly more abstract, provided that the removal does not invalidate the entailment of e.

For example, suppose that a set of conditions sufficient for the breaking of an Iznik jar specifies that the weight of the cannonball hefted at the jar by the sultan's mother was exactly 2 kilograms. On the original Mackie account, you would have to leave this condition in the description; taking it out would leave the weight of the cannonball unspecified, creating the possibility that the ball might weigh only 2 grams, in which case the jar would not have been broken. Thus, on the Mackie account, the exact weight of the ball was a cause of the breaking.

If the account is extended, however, you are allowed to make the description of the weight more abstract. You can replace the condition stating an exact weight of 2 kg with a looser specification, say that the weight was between 1 kg and 10 kg. (Why an upper bound? Even the sultan's mother's strength has its limits.) This replacement can be carried out without invalidating the entailment of the breaking. Result: you can claim, on the extended account, that though the exact weight of the cannonball did not make a difference to the jar's breaking, the approximate weight did; the ball's being quite heavy, but not too heavy to lift, was the difference-maker. Mackie himself, it should be noted, comes very close to spelling out the extended account in chapter 10 of *The Cement of the Universe* (see especially pp. 260–265).

The extended Mackie account explains the peculiarity of symmetric over-determination. Consider a set of sufficient conditions for the intruder's death that includes the chief black eunuch's scimitar throw nonredun-dantly, but that does not mention the chief white eunuch's throw. The conditions entail the scimitar's flying towards the intruder's chest, entering the heart, causing traumatic damage to the heart tissue, and so on. Now remove all the redundant detail, as envisaged by the extended Mackie ac-count. The pared-down sufficient conditions will not specify the precise tra-jectory of the scimitar; rather, they will say just enough about the trajectory to entail that the scimitar strikes the heart. Consequently, they will not en-tail the precise details of the damage caused by the scimitar; rather, they will entail only that massive damage is done to the heart.

But observe: everything that the pared-down sufficient conditions say of the chief black eunuch's throw is also true of the chief white eunuch's throw, because of the inexactness in the description of the trajectory, the damage, and so on. The pared-down conditions say that a scimitar throw caused the death, and they give some details about that throw; yet look-ing at the conditions in isolation, you cannot tell which throw is being described.

Now consider a set of conditions sufficient for the death that describes both scimitar throws. It is possible to remove entirely the conditions describing one of the throws provided that the conditions describing the other are left behind. The pared-down conditions will mention only one throw, then.[8] But, for the reasons given in the last paragraph, there will be nothing left in the conditions to determine which of the two throws is being mentioned.

So what is the cause of the intruder's death? The two throws are not a joint cause of the death, because a set of conditions that mentions both throws can always be pared down so that it mentions only one. But the throws are not separate causes of the death, either. For each to be a cause, there would have to be two sets of pared-down sufficient conditions, one describing how the chief white eunuch's throw led to death and one describing how the chief black eunuch's throw led to death. Instead you have a single set of pared-down conditions mentioning a single throw— but which one is undetermined. This result, I propose, precisely captures the ambivalence we feel in cases of symmetric overdetermination.

5   Mackie Remixed

For all the advantages that it enjoys in handling cases of preemption, the Mackie account faces deep problems of its own. The advantages of the Mackie approach to preemption may be enjoyed only once these problems are addressed; the result is an outline of a theory of causal claims that has a quite different flavor from Mackie's.

According to this reconception of Mackie's theory, the role of causal claims in science and everyday life is not to express basic metaphysical facts about causal connections, but rather to extract from the basic causal facts an understanding of how causal connections work together to bring about certain states of affairs. The question of the meaning of causal claims turns out to be less a question about metaphysics, then, and more a question about understanding or explanation. (Appropriately, the theory of causal claims sketched in what follows was first presented as an account of causal explanation in Strevens 2004.)

If I am right, it will turn out to have been an error—a major and pervasive error—for causal metaphysicians to have focused so great a part of their energies on causal claims. Let me put these strategic remarks to one side, however, to concentrate on the task of providing an account of the truth conditions of causal claims that is adequate to the data, that is, to our intuitive judgments of causal claims' truth and falsehood.

In order to motivate my theory, I will focus on two shortcomings of Mackie's account. The first is independent of the handling of preemption problems discussed above; whereas the second exposes serious difficulties with the handling of those problems. The solution to the first will, however, point the way to the solution of the second.

5.1 Distinguishing Correlation and Causation

The first problem is that of the notorious Manchester hooters (Mackie 1974, p. 81). Let me tell the story in a pre-industrial guise. When the *boru*, or horn, sounds on the European side of the Bosporus, the Rumelian janissaries assemble outside the sultan's New Palace. Similarly, when the *boru* sounds on the Asian side of the Bosporus, the Anatolian janissaries assemble outside the Old Palace. Seeking the sense of order that evades him in his own harem, the sultan insists that the *boru* sound at exactly the same time on both sides of the Bosporus, although the sound does not carry over the water. As a result of this very regular timing, it seems that the Mackie account classes the sounding of the Rumelian *boru* as a cause of the Anatolian janissaries' assembly, even though the Anatolian janissaries cannot hear the Rumelian *boru*.

At the core of the problem is the truth, indeed robustness, of the following generalization: when the *boru* is sounded on the Rumelian side of the Bosporus, the Anatolian janissaries assemble. The generalization, together with the fact that the Rumelian *boru* sounds at a particular time t, entails that the Anatolian janissaries assemble at time $t + 1$. Removing the fact of the Rumelian *boru*'s sounding from this set of sufficient conditions invalidates the entailment. Thus, the sounding of the Rumelian *boru* is an INUS condition for the Anatolian janissaries' assembly. But we do not say that the Rumelian *boru* causes the Anatolian janissaries to assemble.

Mackie's solution to this problem emerges from a rather informal discussion in which he suggests that the Rumelian *boru* does not qualify as a cause of the Anatolian janissaries' assembly because of some combination of (1) considerations concerning the times at which events become "fixed," which are redolent of the screening-off criterion proposed by Reichenbach (1956); and (2) a negative answer to the question whether the sounding of the Rumelian *boru* is linked to the Anatolian janissaries' assembly by a "continuous causal process" (Mackie 1974, pp. 190–192).

It is difficult to extract from this discussion a canonical solution to the *boru* problem, and I will not try to do so here. (If anything, one gets the impression that for Mackie, empiricist that he is, our distinction between the effect of the Rumelian and the Anatolian *borus* is more a human foible than a desirable feature of an ideal science.) Let me point instead to Mackie's own admission (1974, p. 191) that his solution to the *boru* problem will not work in a completely deterministic world. This represents, I think, a fundamental weakness in Mackie's account, if it is construed as an account of the truth conditions for causal claims, rather than as a piece of revisionary metaphysics. Clearly, we do distinguish the effects of the Rumelian and the Anatolian *boru*, and clearly, the question of determinism has no bearing on the distinctions we make.

Why do we deny that the Rumelian *boru* causes the Anatolian janissaries' assembly? Mackie is correct, I think, when he points to our beliefs about continuous causal processes as lying at the root of the denial. There is no causal process linking the sounding of the Rumelian *boru* to the Anatolian janissaries' actions, whereas there is such a process linking the sounding of the Anatolian *boru* to the Anatolian janissaries' actions. It is for this reason, I suggest, that although the sounding of the Rumelian *boru* is an INUS condition for both the Rumelian and the Anatolian janissaries' assembly, it is right to say that the Rumelian *boru* caused the Rumelian janissaries' assembly, but wrong to say that the Rumelian *boru* caused the Anatolian janissaries' assembly.

If this approach is correct, then there must be facts about continuous causal connections that are prior to, and therefore independent of, the facts asserted by causal claims. Mackie, the reader will recall, has an appropriate definition of a continuous causal connection—namely, his relation of causal production described in section 3, characterized in terms of INUS conditions for concrete realizers. It seems that Mackie builds causal connection into his account of causal claims simply by adding to the INUS account a requirement that cause and effect be causally connected in his proprietary sense.

My proposed revision to Mackie's account differs from Mackie's own suggestion in two ways:

1. The facts about causal connection are not defined by INUS conditions for concrete realizers, but are rather read off directly from the relevant causal laws.

2. The requirement of causal connection is not added to the INUS account; rather, the definition of an INUS condition is itself modified to reflect facts about causal connection.

I will discuss each amendment in turn.

First, the source of the facts about causal connection. We hold that the sound of the Rumelian *boru* is causally connected to the Rumelian janissaries' assembly, but not to the Anatolian janissaries' assembly. Why? Because physics says that the sound of the Rumelian *boru* reaches the ears of the Rumelian janissaries, but not the ears of the Anatolian janissaries. Thus the Rumelian *boru* is causally connected to the Rumelian janissaries' actions, but not to the Anatolian janissaries' actions. In general, I claim, you can read off the facts about causal connection from the nomological dependencies spelled out in the laws of physics.

This is a controversial view. But there are various ways to extract causal relations from fundamental physics. One strategy is to found the facts about causal connection using the "process" approach to causation (Dowe 2000); another might employ Lewis's recent account of causal influence (Lewis 2000). (Both authors, of course, have higher ambitions for their theories than this.) Rather than endorse any particular approach, let me simply assume as given the primitive facts about causal connections between events and about the laws in virtue of which the connections exist.

Second, the question of how to build a requirement of causal connectedness into the Mackie account. A part of the answer, sufficient to solve the *boru* problem, is given here; the full answer will be given in section 5.3.

In Mackie's original account, you begin with a set of conditions sufficient to entail that the putative effect *e* occurred. By contrast, I propose that you begin with a set of conditions *causally sufficient* for *e*. The full definition of causal sufficiency will be stated in section 5.3; for now I give just a necessary condition for causal sufficiency: a set of conditions sufficient for *e* is causally sufficient only if each condition characterizes a causal influence on *e*, by which I mean that each condition describes (1) an event that had some causal influence on *e*, (2) a causal law (or set of laws) in virtue of which an event had such an influence, or (3) a background condition necessary for the operation of such a causal law.

Note that, because the background conditions required for the operation of a law are sometimes negative states of affairs—such as nothing's having interfered with the flight of the prince's cannonball—an absence can count as a "causal influence" in my technical sense. This opens the door to causation by omission; however, the treatment of omissions requires some adjustments to my account that I will not pursue here, and so I will have to leave that very interesting topic to another occasion.

The *boru* problem is then solved as you would expect. The Rumelian *boru* is not a causal influence on the Anatolian janissaries' actions, so a set of conditions sufficient for the Anatolian janissaries' assembly that mentions the Rumelian *boru* is not *causally sufficient* for the assembly. Such conditions do not, then, confer causehood on their nonredundant parts.

Why do I appeal to facts about causation in the middle of an account of facts about causes? What big picture legitimates such a move? In the next section I pause to sketch the role, as I see it, played by causal claims in our scientific and ordinary discourse. This discussion will provide the basis for solving the second problem with Mackie's account, in section 5.3.

5.2   The Role of Causal Claims in Understanding

The world, according to physics, is a vast and complex causal web. By this paper's working assumption, it is a deterministic web: the elements and structure of the web are completely determined by the initial conditions of the universe and the fundamental laws of nature. Find any property of any particular region of space-time, and there is some combination of physical facts and laws whose combined causal influence is sufficient for the region's instantiating the property. This much fundamental physics says, or so I suppose.

If we were fully satisfied with knowledge of the facts about causal influence, we would have no need for causal claims. It would be enough, for any event e, to know, concerning any other event c, that c causally influenced e, meaning that you could trace, by way of a series of instantiations of causal laws, a chain of events causally connecting c to e. We would know, to use Mackie's term, that there was a "continuous causal process" connecting c and e.

Just how meager this knowledge is can be seen from my earlier discussion of Mackie's relation of causal production (not quite the same relation that I have described here). The vast mass of the chief white eunuch is causally connected to the sultan's death by poisoning (Smith and Jones being the perpetrators, you will recall), due to the gravitational influence it exerts on the event, as on every other event in the vicinity. Using the laws of physics, that is, you can trace a line of causal influence from the eunuch to the dying sultan. But what does this tell you? Almost nothing of interest.

What we really want to know is what, among all the physical influences on the sultan's dying, *made a difference* to the fact that he died. It is here, I claim, that the INUS apparatus comes into its own. What we want to find are the parts of the causal network that play an essential role in the causation of the death. These may be ascertained by looking to a description of the web of causal influences in which the death is embedded, and finding the parts that play an essential role in entailing the death's occurrence—that is, roughly, the parts that cannot be removed from the description of the web without invalidating the entailment of the death.

What facts about the world, then, are our causal claims supposed to capture? Not the facts about fundamental causal relations—about what causally influenced what—as many philosophers suppose. Rather, causal claims capture higher-level facts about which causal influences played a critical role, which were decisive, in bringing about some high-level (almost never concrete) event. These are the causal influences that—unlike the gravitational influence of sundry large bodies—made a difference between the event's occurring and its failing to occur.

I concur with Lewis and Mackie, then, that causal claims are claims about difference-making. I do not agree that this difference-making is itself the fundamental causal relation. What is fundamental is the web of causal influence. This is the province of fundamental physics. The role of causal claims is to single out the elements of the web that are relevant to the high-level events that matter to us humans—the breakings, the pleasurings, the dyings, and all the rest.[9]

5.3   Spurious Nonredundancy

Over-reliance on the entailment relation can put a philosophical analysis in real peril. For Mackie's account of causal claims, the threat is exemplified by the following recipe.

To show that any event r whatsoever was a cause of a given event e: Take a set of conditions jointly sufficient for e, none redundant. Replace one of these conditions c with the following two conditions: r and $r \supset c$. The new set of conditions is also sufficient for e. The intuitively irrelevant event r cannot be removed from this set without invalidating the entailment of e. Therefore r is an INUS condition for e, and so, according to Mackie's account, r was a cause of e.

Let me give an example. The sultan has been murdered. A set of sufficient conditions for his death involved, nonredundantly, the fact of the grand vizier's poisoning his wine. Earlier, the chief black eunuch sneezed. To show that the sneeze was a cause of the death, take a list of sufficient conditions for death nonredundantly including the grand vizier's poisoning the wine, and replace the poisoning with the fact of the eunuch's sneeze and the following disjunction:

Either the chief black eunuch did not sneeze, or the grand vizier poisoned the sultan's wine.

Then the sneeze is, in virtue of the set of sufficient conditions so constructed, an INUS condition for the sultan's death.

The problem exists because it is so easy to play an essential role in an entailment. If the Mackie account is to be saved, some sort of constraint must be imposed on the kinds of entailments that count for the purpose of determining causes. An entailment involving an irrelevant r and the disjunction $r \supset c$ must be declared, for some reason, illegitimate.

For what reason, then? Let me take as my starting point the amendment made to the Mackie account in response to the *boru* problem. In the determination of the causes of an event e, I proposed, it is not enough that a set of conditions be sufficient for the occurrence of e; it must be *causally sufficient* for e. In section 5.1, I gave a necessary condition for causal sufficiency: all conditions must describe either events that causally influence e or causal laws or background conditions in virtue of which they do so.

This seems not enough in itself to solve the problem of spurious nonredundancy, since the eunuch's sneeze is a causal influence—in the same negligible way as any bystander's gravitational influence—on the sultan's death. In what follows, I complete my account of causal sufficiency so as to rule out the sneeze as a cause of death, taking as a guide the picture of the role of causal claims sketched in section 5.2.

According to that picture, a causal claim picks out a piece of the causal web essential for the production of some event e. The revised Mackie account promises to determine such causes by, first, finding a part of the causal web sufficient for the production of e, described by a sufficient condition for e, and then discarding those elements that are not essential to the production of e, the redundant parts of the sufficient condition.

The sufficient condition for e, then, is supposed to represent a part of the causal process that produced e. Many sets of conditions may entail e and yet not represent any part of the process that caused e; the case of the Rumelian *boru* provides a salient example. It is these conditions that I am trying to rule out of contention for the INUS treatment by my requirement that the conditions not only be sufficient for e, but be causally sufficient.

Causal sufficiency ought to be defined, then, so that a set of conditions is causally sufficient for an event e only if the conditions represent a causal process that produces e. A set of conditions entailing e represents a causal process producing e, I propose, just in case each step in the entailment corresponds to a strand in the relevant causal web.[10]

Take, to choose the simplest possible example, events c and e and a law "All events of type C cause events of type E," where c and e are of types C and E respectively. The occurrence of c and the law entail (when fleshed out) the occurrence of e; but also, this entailment corresponds to a link in the causal chain that produced e, namely, the link between c and e. Call such an entailment a *causal entailment*.

Now consider, by contrast, the case of the eunuch's sneeze. The step in the entailment of the sultan's death that involves the sneeze is the step from the sneeze and the disjunction "Either the chief black eunuch did not sneeze, or the grand vizier poisoned the sultan's wine" to the conclusion that the grand vizier poisoned the sultan's wine. This is not a causal entailment, as it does not correspond to a causal process recognized by the laws of physics. Indeed, it is hard to imagine a physics in which something in the world captured by the description $\sim r \vee c$ could be a part of any story about causal influence.

I define causal sufficiency as follows: a set of conditions is causally sufficient for the occurrence of an event e just in case each step in the entailment of e is a causal entailment. It follows that, because the chief black eunuch's sneeze is an INUS condition for the sultan's death only by way of an entailment that is not causal, the sneeze does not count as a cause of the death. This solution goes to the heart of the problem: when what we regard as an intuitively irrelevant factor r is made essential to the entailment of an event e, it is always by way of a disjunction or other logical construction that links r and e truth-functionally but not causally.

The approach to causal claims taken by my revision of Mackie's account puts a considerable burden on the physical laws: they must determine what primitive causal connections there are in the world, hence determine the structure of the causal web. I think that they are quite capable of bearing the load, and that we do indeed look to the laws as the final arbiters on any question of causal connection. But I will not try to make the case here; it is enough for my present purposes to show that an updated INUS account is not defenseless against the old objections to the Mackie account.

In the course of the defense, Mackie's account has been transformed into something that he would likely not endorse. It is no longer explicitly empiricist—though it is compatible with empiricism, since you may give an empiricist account of causal influence. More important, although it makes use of deductive logic, and in particular the entailment relation, logical constructs and relations do not, as they do in the logical empiricist tradition, replace metaphysics. Rather, they are used to represent metaphysics. No longer does logical necessity take over from some forsaken relation of nomic dependence. Its role in the new account is far more humble—it is used to represent the species of nomic dependence that I am calling causal influence. The Mackie account, by picking out certain propositions as essential to the entailment of the proposition that e occurred, also seeks out the real object of our inquiry, the causal influences essential to the causal production of e itself.

5.4   One More Preemption Scenario

In section 4.2, I mentioned a preemption scenario that would be handled later. Now is the time.[11] The story is as follows. The sultan's mother is determined that a certain hated Iznik jar should be broken. She stations herself near the jar with a cannonball and resolves that, if the jar is still intact in ten minutes' time, she will hurl the cannonball at the jar, of course breaking it. Before the time is up, the prince arrives and breaks the jar himself. Now, just from the fact of the sultan's mother's resolution (and her ability to make good on it), it is sure that the jar will be broken. Therefore, it is possible to construct a set of conditions that is sufficient for the breaking and that mentions only the resolution, saying nothing about the prince. The mother's resolution is nonredundant—it cannot be removed from the conditions without invalidating the entailment of the breaking. It seems that her resolution must be counted as a cause of the breaking.

Although this is a case of preemption, I think that the problem it uncovers in the Mackie account belongs with the Rumelian *boru* and the chief black eunuch's sneeze. In any case, the solution is the same: the sufficient conditions of which the mother's resolution is a nonredundant part are not, given the way the story unfolds, *causally sufficient* for the breaking.

This case is somewhat more complex than the case of the *boru*, since the mother's resolution would have been a straightforward causal influence on the breaking if the prince had never turned up. There are two quite different ways, then, that the resolution-including sufficient conditions for breaking could be satisfied. One way, the conditions are not just sufficient, but causally sufficient: the prince stays away and her resolution causes the mother to hurl the ball. The other way, the conditions are not causally sufficient: they identify neither a cause of the breaking, nor a condition (negative or positive) necessary for such a cause to have its effect. In short, a single, apparently quite univocal set of sufficient conditions turns out to be satisfiable by two different causal scenarios; in one case but not the other, the conditions identify elements of the causal process in question.

It remains only to say that the definitions of causal entailment, and so of causal sufficiency, should be understood so as not to apply to such cases—by specifying, for example, that a set of conditions sufficient for an event e is causally sufficient only if it identifies aspects of the world that play a role in causally producing e in *every one* of its instantiations. It then follows that the identified aspects are required to play a causal role in the actual scenario, as desired.

Notes

1. I learned of this case from an appendix to the augmented edition of Montesquieu's *Persian Letters*.

2. McDermott (1995) offers a treatment of preemption which builds on the Mackie account but is different from both Mackie's and my own. The main difference between McDermott's and my treatments is that McDermott makes no use of the violation of negative conditions. I believe that McDermott's account is unable to handle the problem of the colliding cannonballs presented at the end of section 4.1, but my reasons for thinking so will have to wait until another occasion.

3. It is a matter of controversy whether the primary meaning of our nontechnical term "event" is closer to "concrete event" or to "state of affairs." Davidson (1969) maintains the former position, Kim (1973) the latter.

4. In Mackie 1974, these comments appear before the presentation of the INUS account itself.

5. Most of Mackie's discussion concerns Hart and Honoré's famous case of the desert traveler with the leaky canteen filled with poisoned water. But his treatment of this complex case is supposed to apply equally to other, uncontroversial cases, such as that of the backup Circassian and the case I am about to discuss.

6. Ramachandran proposes a variant of the counterfactual account of causation based on a similar observation (1997, p. 273). This account cannot, I think, handle the case of the colliding balls.

7. Unless, perhaps, this was a case of symmetric overdetermination (see section 4.3).

8. Though they will leave open the possibility that there was more than one throw, on pain of nonveridicality.

9. This provides a way of understanding the claim of Hall (2004) and others that there are two different notions of causation at work in our cognitive economy, without concluding that our causal thinking is ambiguous or confused.

10. Talk of "steps in the entailment" implies an intended proof. The proof can be understood as a causal model, as described in Strevens 2004. For the purposes of this paper, say that causal sufficiency requires the existence of at least one proof, intended or otherwise, in which each step corresponds to a strand in the web.

11. Christopher Hitchcock has urged the importance of this sort of case for Mackie's account.

References

Davidson, D. 1969. "The Individuation of Events." In *Essays in Honor of Carl G. Hempel*, edited by N. Rescher. Dordrecht: D. Reidel.

Dowe, P. 2000. *Physical Causation*. Cambridge: Cambridge University Press.

Hall, N. 2004. "Two Concepts of Causation." In *Causation and Counterfactuals*, edited by J. Collins, N. Hall, and L. Paul. Cambridge, Mass.: MIT Press.

Hall, N., and L. Paul. 2003. "Causation and Preemption." In *Philosophy of Science Today*, edited by P. Clark and K. Hawley. Oxford: Oxford University Press.

Hempel, C. 1965. "Aspects of Scientific Explanation." In C. Hempel, *Aspects of Scientific Explanation*. New York: Free Press.

Hitchcock, C. 2001. "A Tale of Two Effects." *Philosophical Review* 110: 361–396.

Kim, J. 1973. "Causation, Nomic Subsumption, and the Concept of Event." *Journal of Philosophy* 70: 217–236.

Lewis, D. 1973a. "Causation." *Journal of Philosophy* 70: 556–567. Reprinted in Lewis 1986a.

Lewis, D. 1973b. *Counterfactuals*. Cambridge, Mass.: Harvard University Press.

Lewis, D. 1986a. *Philosophical Papers*, vol. 2. Oxford: Oxford University Press.

Lewis, D. 1986b. Postscript to "Causation." In Lewis 1986a.

Lewis, D. 2000. "Causation as Influence." *Journal of Philosophy* 97: 182–197.

Mackie, J. 1974. *The Cement of the Universe*. Oxford: Oxford University Press.

McDermott, M. 1995. "Redundant Causation." *British Journal for the Philosophy of Science* 46: 523–544.

Pearl, J. 2000. *Causality: Models, Reasoning, and Inference*. Cambridge: Cambridge University Press.

Ramachandran, M. 1997. "A Counterfactual Analysis of Causation." *Mind* 106: 263–277.

Reichenbach, H. 1956. *The Direction of Time*. Berkeley, Calif.: University of California Press.

Schaffer, J. 2003. "Overdetermining Causes." *Philosophical Studies* 114: 23–45.

Stalnaker, R. 1968. "A Theory of Conditionals." In *Studies in Logical Theory*, edited by N. Rescher. Oxford: Blackwell.

Strevens, M. 2003. "Against Lewis's New Theory of Causation." *Pacific Philosophical Quarterly* 84: 398–412.

Strevens, M. 2004. "The Causal and Unification Accounts of Explanation Unified—Causally." *Noûs* 38: 154–176.

Yablo, S. 2002. "De Facto Dependence." *Journal of Philosophy* 99: 130–148.

6   Occasional Causes

Russell Wahl

In this essay I will examine some of the issues surrounding occasionalism, and point out that the position is not quite as silly as it has been thought. In fact, occasionalism represents a shift in the concept of causality from that of producing or creating, to the concept of a causal law as a regularity of nature. I also want to defend a sense in which an occasional cause can be said to be a genuine cause—although the advocates of occasionalism, specifically Malebranche, denied this. Finally, I will make some brief remarks about occasionalism in light of the recent criticism of the regularity account of causation by such philosophers as Scriven and Salmon.

The Early Modern Setting

By the advent of the early modern period, causation was seen primarily in Aristotelian terms as a relation between two things, agent and patient, where the one by its power effected a change in the other. The explanation of the end result would involve the preexisting patient (the material cause); the form taken on by the patient (which would have to be in the agent, either "formally" or "eminently"); the agent (as "moving" or "efficient" cause); and the purpose or goal of the activity. The general view was that a form or likeness flowed from the agent to the patient by means of a power contained within the agent.[1] Thus, Francisco Suarez said that physical cause is a "cause truly and really inflowing into an effect" (O'Neill 1993, p. 30).

   As several commentators have pointed out,[2] this account of cause does not lead to what we might think of as causal laws. The concern is with an adequate explanation, in terms of a producing agent, of the being of what we have before us—but not with anything that could be used to predict an outcome. Of particular concern to philosophers in the medieval period was the case of God being the cause of the world. In this case the concern is with an ontological ground of the effect. There is no law that would move from God to the particulars of the world; there was nothing necessary about God's creation. I will call this concept of cause the "production model," since on this view the cause literally produces the effect. When Descartes gave his principles concerning causality in the third meditation, he had this production model in mind. His concern there was not with anything like a modern causal law, so much as with a principle which demands that the cause have enough being to produce the effect.

Philosophers struggled with the production model over the course of the early modern period. The new physics of Galileo and Descartes did away with the various substantial and other forms which were so important in the earlier explanations; and the new physiology called into question the standard explanation of the causal relation between the world and the mind. Philosophers were forced to search for a new account of the causal relation.

The doctrine of occasionalism—the view that there is only one genuine cause, God; and that all other apparent, or secondary causes are merely occasions for the exercise of God's power and have, by themselves, no causal efficacy—is a product of this era. If we understand a genuine cause in the production sense, it becomes less surprising that philosophers who advocated occasionalism thought that material things did not have within them the requisite causal powers.

While Descartes' causal principle did allow that finite created beings can produce others, the mechanism of this creation was something later Cartesians had difficulty with. Some of them—most notably Malebranche—rejected such causation and concluded that God was the sole cause *in this sense of "cause."* It is, I believe, misleading to leave off this last qualifier in a discussion of occasionalism, as it is in the sense of a producer that God is asserted to be the only cause. As we shall see, occasionalists did not deny that created things could be the antecedent conditions of causal regularities.

I claim that occasional causes—which were held not to be genuine causes in the production sense—in many ways fit what we would now think of as genuine causes. This claim is contentious for two reasons: (1)

Malebranche, the most prominent advocate of occasionalism, explicitly denied that occasional causes are genuine causes, and asserted they have no efficacy whatsoever; and (2) Malebranche's arguments for occasionalism attacked a necessary connection between the occasional cause and the effect, an attack that anticipated Hume's. It is easy to think that all we are left with in the order of occasional causes are merely contingent regularities, which are too weak to count as genuine causes. I will argue to the contrary.

Malebranche's Arguments for Occasionalism

Malebranche gave several arguments for occasionalism—in book six of the *Search after Truth*, in the fifteenth of the *Elucidations*, and with the most detail in the *Dialogues on Metaphysics and Religion*. Contrary to popular opinion,[3] occasionalism was not thought of primarily as a doctrine to handle mind-body interaction. The primary target of all of Malebranche's arguments was the attribution of powers—powers of creation, really—to inert pieces of matter. Thus in book six of the *Search* (in a section subtitled "The most dangerous error of the philosophy of the ancients"), Malebranche says,

If we consider attentively our idea of cause or of power to act, we cannot doubt that this idea represents something divine.... We therefore admit something divine in all the bodies around us when we posit forms, faculties, qualities, virtues, or real beings capable of producing certain effects through the force of their nature. (1675/1980, p. 446)

Here Malebranche was concerned to argue that lower bodies cannot act on higher beings, and in particular that we should not believe that bodies are the true causes of the pleasures and ills we feel. The emphasis is on power and production, and what is being called into question here is any role for material bodies in what I have called the "production model" of causation.

Malebranche also called into question any necessary connection except that between God and creatures:

A true cause as I understand it is one such that the mind perceives a necessary connection between it and its effect. Now the mind perceives a necessary connection only between the will of an infinitely perfect being and its effects. Therefore, it is only God who is the true cause and who truly has the power to move bodies. (1675/1980, p. 450)

Here Malebranche is relying on the Cartesian method of examining what is contained in our clear ideas. He first examines his idea of a body, and finds that the idea we have of all bodies "makes us aware that they cannot move themselves." Like Descartes', Malebranche's clear and distinct idea of matter contains only extension and motion; he does not find any force or power contained in this idea. There is more argument with respect to willing beings: "When we examine our idea of all finite minds, we do not see any necessary connection between their will and the motion of any body whatsoever" (1675/1980, p. 448). There is, though, such a connection perceived in the idea of God:

When one thinks about the idea of God, i.e., of an infinitely perfect and consequently all-powerful being, one knows there is such a connection between His will and the motion of all bodies, that it is impossible to conceive that He wills a body to be moved and that this body not be moved. (1675/1980, p. 448)

The element which grounds this connection in the idea of God is omnipotence. It is this property that makes the necessary connection between the will and the effect. It is the lack of such a property, presumably, which enables us to conceive a finite mind willing a motion and that motion not occurring. Malebranche's remarks about the lack of such a connection in the case of finite minds or contained within our ideas of the bodies themselves clearly anticipate the later empiricist (and Kantian) claims that there are no logically necessary connections between causes and effects.

In the *Dialogues on Metaphysics*, Malebranche supplements this argument with a claim that there is a contradiction in supposing finite created beings to be causally efficacious. The argument focuses on motion in material substance, and requires a strong interpretation of the Cartesian claim that there is no real distinction between creation and conservation. The argument is that, if each moment of time is logically and metaphysically independent of each other moment, and there is no distinction between creation and conservation, then God's conservation of any particular individual amounts to a constant recreation of that individual. Now in recreating an individual, God must create that individual in a particular place and shape; therefore, it is God, not any creature, who causes the individual to be in that particular place and have a particular shape:

God cannot do the impossible, or that which contains a manifest contradiction. He cannot will that this chair exist without at the same time willing that it exist either here or there and without His will placing it somewhere, since you cannot conceive of a chair existing unless it exists somewhere, either here or elsewhere. (1688/1997, pp. 111–112)

Malebranche's claim is that in creating the chair, God must create it at a particular place and so, whether it is at rest or in motion, it will be caused at each point by God's creating it. He adds somewhat later, that if God wills a chair or a ball to be at a given point,

all the powers imaginable could not move it, unless God intervenes. For once again, insofar as God wills to create or conserve this ball at point A or at some other point you choose—and it is necessary that He put it somewhere—no force can displace it from there. (1688/1997, p. 116)[4]

The conservation argument again focuses on causality as a production. There is a lack of producing force in any body; and when God produces a body and conserves it, He must conserve it at a particular place, so that for bodies, at least, not only that they are, but the place they are (and therefore their motion) will be entirely a consequence of God's will.

This argument calls into question the causal efficacy of bodies or minds to act on other bodies. The earlier argument called into question the ability of bodies to act on anything. Malebranche had an important moral and theological reason for emphasizing this latter point, as he wanted to emphasize that it was not bodies that were ultimately responsible for either the pleasure or the pain we felt. He also emphasized that bodies were not causally responsible, in this sense, for ideas. On the production model of causes, the only way a body could cause an idea was for the idea to be, in some sense, present in the body and then be transmitted—that is, produced—in the mind by the transfer of the form. This whole picture involves a conception of matter with power, and a conception of form which is at variance with the new conception of bodies as extension.

Malebranche and Leibniz

Malebranche's sweeping arguments, especially the conservation argument, have led many to the conclusion that Malebranche's occasional causes should not be understood as causes in any sense, nor should they be thought to have an explanatory role, and so for Malebranche the only genuine explanation is simply, "God did it."[5] This is a criticism that goes back to Leibniz, who was eager to distinguish his own view of preestablished harmony from Malebranche's occasionalism. Leibniz claimed that on

Malebranche's view there was no difference between ordinary events and miracles—that God was "constantly intervening" in the world.

Before answering this criticism, it would be instructive to contrast Leibniz's treatment of causal relations with Malebranche's; Leibniz is likewise famous for denying that there are any causal interactions among created substances. The model he has for such interactions is the "production model," and the related "influx" model, when dealing with causality between different substances. This model involves either a transfer of a property from one substance to another or the creation of a property in one substance by another. Where Leibniz disagrees with Malebranche is not in rejecting these relations among created substances, but in rejecting Malebranche's arguments that individual created substances have no power. Leibniz's view is that these substances do have power, but only over themselves. Thus the inner transformation which each individual substance undergoes is something that emanates from itself. This is Leibnizian spontaneity. Other substances also go through changes which emanate from themselves. The substances are all in harmony, but each is as if a world apart from each other in terms of genuine causal ties. However, Leibniz does not reject what we would think of as ordinary causal explanation: at the phenomenal level it is correct to see each substance as causally connected to each other, provided we understand the metaphysical analysis of this. The metaphysical analysis involves each substance unfolding on its own and containing within itself an expression (or perception) of each other substance. The real change in substance A is in harmony with a real change in substance B, and for that reason we can say there is a relation between A and B.

Now when Leibniz denied that there are causal relations among objects, he was denying them in the sense of the "production" or the "influx" model of causality. He did not deny that objects obey causal laws, and at the phenomenal level, he thought proper explanation made reference to these laws (including the mechanical models of the corpuscularians).[6] While Leibniz would say that these laws are not necessary in his sense, they do involve a kind of necessity which he calls "certainty." It is a necessity which is not grounded in the law of contradiction, but which, he says, is grounded in God's benevolence—God's choosing the best of all possible worlds.

Those who see that Leibniz is not rejecting causal explanations often see him as quite different from Malebranche and the occasionalists. This is what Leibniz himself also asserted when he contrasted his view of preestablished harmony with the occasionalist view he likened to "a perpetual supervisor who represents in the one everything which happens in the other, a little as if a man were charged with constantly synchronizing two bad clocks which are in themselves incapable of agreeing" (Leibniz 1989, p. 494). Leibniz in the end accused Malebranche of requiring that God is continually performing miracles:

It is quite true that speaking with metaphysical rigor there is no real influence of one created substance upon another and that all things, with all their reality, are continually produced by the power of God. But problems are not solved merely by making use of a general cause and calling in what is called the *deus ex machina*. To do this without offering any other explanation drawn from the order of secondary causes, is, properly speaking, to have recourse to miracle. (Leibniz 1989, p. 457)

As it turns out, this claim is quite unjust to Malebranche.

Malebranche and Causal Laws

When we look at Malebranche's whole philosophy and turn away from Malebranche's diatribes against the causal efficacy (in the sense of the production model) of creatures, we see that he has and needs a view which requires that the secondary causes fit into a general pattern of causal laws. This is forgotten if one just focuses on the initial discussion in the *Search after Truth* and the arguments in the *Dialogues*. When we see the role that general laws play in *The Treatise on Nature and Grace*, and in other parts of the *Search*, we see that causal laws will play the same role in Malebranche's system as they do in Leibniz's.

Malebranche often illustrated this part of his overall view with his discussion of the weather and with the example of a deformed child. He stressed that God does not act by particular volitions but only by general will. He does not will, for example, that children are born deformed, but he wills the general laws of which these are consequences:

God having foreseen everything that had to follow from natural laws even before their establishment, he ought not to have established them if he was going to overturn them. The laws of nature are constant and immutable; they are general for all times and for all places. Two colliding bodies of such-and-such a size and of such-and-such a speed will rebound now in the same way that they rebounded heretofore. If rain falls on certain lands, and if the sun roasts others; if weather favourable for crops is followed by hail that destroys them; if a child comes into the world with a malformed and useless head growing from his breast, and makes him wretched; it is not that God has willed these things by particular wills; it is because he has established laws for the communication of motion, of which these effects are necessary consequences. (1680/1992, p. 118)

Malebranche further suggests that these particulars are foreseen but unwilled consequences:

But one cannot say that God acts through caprice or through ignorance, when a child comes into the world with superfluous members which keep it from living or when a hailstone causes an almost ripe fruit to fall. The reason for this is, that if God causes a fruit to fall through hail before it is ripe, it is not that he wills and no longer wills; for God acts not at all by particular wills, like particular causes. He has not established the laws of the communication of motion with the design of producing monsters, or of making fruits fall before their maturity; he willed these laws because of their fruitfulness, and not of their sterility. (1680/1992, pp. 118–119)

The claim that Malebranche is making here is crucial to his whole theory of grace: God wills that everyone be saved, and yet not everyone is saved. This is to be taken in the same sense that God wills that everything tend to move in a straight line (the laws of motion), and yet things bump into each other and end up moving in circles. God does not will particular events; what God wills are the general laws, and only the very simple general laws.

With respect to the laws of the physical world, Malebranche suggests that there are very few indeed:

I am persuaded that the laws of motion which are necessary to the production and the preservation of the earth, and of all the stars that are in the heavens, are reducible to these two: the first, that moved bodies tend to continue their motion in a straight line; the second, that when two bodies collide, their motion is distributed in both in proportion to their size, such that they must afterwards move at an equal speed. (1680/1992, p. 119)

These laws are not logically necessary, nor did God have to create things according to these laws; yet they do have a kind of necessity. For Leibniz, the law-like relations between various objects do not follow from the law of contradiction, but they do follow from the principle of sufficient reason. For Malebranche, God's wisdom requires that he will a world which conforms to simple, general laws. Malebranche goes so far as to say that this wisdom constrains God's options, making him powerless to act: "God's wisdom makes him powerless in the sense that it does not permit him to will certain things nor to act in certain ways" (1680/1958, vol. 5, p. 180).[7] The simplicity and generality of the laws constrain God's activity, and in that sense make the conformity of motions in the created world to these laws necessary. God's willing is at the level of the general law, not the particular event. Malebranche does not think that occasional causes are simply items which always occur prior to the occasional effects. He thinks that there are general laws which connect the causes with the effects, and it is these general laws, not the particular instances, which have been willed by God and which have a necessity that constrains his particular will.[8]

Given Malebranche's view that what God wills are the laws, not the instances, it is no surprise that Malebranche has the same position on explanation as Leibniz. Explanation should make reference to the occasional cause, and not to God. Given the passage we have cited from the *Treatise*, concerning monsters, it would be especially incorrect to attribute the effect to the will of God, rather than to the laws of motion of which this event was a consequence. But even in the *Search after Truth* we get this remark:

I grant that recourse to God or the universal cause should not be had when the explanation of particular effects is sought. For we would be ridiculous were we to say, for example, that it is God who dries the roads or who freezes the water of rivers. We should say that the air dries the earth because it stirs and raises with it the water that soaks the earth, and that the air or subtle matter freezes the river because in this season it ceases to communicate enough motion to the parts of which the water is composed to make it fluid. (1675/1980, p. 662)

Malebranche goes on to say that what he does not want us to do is to conclude from this point about explanation that there is a power or force within the bodies which does this. What he does think is that, given that God has willed bodies into existence, and that his wisdom requires the conformity of creation to simple laws, the laws of motion and impact are necessary.

It is clear that in the sense of "cause" found in Hume, Malebranche does not deny causal connections. There is nothing, even, that Kant affirms which is denied by Malebranche: Kant certainly did not think that there were real powers in the phenomena which produced or created the next phenomena. Both Kant and Malebranche see the connection between causes and their effects as necessary, although they account for that necessity in quite different ways. Malebranche places it in the general laws which have been willed by God; Kant places it in the human mind.[9] So there is more to Malebranche's notion of occasional cause than constant conjunction: there is an element of necessity to it, a necessity which would support counterfactuals.

Salmon's Critique of Nomic Explanation

While discussion of causality and explanation in the first part of the twentieth century focused on explanation in terms of law-like regularities,[10] within the past few decades there has been a criticism of what we might loosely call the "regularity model" of causation. If we ignore the further metaphysical stories that Leibniz and Malebranche tell about what they take to be genuine causes, their views on what we think of as ordinary causal relations might seem quite similar to the later regularity account of causal laws. Of course, both Leibniz and Malebranche thought there was a further causal story—one that later regularity theorists denied. However, for both of them the account of the genuine cause in terms of God's goodness or simplicity is very general, and is not used in explanation. Explanation is given in terms of causal laws and occasional causes.

Now several writers have pointed out that in certain instances the regularity model does not give us what we mean by "cause," and that the genuine concept of cause is what scientists are (or should be) interested in. Wesley Salmon, in particular, advocated what he called an ontic conception of causal explanation, which he contrasted with the epistemic and modal conceptions (1984, p. 19). The epistemic conception sees explanation as primarily showing how an event was to be expected, by deriving it from a law and the initial conditions; the modal conception sees explanation as showing that the event was necessary, given the initial conditions, again by deriving its occurrence using necessary laws. But simply knowing that there is a law-like regularity, Salmon argued, does not yet answer the question *why* something happened. Salmon's ontic conception of scientific explanation requires that an explanation not simply give a regularity, but that it show how events fit into the causal structure of the world. Salmon and others, such as Scriven (1975) and Ruben (1990), gave several criticisms of the deductive nomological model of explanation. Some of these criticisms exploit the fact that there may be several factors which have a relation of law-like regularity with a given result, yet only one was the actual causal antecedent. The classic example of this problem is the situation of a man who eats arsenic and is subsequently hit by a bus. The law-like regularity between eating arsenic and dying is causally irrelevant in this case. Other criticisms exploit the differences between accidental or noncausal regularities on the one hand, and genuine causal regularities on the other. Salmon gave the example of the correlation between the tides and the phases of the moon (1998, p. 129). The mere correlation, he suggested, did not explain the tides—but Newton's laws did. These criticisms clearly apply to a Humean account of explanation, and would appear to apply to the occasionalists as well. Salmon could say of Malebranche that what he gives us—apart from the deus ex machina—are merely descriptions, not explanations.[11]

I want to make two remarks about these criticisms of causal explanation as deductions from regularities. First, while Salmon advocated a reference to a causal nexus, he did not call for a return to what Malebranche or other occasionalists were rejecting, namely the influx or production model. Salmon said that some regularities are explanatory and some are not (1984, p. 121), suggesting that causal *laws* are an important component of explanation. The causal regularities of Newton's laws were explanatory, while the mere correlations between the moon and the tides were not, nor was Boyle's law (1998, p. 128); while some regularities are not explanatory, some are. He also emphasized propagation and production as a component in causal explanation (1984, p. 139). This latter concept perhaps comes close to the influx or production model, but is still quite different from the production-as-creation model Malebranche was rejecting. In fact, Salmon was wary of bringing back any occult power, which he thought could be subjected to Hume's criticism, and analyzed causal processes in terms of mark transmission, which he saw as "a particularly important species of constant conjunction" (1984, pp. 147–148). Salmon later modified his theory to replace the transmission of a mark with the transmission of a conserved quantity (1998, p. 19); but his account of transmission, in terms of what he calls the "at-at" theory, is something that even an occasionalist could live with (Salmon 1998, p. 197; 1984, p. 153). Salmon's analysis of causal processes and causal interactions goes far beyond the remarks of seventeenth-century philosophers, and of course Malebranche would deny that any of these processes are genuinely causal or any of these events genuinely interactions, given that he saw genuine causality as equivalent to creation. Here, of course, he would be in agreement with Leibniz, who also held that these processes and events are not genuinely causal. But for Malebranche the genuine was not part of explanations, but the occasional causes were.

The second point I want to make is that Malebranche's occasionalism is sensitive to many of the problems raised by the critics of the "regularity model," particularly the case of noncausal regularities and the demand that even when we have a completely general correlation, we do not have a genuine explanation until we have some kind of mechanism. This may come as a surprise to those who have seen Malebranche's occasionalism simply as a precursor to the views of Hume and Kant. When the regularity model is driven by epistemological concerns, it is extremely vulnerable to the charge of being unable to distinguish accidental regularities from causal ones. While Malebranche did occasionally make use of epistemological arguments against the view that there were genuine (production) causes between created things—arguments much more prominent in Hume— most of the arguments he gave were metaphysical, involving God's creative power and the lack of such power in material objects. With respect to explanation, Malebranche thought God willed very few physical laws. Any genuine explanation in nature would have to go back to those laws. This is why Malebranche himself eagerly attempted mechanical models of, for example, the transmission of pressure in the eye and the generation of fire (see elucidation 16 in Malebranche 1675/1980). Malebranche thought that every genuine occasional causal correlation would have to be explained by an underlying mechanism obeying the basic laws of motion. Not any regularity will do for him. There may be regularities which are accidental products of the basic laws of motion, but these regularities require explanation in terms of these basic laws. In these cases, especially, "God wills it" would certainly not be Malebranche's account of the regularities—for on his view God would not have separately willed these regularities any more than he wills monsters and droughts.

Notes

1. These basic claims are common to all the examples of "influxes" discussed in O'Neill 1993. O'Neill's important paper documents various influx models of causa-

tion from the scholastic period to Gassendi. O'Neill is interested in outlining the influx theory which Leibniz contrasts with occasionalism and preestablished harmony. Many of the features required of causes on these models, though, are the very ones that lead Leibniz to preestablished harmony and Malebranche to occasionalism—specifically, the requirement of a power in the agent which acts on the patient, and the demand that the agent be at least as perfect as the patient.

2. See, for example, Falkenstein 1998 and Ishiguro 1977.

3. See Taylor 1974, p. 18.

4. With this last point Malebranche is suggesting that God's will is efficacious, and no other will is. Earlier he said, "No power can convey it to where God does not convey it, nor fix nor stop it where God does not stop it unless God accommodates the efficacy of His action to the inefficacious action of His creatures."

5. For a strong statement of this view, see Watson 1993, pp. 81–91.

6. This point is emphasized in Ishiguro 1977.

7. "La Sagesse de Dieu le rend donc impuissant en ce sens, qu'elle ne lui permet pas de vouloir certaines choses, ni d'agir de certaines manieres." One of the things God's wisdom prevents him from willing into being, says Malebranche, is a single animal which is a monster or has useless limbs.

8. In putting it this way I am rejecting the view that Leibniz suggested, that Malebranche wished to explain things with a deus ex machina. Here I am siding with Fontenelle's objection—as reported by Thomas Lennon in the "Philosophical Commentary" of Malebranche 1675/1980—that things by their natures enter into necessary connections that limit God's action. I think it is hard to read these passages from the *Treatise* in any other way. I also think these passages make it hard to support Nadler's (1993) view that God's general will is a series of particular acts of will in accordance with a general law, understanding a particular will to be an act which does not conform to a general law. In the passage above, Malebranche explicitly denies that God wills that there be a monster. However, Nadler's interpretation does not affect the point I am making in this paper (see Nadler 1993, p. 49).

9. For more on this contrast see Alquié 1974, p. 514.

10. See, for example, Hempel and Oppenheim 1948, pp. 567–579; and Braithwaite 1953.

11. Salmon emphasizes this distinction in the first chapter of 1984.

References

Alquié, F. 1974. *Le Cartésianisme de Malebranche*. Paris: Vrin.

Braithwaite, R. 1953. *Scientific Explanation*. Cambridge: Cambridge University Press.

Falkenstein, L. 1998. "Hume's Answer to Kant." *Noûs* 32: 331–360.

Hempel, C., and P. Oppenheim. 1948. "Studies in the Logic of Explanation." *Philosophy of Science* 15: 135–175.

Ishiguro, H. 1977. "Pre-established Harmony Versus Constant Conjunction: A Reconsideration of the Distinction between Rationalism and Empiricism." *Proceedings of the British Academy* 63: 239–263.

Leibniz, G. 1989. *Philosophical Papers and Letters*. Edited by L. Loemker. Dordrecht: Kluwer.

Malebranche, N. 1675/1980. *The Search after Truth*. Translated by T. Lennon and P. Olscamp. Columbus: Ohio State University Press.

Malebranche, N. 1680/1958. *Traité de la Nature et de la Grace*. In vol. 5 of *Oeuvres Complètes*. Paris: Vrin.

Malebranche, N. 1680/1992. *Treatise on Nature and Grace*. Translated by P. Riley. Oxford: Clarendon Press.

Malebranche, N. 1688/1997. *Dialogues on Metaphysics and on Religion*. Translated by D. Scott and edited by N. Jolley. Cambridge: Cambridge University Press.

Nadler, S. 1993. "Occasionalism and General Will in Malebranche." *Journal of the History of Philosophy* 31: 1: 31–47.

O'Neill, E. 1993. "Influxus Physicus." In *Causation in Early Modern Philosophy*, edited by S. Nadler. University Park, Penn.: Pennsylvania State University Press.

Ruben, D. 1990. *Explaining Explanation*. New York: Routledge.

Salmon, W. 1984. *Scientific Explanation and the Causal Structure of the World*. Princeton: Princeton University Press.

Salmon, W. 1998. *Causality and Explanation*. Oxford: Oxford University Press.

Scriven, M. 1975. "Causation as Explanation." *Noûs* 9.

Taylor, R. 1974. *Metaphysics*, 2d ed. Englewood Cliffs: Prentice-Hall.

Watson, R. 1993. "Malebranche, Models, and Causation." In *Causation in Early Modern Philosophy*, edited by S. Nadler. University Park, Penn.: Pennsylvania State University Press.

7   In Defense of Explanatory Deductivism

Bruce Glymour

Three Varieties of Explanation

For one who is a pluralist about explanation, as I am, explanations are where you find them. And often enough, explanation is to be found in information that reduces one's surprise at whatever event occasions that surprise. On the other hand, explanation is often found in information that conveys some understanding of how the event in question came to occur. Typically, explanations do some of both, but rather more of one than the other.

Suppose I explain Boris's loss in the last hand of poker, despite his apparently good cards, by noting that he was drawing dead—any card he might catch on the river would make him a good hand that would be slightly worse than that of his opponents. You should then be unsurprised at his loss—given the situation, he could win only by some misplay on his opponents' part (say, had he drawn an ace or a 6 to his 2, 3, 4, 5, his straight would have lost to a hidden flush, but had he caught a 7, his 7–5 low would have lost to a hidden 6–4 low). You would also know something about the origins of Boris's loss—though less than you might have (I could have told you, but did not, whether he lost to the flush or the low).

The two varieties of explanation are aimed to reduce quite different sources of cognitive dis-ease. Understanding-conveying explanations fill a cognitive lacuna, a gap in one's information about the origins of an event. Surprise-reducing explanations may fill such gaps, but do so only, as it were, by the by. And in some cases, they do not do it at all. For example, pick any casino you like at which some large number of blackjack hands are played this year. If you are surprised at the casino's success given the slim margin of the house advantage, I might explain this success by pointing out the improbability of the casino loosing money. The explanation need advert only to the number of hands dealt and the actual value of the house advantage; the causal details by which the profit is actually generated are omitted, because otiose given the aims of the explanation.

Understanding-conveying explanations often reduce surprise, but again, as it were, only by the by. And sometimes they do not—or anyway ought not—do even this. It sometimes happens, for example, that a deleterious allele is fixed in a small population of organisms. Such fixation is both surprising and puzzling—that is, we might seek an explanation of such an event that both reduces our surprise at the event, and gives us to understand how the event came to occur. One way to explain such an event is to trace out the details of the reproductive history of each member of the population, noting the particular vicissitudes which lead to early deaths of members not carrying the allele, and the unexpected reproductive success of members carrying the allele.

This explanation will surely convey an understanding, of sorts. It is the kind of understanding Hume is on about when he claims "Did I show you the particular causes of each individual in a collection of twenty particles of matter, I should think it very unreasonable, should you afterwards ask me, what was the cause of the whole twenty" (Hume 1779/1976, p. 218). Moreover, at least in some cases, this sort of Humean understanding is all the understanding there is to have, for there is no overarching reason that the vicissitudes had to work out as they did. Precisely for this reason, the explanation really should not reduce one's surprise at the outcome: the happenstance that just the noted concatenation of causal details should have occurred is really much more improbable than the effect the concatenation is adduced to explain. There are, as it happens, any number of causal stories which lead to the unexpected frequencies (and very, very many more that do not), each with some chance of occurring. So though the allelic frequencies themselves are improbable, the causal details which produce them are even less likely. This permits a nice characterization of the explanatory work Humean explanations of such explananda are meant to carry out: it sometimes happens that we think an event might have been produced by any of several different kinds of causal process, and we care to know which actually did the job; a good Humean explanation tells us just this. But it need not, and in general will not, tell us why just that sort of causal process did occur.

Note that Humean explanations are different in point and content from a more standard picture of understanding-conveying explanations. That picture is best, though not uniquely, exemplified by covering-law models of explanation. These explanations are aimed not simply, or even primarily, to say what produced the explanandum. Instead, they aim to show why the explanandum had to occur, come what may. One is therefore tempted to see these explanations as a species of surprise-reducing explanation. But that is not quite right, since, in the appeal to the natural laws which constrain the operation of causal processes so that, whatever happens—whatever causal processes actually occur—the explanandum and not any alternative to it is produced, covering-law explanations do convey understanding of a sort.

A characterization of the sort of understanding conveyed by covering-law explanations emerges if we ask with what we would need to supplement a Humean explanation of allelic frequencies in order to convert it into a covering-law explanation. What we need is some further fact, presumably a fact about natural laws, which makes it the case that the causal vicissitudes which actually occurred had to occur as a matter of law. Or, better, some further fact which makes it the case that that the fixation of the deleterious alleles had to occur, however the vicissitudes of circumstance might have fallen out. To search for such supplemental information—information that would, if provided, convert a Humean explanation into a covering-law explanation—is to search for a conspiracy, if you will, of nature. Good conspirators arrange things so that all paths lead to victory. Similarly, we have a conspiracy of nature when the laws require that some event occur, no matter what conditions might obtain. To describe such a conspiracy in an explanatory context is to convey understanding. Hence covering-law explanations are essentially understanding-conveying explanations, though of a kind that nearly always serves to reduce surprise.

Conspiracy explanations can be more or less successful even when there is a conspiracy to which one can appeal (as there is not in the case of deleterious alleles). Some conspirators are less than perfect, and so unable to arrange things so that all paths lead to victory, but good enough to ensure that most do. Just so, sometimes the laws of nature cannot of themselves conspire to ensure that a particular event or regularity occurs. They rather require a bit of help from the vicissitudes of circumstance. Fisher's explanation of sex ratios (1930) is of this kind—a conspiracy in which the laws of nature require the collaboration of circumstance. But the fewer the arrangements of circumstance which *do not* lead to the explanandum, and the greater the number which do, the less help the laws require. The less help required by the laws to ensure the explanandum, the better the conspiracy explanation; in Railton's terms (1981), the more *robust* the resulting explanation. It should be clear, however, that even when a conspiracy of laws is insufficient of itself to guarantee the explanandum, the point of such explanations is to describe the conspiracy, such as it is, rather than the particular vicissitudes of circumstance which happen to lead to its success. One seeks a conspiracy explanation when one is less interested in knowing which features of context cause the explanandum, and more interested in knowing in virtue of what laws those features, whatever they may be, do so.

So we have three general classes of explanation. Some explanations aim essentially to reduce surprise. Some explanations aim rather to convey understanding, and of these there are two broadly different kinds—Humean explanations and conspiracy explanations. Humean explanations are appropriate when one thinks that there are several different kinds of processes any one of which could have produced the explanandum, and one wants to know which in fact did. The Humean explanation answers the question by describing the causal details by which an explanandum event is produced. But these explanations do not say much, or even anything, about why an instance of that kind of process did or had to occur. Conspiracy explanations, on the other hand, are concerned exactly with this missing information. They are appropriate when one wants to know why the explanandum rather than any relevant alternative to it occurred, but wants further that this explanation should be more or less independent of the causal details by which the explanandum was actually produced. I hope the difference in the point of conspiracy and Humean explanations is clear enough. This difference in aim implies some differences in content, an issue to which we will return in the final section.

As we have said, sometimes information that reduces surprise also conveys understanding. Explanations of essentially chancy events are often like this, and among these an important group come from classical statistical mechanics (SM).[1] When a gas confined in one half of a partitioned box becomes evenly distributed over the whole volume of the box soon after the partition is removed, the details of the SM explanation give one information which makes the result—the homogenous distribution of the gas—unsurprising. But the explanation also conveys an understanding: one knows not only why, given a probability distribution over initial states of the gas in the box, the statistics require that it is likely that the gas will be evenly distributed; one understands as well something about why the relevant statistical description obtains. In particular, one knows something about the laws governing the evolution of initial conditions into final states, and why the statistical description of the evolution of the gas need not attend to the details of the causal histories of each molecule of the gas.

What are we to make of such explanations of essentially chancy phenomena? What cognitive dis-ease do they aim to remove, and how to they do it?

The Standard View

Over the past half century or so, a more or less standard view about the structure and content of explanations of chancy events has emerged from work on indeterministic causation and scientific explanation. Though accounts vary, especially regarding the structure of explanations, certain features of the standard accounts are shared with sufficient frequency to count as something like an orthodoxy.[2] I take the following to characterize the crucial and generally accepted subset of the claims constituting this orthodoxy.

For any chancy event E which can be explained, there is some theory T and some prior condition C, such that the conjunction of T&C is explanatorily relevant to E because it entails a probability distribution over some set of alternatives, **A**, including a sentence E claiming that E occurs, on which $Pr(E/T\&C) \neq Pr(E/T\&\sim C)$.[3] For any triple of essentially chancy E, class of alternatives **A**, and background presuppositions **P** had by the requestor of an explanation, there is some T and some C such that T&C exhaust the explanatorily relevant information. Furthermore, T&C $\therefore$ E is not a valid argument (were it, E would not be chancy). Call the explanations countenanced by theories of explanation on which the above hold *inductive explanations*, whether or not they have the structure of an inductive argument (on most accounts, they do not).

Inductive explanations may be contrasted either with *deductive* or with *deterministic* explanations. By *deductive* explanation, I mean an explanation which consists in a valid deductive argument from some set of explanans sentences to a sentence E asserting the occurrence of the explanandum event *E*. Inductive explanations are not deductive, and indeed could not be: according to the theories which countenance inductive explanations, that *E* is essentially chancy implies that no deduction from any T&C is possible for a relevant description E of *E*. By *deterministic* explanation I mean an explanation of E which appeals only to deterministic causes or processes or laws governing events of the kind to which *E* belongs—that is, explanations that appeal only to nonstatistical, deterministic, theories and non-chancy initial conditions. Discussions of explanations of chancy events have by and large elided the distinction between deductive and deterministic explanations, and not without reason. It is natural enough, and maybe even right, to think that if *E* is essentially chancy, the processes which produce it and the laws governing that production, causal or otherwise, must be indeterministic, and hence any theory correctly describing these processes or laws must be statistical. Whence it follows that any correct explanation of E must be indeterministic. On the equally natural—though, as I think, mistaken—supposition that there is no explanatorily relevant information I with which to supplement T&C, it then also follows that any explanation of E must be nondeductive.

The orthodoxy commits to some claims about such inductive explanations. First, such explanations are a kind of understanding-conveying explanation.[4] Second, as has been advocated variously by Jeffreys (1971), Humphreys (1989), and Salmon (1984) among others, one can explain unlikely outcomes just as well as one can explain their more probable alternatives. Third, explanations of neither probable nor improbable chancy events can be contrastive, a view most forcefully defended by Salmon (1984). An explanation is contrastive if it is an explanation not merely of E, but of why E rather than F, where F is some alternative to E in **A**.

The first of these has not, I think, been given a principled defense, but is a more or less natural inference from the content of any number of successful explanations of chancy phenomena: these explanations do seem to convey an understanding, and the search for just such understanding might well motivate a question to which the explanation is an appropriate response.

The second and third theses emerge in roughly the following way (I take Salmon 1984 as a guide here). The quality of an explanation is, in the end, to be measured by the understanding it conveys. So suppose a statistical theory T specifies law-like regularities between some prior state described by C and a probability distribution over some set of alternatives including E, on which E is likely, even overwhelmingly likely. Then if by appeal to T&C we can explain E (and everyone now agrees this we can in fact do), T must convey some understanding of why E occurs. But, pretty generally, T&C will convey exactly the same kind of understanding of why ~E occurs on those rare occasions when it does, since what T describes is the way in which the occurrence of C modifies the probability of each of E and its alternatives, for example, ~E. So whether E or ~E occurs, an appeal to T&C will give us to understand that the event in question occurs as a matter of chance, against a probability whose evolution is described by T&C. Since a bit of language is an explanation only to the extent that it conveys understanding, or is capable of so doing; and since appeal to T&C gives us as good an understanding of ~E when it occurs as of E when it does; T&C must give us as good an explanation of ~E as of E. Consequently, the probability of the explanandum event is irrelevant to its explicability: low probability events can be explained just as well as high probability events. Hence thesis 2; call it the thesis of explanatory parity.

If parity is right—if an appeal to T&C would explain ~E just as well as it would E—then there is some question about whether an explanatory appeal to T&C could provide a contrastive explanation of E rather than ~E. For, following van Fraassen (1980), to explain why E rather than ~E is to provide information that favors E over ~E, and this the appeal to T&C cannot do—else the appeal would provide a better explanation, and therefore perforce a better understanding, of E than of ~E. Hitchcock (1999) calls the thesis that chancy events cannot be contrastively explained CEID, short for "contrastive explanation implies determinism." At the price of clumsiness but in aid of clarity, I will call this the thesis of *non-contrastivity*.

The case for non-contrastivity presumes a fourth thesis, which is best illustrated by considering deductive explanations. Deductive explanations are always uncontentiously contrastive, and part of the reason they are is that the explanans of such an explanation provides—constitutes—a reason for the occurrence of E that could not be given as a similarly explanatory reason for the occurrence of any alternative to E, should that alternative have occurred. Did the explanans provide such a reason for some exclusive alternative to E, say F, then F, and therefore ∼E would be derivable from the explanans; hence, the explanans would be inconsistent, and therefore false. I shall take this characteristic of deductive explanations to be definitive of contrastive explanations more generally, and call it the thesis of *nonidentity of reasons*: the reason given for the occurrence of the explanandum by a genuinely contrastive explanation could not be given as a similarly explanatory reason for the occurrence of any alternative, in some space of exclusive alternatives to the explanandum, had that alternative occurred.

The orthodoxy has recently been challenged on two fronts. Hitchcock (1999) has argued that non-contrastivity is mistaken, while Strevens (2000) has argued that parity is mistaken. In fact, Hitchcock's challenge depends implicitly on a failure of parity. I think parity is right in the following sense: the information given by an inductive explanation of an essentially chancy event E conveys as much understanding of alternatives to E as of E itself. For that reason, inductive explanations cannot be seen as understanding-conveying conspiracy explanations. If we relinquish parity by requiring that the explanans increase the probability of the explanandum, then inductive explanations (of more likely outcomes) regain the collusive aspect of conspiracy explanations. But the price of so doing is to forgo the idea that conspiracy explanations convey understanding essentially, rather than accidentally. Inductive versions of conspiracy explanations are merely surprise-reducing.

To see why it is untenable to treat an inductive explanation of a chancy event as of the conspiracy kind without relinquishing parity, consider an example from Strevens. A box is divided into two equal volumes, one filled with a gas, the second empty. The dividing partition is removed, and a brief time latter, the gas is evenly distributed in the entire volume of the box. The SM explanation of the result is something like this. There are various possible initial states for the gas in the container at the moment the partition is removed, given by the values of position and momentum for each particle, call this set **S**. Particles change their position and momenta in accordance with classical dynamics, so each initial state deterministically evolves into some particular future state at t_0, the time at which we observe the distribution of gas in the box. Each initial state is equally likely (with probability 0), but the probability measure over the space of alternative initial states implies that a particular class of states, those that evolve into homogenous distributions of the gas at t_0 (call these C states), is much, much more likely to be instanced than the alternative class (call this alternative class the set of ~C states—the set of states which do not evolve into a homogenous distribution at t_0). Hence it is very, very likely that we will see an approximately homogenous distribution of the gas when we look at t_0 (call this E). This explains why we do see such a distribution when we look.

The untenability of treating this explanation as a conspiracy explanation emerges as follows. The explanation appeals to a theory, SM, from which follows a partition of initial conditions into C and ~C states. The theory also specifies a probability distribution over these initial states, from which in turn follows, as noted by the explanation, a probability distribution over E and ~E. The explanation then asserts that E occurs. But of course, E did not *have* to occur. So if the laws of nature conspire to ensure the even distribution of the gas, they are anyway a little inept, since the laws do not ensure that E occurs, but rather ensure only that E is very, very likely. Law must conspire with circumstance if E is to be produced, though the relevant circumstances turn out to be very probable. Still, few conspirators are perfectly competent, and the explanation looks good enough here.

But conspiracy theory explanations do convey understanding, and for this reason we think parity ought to hold. So we ought to have a similarly good explanation of an inhomogeneous distribution, ~E, should such occur. To construct it, we take our initial explanans and addend as the explanandum ~E in place of E. But now the laws of nature are not merely less than perfectly competent at ensuring the explanandum occurs. To the contrary, they are singularly inept, because ~E is really incredibly unlikely. It is hard to see, then, how this explanation could be a successful conspiracy theory explanation.

Strevens consequently urges that we give up on parity. In particular, he thinks high probabilities play a crucial role in the success of our first SM explanation, and that it is the lack of them which dooms our second SM explanation. But notice that if we follow Strevens here, we are forced to regard explanations of chancy events as surprise-reducing. First, reducing surprise has been made the sine qua non of success. Second, our unsuccessful SM explanation really does convey just as much information about how its explanandum came to occur—and just as much information about why—as did our successful explanation (indeed, it is exactly the same information). So the understanding conveyed by an explanation is irrelevant to its success. Whence it follows that the explanation cannot be aimed to reduce the sort of cognitive dis-ease that conspiracy theory explanations remove.

Parity and Non-contrastivity

Hitchcock (1999) presents a theory of contrastive explanation on which inductive explanations of chancy events can be contrastive. The account is nifty, but, I claim, relies implicitly on relinquishing parity, and so cannot be adopted so long as we think inductive explanations are aimed to convey understanding. The account of contrastive explanation goes roughly as follows.

Take C to be explanatorily relevant to E in background conditions B just in case $Pr(E/C\&B) \neq Pr(E/B)$. Suppose further that "Because C" will be a technically correct answer to the question "Why E?" when C is explanatorily relevant to E, but that such answers may be *pragmatically defective* when C is non-salient. Hitchcock takes it that salience is largely determined by the context in which an explanatory request is phrased, and offers an account of the way in which the features of such contexts constrain salience. Call any proposition accepted, at least for the purposes of argument, by all parties to a conversation within which an explanatory request is voiced an *explanatory presupposition*. According to Hitchcock, a presupposition constrains the range of pragmatically *non*-defective answers to an explanatory why-question, by screening off from the explanandum certain features of the history of the explanandum event which are unconditionally probabilistically relevant to the explanandum. So C will be explanatorily relevant to E under a presupposition P just in case (1): $Pr(E/C\&B\&P) \neq Pr(E/B\&P)$. Hitchcock then suggests that when contrastive why-questions are asked, for example, "Why E rather than F?," the contrast class $\{E, F\}$ implicit in the question sustains a presupposition of the form $P =_{df} (E \vee F)$, where the disjunction is exclusive (here and henceforth "$\vee$" represents an exclusive "or"). Under these conditions, says Hitchcock, indeterministic events E can be contrastively explained, for sometimes there will be some C such that (2): $Pr(E/C\&B\&(E \vee F)) \neq Pr(E/B\&(E \vee F))$.[5] In such cases C is explanatorily relevant to the contrastive question, "Why E rather than F?" Consequently, the response "Because C" should be counted as a successful answer to the question, and hence should be held to contrastively explain E.

We can see, then, how on Hitchcock's account our first SM explanation is contrastive. Since we regard homogeneity—that is, the occurrence of E—as surprising, we must have some background assumptions B on which E is not terribly likely. Our contrastive presupposition is $E \vee \sim E$, and our explanation provides information about a theory T and initial conditions (the probability distribution over states in **S**); call the conjunction of them C. Our explanation is contrastive iff $Pr(E/C\&B\&(E \vee \sim E)) \neq Pr(E/B\&(E \vee \sim E))$. Since $E \vee \sim E$ is logically true, $Pr(E/B\&(E \vee \sim E)) = Pr(E/B)$. This is not particularly high (else we would not be surprised at E), but $Pr(E/C\&B\&(E \vee \sim E))$ is. So our explanation is contrastive.

Hitchcock's proposal depends on rejecting parity. To see why this is so, consider the following example from Hitchcock. A vertically polarized photon is shot at a polarizer oriented at a small angle from vertical, and the photon is transmitted. Ignorant of all details but the facts that the photon is vertically polarized and that it was transmitted, we ask, "Why was the photon transmitted rather than absorbed?" Our contrastive presupposition is $P \equiv (A \vee R)$, with A standing for absorption and R for transmission. We are answered, "Because C," where C stands for the fact that the polarizer was oriented very close to the vertical. As it turns out, $Pr(R/C\&P)$ is greater than $Pr(R/P)$. Hence the explanation is contrastive.

But suppose—contrary to fact—that the photon were absorbed. Then, because $Pr(A/C\&P)$ will be less than the $Pr(A/P)$, "Because C" will count as a contrastive explanation of why A rather than R. Passing by the strongly counterintuitive nature of that result, it clearly violates the non-identity of reasons unless we claim that "Because C" is a better explanation of R, when it occurs, than it is of A, when it occurs—thereby implicitly rejecting parity. In order to preserve the non-identity of reasons, Hitchcock could insist that explanatory relevance under a contrastive presupposition requires the satisfaction of inequality (3) (see note 5, above), rather than the weaker inequality (2). Since $Pr(A/C\&P) < Pr(A/P)$, rather than the converse, (3) is not satisfied; and so on this reading "Because C" does not contrastively explain A rather than R on those occasions where A occurs. But that is a problem. If "Because C" does not contrastively explain A, then neither does "Because C and T," where T is the complete relevant theory covering such cases. On the other hand, we have already assumed that "Because C" does contrastively explain R rather than A; so "Because C and T" must do so as well. But this clearly violates explanatory parity. Hence, Hitchcock's proposal requires that we reject parity. And to reject parity for inductive explanations is to reject the idea that they are aimed to convey understanding.

Deductive Explanations?

Inductive explanations look to be in trouble. They are most naturally in terpreted as a species of conspiracy explanation. As such, they are essentially contrastive: conspirators conspire to produce one outcome as against its alternatives. On the other hand, conspiracy explanations are also aimed to convey understanding. But the information contained by those explanations conveys as much understanding of alternatives as of the explanandum. If we insist—explicitly with Strevens or implicitly with Hitchcock—that the explanantia of inductive explanations must increase the probability of their explananda, we can recover the collusive aspect of a conspiracy explanation, and with it inductive explanations become contrastive. But the price of so doing is to relinquish the idea that inductive explanations are essentially aimed to provide a kind of understanding.

Must we then see SM explanations in particular as non-understanding-conveying, surprise-reducing explanations? I think not. There is a different picture of SM explanations, and an available understanding of the explanations so pictured, on which they do in fact convey understanding. The picture is called by Strevens the "brute fact" account (see Railton 1981). This account faces a problem, which I claim is avoided if we take brute fact SM explanations to be a species of Humean explanation.

The brute fact SM explanation of our gas in the box goes as follows. The gas is composed of molecules, each with a position, energy and momentum. These variables change in accordance with classical dynamics. When the partition is removed, the gas is in some initial state Ci. The set of possible initial states S can be divided into two subsets: C states are such that they will, following the rules of classical dynamics, evolve into homogenous distributions at t_0, the time at which we observe the distribution of the gas; $\sim$C states are such that they will evolve into inhomogeneous distributions at t_0. Every individual state has an equal probability of occurring, but according to the probability distribution assumed by the theory, it is much, much more likely that the actual state will be a C state than $\sim$C state; consequently it is very, very likely that our system is in a C state. As it happens, *Ci is* a C state. Hence, at t_0, we observe a homogenous distribution.

Strevens thinks the brute fact account faces insuperable difficulties. Before addressing them, we should see how the explanation functions to Humean ends. First, the explanation describes a large class of causal processes—those in which molecules of a gas causally interact in the ways specified by classical dynamics. Second, it individuates two distinct kinds of processes in this class. The individuation turns directly on a partition of the possible initial conditions, but this in turn depends on a partition of the possible effects. C processes are those which produce homogenous distributions of the gas at t_0, while ~C processes are those which produce inhomogeneous distributions at t_0. Finally, the explanation claims that a process of only one of these kinds, a C process, actually produced the distribution of the gas at t_0. It follows deductively from this that E, the homogenous distribution of the gas at t_0, occurs. The deductive explanation is possible here because the relevant causal processes have been individuated in part by appeal to initial conditions, but also as well by appeal to their ultimate effect. This turns out to be a general feature of Humean explanations of chancy events. The explanation will serve Humean ends, provided there are legitimate questions which are answered by SM explanations in virtue of their individuating between C processes, ~C processes, and perhaps alternatives which are of neither kind. That there are such questions, at least potentially, emerges from a consideration of Strevens's challenge to brute fact SM explanations.

What then is the problem brute fact explanations face, according to Strevens? Strevens claims that a brute fact SM explanation of the second law of thermodynamics must be empty in a particular sense. According to Strevens, an explanation is empty if it conveys no understanding, and an explanation will convey no understanding if it explains equally well a contrary result (see Strevens 2000, p. 375).[6] How then does a brute fact explanation of the second law go, and why is it empty? Taking such an explanation to be Humean, it will go something like this. Systems are composed of molecules, with positions, energies, and momenta evolving over time according to classical dynamics. At any given time, systems can be in C or ~C states: C states lead to thermodynamic equilibrium at the moment of observation; ~C states lead to thermodynamic disequilibrium at the moment of observation. Each state is equiprobable; but it is much, much more probable that, at any given time, a system is in a C state than in a ∼C state. As it happens, most actual systems are in C states most of the time. Hence, the second law is (almost) never violated.

The problem, says Strevens, is that were the second law systematically violated, we could explain that as well, simply by changing the penultimate sentence so that it asserts that ∼C states occur more or less uniformly. No claim in SM proper is thereby changed, so—on this view of SM explanations—SM appears to explain a systematic failure of the second law just as well as its holding. Hence SM explanations are empty. As Strevens puts it, "I say that the explanation is empty because it conveys no understanding of why heat flows one way [from hot things to cold] but not the other, which is just to say that it conveys no understanding of why the second law of thermodynamics is true" (2000, p. 375).

I think Strevens is seriously misguided here by thinking of understanding-conveying explanations as conspiracy explanations. If what it is to convey an understanding of why the second law holds is to show why it has to hold come what may, no matter how the circumstances turn out, then the brute fact explanation is in trouble. If we are searching for some general, noncircumstantial feature of the world which conspires to generate the second law, we are out of luck; there is no such fact. But note that this is true no matter how we read the SM explanation of the second law: the law does not have to hold; its holding is a chancy fact, since nothing makes it the case that systems are virtually never in ∼C states. Conspiracy explanations are simply not on when events are chancy, because when events are chancy their effects occur at all only when general features—that is, laws—conspire with a happenstance decided by a roll of the dice.

If the explanation is understood to be of the Humean variety, then things are rather different. Whether or not SM says anything about why the second law holds, the explanation does. It says that, given SM, the second law holds because most systems are in C states most of the time. Exactly that feature of the explanation is false in the counterfactual case Strevens envisages: SM still holds, but by chance, systems are nearly always in ∼C states. Strevens is not blind to this—there is in fact a difference between the brute fact SM explanation of equilibrium (whether a particular case or the general fact of it), and the SM explanation of disequilibrium.

The problem for Strevens is that the difference does not lie in the theory, but rather in the chancy circumstances to which it applies. This would seem to indicate that SM plays no essential role in explaining why heat flows from hot objects to cold, rather than the other way round, and so has no essential role to play in explaining why the second law holds. And of course SM does play such a role; so the brute fact explanation must be mistaken.

Again, Strevens is misled by thinking of the explanation as a conspiracy explanation rather than a Humean explanation. Understood as a Humean explanation, the brute fact explanation of the second law is not empty, and its content depends essentially on SM, but to see this one has to consider a different contrast. Suppose tomorrow we begin witnessing systematic disequilibrium. There are two possible reasons for such an occurrence. It might be that, simply by chance, on the morrow systems begin systematically to occupy ~C states. Or differently, it might be that God changes the rules so that the nonrealists are right in the long run—beginning on the morrow there are no atoms, and consequently SM presents a radically false account of how physical systems evolve with respect to thermodynamic properties. A relevant—maybe the relevant—question to ask under these circumstances is which of the two scenarios gets it right?

The brute fact explanation of the occurrence of disequilibrium given above is exactly the sort of explanation we would then need. Would SM play a crucial role in that explanation? Certainly. What differentiates the two possibilities is exactly that SM processes are still at work in the world if our brute fact SM explanation is right, but are not if God has changed the rules. If the brute fact explanation of disequilibrium is right, it is just that the SM processes in question are those terribly unlikely ~C processes. But they are no less SM processes for that, and it is for this reason that the explanation is informative. For, given persistent disequilibrium, that the processes producing it are *not* SM process becomes a real possibility. The exclusion of that possibility is informative.

Just so, in cases of actual violations of the second law, the Humean explanation will be informative. If one presents a physicist with an apparent violation of the second law the standard response (at least among the physicists I've talked to) is to deny that the description of the situation is accurate. The physicist presumes that one of those terribly unlikely ~C processes did not, in fact, occur, but rather, that some relevant feature of the circumstance has been omitted. When this relevant feature is included, it turns out that the process which actually occurred is very, very likely. If one adds dye, for example, to a beaker of liquid; stirs in one direction, and then very carefully reverses the motion; and the dye returns to something like its initial position, the presumption will be that the liquid is not water, but, say, glycerin. But if the actual case really has been completely described—if it really does involve water and not glycerin—and so really does involve a terribly unlikely $\sim$C process, a Humean explanation of the restored position will be correctly informative. Even if the physicist is inclined not to accept the explanation, she would learn, did she accept it, what produced the result.

For similar reasons, the brute fact explanation of the more normal case of equilibrium, considered as a Humean explanation, really is informative if we put ourselves in the position of a scientist worried about thermodynamics in the latter half of the nineteenth century. For her, there are several (epistemically) possible processes which, had they occurred, would have produced the homogenous distribution of the gas. She is concerned to discover which actually did the work; this is exactly what the Humean explanation tells her.

So, I claim, brute fact SM explanations are understanding-conveying. They are a species of Humean explanation. These explanations work by specifying which of a range of possible causal processes actually did produce the explanandum. Those processes are individuated by appeal to theory, but also by appeal to initial conditions and ultimate effects. In contrastive cases in which the explanandum fails to occur, this can result either from the chance absence of the appropriate initial condition or causal process, or because the theory used to individuate the processes fails for the particular case. We may be in doubt as to which, and a Humean explanation of the contrasting result, employing the same theory, is therefore informative—it tells one that the contrasting alternative occurs as a result of well-understood processes and conditions, which obtain as a matter of chance, rather than as a result of the failure of one's theory. Hence, it is a mistake to infer from the fact that a theory can be used to explain both E and $\sim$E, either that the theory plays no essential role in the explanation of E, or that the explanation of E is empty.

Extending the Program

The cases considered so far have been classical rather than quantum. And indeed it is crucial that this be so: Humean explanations of quantum phenomena cannot be given, or anyway cannot be given in quite the same way (though we haven't here the space to discuss the reasons for this). One may be in doubt, then, about whether probabilistically caused but non-quantum phenomena can really be given Humean explanations. We do not have the space here to detail a full account, but some observations are relevant and sufficiently brief to be worth making.

Humean explanations of chancy but non-quantum phenomena can be given, provided we individuate probabilistic causal relations in the right way. Standard treatments of probabilistic causation have tended to differentiate between causal processes only by appeal to differences between causes. So, for example, that a person was exposed to UV B photons sometimes explains his subsequent cancer. When this is so, exposure to UV B photons is a cause of cancer, distinguished from other causes of cancer in that it is UV B photons—rather than, say, molecules of arsenic—that account for the change in the probability that cancer occurs. But note that, so individuated, one and the same causal process relating UV B photons and cancer is instanced both in those cases in which exposure leads to cancer, and in those cases in which it does not. The same process is instanced in both cases, because in both cases exposure to UV B has changed the *probability* that cancer occurs.

Causal processes may also be distinguished by appeal to their effects. So, for example, both arsenic and UV B photons cause cancer. But they do so by causing different kinds of mutations. UV B photons cause a particular kind of point mutation—a transition; while arsenic tends to cause extremely large ($\sim$1 million base pair) deletions, or, more rarely, a different kind of point mutation called a transversion. A cancer produced by a large deletion is almost certainly not the result of UV B photons acting alone. Hence, a description of the process leading to, say, Igor's cancer that identifies such a deletion as the basis for the cancerous cells, individuates the process in question as an instance of some process other than that relating UV B photons and cancer. If one individuates a process by appeal to both the cause and some effect, one and the same process cannot be instanced on both those occasions when the cause and the effect are instanced, and on those occasions on which merely the cause is instanced. So, contrary to some views about probabilistic causation, it is possible to say which of two potential probabilistic causes of cancer, say, are actually responsible for a particular case of cancer: to say of Igor that his cancer is caused by exposure to arsenic, which produced a very large deletion in some particular gene, is to make a claim which is incompatible with UV B photons causing the cancer, even if Igor is exposed to such photons as well as to arsenic.

One may also individuate one process, as against others, by describing the relation between cause and effect—that is, by appeal to some theory or law. This is commonly (though not always) done by offering an algebraic expression which describes a relation between magnitudes of causal variables and effect variables. So, for example, although Kepler failed to identify the causal process we call gravity, he did individuate that process insofar as he showed that gravitational force did not, as it might have done, decrease as one over the distance or one over the distance cubed. Explanations in physics tend to explicitly individuate causal processes only by appeal to such algebraic descriptions: according to the Newtonian theory of gravity, one and the same process explains the gravitational force exerted by the Sun on Jupiter and the force exerted by the Sun on the Earth. Differences in those forces are explained not by appeal to different processes, but by appeal to different masses and distances, that is, different initial conditions. As we have seen, however, such conditions may be embedded in the individuation of the process itself—doing this plays a crucial role in the brute fact SM explanation, for if the processes are not so individuated the brute fact explanation must be seen as a failed conspiracy explanation.

How one individuates the processes responsible for an explanandum event depends on the aim of the explanation in which that individuation occurs. It will not do in a conspiracy explanation to individuate processes by appeal either to those initial conditions which are causally active, or to the effect of the causal process. To so individuate the responsible processes would make it impossible to satisfy the aim of a conspiracy explanation—namely, to identify reasons for the occurrence of the explanandum event which are independent of the vicissitudes of circumstance. When law and fact must conspire together to produce the explanandum, the reasons of interest to the conspiracy explanation are, as it were, not features of circumstance but instead the reasons for which those features produce the explanandum. The same is not true of Humean explanations, and for them, individuations of causal processes which appeal to the causally active features of circumstance and/or their effects are perfectly innocuous.

When probabilistic causal relations are individuated in this way, deductive, Humean explanations of probabilistically caused phenomena are possible. We wonder whether Igor's cancer was caused by exposure to UV B or to arsenic (if the latter, the city water company is in big trouble). So we ask, "Why did Igor get cancer?" An explanatory answer will specify the process which actually produced Igor's cancer—exposure to arsenic produced a huge chromosomal deletion, which included the c-ras^K allele, and this absence produced a squamous cell carcinoma. Hence, Igor got cancer.

The explanation is deductive, despite the essential chanciness of the explanandum. Because the explanation is deductive, it is contrastive as well. The explanation, though different, is no worse if we substitute "Hence, Igor got cancer rather than not" for the explanandum. But the explanation is not surprise-reducing—it is much more likely that Igor will get cancer than that he will get it in the way specified by the explanation. And the explanation does not identify a conspiracy in virtue of which Igor's cancer had to occur. It did not have to occur; that it did depended on the chance occurrence of a particular, and more or less unlikely, causal process.

I suggest, then, that there are a variety of ways in which one can individuate the processes responsible for the production of a particular explanandum; each way is appropriate to different kinds of explanations, and differs in aim. Humean, but not conspiracy explanations, may legitimately individuate the causal process producing an explanandum by appeal both to the particular features of circumstance which do the causing, and as well by appeal to the effects of such a process. Individuations that make either sort of appeal are illicit in the context of a conspiracy explanation precisely because the point of such an explanation is to elucidate the reasons an explanandum occurs which are independent of the particular circumstances; conspiracy explanations aim to identify the reasons such features of circumstance do in fact produce the explanandum. But for Humean explanations, individuation by appeal to the effect of a process is licit because each of the processes regarded as possible by the requester of the explanation would produce the explanandum, did that process occur. Appeal to features of circumstance is legitimate because the requester is indifferent to the degree to which the operation of the relevant process is dependent on circumstance. So, I claim, causal explanations of essentially chancy events are essentially Humean, that is, they aim to say which of several alternative processes which might have produced the result actually did so. Because Humean explanations individuate processes with respect to their effects, they can have a deductive structure even when their explananda are essentially chancy. Because they have that structure, they are essentially contrastive: non-contrastivity is mistaken. But their success is independent of the probability that the explananda occur, of the probability that the processes which produce the explananda occur, and of the probability that the relevant initial conditions obtain. That is to say, given a chancy event E, the theory T describing the evolution of its probability, and a complete description of the initial conditions C, T and C convey as much understanding of $\sim E$, when it occurs, as of E, when it occurs. Parity holds. Finally, when identical initial conditions lead, by chance, to different outcomes, different processes, as individuated by their effects, occur; hence Humean explanations of the two kinds of cases provide different reasons for the outcome in each kind of case: non-identity of reasons holds. The happy results depend on one crucial move: understanding-conveying explanations of chancy events have, either explicitly or implicitly, a deductive structure.

Acknowledgments

My thanks to Christopher Hitchcock for illuminating conversation, which led to the avoidance of several errors here.

Notes

1. Note that for me an event is essentially chancy even if it is deterministically caused, so long as the cause is itself an essentially chancy event.

2. There are, of course, dissenters; among those not here explicitly considered, Paul Humphreys (1989) figures importantly.

3. I will use capital letters for descriptions; italic capitals for things described; and underscored capitals for sets. On various accounts an explanation of E may be partial, in that T and/or C may be only partly specified; T, especially, may not be explicitly mentioned at all.

4. Though, again, see Humphreys (1989) for a dissenting voice.

5. In fact Hitchcock is ambiguous about whether A contrastively explains P rather than Q when the inequality (2) holds; or whether he demands, for contrastive explanation, the stronger condition of inequality (3): $Pr(E/C\&B\&(E \vee F)) > Pr(E/B\&(E \vee F))$. His formal representations all give inequality (2), but every one of his examples satisfies inequality (3). With only explicit exceptions below, I take him to have insisted on (2); but little of what I say below depends on that reading. Anyone inclined to adopt the thesis of the non-identity of reasons ought to regard (2) as immediately suspicious.

6. Note that Strevens is here endorsing non-identity of reasons for all understanding-conveying scientific explanations.

References

Fisher, R. 1930. *The Genetical Theory of Natural Selection*. Oxford: Oxford University Press.

Hitchcock, C. 1999. "Contrastive Explanation and the Demons of Determinism." *British Journal for the Philosophy of Science* 50: 585–612.

Hume, D. 1779/1976. *Dialogues Concerning Natural Religion*. In *The Natural History of Religion and Dialogues Concerning Natural Religion*, edited by J. Price. Oxford: Oxford University Press.

Humphreys, P. 1989. *The Chances of Explanation*. Princeton: Princeton University Press.

Jeffreys, R. 1971. "Statistical Explanation vs. Statistical Inverence." In *Statistical Explanation and Statistical Relevance*, edited by W. Salmon, R. Jeffrey, and J. Greeno. Pittsburgh: University of Pittsburgh Press.

Railton, P. 1981. "Probability, Explanation, and Information." *Synthese* 48: 233–256.

Salmon, W. 1984. *Explanation and the Causal Structure of the World*. Princeton: Princeton University Press.

Strevens, M. 2000. "Do Large Probabilities Explain Better?" *Philosophy of Science* 67: 366–390.

van Fraassen, B. 1980. *The Scientific Image*. Oxford: Oxford University Press.

8 Goal-Directed Action and Teleological Explanation

Scott R. Sehon

We typically explain human behavior by citing the agent's *reasons*. Forty years ago, Donald Davidson (1963) convinced most of the philosophical world that such explanations are causal. However, a few holdouts[1] have claimed that action explanation is irreducibly teleological. I am here to defend the holdouts. According to this view, which I will call *teleological realism*, when we explain an agent's behavior by citing her *reason*, we explain the behavior by specifying the state of affairs towards which the behavior was directed. The canonical form would be:

X ϕ'd in order to ψ.

Many explanations of action are already teleological in form:

Joan went to the kitchen in order to get wine.

The quarterback threw the ball out of bounds to avoid a sack.

Other explanations of action have a superficially different form:

Joan went to the kitchen because she wanted wine.

The teleological realist says that the "because" is teleological, and construes the explanation as saying:

Joan went to the kitchen in order to satisfy her desire for wine.

Or as:

Joan went to the kitchen in order to bring it about that she got wine in the way she desired.

For the teleological realist, the concept of *goal-direction* is fundamental to agency and is not reducible to causal concepts.

In a recent paper, Alfred Mele (2000) has defended the causal theory of action explanation and has argued against teleological realism. I want to defend teleological realism against Mele's attack, and I also hope to clarify the nature of the view (at least as I see the position; I cannot claim to speak for the other holdouts from causalism).

Mele's Challenge

Mele begins with a general challenge: "In virtue of what is it true that a person acted in pursuit of a particular goal? No proponent of [teleological realism], as far as I know, has offered a plausible, informative answer to this question" (2000, p. 280). Mele repeats this general challenge in similar words at a number of points. However, at least on one reading, Mele's demand begs the central question at issue. The teleological realist says that teleological explanations are not reducible to nonteleological concepts. By asking, "In *virtue of what* is it true that a person acted in pursuit of a particular goal?" Mele seems to be demanding an account of teleological concepts in nonteleological terms. But that is precisely what cannot be done, if teleological realism is correct.

According to the teleological realist, teleological connectives are primitive. It is not such an embarrassment to have an irreducible primitive. After all, I doubt if anyone can give a reductive analysis of what it means to say "*x* caused *y*," but that does not mean that causal claims are useless or incoherent. Similarly, I cannot give a reductive analysis of "X φ'd in order to ψ," but that, by itself, does not make such claims worthless.

The causalist account does promise to be more parsimonious, for it has one primitive (*causation*) as opposed to two (*causation* and *goal-direction*). That would indeed be a compelling consideration in favor of causalism, *if* one could actually produce a successful reductive analysis of *goal-direction*, and thereby show that one can get by with just the one primitive. But Mele acknowledges (2000, p. 296) that he is not offering any analysis of the fundamental notion of *action*, and I and others (especially George Wilson) have argued that the extant attempts at such an analysis fail.[2] So, even if we do not like it, we may just have to live with both *causation* and *goal-direction* as irreducible primitives.

Nonetheless, even if we cannot analyze teleology in causal terms, we do need some account of how we identify and justify teleological explanations. We might characterize what is needed as the epistemology of teleological explanation. I would acknowledge that the efforts in this direction so far by teleological realists have been inadequate, and some of Mele's arguments highlight that inadequacy.

The heart of Mele's argument is an example involving a man named Norm and some powerful Martians. Mele writes:

[The Martians'] aim was to make it seem to [Norm] that he is acting while preventing him from even *trying* to act by selectively shutting down portions of his brain. To move his body, they zap him in the belly with M-rays that control the relevant muscles and joints. When they intervene, they wait for Norm to begin a routine activity, read his mind to make sure that he plans to do what they think he is doing … and then zap him for a while—unless the mind-reading team sees him abandon or modify his plan. When the team notices something of this sort, the Martians stop interfering and control immediately reverts to Norm.

A while ago, Norm started climbing a ladder to fetch his hat. When he reached the midway point, the Martians took over. Although they controlled Norm's next several movements while preventing him from trying to do anything, they would have relinquished control to him if his plan had changed (e.g., in light of a belief that the location of his hat had changed). (2000, pp. 284–285)

So in this case, Norm *intends* to move up the ladder, *thinks* that he is directing his behavior, he is *aware* of what he is doing, and his behavior is even sensitive to changes in his plans—for if his intentions change, the Martians will relinquish control and Norm will act in accord with his new plan. Norm seems to meet the requirements that teleological realists have typically put forward as indicative of goal-directed activity. And yet, Mele says, it is clear that Norm was not acting at all, for the Martians were in complete control of his body, and prevented him from so much as *trying* to fetch his hat. Mele's suggestion is that the causalist, but not the teleological realist, can explain why Norm's motion up the ladder fails to be a goal-directed action.

It is worth noting that it is not *trivial* for the causalist to explain why Norm's behavior fails to count as an action. After all, by hypothesis, Norm's intention *did* cause his bodily motion—albeit via an indirect route involving Martians. The causalist will have to say that in this case the desire did not cause the bodily motion "in the right way." And that, in turn, can land the causalist in a long debate. However, I will accept, for the sake of argument, that the causalist has no problem with this case. The challenge is to provide an account of the epistemology of teleology that correctly covers Norm. My approach here will resemble, and is certainly influenced by, the work of Donald Davidson and Daniel Dennett, although neither of them would agree that action explanation is irreducibly teleological.

A couple of caveats before proceeding. First, the account will be more general than is necessary to answer the specific example, since I am hoping to illuminate the position as well as respond to Mele. Second, at the same time, the account is still somewhat sketchy; there is much more to be said.

The Epistemology of Teleology

Theorizing in physical science is governed at least in part by a principle of simplicity, which I would express as follows:

(S)   Given two theories, it is unreasonable to believe the one that leaves significantly more unexplained mysteries.

Thus, as our physical theory of the world improves, it gradually leaves fewer and fewer unexplained mysteries. Something is mysterious, roughly speaking, when it is unexpected; we explain apparently mysterious events by giving a theory according to which events like that would be expected. Within physical science, there is no further requirement that events be *justified* or make *rational sense*. For example, if we can explain a tornado's occurrence in terms of general laws and existing meteorological conditions, we do not ask what justifiable purpose it served. The tornado serves no justifiable or reasonable purpose, but this fact does not count as an unexplained mystery for our meteorological theory.

When our subject matter includes agents and their behavior, things are different. When theorizing about an agent, we aim for a theory according to which the agent is rational and her behavior makes sense. In the course of constructing such a theory, we will be guided by the simplicity principle, but we will also be guided by an additional maxim:

(R)   Given two theories of an agent, it is unreasonable to believe the one according to which the agent is significantly less rational.

As Davidson puts it, when we are dealing with an agent, "In our need to make him make sense, we will try for a theory that finds him consistent, a believer of truths, and a lover of the good (all by our own lights, it goes without saying)" (1980, p. 222). (R) by itself does not provide us much guidance on exactly how to do this, for (R) is phrased quite generally, and it is not immediately obvious how it applies to individual items of behavior.

Indeed, by the very nature of the principle, it cannot simply be applied, in a vacuum, to a single piece of behavior. We determine the purpose of behavior against the background of a more general theory of the agent.

So we will need to explore further to see what sorts of explanation make better sense of a behavior. But we can note a couple of points at the outset. First, the idea behind R is that agents are basically rational. To quote Davidson again: "Global confusion, like universal mistake, is unthinkable, not because imagination boggles, but because too much confusion leaves nothing to be confused about and massive error erodes the background of true belief against which alone failure can be construed" (1980, p. 221). Second, in the context of explaining behavior, the rationality of a piece of behavior can be measured along two axes—the extent to which the behavior is appropriate for achieving the agent's goal, and the extent to which the goal itself is of value from the agent's perspective. If an agent is ineffective at achieving her goals, then she is, to that extent, not rational; but an agent is also irrational insofar as her goals themselves have no value. Accordingly, built into (R) is the expectation that agents will be effective in achieving their goals and that their goals will be of value. Of course, we do not expect perfect efficiency or an ideal set of goals of every agent. Instead, the twin expectations built into (R) will be something like the following:

(R_1) Agents act in ways that are appropriate for achieving their goals, given the agent's circumstances, epistemic situation, and intentional states.

(R_2) Agents have goals that are of value, given the agent's circumstances, epistemic situation, and intentional states.

I will approach the issue of how we apply (R) via a related discussion by the biologist Richard Dawkins (1995).[3] Suppose you are confronted by an unknown object, and you want to determine the purpose (if any) for which it was designed. Dawkins says that you will employ reverse engineering. You assume, as a working hypothesis, that the object was well-designed for achieving some end. To determine what end, we ascertain the object's *utility function*, meaning that which is maximized or optimized by the operation of the object. Roughly speaking, we then assume that the utility function of the object is its intended purpose. For example, if someone unfamiliar with baseball saw a catcher's mask, he might be initially puzzled. But upon examining the straps, the metal bars in front, the padding around the edges of the bars, he might quickly infer that this would be a good device for fitting over someone's head and protecting the face from ball-sized objects.

Dawkins's specific question is whether living bodies are themselves the result of intelligent design. He argues that "the true utility function of life, that which is being maximized in the natural world, is DNA survival" (Dawkins 1995, p. 85). Thus, the utility function of living bodies is not the good of the individual or the welfare of the species; even when those goods happen to be served, this is a secondary consequence of the primary function of DNA survival. As Dawkins puts it: "Nature is neither kind nor unkind. She is neither against suffering nor for it. Nature is not interested in suffering one way or the other unless it affects the survival of DNA" (1995, p. 85). Here Dawkins talks as if Nature is a designing agent, albeit an agent that is interested only in survival of DNA and is indifferent to suffering. But Dawkins contends that this supposed indifference actually shows that living bodies are not the products of intelligent design at all:

> In a universe of electrons and selfish genes, blind physical forces and genetic replication, some people are going to get hurt, other people are going to get lucky, and you won't find any rhyme or reason in it, nor any justice. The universe that we observe has precisely the properties we should expect if there is, at bottom, no design, no purpose, no evil and no good, nothing but pitiless indifference. (Dawkins 1995, p. 85)

Dawkins's point is this: if we are to vindicate the working assumption that a thing was designed for a purpose, then we must do more than show that it *has* a utility function; in addition, the utility function must be of the right sort. In particular, we should conclude that the thing has a purpose only if the utility function exhibits rhyme, reason, or justice. That is to say, the utility function must be of some sort of intelligible value.

To summarize, on Dawkins's account, when we attempt to ascertain whether and what purpose an object has, we presuppose two principles:

If an object has an intended purpose, then its purpose is its utility function.

An object has an intended purpose only if its utility function has rhyme and reason.

The question of whether an object was *designed* by an agent is of course different from the question of whether something *is* an agent, and it is also different from the question of whether a bodily motion was directed by an agent. Nonetheless similar considerations are involved. We apply something like the reverse engineering approach, but instead of deciding whether the object itself was designed, we look to see whether the object's behavior is "designed"—that is, directed—and, if so, to what end. Accordingly, if we were to apply Dawkins's account directly to this task, we would assume the following two principles:

(D_1)   If a behavior is directed to a goal, then its goal is its utility function.

(D_2)   A behavior is directed toward a goal only if the utility function of the behavior has intelligible value.

These principles constrain what can count as the goal of a piece of behavior. (D_1) tells us that the goal, if there is one, has to be the utility function of the behavior, and, according to (D_2), for the utility function to be a goal, it must have intelligible value. (D_1) and (D_2) have a fairly obvious correlation with the two axes of rationality noted above in (R_1) and (R_2). According to (R_1), agents act in ways that are appropriate to achieving their goals, modulo the agent's circumstances and epistemic situation; (D_1) takes this somewhat further by specifying that the goal of a behavior is precisely that which the behavior is most effective at obtaining. (R_2) says that agents have goals that are of value from their perspective, and the correlation between this and (D_2) is even more direct. There is, I claim, something importantly correct about (D_1) and (D_2); however, the account will require some refinement before it accurately reflects our practice of giving teleological explanations.

To see the need for refinement, it will help to consider another example. During the course of a commencement speech, Ben, who has never seen or heard of American Sign Language, notices someone standing to the side of a podium making (to his mind) strange gesticulations, and he wonders what the person is doing. The person's behavior would be good for accomplishing any number of aims: signing is a good way of burning a certain number of calories per hour; it is a good way of demonstrating one's ability for certain kinds of hand and arm motions; and it is a good way of displacing a certain number of air molecules. Ben quite rightly does not consider such possible objectives, for he would find it hard to imagine that these goals would have any particular value for the agent in these circumstances. Ben might notice that the signer's hand motions have a certain correspondence to the speaker's words—when the speaker pauses, the hand motions cease soon thereafter, and when the speaker resumes, the hand motions begin again. The signer could be responding to the speaker's words in the way that a dancer responds to music, but this would rightly strike Ben as a goal that would be of dubious value in the circumstances. Ben might hit upon the idea that if the hand motions are used as symbols, they might be a good way of expressing the speaker's words. Why would this be of value? It would not benefit those who can already clearly hear the speaker's words, but it could help the hearing-impaired members of the audience. Ben tentatively concludes that this is the goal of the behavior. Further investigation could then serve to confirm this hypothesis.

I have belabored this rather obvious example in order to highlight a number of points about how teleological interpretation works. First, while we do ascertain what the behavior would be good for, we do not assume that its goal is the one state of affairs that the behavior is best suited to achieve. In the case of the person signing, the behavior would be an effective means for bringing about any number of states of affairs, and it is not at all clear that there is *one* state of affairs for which the behavior is most appropriate. And the point is quite general: given any piece of behavior, we can postulate any number of outcome states for which the behavior is well suited. Items of behavior do not typically have any *one* utility function. Many possible goals are ruled out (or never even brought into consideration) if they have no obvious value in the circumstances. So we might try revising (D_1) by saying that if a behavior is directed to a goal, then the behavior must be *optimal* for achieving that goal, where this leaves open the possibility that a given behavior could be optimal for achieving any number of goals. We would then rely on (D_2) to exclude those candidate goals that have no intelligible value.

However, we will need to revise (D_1) and (D_2) even further, for in fact we do not assume that a piece of behavior must be optimal for achieving its goal; indeed, we do not necessarily assume that the behavior is even effective at all. The person making the hand motions might be an incompetent signer, and hence is not communicating anything to anyone. Or consider a different example: a car owner (okay, it was me) places a new car battery into the car and then attaches the red cable to the negative terminal and the black cable to the positive terminal. This behavior would be well suited to frying the cable wires, but that is not the goal towards which it was directed. The car owner was attempting to replace the car battery and get the car in working order again; but his behavior was in fact optimally suited to damaging the car rather than restoring it to operation. The lesson is this: when ascertaining the purpose of a behavior, we will allow for various failings on the part of the agent, especially mistaken beliefs and failures of execution.

So if we are to explain the agent's ϕing by saying that it was directed at ψing, we need not claim that ϕing would be optimal for ψing; however, ϕing still must be *appropriate* for the goal of ψing. Behavior can be appropriate, even if it is not effective, if it is at least a reasonable sort of thing to try given the agent's situation. Given that the car owner thought that the terminals on the new battery would have the same relative position as the terminals on the old battery, his actual hand motions in attaching the cables were appropriate for the goal of restoring the car to working order. His mistake is at least comprehensible. And the point here is general. We improve the intelligibility of a teleological explanation to the extent that the behavior is appropriate to achieving the hypothesized goal state, modulo the agent's epistemic circumstances and intentional states.

We can summarize this as follows. In trying to find a teleological explanation according to which an agent ϕ'd in order to ψ, we do the following:

(I_1)   Find a ψ such that ϕing is optimally appropriate for ψing, given a viable theory of the agent's intentional states and circumstances.

In the limit case, where ϕing is not even the right sort of thing to try, then the purported explanation loses sense altogether. If an ordinary car owner were to bludgeon the engine of her car repeatedly with a sledgehammer, then, in the absence of an incredibly compelling story, it would simply make no sense to suggest that she was doing this in order to restore the car to working order. Similarly, in the sign language example above, Ben never considers the possibility that the agent is making the hand motions in order to fly to the moon. In the course of teleological interpretation, we restrict our attention to outcome states for which the behavior would be a reasonable or comprehensible means.

In one sense, (I_1) is less restrictive than the Dawkins-inspired (D_1), for the goal need not be that which the behavior is best suited to accomplish. If the agent falsely believes that ϕing will be very appropriate for ψing, then the requirements of (I_1) could be met even if ϕing fails miserably at ψing. On the other hand, (I_1) is intended to include an idea that may be stronger than Dawkins's corresponding formulation: there should not be another action that would have been obviously more appropriate for ψing. In most circumstances we will want to go beyond finding a goal for which the behavior is minimally appropriate. For example, suppose a carpenter attaches a piece of nosing to a cabinet top; she uses glue and very small nails which she taps in below the surface of the wood and covers with tiny bits of wood fill. This complex behavior is effective at attaching the nosing to the cabinet, but this behavior is not optimally appropriate if the goal were *simply* to attach the nosing. If that were the goal, we would want to know why the carpenter did not take the easier and equally effective course of simply driving a few reasonably large nails in. Given the availability of a much simpler way of attaching the nosing, the carpenter's complex and painstaking behavior would not be highly appropriate for that goal. Instead, we would conclude that the carpenter was directing her behavior at some goal beyond that of attaching the nosing—the behavior was also directed at the goal of making the final result aesthetically pleasing. Since most people would think that visible nails in a finished piece of furniture are ugly, the carpenter's added effort is highly appropriate to the more complex goal of attaching the nosing in an aesthetically pleasing fashion. Put in general terms, even if ψing is the state of affairs that is best accomplished by ϕing, ϕing would not be optimally appropriate if there were some other action that would be obviously more effective at ψing (given a viable theory of the agent's intentional states and circumstances).

As was the case with (D_1), (I_1) by itself would seriously underdetermine teleological explanation; as we saw in the case of Ben and the person communicating in American Sign Language, there are any number of conceivable goals for which the signer's hand motions would be quite appropriate. However, Ben will rightly fail to consider possible goals that would be of no intelligible value. Accordingly, we will need an analogue to (D_2), one which also makes it explicit that we are operating within the context of an overall theory of the agent. Specifically, when trying to find a teleological explanation according to which an agent ϕ'd in order to ψ,

(I_2) Find a ψ such that ψing is the most valuable state of affairs toward which ϕing could be directed, given a viable theory of the agent's intentional states and circumstances.

Thus in explaining behavior, we do the best we can in jointly satisfying instructions (I_1) and (I_2). When Ben saw the person translating the commencement speech into American Sign Language, he tried to determine what the arm motions might accomplish that would also be of intelligible value. We adopt the same approach in utterly routine cases as well; if I see a student raise her hand in my class, I understand that this behavior is likely to be directed at indicating that she has something she wishes to say. Given the circumstances, including accepted conventions, raising her hand would be a highly appropriate means of achieving that end, and doing so is likely the most valuable goal she could achieve by that behavior under the circumstances. Of course, there is room for error. If she had nothing that she wished to say, and her head itched, then scratching her head would perhaps have been the most valuable thing that could be accomplished by moving her hand at that time. Further inquiry presumably settles the issue.

There are times, of course, when no explanation seems to be in accord with the instructions. If I see a student suddenly collapse into a motionless heap while walking out of class, no teleological explanation leaps to mind. Such behavior would be a good way of inciting a certain amount of attention and inquiry from bystanders, but the sort of attention received would be valuable only given a rather odd set of intentional states. Attributing these states to the agent might be the best interpretation, but, without specific evidence in favor of such a theory, it does not seem likely. In a case like this, we might well conclude that there is no ψ such that, given a viable account of the agent's intentional states and circumstances, (1) the observed behavior is appropriate for ψing, and (2) ψing would have intelligible value. That is to say, there is no ψ that would allow us to satisfy both (I_1) and (I_2) in anything beyond a degenerate way. In such cases we would conclude, at least provisionally, that the behavior was involuntary and not goal-directed at all.

Application to the Mele Cases

Let us return now to Norm, who was fetching his hat when the Martians took control of his body, all the while making it seem to Norm that he was still in control. I first want to make some general comments about the case, and then look at it in relation to the account just given of the epistemology of teleological explanation.

First, given the small amount of information we have about the case, it is not completely *obvious* that Norm's behavior fails to be an action. Suppose that instead of fetching his hat, Norm was doing something of grave moral concern; suppose he was murdering his philosophy professor. At the key moment when Norm is picking up the gun and about to shoot it, the Martians take over his body and make it carry out the dirty deed. However, they make it seem to Norm as if he is acting, and if Norm had changed his mind and decided to put the gun down, the Martians would have immediately relinquished control, and Norm would not have committed the murder. Now, at his murder trial, it comes out that the Martians controlled Norm's body at the time of the shooting. Does this completely absolve Norm of responsibility for shooting his professor? Should the district attorney only charge Norm with having a plan to commit murder, and drop the actual murder charge? It is not obvious to me how to answer these questions. Accordingly, even in the routine case of going up the ladder, I take it not to be obvious that Norm failed to act.

What we say about such examples might depend on further details about the supposedly controlling agent. What if it were God, instead of Martians? And suppose God never relinquished control, but always moved our bodies exactly in accord with our intentions and plans? This would look like a variety of occasionalism, and I lose any strong intuition that we would fail to be agents of our behavior.

I am willing to grant Mele that Norm's behavior is not an action, but I think that these observations shed light on the oddity of the example. (And I do not mean the oddity of M-rays, and of interveners taking control of our bodies; for better or worse, we philosophers are used to that sort of oddness.) What is odd about the case is the motivation of the Martians. They periodically take control of Norm's body, but only to make him do exactly what he planned to do anyway. Why? What's in it for the Martians? One senses that the Martians are giving a benign demonstration of a powerful technology that could easily be put to much more nefarious use. And in this implicit feature of the example lies the reason we are inclined to think Norm's behavior was not an action. Mele stipulates that the Martians are going to make Norm's body do exactly what Norm planned to do anyway. If this were an ironclad promise from the Martians, or, better yet, something that followed necessarily from their good nature, then we would be back at something very like occasionalism, and I have little problem saying that Norm *is* still acting, despite the fact that the causal chain involved is an unusual one. If he commits a murder under these circumstances, we will definitely not let him off.

However, since Mele uses Martians rather than God, he thereby suggests that their plan—to relinquish control if Norm changes his mind—is a contingent one. The Martians have chosen not to disrupt Norm's plans on this occasion, but there are no guarantees that they will always use their powerful technology in such a benign manner. If the desires and intentions of the Martians had been different, then Norm's body would have moved very differently. For example, if the Martians had decided to make Norm's body jump off of the ladder's top rung, then that is what would have happened. How Norm's body moves at the time is completely at the whim of the Martians. For a wide range of counterfactual situations, namely those involving different desires on the part of the Martians, Norm's behavior will be far from appropriate for achieving his goals.

In terms of my account of the epistemology of teleology, this means that, at the moment in question, Norm fails to satisfy the condition imposed by (R_1). His behavior is ultimately appropriate to the goals and values of the Martians, rather than his own. As it happens, Norm's body does move in accord with his goals, but this is only because of the happy fact that the Martians made that decision. The Martians also happen to have made the decision that if Norm's plans change, they will stop the M-rays, and Norm will be back to normal. But again, so long as these are just decisions that the Martians happen to have made (for no especially compelling reason), then there are plenty of very nearby counterfactual circumstances in which Norm's behavior is not appropriate to achieving his goals. Since Norm fails, at that time, to satisfy the condition imposed by (R_1), his behavior does not count as goal-directed behavior on my account of the epistemology of teleology. And thus my account is in accord with our intuitions about the case.

One might reply by trying to seal off those counterfactual possibilities; for example, one might stipulate that it is in the Martians' *nature* that they only want to see Norm's plans fulfilled. In that case, (R_1) is still true of Norm, and it looks as if I have to say that his behavior is goal-directed. However, with this revision to the example, it seems to me that this is the right thing to say, for I lose the intuition that Norm's behavior was a nonaction. If the Martians are God-like in their intentions and effectiveness, then the situation looks again like a temporary occasionalism, and I would suggest that Norm's agency is intuitively still intact. So with either version of the example, teleological realism gives an intuitively acceptable diagnosis of the case of Norm and the Martians.

Mele's objection had been that the teleological realist's account was too liberal—the criteria given would count Norm as genuinely acting when our intuitive judgment is that he was not acting. I have argued that this is mistaken, and that the teleological realist is able to accommodate our intuition that Norm is not acting. One might fear that I have gone too far in the other direction, and that my account is now too restrictive or chauvinistic, in that it will fail to count as goal-directed some behaviors that are, intuitively speaking, goal-directed. Consider a different person,[4] Sally, who is about to pull the trigger of a gun, thereby murdering her philosophy professor. Sally has an odd neurological disorder, such that when she attempts to make a finger-pulling motion of the required sort, it is very often the case that her finger becomes paralyzed, and instead of the finger pulling motion, her body goes through any number of other random motions. However, as things happen, she pulls the trigger successfully, and murders the professor. Intuitively, it seems reasonably clear that her behavior counts as a goal-directed action.

In Norm's case, I argued that, at t, Norm's motion is not that of an agent because in a range of nearby counterfactual situations, his behavior is not appropriate to his goals. Specifically, in all those situations in which the Martians simply change their mind about what to have Norm's body do, Norm's body will do something quite different. In Sally's case, let us suppose that whether her finger makes the intended motion, or instead becomes paralyzed, depends on some more or less random events in her nervous system. Had those events gone differently, her behavior would not have been appropriate to her goals. So the suggestion is that, like Norm, Sally fails to satisfy the condition imposed by (R_1), and thus teleological realism should not count her as a genuine agent at the time in question.

However, I think that the teleological realist can distinguish between the cases of Norm and Sally. The basic idea is this: in Norm's case, his behavior fails to be appropriate to his goals in a much wider array of nearby counterfactual situations than in Sally's. For example, if the Martians had decided to make Norm's body leap off the ladder, then that is what Norm's body would have done, regardless of Norm's intentions or desires. In other words, depending on the whim of the Martians, Norm's bodily motions might have no connection at all to his desires and intentions. In Sally's case, given that she decides to make a trigger-pulling motion with her finger, there are a number of nearby counterfactual situations in which her body does something else, for we have assumed that Sally has a strange neurological disorder that leads to random bodily motions much of the time when she starts to pull her finger. However, we are also assuming that her behavior is only subject to these flukes when it involves a finger-pulling. If Sally had decided not to shoot the gun, to put it down, to do a jumping jack, to scream, and so forth, then in all those circumstances her behavior presumably would have been appropriate to her goals. So, given the scenario as described, her behavior is generally very sensitive to her goals. So Sally, unlike Norm, does satisfy the condition imposed by (R_1) well enough to make her an agent at the time in question.

One could alter the Sally case such that her neurological disorder is much more general, and that she rarely does what she intends; but in that case, my intuitions about the case grow flimsy. I am not sure what to say about her agency in such a case, and I am not too troubled by the conclusion that she is not exhibiting genuine goal-directed behavior at any particular moment.

Conclusion

To sum up very briefly, I have defended teleological realism by doing several things. I have rejected Mele's demand for a reductive or metaphysical account of the nature of teleological explanation. At the same time, I have acknowledged that his attack does indicate the need for an appropriate epistemology of teleology—an account of how we make and justify teleological explanations. I have tried to provide the beginnings of such an account, and I have tried to show that the account is adequate to defuse Mele's argument.

Acknowledgments

Thanks to Al Mele, G. F. Schueler, and George Wilson for helpful commentary on earlier versions of this material.

Notes

1. Wilson (1989), Collins (1987), Schueler (2003), and Sehon (1994, 1997, 1998, and 2000), for example. There are other non-causalists, but most of them do not explicitly claim that action explanation is *teleological*.

2. See Wilson 1989 and Sehon 1997.

3. Dawkins in turn acknowledges that his discussion was highly influenced by the writings of Daniel Dennett.

4. This objection was raised by a member of the audience when I presented the material at the INPC conference on 4 May 2003.

References

Collins, A. 1987. *The Nature of Mental Things*. South Bend, Ind.: Notre Dame University Press.

Davidson, D. 1963. "Actions, Reasons, and Causes." Reprinted in Davidson 1980.

Davidson, D. 1980. *Essays on Actions and Events*. Oxford: Clarendon Press.

Dawkins, R. 1995. "God's Utility Function." *Scientific American* (November 1995): 80–85.

Dennett, D. 1987. *The Intentional Stance*. Cambridge, Mass.: MIT Press.

Mele, A. 2000. "Goal-Directed Action: Teleological Explanations, Causal Theories, and Deviance." *Philosophical Perspectives* 14: 279–300.

Schueler, G. 2003. *Reasons and Purposes: Human Rationality and the Teleological Explanation of Action*. Oxford: Oxford University Press.

Sehon, S. 1994. "Teleology and the Nature of Mental States." *American Philosophical Quarterly* 31: 63–72.

Sehon, S. 1997. "Deviant Causal Chains and the Irreducibility of Teleological Explanation." *Pacific Philosophical Quarterly* 78: 195–213.

Sehon, S. 1998. "Connectionism and the Causal Theory of Action Explanation." *Philosophical Psychology* 11: 511–531.

Sehon, S. 2000. "An Argument against the Causal Theory of Action Explanation." *Philosophy and Phenomenological Research* 60: 67–85.

Wilson, G. 1989. *The Intentionality of Human Action*. Stanford, Calif.: Stanford University Press.

9 Van Fraassen's Dutch Book Argument against Explanationism

Dorit Ganson

> Quiet, don't explain.
> What is there to gain?
> Skip that lipstick.
> Don't explain.
> —Billie Holiday

As I am reminded by my four-year-old daughter, who loves to ask strings of why-questions to the point where our explanatory resources give way, the desire for explanation, the need to make sense of the world in order to understand it and change it, is deeply human and, for most people (save a few constructive empiricists such as Bas van Fraassen), irresistible. Sadly, our desires often exceed our abilities to satisfy them, and we wind up fabricating explanatory stories far beyond the limits of reason alone. And even when we are faced with explanations that seem genuinely satisfying to us, it is far from obvious that there is something good and general to say about what epistemic attitude we *ought* to take to them. Against the backdrop of a growing skepticism about the notion that philosophers have special resources for understanding what the aims of human inquiry really are or should be as well as what we need to do or think, or not do or not think, in order to help us get there, or never get there, the prospects for acquiring specifically philosophical insight into whether or when to believe our best explanations do seem grim.

Despite worries about the legislative role of epistemology, commitments concerning the epistemic status of explanatoriness—its relevance to a theory's likelihood of truth and rational acceptability—are quite widespread in contemporary philosophy, often under the guise of an expressed attitude towards "inference to the best explanation" (IBE). Though there is little by way of positive defense of the legitimacy of such a form of inference, among those who believe in it, various substantive projects in epistemology and metaphysics rely on this variety of reasoning.[1]

Nowhere is controversy over the epistemic force of explanatoriness quite as lively and significant as in the debates over scientific realism; here, whether you accept or reject IBE (under various interpretations of what such stances really amount to) seems to determine which side of the conflict you fall on. Despite the plurality of approaches and aims in work done on behalf of scientific realism, one unifying theme is that rationality sometimes demands that we regard the best explanation of puzzling phenomena as more likely to be true than explanatorily inferior rivals—even those which are equally empirically adequate.[2] Antirealism, on the other hand, involves the view that, in so far as explanatoriness trades on features of theories that go beyond considerations of logical consistency and empirical adequacy, we ought to regard explanatoriness as epistemically irrelevant: explanatoriness is never a good reason to increase our confidence in a theory's truth. Such a virtue in a theory speaks only to its pragmatic advantages. So, for a realist, there will be episodes in scientific inquiry where the explanatory strength of a particular theory or hypothesis should affect our conception of its likelihood of truth; for an antirealist, it should not.

Since a fair amount of substantive philosophical work depends on accepting explanatoriness as a potentially epistemic virtue—a view I shall call "explanationism"—it would be nice to have a clearer sense of whether this view is at all defensible. Can we even begin to answer the most weighty and seemingly decisive arguments against it?

We shall focus here on the most devastating of the bunch—van Fraassen's clever Bayesian Peter argument, which appears in his second major antirealist tract, *Laws and Symmetry* (1989). Recounting the travails of hapless Peter, who is so foolish as to heed the advice of an evangelist for inference to the best explanation, van Fraassen tries to show that anyone who allows explanatoriness to enhance her degree of credence in accordance with a rule is susceptible to a Dutch book.[3] This sorry predicament indicates that accepting explanationism leads to an unacceptable incoherence in one's belief state.

In van Fraassen's parable, Peter has fallen under the influence of an explanationist preacher who urges him, as a general rule, to increase his epistemic confidence in hypotheses which emerge as best explanations. Peter is confronted with an alien die with a bias of any one of $X(1), X(2), \ldots, X(10)$, he knows not which; (a bias of $X(n)$ indicates that the probability of ace on any single proper toss is $n/10$). Given outcomes E, the die coming up aces for four consecutive tosses; and H, the die coming up ace on the fifth toss; his opinions about the likelihood of E, and of E and $-H$, are determined by taking an equally weighted average of the probability of these outcomes for each of the ten possible scenarios, bias $X(1)$, bias $X(2)$, and so on. A friend comes along, and they negotiate bets on $E\&-H$, $-E$, and E, which Peter regards as fair since their price is properly based on his probability assignments. In the course of the game, a string of four aces is tossed. Thinking that the best explanation of this occurrence is a hypothesis of high bias, and mindful of the preacher's urgings, Peter raises his current probability for the event "the fifth toss shows ace" turning out true from 0.87, the result obtained from a routine application of Bayes' Theorem, to 0.9. After further betting negotiations with his friend, which again are fair according to Peter's updated probability assignments, he winds up with a Dutch book.[4] Van Fraassen triumphantly concludes: "What is the moral of this story? Certainly, in part that we shouldn't listen to anyone who preaches a probabilistic version of Inference to the Best Explanation, whatever the details. Any such rule, once adopted as a rule, makes us incoherent" (van Fraassen 1989, p. 169).

There are a number of possible responses to van Fraassen's argument, several of which are suggested, if not always fully developed, in the fairly extensive literature which aims to confront his criticisms of inference to the best explanation and scientific realism. One tends to find in this literature an underestimation of the multiplicity of defensive options, as well as a failure to acknowledge the deeper problems inherent in the project of trying reconcile explanationism with Bayesian accounts of confirmation—problems which remain even after the shortcomings of van Fraassen's way of demonstrating the diachronic incoherence of explanationism have been exposed. First, however, we shall examine the wide array of potential solutions to the Bayesian Peter objection.

Peter's Carelessness

Douven (1999), Kvanvig (1994), and Ganson (2001) all explore some version of the criticism that Peter does not seem to look before he leaps: it is far from clear that a more conscientious Peter—one who is more alert to what his rules for belief revision actually are—would accept his friend's initial bets as fair. Van Fraassen nonchalantly states at the beginning of the tale that, before any evidence comes in, Peter will calculate his personal probability for $E\&\text{-}H$, the object of bet 1, by taking the average of $p(E\&\text{-}H/\text{bias } X(1)), \ldots, p(E\&\text{-}H/\text{bias } X(10))$. This result follows from a simple application of the theorem of total probability since the mutually exclusive and jointly exhaustive hypotheses of bias are initially equiprobable, each having probability $1/10$: using $p_n(Y)$ as shorthand for $p(Y/\text{bias } X(n))$,

$$p(E\&\text{-}H) = p_1(E\&\text{-}H)p(\text{bias } (X1)) + \cdots + p_{10}(E\&\text{-}H)p(\text{bias } (X10))$$

$$= \frac{\Sigma(i/10)^4(10 - i/10)}{10} = .032505$$

Since $p(\text{-}H/E) = p(E\&\text{-}H)/p(E) = .032505/.25333 = 0.13$, Peter has already essentially committed himself to a value for this conditional probability—a value at odds with the assignment he offers later on in the story, $p(\text{-}H/E) = 0.1$. For Peter, once E happens, the hypothesis of high bias gets "bonus points" on account of its explanatory success, and this increase in credence in turn affects his personal probability for the fifth toss being, or not being, an ace.

Van Fraassen's calculation of $p(E\&\text{-}H)$ on Peter's behalf, one could suggest, takes no accounting of the fact that Peter is the sort of explanationist whose probability values for fifth-toss events like H or $\text{-}H$ will be affected by whether E happens. As such, the calculation is not really true to the rules which govern Peter's degree of belief assignments. Given the necessary interdependence between $p(E\&\text{-}H)$ and $p(\text{-}H/E)$, any determination of $p(E\&\text{-}H)$ will somehow have to incorporate Peter's explanationism as well, a requirement which is violated by van Fraassen's method, the averaging of values for $p_n(E)p_n(\text{-}H/E)$ given equally weighed biases. Who knows exactly what peculiar methods or rules Peter *would* want to use, to set a value for $p(E\&\text{-}H)$? But we do know, from what happens toward the end of the tale, that $p(\text{-}H/E) = 0.1$. Consequently, supposing Peter would still set $p(E) = 0.25333$, we could picture him assigning $p(E\&\text{-}H) = p(E)p(\text{-}H/E) = (.25333)(.1) = 0.025333$; and Peter's fair price for bet 1, which pays $10,000 if $E\&\text{-}H$, would then be $253.30. If we use this value, and follow along with the rest of Peter's adventures, he would end up gaining three cents.[5] Three cents is a fairly insubstantial amount, but it is enough to save him from the perils of his friend's Dutch book.

In the discussion before the Bayesian Peter story is presented, van Fraassen creates the misleading impression that his argument will show that any "ampliative" rule of inference to the best explanation leads to incoherence: allowing explanatoriness, and not just predictive capacity, to factor in as a feature relevant to revising our degree of belief as evidence comes along, will in general be irrational. The Peter of the original parable is hardly an adequate representative of this sort of broad explanationist view. Instead, according to the response we have been exploring, he turns out to be a particularly unlikely sort of philosophical victim whose real problem is not his belief in the relevance of explanatoriness to likelihood of truth; but rather his tendency not to think very carefully ahead of time of what his rules for degree of belief revision actually are. If the Peter in van Fraassen's version of the story had been attentive to his own rules for updating his probability function in light of evidence, his explanationism would not have been ignored in his determination of $p(E\&\text{-}H)$, and he would never have been duped in the first place.

Van Fraassen almost seems to anticipate this kind of response in a brief discussion of the preacher's doctrine which precedes the main argument. Here, the preacher protests:

> Your problem was that you did not give up enough of your pagan ways. This probability of .87 had already become quite irrelevant to any question of what would happen after an initial run of four aces. If you had followed the rule properly, you would not only have foreseen that your new probability afterward would become 0.9. You would also now have had as conditional probabilities, those probabilities that you would get to have, after seeing such an initial run of aces. Thus the leavening effect of explanatory power in our lives, although activated properly only after seeing explanatory success, reaches back from the future into the present as it were, and revises our present conditional opinions. (van Fraassen 1989, p. 167)

Peter's friend apparently dodges these protestations by, in van Fraassen's words, being "careful not to propose any conditional bets" as he generates a Dutch book against Peter. But these maneuvers only superficially avoid such bets, since the combination of bets 1 and 2 is equivalent to a conditional bet on $\text{-}H$ given E which costs \$1300. Van Fraassen himself admits as much, in a different context, when he tries to show that violating the principle of reflection leads to incoherence. Of a bet 1 which pays y if $\text{-}H\&E$, and a bet 2 which pays yx if $\text{-}E$; where $x = p(\text{-}H\&E)/p(\text{-}E)$, as in the Bayesian Peter example[6] (the only difference being that in the reflection argument $y = 1$, so that the cost of bet 2 is simply x); he says: "It helps to observe that I and II together form in effect a conditional bet on $-H$ on the supposition that E, which bears the cost x and has prize 1, with the guarantee of your money back should the supposition turn out to be false" (van Fraassen 1984, p. 240).[7]

An Implausible Explanationist Rule

We should hardly expect that a real explanationist would, or would have to be, as foolhardy as Peter. Ignoring your own rules for probability function revision at the beginning of betting, even though they are relevant to assessing subjective probability values for particular events which form the object of bets, and then letting these rules influence your probability assignments and choice of further betting arrangements later on (in a predictable way), clearly creates opportunities for clever bookies. What's more, even if Peter had been more attentive to his updating rules from the very start, in the manner suggested above, the results are far from satisfying. Peter's explanationist principle seems to commit him to a somewhat perverse value for $P(-H\&E)$, one wholly at odds with a straightforward, well-justified method for determining prior probability assignments. There is nothing inherently incoherent about setting priors in an unreasonable or wacky way, though of course assignments which satisfy the minimal formal requirements of probabilistic coherence can still be criticized on other grounds. Could a sensible explanationist ever be drawn to Peter's rule?

The rule in question is highly general: the explanatoriness of a hypothesis should make you increase your degree of credence, even beyond what would be recommended by what could be called a "neutral" application of the probability calculus. When you update your probability function in an alien die case, for instance, where the competing hypotheses *high bias, low bias* start out with the same prior probability, you should not simply take into account how each hypothesis weighs the evidence (i.e., how probable the evidence is under the assumption that the hypothesis is true); you should add on bonus points once a hypothesis becomes explanatory. This increase in credence will in turn lead to additional increases or decreases in your probability assignments for events (such as, in the case at hand, *the fifth toss shows ace*) which are statistically affected by whether or not the hypothesis is true.

The credence boost in this instance seems highly unmotivated. When we actually make a judgment about which hypothesis, *high bias* or *low bias*, is the best explanation in light of the evidence, there is no information relevant to our decision beyond how each hypothesis weighs the evidence. All that grounds the explanatory superiority of the *high bias* is its greater predictive success; so we would hardly expect to be able to raise our credence over and above what is suggested by a routine, neutral application of Bayes' Theorem.

The most reasonable explanationists will recognize that there are many cases, especially in normal science, where hypotheses—all with the same prior probabilities—are essentially distinguishable by the different weights which they accord to various sorts of outcomes. In such cases, the best explanation will simply be the hypothesis which achieves the greatest predictive success. Special bonus points for being the best explanation will not be added (though the best explanation will still be taken to be more likely to be true than the alternatives, on normal Bayesian grounds). The reasonable explanationist, then, would not agree that we should follow Peter's peculiar rule.

This is not to say that the explanationist would never recommend a boost in credence beyond what would be suggested if we simply took predictive success into account. Explanatory superiority is a property sometimes wholly grounded in greater predictive success, and sometimes not. When it is not (and there are different views about what more it could consist of), we might find ourselves with additional information which is relevant to our probability assignments. That the explanationist would feel that such a situation can arise is particularly clear when we look at the sorts of examples which most notoriously divide realists and antirealists—cases where we are faced with incompatible, but equally empirically adequate theories with different degrees of explanatoriness. The realist/explanationist—against the antirealist/anti-explanationist— will insist that there are sometimes cases in which we are rationally constrained to regard the best explanation as more likely to be true than the available alternatives, even when these rivals are equally empirically successful.

A somewhat similar response to the Bayesian Peter objection is suggested in Ben-Menahem 1990. Ben-Menahem, like Day and Kincaid (1994) and Douven (1999), stresses the importance of acknowledging the contextual character of explanatoriness. In some contexts, explanatory superiority is judged on the basis of what she calls "structural" considerations—by which she appears to mean highly general, formal features of theories, such as simplicity. In other (notably nonphilosophical) contexts, judgments of explanatory superiority are made on the basis of appeal to "broad empirical considerations," that is, general facts or claims which have been sanctioned by empirical research. The best explanation is the hypothesis judged to be most credible in light of our background empirical knowledge. Only in the latter contexts is explanatoriness linked to likelihood of truth; and so only in these contexts does inference to the best explanation genuinely and legitimately enter into our deliberations.

The problem with van Fraassen's use of the Bayesian Peter story to illustrate the flaws of inference to the best explanation, according to Ben-Menahem, is that the context in question is one where broad empirical considerations play no role in the determination of the best explanation: which hypothesis is the best explanation, in the end, is simply a matter of which hypothesis accords the highest probability to the data. Purely formal criteria are involved in determining the best explanation, so adding bonus points beyond what purely formal probabilistic considerations dictate is unwarranted. Inference to the best explanation does not really enter into the picture:

[W]hen the only criterion for evaluating the explanatory power of a hypothesis is the degree of probability conferred by that hypothesis on the data, one cannot use this evaluation of explanatory power to redistribute the probabilities ... I welcome van Fraassen's argument for it adds further weight to a point I have stressed several times above: the rationality of IBE depends on the standards we use to assess explanatory power. Where there are not explanatory merits except the structural ones, there is no room for the application of IBE. (Ben-Menahem 1990, p. 330)[8]

Though Ben-Menahem is right to insist that the context of the Bayesian Peter argument is one where bonus points are not warranted, her justification for this claim is somewhat problematic. Ben-Menahem suggests that inference to the best explanation is not really involved when determining explanatory superiority is just a matter of judging which hypothesis accords the highest probability to the data. This move seems ill-advised. As we shall see in the next section, some explanationist philosophers, such as Harman, think that it is precisely in the assignment of likelihood (conditional probability, $p(e/Hi)$) and prior probability ($p(Hi)$) that considerations of explanatoriness find their expression. The best explanation, in any context, will be the hypothesis which wins out over others with respect to the dual consideration of its initial plausibility, and the weight it accords to the evidence which unfolds (in accordance with Bayes' Theorem). Even if it should turn out that Harman's suggestion cannot accommodate all cases where explanatoriness bears on one's degree of belief, we can grant that many cases will nicely fit his proposal: for example, after I cough up bloody sputum, the best explanation for my continuing cold symptoms is that I have a secondary bacterial infection, instead of simply a viral infection, since bloody sputum is more likely given the former hypothesis than given the latter hypothesis. I see no reason to deny that this case involves inference to the best explanation, even though which explanation wins out is simply a matter of determining which hypothesis accords the highest probability to the data at hand.

Ben-Menahem further distinguishes the Bayesian Peter case from contexts where inference to the best explanation is genuinely and legitimately involved by noting that, in the Peter case, no background empirical considerations or generalizations are invoked in deciding which hypothesis is most credible. She seems to suggest that because only purely formal, a priori considerations play a role in the relevant probability assignments, inference to the best explanation does not or should not really enter into Peter's deliberations. But even this conclusion is subject to some doubt. Peter does implicitly rely on substantial background empirical commitment: for example, he presupposes that there are no environmental factors (magnetic fields, hidden wires, and such) which might distort the frequency of tossing an ace, given a particular bias. This commitment has a bearing on his likelihood assignments, and hence on his judgment of which hypothesis accords the highest probability to the data.

Put It in the Priors

Day and Kincaid (1994), Harman (1999), and Okasha (2000) also develop the criticism that van Fraassen presupposes an idiosyncratic and uncharitable construal of inference to the best explanation. These authors all conclude that van Fraassen misidentifies the way attentiveness to explanatory factors could be reasonably thought to enter into our deliberations. Rather than warranting a boost in credence after the evidence comes in, such factors, first of all, may be crucial in our initial efforts to establish which candidate hypothesis should be taken seriously (Okasha 2000; Day and Kincaid 1994). The background empirical assumptions or specific causal commitments which inform our judgments of explanatory strength help us to determine which hypotheses are worth considering, as well as to decide when this set of alternatives is too limited, and what new options are available in light of the limitations of previous theories.

Second, we appeal to explanatory considerations to help us assign prior probabilities and likelihoods. Though the authors who pursue this line of response have somewhat different views on what these considerations involve (context-specific background knowledge of causal processes, for Day and Kincaid; constraints of conservatism, simplicity, and degree of data accommodation for Harman), all agree that explanatory considerations help us determine the initial degree of plausibility of the available options, as well the likelihood of certain data and experimental outcomes given the various alternatives. Any factor that would enter into the evaluation of hypothesis 1 as a better explanation than hypothesis 2 would be reflected in higher prior probabilities and/or likelihoods.

This effort to reconcile explanationism with Bayesian demands seems to work well enough for a wide range of cases, but as we shall see after we look at one final response to van Fraassen's argument, another Bayesian puzzle will expose its limitations.

The Illegitimacy of Diachronic Dutch Book Arguments

Even some hard core Bayesians, such as Howson and Urbach, believe that only synchronic Dutch books—Dutch books built up from simultaneous degrees of belief ascriptions, and bets the agent simultaneously regards as individually fair—highlight genuine failures of rationality. "Coherence," according to this view, is a term which has legitimate application only when used to describe belief states at particular points in time, as opposed to sets of belief states over stretches of time. It is no more incoherent to make degree-of-belief assignments at different times which correspond to bets which ultimately cannot be regarded as simultaneously fair, than it is inconsistent to believe p at one point and $-p$ later. The probability calculus, then, like the laws of logic, places rationality or coherence constraints on the structure of our belief state at a given moment; both formal systems have much less to say on how our belief state at one time should relate to our belief state at a later time, to preserve rationality.

On the assumption that this view is correct (an assumption I defend in Ganson 2001), we have yet another reason for dismissing van Fraassen's Bayesian Peter objection, which takes the form of a diachronic Dutch Book argument.[9] Unfortunately for the explanationist, however, we do not really need to rely on the charge of diachronic incoherence to show that trouble arises when explanationists try to respect Bayesian principles.

Another Bayesian Puzzle

We do not need a complicated and somewhat misleading story about the follies of Bayesian Peter to see that it might be difficult to conform to the probability calculus, as evidence comes along, once we allow explanatory power to influence our judgments about likelihoods or likelihood comparisons. Examining Bayes' Theorem,

$$p'(Hi) = p(Hi/e) = \frac{p(e/Hi)\,p(Hi)}{p(e/H1)\,p(H1) + p(e/H2)\,p(H2)\cdots + p(e/Hn)\,p(Hn)}$$

we see that we can compare the $p(Hi/e)$'s just by looking at the $p(e/Hi)\,p(Hi)$'s, since the denominator is the same for all the $p(Hi/e)$'s. Imagine a situation where:

1. $H1$ and $H2$ are both accorded the same initial probability; say that prior to exposure to startling evidence, both are considered equally likely.

2. e is considered equally likely on $H1$ and $H2$: $p(e/H1) = p(e/H2)$; suppose e is a deductive consequence of both hypotheses, given certain background assumptions.

3. We affirm that $H1$ is a better explanation for e, than is $H2$.

We might be tempted to say $p(H1/e) > p(H2/e)$ because of $H1$'s capacity to explain e in a more satisfactory way, but a quick glance back at Bayes' Theorem shows us that we cannot consistently do so.

We have noted that the realist/explanationist accepts that there are cases where greater explanatoriness warrants a boost in credence above and beyond what we would assign if we took only predictive success or empirical adequacy into account: we are sometimes rationally constrained to regard the best explanation as more likely to be true than equally empirically adequate rivals. We are rationally constrained, for example, to think that the best explanation for the phenomenon of Brownian motion (e)—namely, the molecular hypothesis ($H1$)—is more likely to be true than the hypothesis that matter is continuous ($H2$), even if this radical hypothesis could in principle be incorporated into a non-discrete theory of matter which is empirically equivalent to molecular theory. In other words, once we witness and accept e ($p'(e) = 1$), our revised probability function p' must assign a higher value to $H1$ than $H2$,

$$p'(H1) = p(H1/e) > p'(H2) = p(H2/e),$$

even though $p(e/H1) = p(e/H2)$. If we accept Bayes' Theorem, how is this possible?

We have already explored one solution which will usually work quite well, and is certainly appropriate in the Brownian motion case: accommodate for the differences in value between $p(H1/e)$ and $p(H2/e)$, despite the equality of $p(e/H1)$ and $p(e/H2)$, by making $p(H1)$ higher than $p(H2)$. For example, the prior probabilities $p(H1)$ and $p(H2)$ may reflect $H1$ and $H2$'s differing degrees of plausibility in light of constraints of conservatism, simplicity, and so on, as Harman would suggest, or differing degrees of fit to background empirical commitments and causal principles, as Okasha, and Day and Kincaid would propose (again, independent of considerations of fit with data).[10] The factors which make $H1$ a better explanation than $H2$ are already taken into account in $H1$ and $H2$'s prior probability assignments.

The fact that $p(H1/e) > p(H2/e)$ even though $p(e/H1) = p(e/H2)$ cannot, however, always be grounded in differences in prior probability assignments to $H1$ and $H2$, as Harman et al. would hope. We might come across a situation wherein which hypothesis is ultimately the most plausible in light of the relevant background constraints and commitments will depend on what sort of empirical data comes along. Say that two hypothesis $H1$ and $H2$ are, before the evidence comes in, equally plausible in light of background theory, or equally recommended by our causal principles: $p(H1) = p(H2)$. Two possible, incompatible events are $e1$ and $e2$, and $p(e1/H1) = p(e1/H2)$, $p(e2/H1) = p(e2/H2)$; but $H1$ will emerge as the best explanation if $e1$ happens, and $H2$ will count as the best explanation if $e2$ happens. (Perhaps $H1$ explains $e1$ better than $H2$ does, and $H2$ explains $e2$ better than $H1$ because $H1$ and $H2$ focus on different types of phenomena; or perhaps $H1$ will fit better with background theory/causal principles than $H2$ if $e1$ happens, and $H2$ will fit better with background theory/causal principles

than *H*1 if *e*2 happens.) We do not know what evidence we will end up fac-
ing, so which hypothesis is most explanatory cannot be settled ahead of
time and reflected in our prior probability assignments $p(H1)$ and $p(H2)$.
Nonetheless, since greater explanatoriness should have a positive impact
on our degree of credence, we want to say that $p'(H1) > p'(H2)$ if *e*1 happens, or $p'(H2) > p'(H1)$ if *e*2 happens; but how can we square this probability assignment with Bayes' Theorem, given that all the relevant prior
probabilities and likelihoods are the same? Must we abandon our explanationist inclinations in this example, and concede that $p'(H1) = p'(H2)$?

For explanationists, whether *H*1 or *H*2 turns out to be explanatorily superior is as relevant to our degree of belief revisions as whether *e*1 or *e*2 happens. It would be quite natural for explanationists, then, to acknowledge
that the information about which hypotheses possess the highest degree
of explanatoriness is as significant a constraint on our evolving probability
function as is the raw evidence itself. We will need to take this new constraint into account if we are to have any hope of successfully applying
Bayes' Theorem to the case at hand.

Just as we specify a range of significant outcomes for the raw evidence, *e*1
and *e*2, we specify a range of outcomes for the new constraint "information
about explanatory superiority":

*d*1 = *H*1 is the best explanation—it fits best with the background theory/
causal principles once the evidence comes in.

*d*2 = *H*2 is the best explanation—it fits best with the background theory/
causal principles once the evidence comes in.

We will then conditionalize on one of *e*1&*d*1, *e*1&*d*2, *e*2&*d*1, and *e*2&*d*2
(depending on what happens) when we update our probability function
from *p* to *p*'. So, for example, if *e*1&*d*1 turns out to be true, $p'(e1\&d1) = 1$,
$p'(H1) = p(H1/e1\&d1)$, and $p'(H2) = p(H2/e1\&d1)$. We can use Bayes'
Theorem to calculate these latter two values:

$$p'(H1) = p(H1/e1\&d1) = \frac{p(e1\&d1/H1)p(H1)}{p(e1\&d1)}$$

$$p'(H2) = p(H2/e1\&d1) = \frac{p(e1\&d1/H2)p(H2)}{p(e1\&d1)}$$

Now we see that there is no longer a difficulty with maintaining explanationist inclinations and respecting Bayes' Theorem for the problematic

sort of case: $p'(H1) > p'(H2)$, since $p(H1) = p(H2)$, and $p(e1\&d1/H1) > p(e1\&d1/H2)$. (Explanationists will think that it is more likely that $e1$ happens and $H1$ turns out to be the best explanation if $H1$ is in fact true, than if $H2$ is in fact true.)

Neither van Fraassen's argument nor more general probabilistic considerations show that commitment to explanationism results in probabilistic incoherence. Instead, the most significant moral to be drawn from reflections on Peter's foibles and attendant worries about the compatibility of explanationism and Bayesianism is that explanationists need to fill in the details of their position by specifying when explanatoriness allows us to boost our degree of belief, and how this boost should be incorporated into our changing belief state.

Acknowledgments

Many thanks to Brad Armendt, Nancy Cartwright, and especially Martin Thomson-Jones for helpful comments and discussion; as well as to our INPC hosts, Michael O'Rourke and Joseph Keim Campbell, for putting together such a pleasant and engaging conference.

Notes

1. IBE has been thought to be potentially helpful in helping us combat Cartesian skepticism: our ordinary, commonsense conception of the world is rational and justified—despite the existence of radical alternatives which are equally compatible with our evidence—because the commonsense conception offers a better explanation for the play and patterns of our sensory appearances. Bertrand Russell, Jonathan Vogel, Paul Moser, Alan Goldman, Frank Jackson, J. L. Mackie, and James Cornman all pursue some version of this approach. Gilbert Harman designates IBE as the most fundamental form of inductive inference and, along similar lines, Laurence BonJour depicts explanatory connections between beliefs as a major contributor to a belief system's coherence, and hence as a central factor in his accounts of justification. He also appeals to inference to the best explanation in his early efforts to defend the idea that coherence in the sense he describes is relevant to a belief system's likelihood of truth. Abductive arguments for realism, whereby the approximate truth of our scientific theories is offered as the best explanation for their empirical success, have been advocated with varying degrees of refinement by J. J. C. Smart, Hilary Putnam, Richard Boyd, and, most recently, Philip Kitcher. In his scathing critique of contemporary analytic metaphysics, Bas van Fraassen portrays IBE as a harmful enabler of this problematic philosophical enterprise, citing David Lewis's defense of possible

worlds and David Armstrong's defense of universals as examples. IBE has played a longstanding role in the philosophy of religion on account of its operation in both classic and newfangled arguments from design ("intelligent design theory," the latest offering from members of the creationist camp).

2. Acceptance of IBE might seem essential to scientific realism, on account of the role abductive arguments have often played in the defense of scientific realism; but Miller (1987) and Ganson (2001) offer approaches to defending realism which do not depend on such arguments.

3. Developing a Dutch book is a way of showing how certain epistemic decisions are irrational or incoherent—in violation of the axioms of probability. An implicit assumption in such an approach is that any time a bookie could use an awareness of your principles for probability assignment to sell you a series of individually fair bets which would in combination represent a sure loss for you, regardless of outcomes, your assignments (and the principles dictating such assignments) are irrational. Given that a fair price for a bet on A which pays W if you win (0 if you don't) is $p(A)W$, a bookie can determine which bets you would consider fair on the basis of your degrees of belief and rules for degree of belief revision. If he can then offer you a series of individually fair bets which would lead to a certain loss, your belief state as a whole must contain a structural inconsistency.

4. Here is a more thorough version of the Bayesian Peter story: Peter is confronted with an alien die with a bias of any one of $X(1), X(2), \ldots, X(10)$, he knows not which; (again, a bias of $X(n)$ indicates that the probability of ace on any single proper toss is $n/10$.) A friend comes along, and proposes some bets. Given proposition E, the first four tosses of the alien die show ace; and proposition H, the fifth toss shows ace:

Bet 1 pays $10,000 if E is true and H is false;

Bet 2 pays $1300 if E is false;

Bet 3 pays $300 if E is true.

   At the beginning of the die tossing, when Peter has the same initial probabilities as his friend, they both evaluate the fair cost of each bet in accordance with the laws of the probability calculus.

The initial probability that E is true = the average of $(.1)^4, (.2)^4, \ldots, (1)^4 = 0.25333$

Initial probability that E is false $= 1 - 0.25333 = 0.74667$

Initial probability that E is true and H is false = the average of $(.1)^4(.9), \ldots, (.9)^4(.1)$, $0 = .032505$

The fair cost of a bet that pays x if y is xp(y) so:

Bet 1 costs $325.05

Bet 2 costs $970.67

Bet 3 costs $76.00

Peter buys all three bets from his friend ($1,371.72). We see that if all four tosses do not come up ace, Peter loses bets 1 and 3, and wins bet 2. In this case, Peter's losses amount to $1,371.72 − $1,300 = $71.72.

Van Fraassen asks us to assume that E turns out true. Peter wins bet 3 and loses bet 2, so he is paid $300. So far he has a net loss of $1,071.72. At this point, information from an earlier part of the story which I have not yet included becomes relevant. Before running into his friend, Bayesian Peter was confronted by an IBE preacher who convinced him that the explanatory power of a hypothesis allows him to raise his credence. Peter came to believe that posterior probability can be fixed by prior probability, outcomes, and explanatory success (see van Fraassen 1989, p. 166).

In light of this belief and the string of four ace tosses, which is best explained by a hypothesis of high bias, Peter raises his probability for H being true from 0.87 (the result obtained from a routine application of Bayes' Theorem), to 0.9. Peter sells bet 1 to his friend for $1,000 (the payoff is $10,000, and the probability that H is false is 0.1).

Thanks to the influence of the IBE preacher, Peter winds up with a Dutch book. Now that he has sold bet 1, he must count his net losses at $1,071.72 − $1,000 = $71.72. He could have seen at the beginning of the game that he was bound to lose $71.72, whether E and H turned out to be true or false.

5. Before he embarks on his final transaction and sells bet 1 for $1,000, he has spent a total of only $999.97, not $1,071.72 as in the original version of the parable.

6. To see that the Bayesian Peter bets do have this structure, note that $y = 10,000$; $x = p(\text{-}H\&E)/p(E) = 0.13$; and the cost of bet 2 = xy = $1,300.

7. More generally, bets 1 and 2 together are essentially equivalent to a bet on $\text{-}H$ given E which costs xy and pays y. The total cost of these bets is $yp(\text{-}H\&E) + xyP(\text{-}E) = yP(\text{-}H/E)P(E) + xyP(\text{-}E) = yxP(E) + xyP(\text{-}E) = xy(P(E) + P(\text{-}E)) = xy$. If $\text{-}E$ happens, the agent wins her money back.

8. Though not his primary criticism of van Fraassen's argument, Douven (1999) draws a similar conclusion:

> Presumably not even the staunchest defender of IBE would want to hold that IBE is applicable in every context. Indeed, it is exactly the sort of context in which van Fraassen puts the discussion that seems not to license an inference to the best explanation.... IBE is a contextual principle in that it draws heavily upon background knowledge for its application, e.g., in order to judge which hypothesis among a number of rivals is the best explanation for the data gathered. However, in van Fraassen's model there is no such knowledge to invoke. (Douven 1999, p. 426)

9. Kvanvig (1994) and Leeds (1994) also criticize van Fraassen's argument by noting that van Fraassen needs to say more to defend the notion that diachronic incoherence is indicative of a failure of epistemic rationality, though there are flaws in the way they develop this objection. Kvanvig claims that diachronic Dutch books, unlike synchronic ones, illegitimately rely on the bookie's possessing "special information," namely knowledge of the future. According to Kvanvig, being susceptible to a certain

loss when dealing with a prescient bookie is not epistemically telling—after all, we would all be susceptible to certain loss if we accepted bets from omniscient bookies. This observation hardly seems to capture why the epistemic implications of synchronic and diachronic incoherence may be fundamentally different: the bookie in a diachronic Dutch book has no uncanny knowledge of the future; he simply knows your current degrees of belief and rules for degree of belief revision, and hence knows which bets you will regard as fair over time.

Leeds casts doubt on the epistemic implications of probabilistic incoherence by noting:

> [I]f we reject the operationalist idea—prevalent for so long in both psychology and economics—that we need to define the notion of degree of belief in terms of betting behavior, then we will have no reason to think there are such tight conceptual connections between betting and believing as Lewis' argument requires. (Leeds 1994, p. 211)

We can adequately justify taking Dutch books (at least synchronic ones) as epistemically relevant, however, without presupposing that degree of belief needs to be defined in terms of betting behavior. As Howson and Urbach (1993) suggest, a belief in A to degree $p(A)$ implies that the agent would at least regard a bet on A costing $p(A)w$ with payoff w as fair, i.e., as offering zero advantage to either side of the bet, given the way the world appears to the agent. If the agent simultaneously regards particular individual bets as fair (offering neither advantage nor disadvantage), the sum of such bets should also offer neither advantage nor disadvantage. In the case of Dutch books, however, it turns out that the sum, by guaranteeing a net loss if purchased, offers a definite disadvantage and hence cannot be fair. If a Dutch book has been developed from bets the agent simultaneously regards as individually fair, we see that there must have been a clash in her original simultaneous degree of belief assignments, a lack of coherence among those values which dictate which bets she counts as fair.

In light of the Dutch Book theorem, this line of thought provides an excellent justification for the view that our simultaneous degree-of-belief assignments have to conform to the axioms of probability in order to be rational.

Leeds also criticizes van Fraassen for failing to explain why there is an epistemically relevant difference between violating conditionalization by a rule, and not by a rule. But it should be clear why van Fraassen thinks there is such a difference: in the former case, the bookie is in a position from the start to offer a series of bets which lead to *certain* loss; in the latter, he is not.

10. In the discussion which follows I do not presuppose any specific account of what more of epistemic significance there is to good explanation. All that we are concerned with here is the general view that explanatoriness is sometimes relevant to degree of credence, even when the explanatory superiority of a favored hypothesis is grounded in more than its predictive success. The reader should keep in mind, however, that explanationists have contrasting conceptions of what can make explanatoriness epistemically relevant.

References

Ben-Menahem, Y. 1990. "The Inference to the Best Explanation." *Erkenntnis* 33: 319–344.

BonJour, L. 1985. *The Structure of Empirical Knowledge*. Cambridge, Mass.: Harvard University Press.

Boyd, R. 1991a. "On the Current Status of Scientific Realism." In *The Philosophy of Science*, edited by R. Boyd, P. Gasper, and J. Trout. Cambridge, Mass.: MIT Press.

Boyd, R. 1991b. "Observations, Explanatory Power, and Simplicity: Toward a Non-Humean Account." In *The Philosophy of Science*, edited by R. Boyd, P. Gasper, and J. Trout. Cambridge, Mass.: MIT Press.

Boyd, R. 1996. "Realism, Approximate Truth, and Philosophical Method." In *The Philosophy of Science*, edited by D. Papineau. Oxford: Oxford University Press.

Cornman, J. 1980. *Skepticism, Justification, and Explanation*. Dordrecht: Reidel.

Day, T., and H. Kincaid. 1994. "Putting Inference to the Best Explanation in Its Place." *Synthese* 98: 271–295.

Douven, I. 1999. "Inference to the Best Explanation Made Coherent." *Philosophy of Science* 66: 424–435.

Ganson, D. 2001. *The Explanationist Defense of Scientific Realism*. New York: Garland Publishing.

Goldman, A. 1988. *Empirical Knowledge*. Berkeley, Calif.: University of California Press.

Harman, G. 1965. "The Inference to the Best Explanation." *Philosophical Review* 74: 88–95.

Harman, G. 1999. *Reasoning, Meaning, and Mind*. Oxford: Oxford University Press.

Howson, C., and P. Urbach. 1993. *Scientific Reasoning: The Bayesian Approach*. Chicago: Open Court.

Jackson, F. 1986. *Perception: A Representative Theory*. Cambridge: Cambridge University Press.

Kitcher, P. 2001. "Real Realism: The Galilean Strategy." *Philosophical Review* 110: 151–191.

Kvanvig, J. 1994. "A Critique of van Fraassen's Voluntaristic Epistemology." *Synthese* 98: 325–348.

Leeds, S. 1994. "Constructive Empiricism." *Synthese* 101: 187–221.

Mackie, J. 1976. *Problems from Locke*. Oxford: Clarendon Press.

Miller, R. 1987. *Fact and Method*. Princeton: Princeton University Press.

Moser, P. 1989. *Knowledge and Evidence*. Cambridge: Cambridge University Press.

Okasha, S. 2000. "Van Fraassen's Critique of Inference to the Best Explanation." *Studies in the History of Philosophy* 31: 691–710.

Putnam, H. 1975. *Mathematics, Matter, and Method*. Cambridge: Cambridge University Press.

Russell, B. 1997. *The Problems of Philosophy*. Oxford: Oxford University Press.

Smart, J. J. C. 1968. *Between Science and Philosophy*. New York: Random House.

van Fraassen, B. 1984. "Belief and the Will." *Journal of Philosophy* 81: 235–256.

van Fraassen, B. 1989. *Laws and Symmetry*. Oxford: Oxford University Press.

van Fraassen, B. 2002. *The Empirical Stance*. New Haven, Conn.: Yale University Press.

Vogel, J. 1990. "Cartesian Skepticism and Inference to the Best Explanation." *Journal of Philosophy* 87: 658–666.

10 Counterfactuals in Economics: A Commentary

Nancy Cartwright

Introduction

Counterfactuals are a hot topic in economics today, at least among economists concerned with methodology. I shall argue that on the whole this is a mistake. Usually the counterfactuals on offer are proposed as *causal surrogates*. But at best they provide a "sometimes" way for finding out about causal relations, not a stand-in for them. I say a "sometimes way" because they do so only in very special—and rare—kinds of systems. Otherwise they are irrelevant to establishing facts about causation. On the other hand, viewed just as straight counterfactuals, they are a washout as well. For they are rarely an answer to any genuine "What if ...?" questions, questions of the kind we pose in planning and evaluation. For these two reasons I call the counterfactuals of recent interest in economics, *impostor counterfactuals*.

I will focus on Chicago economist James Heckman, since his views are becoming increasingly influential. Heckman is well known for his work on the evaluation of programs for helping workers more effectively enter and function in the labor market. I shall also discuss economist Stephen LeRoy, who has been arguing for a similar view for a long time, but who does not use the term "counterfactual" to describe it. I shall also discuss recent work of Judea Pearl, well known for his work on Bayesian nets and causality, and economist/methodologist Kevin Hoover, as well as Daniel Hausman. I shall begin with a discussion of some counterfactuals and their uses that I count as genuine, to serve as a contrast with the impostors.

Before that I need one technical remark. I shall talk about causal models. As I shall use the term, a causal model for a given system or kind of system (such as a toaster of a given make, or the UK economy in 2003) is a set of equations that represent a (probably proper) subset of the causal principles by which the system operates. The equations are supposed to be functionally true. In addition, the quantities on the right-hand side are supposed to represent a complete and minimal set of causes for the quantity represented on the left; to signal this I use not an ordinary equal sign but rather "$c =$."

The equations may represent deterministic principles, or they may contain random variables that do not represent real quantities but serve to allow for a purely probabilistic relation between a full set of causes and their effect. In this case, the causal model must also specify a joint probability distribution (that I shall designate by μ) over these "dummy" variables. For simplicity of presentation I will assume that the contributions of the different causes are additive. I also assume that causality is asymmetric, irreflexive, and functionally transitive.[1] So a causal model will look like this:

(CM) $x_1 c = z_1$

$$x_i c = \sum_{j<i} a_{ij} x_j + z_j$$

$$x_n c = \sum_{j<n} a_{nj} x_j + z_n$$

$\mu(z_1, \ldots, z_n)$.

The x's represent known quantities. The z's are random variables, which may either represent the net effect of unknown causes or may be dummy variables that allow for the representation of probabilistic causality. (Note that my characterization is not the same as Judea Pearl's, because Pearl does not allow for purely probabilistic causation.)

1   Genuine Counterfactuals

1.1   The Need for a Causal Model

Daniel Hausman tells us, "Counterfactual reasoning should permit one to work out the implications of counterfactual suppositions, so as to be prepared in case what one supposes actually happens" (Hausman 1998, p. 119). My arguments here will echo Hausman. The counterfactuals that do this for us provide genuine answers to genuine what-if questions; and they play a central role throughout economics. When we consider whether to implement a new policy or try to evaluate whether a trial program has been successful, we consider a variety of literally intended counterfactual questions: What if the policy were put in place? What if the program had not existed?

These are just the kinds of questions Heckman considers in his applied work, where he is at pains to point out that the question itself must be carefully formulated. We may for instance want to know what the wages of workers in the population at large would have been had the program not existed; more commonly we end up asking what the wages of workers *in the program* would have been. Or we may want to know what the GDP would have been without the program. We also need to take care about the contrast class: do we want to know the difference between the results of the program and those that would have occurred had no alternatives been present, or the difference compared to other programs, real or envisaged?

To evaluate counterfactuals of this kind we need a causal model; and the causal model must contain all the information relevant to the consequent about all the changes presumed in the antecedent. There is no other reasonable method on offer to assess counterfactuals. We may not always produce a model explicitly, but for any grounded evaluation there must be a causal model implicit; and our degree of certainty about our counterfactual judgments can be no higher than our degree of certainty that our causal model is correct.[2]

As an aside: David Lewis and his followers suppose that we need a model containing the principles by which the system operates (a *nomological* model) to assess counterfactuals, but not a *causal* model. I do not agree. But it is not this distinction between a Lewis-style, merely nomological model, and a causal model that I want to discuss here. Rather I want to focus on the difference between the causal models that support the counterfactuals we use directly in policy deliberations and those associated with impostor counterfactuals.

For purposes of evaluating a counterfactual, besides our causal model we will need to know what changes are envisaged—usually these are changes under our control. Before that we will need to know what changes are possible. This will depend on the structure of the system and the principles under which it operates. For this question, a causal model as I have characterized it is insufficient, for the causal model does not yet carry information about what can and what cannot be changed. I will turn to this question first, in section 1.2, then in 1.3 take up the relation between counterfactuals and the changes they presuppose.

1.2 What Can Be Changed?

Some people take there to be a universal answer to the question of what can (and should) be changed in assessing counterfactuals: every separate causal principle can be changed, leaving everything else the same, including all other causal principles, all initial values, and all conditional probability distributions of a certain sort. Judea Pearl claims this; so do James Woodward and Daniel Hausman.

Hausman and Woodward defend this view by maintaining that the equations of a causal model would not represent *causal* principles if this were not true of them. I have, however, characterized the equations in such a way as to give a different job to them: they are to be functionally correct and to provide a minimal full set of causes on the right-hand side for the quantity represented on the left. The two jobs are different, and it would be surprising if they could both be done in one fell swoop as Hausman and Woodward claim.

Hausman and Woodward object that the jobs cannot be different since the following is true by virtue of the very idea of causation: if a functional relationship between a set of factors (represented by, say, $\{x_j\}$) and a different quantity (say x_e) is functionally correct and the set $\{x_j\}$ is a minimal full set of causes then it must be possible to change this functional relationship, and indeed to stop every one of the x_j from being a cause of x_e, without changing anything else. The x_j would not be causes of x_e were this not true.

I think this claim is mistaken. There is any number of systems whose principles cannot be changed one at a time without either destroying the system or changing it into a system of a different kind. Besides, this assumption does not connect well with other features of causality, described in other accounts, such as probabilistic theories, causal process theories, or manipulation accounts.[3]

Pearl has another argument. He says that this assumption is correct because otherwise counterfactuals would be ambiguous. As far as I can tell, the argument must go like this:

1. Before we can evaluate $c \mathbin{\square\!\!\rightarrow} e$ we must know how c will change, otherwise the counterfactual will be ambiguous.

2. But counterfactuals should not be ambiguous.

3. We can make them unambiguous by assuming that there is a single rule, the same one all the time, about how c will be brought about.

4. The rule that says, "Bring c about by changing the principles that have c as effect to 'Set $c = \cdots$'," is such a rule.

5. Therefore we need this rule.

6. But this rule will not be universally applicable unless this kind of change is always possible.

7. Therefore this kind of change must always be possible.

I have written the argument out in detail to get you to have a look at it. It is obviously fallacious. It infers from the fact that the rule in question does a needed job that it must be the rule that obtains, which is just to mistake a sufficient condition for a necessary one. So I do not think Pearl's argument will support the conclusion that changes in one principle holding fixed "everything else" are always possible and indeed are the only possibilities that matter in the evaluation of counterfactuals.

Another similar assumption that is sometimes made is that for purposes of assessing counterfactuals, changes in x_j are always presumed to be brought about by changes in z_j. But this does not fit with either interpretation I have given for the z's in a causal model. There is no reason that the unknown causes should be just the ones that can change; and when the z's simply serve to introduce probabilities, there isn't even a quantity there to change. To make sense of the assumption we might instead think of the z's as exogenous, in the sense of determined outside the equations that constitute the causal model. This, though, will still not guarantee that they can be changed, let alone changed one at a time. Some quantities not determined by the equations of the model will nevertheless be determined by principles outside it, some may not; and some of these outside-the-model principles may be changeable and some may not.

When we consider counterfactuals for the purposes of policy and evaluation, we assume that change is really possible—change without threatening the identity of the system under study. And sometimes it is. What changes are possible and in what combinations, then, is additional information we need to put into the causal model or the causal model will not be able to tell us which counterfactuals make sense in the first place, before we begin to assess their truth and falsity.

In the economics literature Kevin Hoover (2001) makes this point explicitly. Hoover distinguishes what he calls *parameters* from *variables*. Both vary, but only parameters can be changed directly—any change the value of a variable might undergo will be the result of a change in a parameter. In formulating a causal model, then, we are to distinguish between the parameters and the variables. Moreover, each different parameter is supposed to represent a quantity that can be changed independently of every other. This implies that the quantities represented by parameters can take any combination of values in their allowed ranges; they are, formally speaking, "variation free": $Range(a_1, a_2, \ldots, a_n) = Range(a_1) \cdot Range(a_2) \cdot \ldots \cdot Range(a_n)$. We should note, though Hoover himself does not make much of this, that this is not generally the distinction intended between parameters and variables. So we must use care in taking over already formulated causal models that may distinguish parameters and variables in some other way.

1.3   What Is Envisaged to Change?

Once we have recorded what things can change, we know what counterfactuals make sense. But to assess the truth-value of any particular counterfactual, we will need to know what changes are supposed to happen. Often the exact details matter. For instance, many people feel they would not be opposed to legalizing euthanasia, *if only* it could be done in a way that would ensure that abuses would not occur.

Sometimes when we consider a policy we have a very definite idea in mind how it will be implemented. I shall call the related counterfactuals, "implementation specific." At the other end of the scale, we might have no idea at all; the counterfactuals are "implementation neutral." When we evaluate counterfactuals, we had better be clear what exactly we are presuming.

For counterfactuals that are totally implementation specific, we know exactly what we are asking when we ask, "What would happen if ...?"[4] For others there are a variety of different strategies we might adopt. For one, we can employ the usual devices for dealing with epistemic uncertainty.

We might, for instance, assess the probabilities of the various possible methods of implementation and weight the probability of the counterfactual consequent accordingly. In the methodology of economics literature we find another alternative: Stephen LeRoy and Daniel Hausman focus on counterfactuals that would be true *regardless* of how they are implemented. I begin with LeRoy.

LeRoy's stated concern is with causal ordering among quantities, not with counterfactuals. But, it seems, he equates "*p* causes *q*" with "if *p* were to change, *q* would change as well"—so long as we give the "right" reading to the counterfactual. It is his proposed reading for the counterfactual that matters here. It may help to present his brief discussion of a stock philosophical example—the case of birth control pills and thrombosis—before looking to more formal cases.

Birth control pills cause thrombosis; they also prevent pregnancy, which is itself a cause of thrombosis. LeRoy assumes that whether a woman becomes pregnant depends on both her sexual activity and whether she takes pills. Now consider: "What would happen vis-à-vis thrombosis were a particular woman to become pregnant?" That, LeRoy, points out, is ambiguous—it depends on whether the change in pregnancy comes about because of a change in pill-taking or because of a change in sexual activity.

In his formal characterization LeRoy treats systems of linear deterministic equations. We may take these to be very sparse causal models. They are what in economics are called "reduced form equations": "In current usage an economic model is a map from a space of exogenous variables—agents' characteristics and resource endowments, for example—to a space of endogenous variables—prices and allocations" (LeRoy 2003, p. 1). The equations are expected to be functionally correct, but not to represent the causal relations among the variables, with one exception. Variables designated as "exogenous" are supposed not to be caused by any of the remaining (endogenous) variables. Since they are functionally related to the endogenous variables, we may assume that either they are causes of some of the endogenous variables or are correlated with such causes. For LeRoy's purposes I think we must suppose they are causes.

In the context of our discussion here, with Hoover in mind, we should note one further assumption LeRoy makes. The possible sources of change in an endogenous variable are exactly the members of the minimal set of exogenous variables that, according to the economic model used to evaluate the counterfactuals, will fix the value of the endogenous variable. LeRoy considers a familiar supply and demand model:

(I) $q_s = a_s + a_{sp}p + a_{sw}w$

$q_d = a_d + a_{dp}p + a_{di}i$

$q_s = q_d = q$

Here p is price; q, quantity; w, weather; i, income. LeRoy asks what the effect of a change Δ in price would be on the equilibrium quantity. By the conventions just described, a change in price can come about through changes in weather, income, or both, and nothing else. But, LeRoy, notes, "any of an infinite number of pairs of shifts in the exogenous variables 'weather' and 'income' could have caused the assumed changes in price, and these map onto different values of q" (LeRoy 2003, p. 6). Thus the question has no definite answer—it all depends on how the change in p is brought about.

LeRoy contrasts this model with a different one:

(II) $q_s = a_s + a_{sw}w + a_{sf}f$

$q_p = a_p + a_{dp}p + a_{di}i$

$q_s = q_d = q$

Here f is fertilizer. Fertilizer and weather can change the equilibrium quantity, and no matter how they do so, the change in price will be the same. In this case Leroy is content that the counterfactual, "If q were to change from Q to $Q + \Delta$,[5] p would change from $P = (Q - a_p - a_{di}I)/a_{dp}$ to $P = (Q + \Delta - a_p - a_{di}I)/a_{dp}$," is unambiguous (and true). The lesson he draws is the following (where I substitute counterfactual language for his causal language): "[Counterfactual] statements involving endogenous variables as [antecedents] are ambiguous except when all the interventions consistent with a given change in the [antecedent] map onto the same change in the [consequent]" (LeRoy 2003, p. 6). I think the statement as it stands is too strong. Some counterfactuals are, after all, either implicitly or explicitly implementation specific. What LeRoy offers is a semantics for counterfactuals that are, either implicitly or explicitly, implementation neutral. In this case the consequent should obtain *no matter what possible change occurs to bring the antecedent about.*

Dan Hausman seems to have distinguished between implementation specific and implementation neutral counterfactuals, too, as I do here, though I do not think he explicitly says so. He considers an example in which engineers designing a nuclear power plant ask, "What would happen if the steam pipe were to burst?" The answer, he argues, depends on how it will burst. "Responsible engineers," he argues, must look to the origins of the burst "when the consequences of the pipe's bursting depend on what caused it to burst" (Hausman 1998, p. 122).

On the other hand, when Hausman turns to providing some constraints that a possible-world semantics for counterfactuals must satisfy, he seems to be concerned with implementation neutral counterfactuals. The results are similar to LeRoy's: any semantics that satisfies Hausman's constraints should give the same result as LeRoy's prescription when restricted to counterfactuals evaluated via what LeRoy calls an "economic model." The Hausman constraint on the similarity relation between possible worlds that matters to our discussion here is:

SIM 2. *It doesn't matter which cause is responsible.* For any event b, if a and c are any two causes of b that are causally and counterfactually independent of one another, there will be non-b possible worlds in which a does not occur and c does occur that are just as close to the actual world as are any non-b possible worlds with a and without c, and there will be non-b possible worlds without a and with c that are just as close to the actual world as are any non-b possible worlds without both a and c. (Hausman 1998, p. 133)

Look back at LeRoy's model (I) for illustration, where weather and income are the causes by which either price or quantity can change. It is easiest to see the results if we first solve for p and q:

$$q = (\alpha_{dp}\alpha_s - \alpha_{sp}\alpha_d + \alpha_{dp}\alpha_{sw}w - \alpha_{sp}\alpha_{di}i)/(\alpha_{dp} - \alpha_{sp})$$

$$p = (\alpha_s - \alpha_d + \alpha_{sw}w - \alpha_{di}i)/(\alpha_{dp} - \alpha_{sp})$$

If p changes by ΔP with w fixed, then i must have changed by $\Delta P(\alpha_{sp} - \alpha_{dp})/\alpha_{di}$ and so q will change by $\Delta Q = \alpha_{sp}\Delta P_i$. If on the other hand i is fixed, then w must have changed by $\Delta W = \Delta P(\alpha_{dp} - \alpha_{sp})/\alpha_{sw}$ and so $\Delta Q = \alpha_{dp}\Delta P$. Now we can bring in SIM 2. If q changes (q is here the analogue of b in SIM 2) some world in which w (the analogue of a) changes will be just as close as any world in which i (the analogue of c) changes. But the world in which w changes and i stays fixed, and the world in which i changes and w stays fixed, have different values for the change in q. Yet they are equally close. So the truth value of counterfactual claims about what would happen to q, were p to change by ΔP are undefined.

So we may have counterfactuals that are implementation specific; we may have ones that assume some one or another of a range of possible implementations; and we may have implementation neutral ones where we wish to find out what would happen no matter how the change in the antecedent is brought about. For thinking about policy we had better know which kind of counterfactual we are asserting, and ensure that our semantics is appropriate to it.

2 Impostor Counterfactuals

The kinds of what-if questions we ask in planning and evaluating are in sharp contrast with a different kind of "counterfactual" that occupies economists as well—the impostor counterfactuals. Like the counterfactuals I have so far been discussing, these too are evaluated relative to a causal model. But they are not used directly in planning and evaluation. Rather they are used to define certain causal concepts. For Heckman the relevant concept is *causal effect*; for LeRoy, *causal order*. I shall discuss LeRoy first.

2.1 LeRoy

I have urged that in order to assess counterfactuals, we need a causal model. Recall that LeRoy begins with a sparse causal model—a reduced form equation that links the endogenous variables to a set of exogenous variables, where he supposes that no exogenous variables are caused by any endogenous ones, and that the exogenous variables completely determine the values of the endogenous variables.[6] The task is to say something about the causal order of the endogenous variables and, I take it, about the strength of influence of one on another. Let Z_j be the minimal set of exogenous variables that determine x_j and define Z_{ji} as $Z_j - Z_i$. Then x_c causes x_e if and only if there is a (scalar) γ_{ec} and a (vector) δ_{ec} such that

$$x_e = \gamma_{ec} x_c + \delta_{ec} \bar{Z}_{ec}.$$

This means that x_e is determined completely by x_c plus a set of exogenous variables that do not participate in determining x_e; that is, there is no z that both helps fix the first term in the above equation and also helps fix the second.

What what-if question does γ_{ec} answer? It answers an implementation neutral counterfactual: by how much would x_e change were x_c to change by a given amount, no matter how the change in x_c is brought about? This is often an important question for us to be able to answer. It may also important to know whether, for the system we are dealing with, it has no answer: there is nothing general, or implementation neutral, that we can say; how much the effect changes cannot be calculated without knowing what the method of implementation will be.

There are two points I would like to make about LeRoy's approach. First, I admit that these counterfactuals are in no way "impostors"—they ask genuine what-if question whose answers we frequently need to know. Nevertheless, they are severely restricted in their range of application. For vast numbers of systems the answer to LeRoy's counterfactual question will be that it has no answer: there is no implementation neutral change that would occur in the effect consequent on a change in the cause.

Second, LeRoy's definition answers one very special kind of causal question—it asks about how much, if one factor changes in any way whatsoever, a second factor will change. But it does not answer the question of how much one factor *contributes* to another. For a simple example of where the two questions have different answers, consider a system governed by the following two causal laws:

(CM1) $q = a_{qz}z$

         $p = a_{pz}z.$

Compare this with a system governed by different laws

(CM2) $p = a_{pz}z$

         $q = a_{qp}p.$

It should at least in principle be possible for two such systems to exist. The two systems have different causal structures and different answers to the question, "How much does p contribute causally to q?" In the second system the answer is given by a_{qp}. In the first the answer is, "Nothing." Yet in cases where $a_{qz} = a_{qp}a_{pz}$ there will be exactly the same answer to LeRoy's counterfactual question: if p were to change by Δp, no matter how it does so, q would change by $a_{qz}\Delta p = a_{qp}a_{pz}\Delta p$.

In my view we have a large variety of causal concepts, applicable to a variety of different kinds of systems in different situations; and there is also a large variety of different kinds of causal and counterfactual questions we can ask, many of which only make sense in particular kinds of systems in particular circumstances. LeRoy asks a specific, explicitly articulated counterfactual question, and I take it that that is all to the good. We must be careful, however, not to be misled by his use of the language of "causal order" to suppose it tells us whether and how much one quantity causally contributes to another.

2.2 Heckman

Heckman also uses counterfactuals to answer what he labels as causal questions. I find his usage of them less transparent. Like LeRoy, Heckman asks an explicit, well articulated counterfactual question, in his case an implementation specific question. Again, as with LeRoy, the question has an answer only in certain very restricted systems—essentially, as I shall explain, in Galilean-style experiments. As far as I can see, the primary interest in Heckman's counterfactuals is that they serve as a tool for answering a noncounterfactual question, a question about causal contributions. But questions about causal contributions can be asked—and answered—for situations that are not Galilean experiments, where the counterfactuals Heckman introduces do not make sense. This is why I say that they are impostors. They seem to be the issue of interest; they are certainly the *topic*. But in fact they are only a tool for answering a different question—a causal question—and at that, for answering that question only in very restricted kinds of systems, kinds that are not generally those which concern us.

Before we turn to Heckman it may be helpful to begin with work that will be more familiar to philosophers, from the book *Causality* by Judea Pearl. Pearl gives a precise and detailed semantics for counterfactuals. But of what is this semantics a semantics? What kinds of counterfactuals will it treat, and in what kinds of contexts? Since Pearl introduces them without comment we might think that he has in mind natural language counterfactuals. But he presents only a single semantics with no context dependence, which does not fit with natural language usage.

Worse, the particular semantics Pearl develops is unsuited to a host of natural language uses of counterfactuals, especially those for planning and evaluation of the kind I have been discussing. That is because of the very special way in which he imagines that the counterfactual antecedent will be brought about—by a precise incision that changes exactly the counterfactual antecedent and nothing else (except what follow causally from just that difference). But when we consider implementing a policy, this is not at all the question we need to ask. For policy and evaluation we want generally to know what would happen were the policy really set in place. And whatever we know about how it might be put in place, the one thing we can usually be sure of is that it will not be by a precise incision of the kind Pearl assumes.

Consider for example Pearl's axiom of composition, which Pearl proves to hold in all causal models, given his characterization of a causal model and his semantics for counterfactuals. This axiom states that "if we force a variable (W) to a value w that it would have had, without our intervention, then the intervention will have no effect on other variables in the system" (Pearl 2000, p. 229). This axiom is reasonable if we envisage implementations that bring about the antecedent of the counterfactual in as minimal a way as possible. But it is clearly violated in a great many realistic cases. Often we have no idea whether the antecedent will in fact obtain or not, and this is true even if we allow that the governing principles are deterministic. We implement a policy to ensure it will obtain—and the policy may affect a host of changes in other variables in the system, some envisaged and some not.

We should note that the same problem arises for Lewis-style semantics. If the antecedent of a counterfactual obtains, then our world, with things as they actually happen in it, is the nearest possible world for evaluating the truth value of the counterfactual. There is no room then for anything to change as a result of the antecedent being implemented.[7]

Heckman, unlike Pearl and Lewis, is keen that causal models *model* how change is brought about. So in defining causal efficacy he does not adopt Pearl's semantics in which laws are changed deus ex machina. But he does adopt a similar device. Pearl limits his causal definitions to systems in which the principles responsible for a given factor, with all their causes, can be changed to produce any required value for that factor, without changing any other principles or other "initial" values. Heckman limits his definitions to causal principles in which the causes are variation free. This means that if only the system runs "long enough," the effect (intended as the antecedent of the counterfactual) will naturally take any required value, while the remaining causes, all other principles, and all other initial values stay the same. The counterfactual change in an antecedent with "everything else" the same will "eventually" be factual. Heckman stresses, thus, that what matters for his definitions is natural variability within the system, not changes in the principles under which it operates.

Heckman begins his treatment with *causal functions*. These govern very special kinds of causal systems, systems that mimic experiments:

Causal functions are ... derived from conceptual experiments where exogenously specified generating variables are varied.... The specification of these hypothetical variations is a crucial part of model specification and lies at the heart of any rigorous definition of causality. (Heckman 2001, p. 14)

Heckman tells us three things about causal functions:

1. They "describe how each possible vector of generating variables is mapped into a resulting outcome," where the generating variables "completely determine" the outcome (Heckman 2001, p. 12).

2. They "derive from"—or better, I think, "describe"—conceptual experiments.

3. Touching on questions of realism and of model choice, models involving causal functions are always underdetermined by evidence; hence, as Heckman sees it, causality is just "in the head" since the models relative to which it is defined are just in the head.

From this I take it that causal functions represent (a probably proper subset of) the causal principles under which these special experiment-like systems operate, where the right-hand-side variables—the ones Heckman calls the "generating variables"—form a minimal complete set of causes of the quantity represented on the left[8] and where each cause can vary independently of the others.

Imagine that the causal function for an outcome y is given by

$$y = g(x_1, \ldots, x_n).$$

We can now define the *causal* or *counterfactual effect* of x_j on y fixing the remaining factors in the causal function (Heckman seems to use the terms "causal effect" and "counterfactual effect" interchangeably):

Causal effect of x_j on y:

$$[\Delta y / \Delta x_j = x_j' - x_j''] =_{df} g(x_1, \ldots, x', \ldots, x_n) - g(x_1, \ldots, x_j'', \ldots, x_n).$$

As Heckman insists, in order for this definition "to be meaningful requires that the x_j can be independently varied when the other variables are fixed so that there are no functional restrictions connecting the arguments ... it is thus required that these variables be variation-free" (Heckman 2001, p. 18). I shall call the counterfactual effect as thus defined a *Galilean counterfactual* since, as I remarked, it is just the kind effect we look for in a Galilean experiment.

I should note that Heckman himself treats of double counterfactuals since the outcome variables he discusses are often themselves counterfactuals—y_0 is the value a given quantity would take were a specified "treatment" to occur; y_1, the value it would take were the treatment not to occur. These values, he supposes, are fixed by deterministic causal functions. Relative to these causal functions we can then ask about the causal efficacy of a certain quantity—including the treatment itself—on the counterfactual quantities y_0 and y_1. So we can consider, for example, what difference a change in social security regulations would have on the amount of savings that would obtain if there were a tax cut, versus the difference the change would make were there no tax cut. I will not be concerned with these double-barreled counterfactuals here. They do not appear in Heckman's discussion of the supply and demand equations, which will suffice as illustrations of my central point.

Heckman considers simultaneous supply and demand equations. For simplicity we can look at the specific equations that we have already considered above, where I have added the additional equilibrium constraint on price:

$$(\text{I}') \qquad q_s = a_s + a_{sp}p_s + a_{sw}w$$

$$q_d = a_d + a_{dp}p_d + a_{di}i$$

$$q_s = q_d = q$$

$$p_s = p_d = p.$$

Heckman points out that these equations do not fit Pearl's scheme since they are not recursive, and hence Pearl's method for assessing counterfactuals will not apply. This fits with familiar remarks about these kinds of systems—p and q are determined jointly by exogenous factors. It seems then that it makes no sense to ask about how much a change in p will affect a change in q. To the contrary, Heckman points out: we can still assess causal efficacy using his definition—so long as certain "exclusion" conditions are met.

Say we want to assess the causal/counterfactual effect of demand price on quantity demanded. We first look to the reduced form equations

$$q = (z_d, z_s)$$

$$p = (z_d, z_s)$$

where z_d is the vector of exogenous variables in the demand equations, and z_s, those in the supply equations. In LeRoy's equations (I'), $z_d = i$ and $z_s = w$. Heckman takes these to be causal functions, otherwise the causal model has not properly specified the "exogenous" variables. That means that the exogenous variables are "generating variables" for p and q, and that they are variation free. Now the task is easy:

Assuming that some components of $[z_d]$ do not appear in $[z_s]$, that some components of $[z_s]$ do not appear in $[z_d]$, and that those components have a non-zero impact on price, one can use the variation in the excluded variables to vary $[p_d$ or p_s in the reduced form equations] while holding the other arguments of those equations fixed. (Heckman 2001, p. 36)

The result (using the equality of p_d and p_s and of q_d and q_s) is

$$\partial q_d / \partial p_d = (\partial q / \partial z_s(e)) / (\partial p / \partial z_s(e))$$

where $z_s(e)$ is a variable in z_s that is excluded from z_d and that, as he puts it, "has an impact on" p_d. In (I') this job can be done by w; the causal effect thus calculated of p_d on q_d is α_{dp}.

Notice how much causality is involved here. By definition we are supposed to be evaluating the change in q_d, holding fixed all the factors in a causal function for q_d except p_d. What we actually do is hold fixed z_d while z_s varies. Presumably this is okay because z_s is a cause of p_d that can produce variations in p_d while z_d is fixed; and z_d being fixed matters because z_d constitutes, along with p_d, a minimal full set of causes of q_d. So when the exclusion condition is satisfied, the demand equation is a causal function and the counterfactual definition of causal effect is meaningful.

Now consider a slightly altered set of equations:

$$(I'') \qquad q_s = \alpha_s + \alpha_{sp} p_s + \alpha_{sw} w + \alpha_{si} i$$

$$q_d = \alpha_d + \alpha_{dp} p_d + \alpha_{di} i + \alpha_{dw} w$$

$$q_s = q_d = q$$

$$p_s = p_d = p.$$

Now the demand equation cannot be treated as a causal function, and the question of the causal effect of demand price on quantity demanded is meaningless. This is true despite the fact that a_{dp} still appears in the equation and it still represents something—something much the same one would suppose—about the bearing of p_d on q_d. The intermediate case seems even stranger. Imagine that $a_{sw} = 0$. Now a_{sp} measures a counterfactual effect, but a_{dp} does not.

2.3   Cartwright

I have an alternative. But I should note that I have a stake in this discussion, since I have been stressing the importance of independent variability for over fifteen years; I just think it plays a different role than Heckman (and Pearl and Hausman and Woodward) ascribe to it.

I begin with causal principles. At this level of discussion I myself am a realist about the principles of our causal models: they are correct if and only if they approximate well enough to the causal laws that govern the operation of the system in question. Heckman, it seems, is not a realist. But that does not matter here since he himself has introduced the notion of a causal function. A causal principle is just like a causal function, but without the restriction that the causes (or "generating variables") are variation free. I shall continue to restrict attention to linear causal models. Then, for a given causal model, *the contribution a cause x_c makes to an effect x_e is just the coefficient of x_c in any causal principle for x_e in the model*.[9] It is easy to show for linear models that where Heckman's measure for the causal/counterfactual effect of x_c on x_e applies, it will have the same value as the contribution x_c makes to x_e.

Given this characterization we see that the contribution of p_d to q_d is the same in (I′) and (I″). What is different is that in (I′) we have a particular way to find out about it that is not available in (I″). (I′) is what I have called *an epistemically convenient system*.[10] It is a system in which we can find out what a cause, x_c, contributes to an effect, x_e, in one particular simple way: hold fixed all the other contributions that add up to make the effect the size it is; then vary the cause and see how much x_e varies. Any difference has to be exactly the contribution that x_c adds. This does not mean, however, that for systems where this independent variation is not possible, all is lost. There are hosts of other legitimate ways of defending claims about the size of causal contributions that apply both in systems with independent variation and in ones without.[11]

3   Epistemic Convenience versus External Validity

I began my discussion with reference to impostor counterfactuals. There is a sense in which the counterfactual questions that Heckman focuses on are genuine. If we are talking about the right kinds of systems—epistemically convenient ones—they ask genuine, implementation specific what-if questions. But there are two problems. First, few systems we confront are epistemically convenient. The vast majority are not. For these Heckman's measures are irrelevant.

Second, even if we are studying an epistemically convenient system, there is a puzzle about why we should wish to ask just these implementation specific questions. If we were thinking of setting policy or evaluating the success of some program in the system, then these, with their very special method of implementation, might be relevant sometimes. But there is no necessity to implement policies in the single way highlighted by Heckman; generally we would want to consider a variety of different methods of implementation and frequently to assess implementation neutral counterfactuals as well. Even in epistemically convenient systems, the Galilean counterfactuals that Heckman studies often have no privileged role.

There are two familiar enterprises where they do have a special role. The first is in trying to determine if, and to what degree, one factor contributes causally to another. In an epistemically convenient system we can ask Galilean-type counterfactual questions; and the answers we obtain will double as answers to our causal questions. They are a tool for finding out answers to our causal questions. But note that they are only a tool for finding out about causes in our special epistemically convenient systems. For other systems we cannot even ask these counterfactual questions, let alone let the answers to them supply our causal answers as well.

The other is in Heckman's own field, evaluation. In setting up new programs, we might try to set them up in such a way that the causal contribution they make to the result can be readily disentangled from the contribution of other factors. Of particular concern are other factors that might both contribute to the effect independently of the program, and also make it more likely that an individual entered (or failed to enter) the program. If we can arrange the setup of our program so that it is epistemically convenient, then again we can answer Galilean counterfactual questions— "What difference would there be in outcome with the program present versus the program absent, holding fixed all other contributions to the outcome?" And again, these counterfactual questions will tell us the contribution the program makes, since in these circumstances the difference in outcome between when the program is present and when it is absent must be exactly the contribution the program makes. So we can use information about Galilean counterfactuals to learn about the causal contributions of the program we set up. Still, all we learn is about that program in those special epistemically convenient circumstances.

In either case, whether it be experimental systems or program setups that we engineer to make the measurement of causal contributions easy, we need to ask, why should we be interested in causal contributions in these very special—and rare—kinds of systems? The answer is clear. Generally we want this information because it will tell us something about causal contributions in other systems as well. But we confront here the familiar problem of internal and external validity. In an epistemically convenient (linear) system, using counterfactual differences as a measure of causal contributions is provably valid: internal to the situation, this method is bound to give us correct results about the question of interest. But nothing said in this discussion bears on external validity: when will the results that we can be sure are correct in a convenient system hold elsewhere?

Sometimes this issue is discussed in the economics methodology literature under the heading "invariance." This is often with something like equation set (I′) in mind. Here we can find out the causal contribution, a_{dp}, of p_d to q_d by calculating the difference in Galilean counterfactuals as p_d changes via w holding fixed i. Then we might imagine that everything already in place about the causal principle for q_d would stay the same even if weather became an influence on quantity demanded. Thus we suppose that the second equation can be replaced with

$$q_d = a_d + a_{dp}p_d + a_{di}i + a_{dw}w.$$

We then say that the equation for q_d remains *invariant* as a_{dw} changes from zero to nonzero, or possibly we suppose it invariant over any range of values for a_{dw}. This, though, is only one kind of assumption we might make about the use to which we can put the information we learn about the causal contribution one factor makes to another. Since I have written at length elsewhere about this topic (Cartwright 1989, 1999), I will not pursue it further here.

There are two points that matter to my argument here. The first is that assumptions about where this information can be put to use are not justified by anything we have discussed so far, and in particular not by any information about counterfactuals of the kinds I have explored. Showing that results on causal contributions have external validity—and how far and of what kind—requires a different methodology altogether.

Second, when we export the information gleaned from Galilean counterfactuals in epistemically convenient systems elsewhere, it is not as information about counterfactuals but rather as information about causal contributions. In most systems to which we will carry our results, Galilean counterfactual questions do not even make sense. This supports my claim that both as counterfactuals and as causal surrogates, Galilean counterfactuals are impostors. They do not carry over as counterfactuals to non–epistemically convenient systems; and in epistemically convenient ones they are usually of interest, not on their own as genuine what-if hypotheses, but only as tools for measuring causal contributions. Even then the results about causal contributions are of use outside the highly restricted systems in which they are established only if specific assumptions about the external validity of the results are warranted.

4   Causal Decision Theory

As another illustration of the conflation of Galilean counterfactuals with more realistic implementation specific ones, consider causal decision theory. Various versions of causal decision theory made the same mistake I am pointing to, but in reverse: the aim was to evaluate genuine counterfactuals, but ended up with a measure that measured the causal contribution of a factor, and not the counterfactual effects of the factor being implemented. Let us consider a very simple case.

Given my fear of lung cancer, should I quit smoking? Presumably the answer is yes, if the expected utility if I were to quit is greater than if I were to continue; or

Counterfactual decision formula:

$$P(S \mathbin{\square\!\!\rightarrow} L)U(S\&L) + P(S \mathbin{\square\!\!\rightarrow} \neg L)U(S\&\neg L) < P(\neg S \mathbin{\square\!\!\rightarrow} L)U(\neg S\&L)$$
$$+ P(\neg S \mathbin{\square\!\!\rightarrow} \neg L)U(\neg S\&\neg L)$$

Here $S = I\ smoke$, $L = I\ get\ lung\ cancer$, $U(X) =$ utility of X, and I shall assume the probabilities are personal probabilities read off from the population probabilities.

Conventionally in decision theory $P(B/A)$ appeared in this formula instead of $P(A \mathbin{\square\!\!\rightarrow} B)$:

"Conventional" decision formula:

$$P(L/S)U(S\&L) + P(\neg L/S)U(S\&\neg L) < P(L/\neg S)U(\neg S\&L) + P(\neg L/\neg S)U(\neg S\&\neg L)$$

But it became apparent that this would not do. As the slogan has it: the probability of a counterfactual conditional is not a conditional probability. I can illustrate why with a caricature of a hypothesis mooted by R. A. Fisher. Perhaps smoking does not cause lung cancer; rather, the observed probabilistic dependence of lung cancer on smoking arises entirely because both are the result of some gene that is prevalent in the population. Then it might well be the case that $P(L/S) \gg P(S/\neg L)$, but it would not make sense to give up smoking, if one loved it, in order to avoid lung cancer. To keep the example simple I shall suppose that there is no other cause of lung cancer besides the two possible causes, smoking and the gene.

Since on the Fisher hypothesis, the probabilistic dependence between S and L is due entirely to the fact that each is itself dependent on the gene, the dependence between them should disappear if we condition on the presence or absence of the gene. This led causal decision theorists to substitute the partial conditional probability $P(L/\pm S\&G)$ for $P(L/\pm S)$, depending on whether I do indeed have the gene or not ($G = I\ have\ the\ smoking/ lung\ cancer\ gene$). If, as we might expect, I have no idea at all whether I have the gene, then I should average over $P(L/\pm S\&G)$, where the weights for the average would reasonably be based on the frequency with which G appears in the population: $P(+G)$, $P(\neg G)$. In case we can make the additional assumption that the only bearing that the gene has on my utility is through smoking and lung cancer,[12] this line of reasoning results in

Causal decision formula:

$$[P(L/S\&G)P(G) + P(L/S\&\neg G)P(\neg G)]U(S\&L) + [P(\neg L/S\&G)P(G)$$
$$+ P(\neg L/S\&\neg G)P(\neg G)]U(S\&\neg L) < [P(L/\neg S\&G)P(G)$$
$$+ P(L/\neg S\&\neg G)P(\neg G)]U(\neg S\&L)$$
$$+ [P(\neg L/\neg S\&G)P(G) + P(\neg L/\neg S\&\neg G)P(\neg G)]U(\neg S\&\neg L)^{13}$$

In the case when G is independent of S $(P(\pm G/\pm S)) = P(\pm G)$, this formula reduces to the "conventional" formula.

Notice that the difference $P([S \dashrightarrow L]/\pm G) - P([\neg S \dashrightarrow L]/\pm G)$ is given by $P(L/S\&\pm G)P(\pm G) - P(L/\neg S\&\pm G)P(\pm G)$. This latter formula is a direct analogue to Heckman's formula for the causal/counterfactual difference for values: hold fixed the other causes of the effect in question, and see what difference occurs when the targeted cause varies on its own; only in this case we look not to the difference in values of the effect as the cause varies, but rather to the difference in probabilities. I shall, by extension, call this the *probabilistic causal/counterfactual difference*. It is clearly not defined if S and G are not variation free; when it is defined and they are variation free, we can also by analogy take the formula to provide a measure of the *probabilistic causal contribution* of S to L given G or given $\neg G$.[14]

Like the value-based causal/counterfactual difference, this also is more like the counterfactual difference we look for in a Galilean experiment than the implementation specific difference that might occur in real cases. The particular example I have chosen tends to obscure this point (as did many others that received attention in the early days of causal decision theory). In our case we have only one other cause on the tapis, and it is unlikely to be changed by any method by which we might come to stop smoking. But suppose that the way in which I will be brought, or bring myself, to stop smoking has some chance of altering whether I have the relevant gene or not. In that case, if we assume that the causal contributions of separate factors are additive, a better formula for the implementation specific, probabilistic counterfactual difference might be,[15] (letting $cc(A, B/C)$ stand for the causal contribution of A to B in the presence of C):

$$P([S \dashrightarrow L]/\pm G) - P([\neg S \dashrightarrow L]/\pm G) = cc(S, L/\neg G)P([S \dashrightarrow \neg G]/\pm G)$$
$$+ [cc(S, L/G) + cc(G, L/S)]P([S \dashrightarrow G]/\pm G).$$

I offer this formula as an illustration to make a specific point. Behind the story is a small causal model based on the little story I told about smoking, the gene, and lung cancer, plus the assumption that contributions from separate causes combine additively. And that buys us some advance. But it does not eliminate the counterfactuals altogether. We still need a model involving the implementation variables and the relation to the system to calculate the probability of the remaining counterfactuals. The second model in cases like this will often be far more ad hoc and involve far more local knowledge than the one that models the basic system itself.

The overall point of this discussion, however, is that causal decision theories typically employ a measure that depends entirely on the causal contribution of the action in question. But what is needed, as in policy deliberations in general, is a formula that involves implementation specific counterfactuals across the range of implementations that might in fact obtain—that is, "genuine" counterfactuals.

5 Conclusion

I have claimed that the impostor counterfactuals of current interest in economics provide a tool to measure causal contributions, though this tool is limited in its use to Galilean experiments. It is important to stress that questions about causal contributions are central questions that definitely need answering for the kinds of systems we live in and use. I began with genuine counterfactuals. For purposes of planning and evaluation we need answers to genuine what-if questions—both implementation specific questions and implementation neutral ones. But I have now come full circle. We cannot evaluate the counterfactuals unless we have a causal model. And what is a causal model, in the context of answering genuine what-if questions? A causal model is a set of causal principles that represent our hypotheses about just the causal issue I describe—to what degree one factor contributes causally to another. This is the information we need for genuine counterfactuals, and impostors play at best a very indirect role in helping to provide it.

Acknowledgments

Research for this paper was supported by an AHRB grant, *Causality: Metaphysics and Methods*, and by a grant from the Latsis Foundation. I am grateful for both. Many of the ideas were developed jointly with Julian Reiss (see Reiss and Cartwright 2003). I also want to thank him.

Notes

1. The system is functionally transitive iff $x_k c = f(\ldots x_j \ldots)$ and $x_j c = g(\ldots) \rightarrow x_k c = f(\ldots g(\ldots) \ldots)$.

2. Or, more carefully, our confidence in a counterfactual can be no higher than our confidence that our causal model will produce correct predictions about this counterfactual.

3. Hausman (1998) aims to make this connection. But as his title, *Causal Asymmetries* suggests, generally what he succeeds in doing is using his claims to obtain causal order. For instance, he shows that, given his claims about the independent variability of causal principles, if b counterfactually depends on a, then a causes b. This is an important result. But to establish it requires the prior assumption that if a and b are counterfactually connected then either a causes b, or the reverse, or the two have a common cause, plus his own (as opposed for instance to David Lewis's) constraints on the nearness relation for a possible-world semantics for counterfactuals (which I describe below in discussing implementation neutral counterfactuals). Hausman and Woodward (1999) also claim that the independent variability assumption implies the causal Markov condition. But they do not show that the assumption implies the causal Markov condition, which is false; but rather that there are some systems of equations in which both are true and that it is, roughly speaking, "the same" features of these systems that guarantee both assumptions (see Cartwright 2002, forthcoming).

4. Or rather, we know this relative to the factors included in the causal model. Presumably no causal model will be complete, so this remains as a source of ambiguity in our counterfactual claims.

5. I shall follow LeRoy's convention throughout and use lowercase letters for variables, and uppercase for their values.

6. Note that the reduced form equation need not be a causal function in the sense that I shall introduce from Heckman, since LeRoy allows that the external variables may not be variation free, though he thinks it would be odd if they were not.

7. For a longer discussion of Pearl and Lewis, see Reiss and Cartwright 2003.

8. Or, keeping in mind Heckman's view that causality is only relative to a model, the right-hand-side variables record what the model designates as causes.

9. Recall that the discussion here is limited to linear systems; the concept of a causal contribution is more complex in nonlinear systems. Also note that this supposes that

all principles in the model with x_c on the right-hand side and x_e on the left will have the same coefficient. This will be the case given a proper statement of "transitivity" and the definitions for the form of causal principles sketched in Cartwright 2003.

10. For a definition see Cartwright 2003.

11. For further discussion see Cartwright 1989. It should be admitted, of course, that once the causes need not be variation free, the simple operational way of defining causal contribution in a way analogous to Heckman's definition of causal/ counterfactual effect is not available. But, as we know, there are compelling arguments in the philosophical literature to establish that demanding operational definitions is both too strong and too weak a requirement—it lets in concepts that do not make sense, and does not provide a proper understanding of those that do.

12. So that $U(\pm S \pm L \pm G) = U(\pm S \pm L)$.

13. When there is more than one common cause involved, the usual generalization of this formula conditions on the state descriptions over the common causes, weighted with the probabilities with which each state description obtains.

14. In the linear models assumed in section 2, the coefficients of each variable are assumed to be functionally independent of the values of all variables, so relativization analogous to the relativization to $+G$ and $\neg G$ here was not necessary. The assumption here, analogous to that in section 2, would be that S's contribution to L is the same in the presence and in the absence of G.

15. I offer this as a plausible example. Whether it is the "correct" formula or not will, as I have argued, depend on the details of the causal model; and, as I have also already noted, we do not yet have very good prescriptions for getting from the great variety of different kinds of models we employ, to methods of evaluating the various different kinds of implementation neutral and implementation specific counterfactuals we may need for policy.

References

Cartwright, N. 1989. *Nature's Capacities and Their Measurement*. Oxford: Clarendon Press.

Cartwright, N. 1999. *The Dappled World: A Study of the Boundaries of Science*. Cambridge: Cambridge University Press.

Cartwright, N. 2002. "Against Modularity, the Causal Markov Condition, and Any Link between the Two: Comments on Hausman and Woodward." *British Journal for the Philosophy of Science* 53: 411–453.

Cartwright, N. 2003. "Two Theorems on Invariance and Causality." *Philosophy of Science* 70: 203–224.

Cartwright, N. Forthcoming. "From Metaphysics to Method: Comments on Manipulability and the Causal Markov Condition."

Hausman, D. 1998. *Causal Asymmetries*. Cambridge: Cambridge University Press.

Hausman, D., and J. Woodward. 1999. "Independence, Invariance, and the Causal Markov Condition." *British Journal for the Philosophy of Science* 50: 521–583.

Hausman, D., and J. Woodward. 2004. "Modularity and the Causal Markov Condition: A Restatement." *British Journal for the Philosophy of Science* 55: 147–161.

Heckman, J. 2001. "Econometrics, Counterfactuals, and Causal Models." Keynote address, International Statistical Institute, Seoul, Korea.

Hoover, K. 2001. *Causality in Macroeconomics*. Cambridge: Cambridge University Press.

LeRoy, S. 2003. "Causality in Economics." Manuscript, University of California, Santa Barbara.

Pearl, J. 2000. *Causality: Models, Reasoning, and Inference*. Cambridge: Cambridge University Press.

Reiss, J., and N. Cartwright. 2003. "Uncertainty in Econometrics: Evaluating Policy Counterfactuals." *Causality: Metaphysics and Methods Technical Report*. Centre for the Philosophy of Natural and Social Science, LSE CTR 11-03.

11 Why Don't You Want to Be Rich? Preference Explanation on the Basis of Causal Structure

Till Grüne-Yanoff

To explain people's behavior, we often cite their preferences. It is commonly accepted that to be explanatory, a preference—in combination with other mental states—must have brought about the behavior in question in the appropriate way. One condition for being an appropriate preference for this purpose is that the preferred alternative stands in a relevant relation to the behavior in question. This restricts the explanatory use of many preferences. For example, an agent's preference for coffee over brandy at this moment (at 8 a.m., after waking up) does not explain her choice of coffee over brandy at the end of the dinner party yesterday night. Instead, to explain yesterday's choice requires a preference over alternatives that stand in some abstracting relationship to yesterday evening's choices—maybe a preference for coffee over brandy after dinners, or a preference for nonalcoholic beverages. In order to be explanatorily useful, the most preferred alternative has to exhibit a degree of abstraction, so that the behavior in question can be related to it.

This condition easily comes into conflict with the need to empirically justify preference ascriptions. Preferences are mental states. Given that introspection does not provide a reliable epistemic basis, preferences cannot be directly observed, but can only be derived indirectly from observed behavior. From choices, however, one can only infer preferences over specific states of the world. For example, observing an agent choosing coffee over brandy for breakfast does not justify attributing to her a general preference for coffee over brandy. Even attributing to her a general preference to have coffee for breakfast, rather than brandy, would require observing her breakfast behavior under many different circumstances. Choice observations only justify attributing preferences over the very specific circumstances in which the choice was observed.

This presents a problem for explaining behavior with preferences. Only the most specific preferences can be derived from an agent's observable behavior. But if the outcomes over which preferences are defined are very specific, then they cannot be employed in explaining any behavior except for the very choices that justified their attribution in the first place. Such explanations would be trivial. So how can one ascribe preferences that are sufficiently abstract for explanatory purposes, in an empirically justified manner?

What is needed is a way to construct abstract preferences on the basis of specific preferences, such that the empirical justification of the specific preferences, based on observed choices, is preserved in the derived abstract ones. Indefinitely many degrees of abstraction can be distinguished. For simplicity, only two levels of abstraction are distinguished here—specific preferences over *worlds*, and abstract preferences over *prospects*. This paper develops a *principle of preference abstraction* that connects world-preferences with prospect-preferences. The basis of this link, I will argue, is a model of causal belief.

It has been claimed that world preferences are not basic in decision making, and that instead we make decisions from prospect preferences to world preferences.[1] Based on this claim, some have argued against the methodological construction of abstract preferences from more specific ones.

For a disposition to choose to count as a preference, it must be a disposition to choose with a reason—a disposition to choose on the basis of the properties displayed by the alternatives.... The equation of preferences with such brute [mere behavioral] dispositions is bound to seem inappropriate under the assumption of desiderative structure. And rightly so. After all, even if a person is disposed to choose one unconsidered prospect rather than another, he will be equally disposed, if possible, to consider the properties before making his choice. (Pettit 2002, p. 209)

This may be an argument against a kind of methodological behaviorism, but not against the methodological identification of prospect preferences from behavioral data. What needs to be distinguished is a metaphysical from a methodological meaning of "basic." While the atomism-holism debate remains undecided, it is not methodologically controversial that the prime empirical justification of preferences can be obtained from choice observations. The principle of preference abstraction presented here, therefore, does not take a stance on the former debate, but is only constructed to clarify the role of preferences in explanation of behavior.

Section 1 presents the principle of abstraction as a selection problem of the worlds relevant for defining a preference relation between two prospects. Various restrictions on that function are proposed—first for conjointly exhaustive prospects only, and then for prospect pairs that are not exhaustive. Last, the specific problem of actions is discussed. Section 2 presents a model of the agent's causal beliefs. On the basis of this model, the selection function is specified. The resulting definition of prospect preferences allows characterizing the conditions under which this relation is reflexive, transitive, and complete. Section 3 addresses two problems for further research, and concludes the essay.

1 Prospect Preferences

To formally present this principle, I will make a number of assumptions. First, I assume that there exists a level of maximally specific states of the worlds, denoted $w_1, \ldots, w_n$. Second, a weak preference pre-order (i.e., a binary relation over worlds that is reflexive and transitive) is defined over these worlds, based on the agent's choices. For simplicity reasons, it will be assumed that all choices are made over certain outcomes.[2] Choices are made over certain, most specific outcomes—over worlds. Preferences over worlds are derived from these choices as follows: An agent (weakly) prefers w_i to w_j ($w_i \geq w_j$) if she chooses w_i over the available w_j. She is said to be indifferent between w_i and w_j ($w_i \approx w_j$) iff both $w_i \geq w_j$ and $w_j \geq w_i$. She is said to (strictly) prefer w_i to w_j iff $w_i \geq w_j$ and not $w_i \geq w_j$.[3]

Third, I assume that worlds are fully analyzable into conjunctions of certain prospects. A prospect can be the particular realization of a property, or a conjunction thereof, or the fact that a property is realized at all. Trivially, worlds are prospects as well. A further restrictive assumption I make is that of determinism. Ultimately, there is no uncertainty in any world; hence every world is fully analyzable into certain prospects. Prospects are denoted p, q, r and worlds are sets of the prospects into which they are analyzable—for example, $p \in w_i$.

Last, I assume deterministic causal relations to be defined over certain prospects. This relation is irreflexive, asymmetric, and acyclical, but not complete. It is interpreted as the beliefs an agent holds about the causal dependence of particular prospects.

The principle of abstraction that I propose comes in the guise of a definition of the preference relation $\succeq$ over prospects $p, q, \ldots$ in terms of the preference relation $\geq$ over worlds $w_1, w_2, \ldots$ It employs a representation function f that picks out pairs of worlds $\langle w^p, w^q \rangle$ for each pair of propositions $\langle p, q \rangle$:

Definition 1. $p \succeq q \Leftrightarrow w_i^p \geq w_i^q$ for all $\langle w_i^p, w_i^q \rangle \in f(\langle p, q \rangle)$

Definition 1 is trivial if the propositions p and q are worlds themselves. It becomes interesting if p and q are more abstract than the respective worlds. Then, from left to right, f picks out all those worlds that are specifications of the preference between p and q. Conversely, the preferences between all worlds picked out by f determine the preference between the prospects p and q.[4]

I will discuss the form of f in two separate installments. In the first step, I will focus on the special case where prospect preferences are only defined over a prospect p and its negation $\neg p$. In such a preference, mutually exclusive and conjointly exhaustive prospects are compared.[5] In the second step, I will discuss prospect preferences defined between mutually exclusive, but conjointly not exhaustive prospects.[6] This distinction is important, because the latter prospects feature in preference orderings beyond the pairwise level, while the former do not. Thus preferences over mutually exclusive, but conjointly not exhaustive prospects are subject to the transitivity property, and I will present an interesting result here.

1.1 Mutually Exclusive and Conjointly Exhaustive Prospects

In this subsection I will restrict myself to cases where definition 1 defines preferences over prospects and their negations only; preferences of the sort $p \succeq \neg p$. The way f picks out worlds is of central importance for the preference relation between prospects; definition 1 says nothing about it. There are at least three different doctrines about how to specify f.

The *absolute* preference approach stipulates that all worlds that are logically compatible with a prospect have to be taken into account. That is, any world w^p that contains a prospect p has to be preferred to any other world $w^{\neg p}$ that does not contain the prospect p. This very quickly leads to enormous numbers of world-comparisons necessary for the derivation of a prospect preference. For example, imagine worlds were differentiated by only four prospects, p, q, r, s. Then there would be $2^3 = 8$ different worlds that contain p, and 8 that do not. In the absolute preference approach, all possible $8^2 = 64$ comparisons between p-worlds and $\neg p$-worlds have to show a preference for p worlds, in order to derive the prospect preference $p \succeq \neg p$ from it.

In such a universe, let p be the agent's consumption of Marmite, q and r prospects irrelevant at the moment, and s the case that the agent is allergic to Marmite. Now, whether q and r are realized or not, as long as s is not, the agent prefers the world in which she consumes Marmite to the one where she does not. But, quite understandably, she does prefer the world where she is allergic to the stuff and does not consume it to worlds where she does consume it and suffers the allergic consequences of her actions. Should her preference between those last two worlds determine her prospect preference over Marmite consumption? I don't think so. The scenario is *counterfactual*; she does not actually suffer from the allergy. This does not mean that counterfactual scenarios do not have any influence on prospect preferences; I will show further down that they do. But in this case, the counterfactual scenario is *causally independent* of the prospect in question; Marmite consumption does not cause Marmite allergy. The absolute account does not allow this abstraction and thus should be discarded.

The *ceteris paribus* preference approach stipulates that only those worlds are taken into account, which are as similar as possible to each other, while realizing and not realizing the prospect in question respectively. That is, any world w^p that contains a prospect p has to be preferred to that other world $w^{\neg p}$ which is as similar to w^p in as many aspects as possible.[7]

For illustration, let's imagine that the four aspects of our four-aspect worlds are logically independent. Then, clearly, there is exactly one w^p-world that is most similar to one $w^{\neg p}$-world: namely that world that shares with w^p the realization or nonrealization of all aspects but p. According to the ceteris paribus approach, then, there are only eight comparisons between the four-aspect-worlds necessary to establish prospect preferences. This can be illustrated in table 11.1, where the numerals in the columns signify the realization or nonrealization of an aspect in the respective world.

Table 11.1 shows the sufficient conditions for $p \succeq \neg p$ according to the ceteris paribus approach. Each world in which p is realized is compared with the world in which p is not realized, but which is otherwise as similar as logically possible. If all aspects are logically independent—that is, no aspect is implied by any other aspect nor implies any other aspect—then the

Table 11.1
Ceteris paribus comparisons

w_i^p	p	q	r	s		$w_i^{\neg p}$	p	q	r	s
(1)	1	0	0	0	$\geq$	(1)	0	0	0	0
(2)	1	1	0	0	$\geq$	(2)	0	1	0	0
⋮	⋮	⋮	⋮	⋮	⋮	⋮	⋮	⋮	⋮	⋮
(8)	1	1	1	1	$\geq$	(8)	0	1	1	1

two worlds compared differ only in the realization of p. As we are free to choose how to partition the worlds into prospects, we can avoid partitions with logically dependent prospects. Thus the comparisons will always look like the one illustrated in table 11.1.

There are two fundamental problems with the ceteris paribus account. First, it rests on a concept of logical possibility, which is too wide for the purpose at hand. Second, it disregards the world the agent is in when making the comparison. The following example will illustrate both of these shortcomings.

Diogenes Laertius, the ancient chatterbox, tells of an incident where Alexander the Great puts Diogenes of Sinope to the touch. "Ask of me any boon you like," the Macedonian is reported to have offered; to which the reply came, "Stand out of my light."[8] The anecdote is quite popular, and rightly so. At first sight, Diogenes seems to act contrary to a knee-jerk reaction of most of us. You are offered wealth or power for free—then take it! In this version of the story, Alexander embodies the ancient idea of Kairos, Machiavelli's Fortuna or, if you will, one of the brothers Grimm's good fairies. When Diogenes declines the seemingly irresistible offer, he must have good reasons for it.

As revealed in his choice, Diogenes prefers a world w^u undisturbed by any patron, however powerful, to a world w^o which promises all the wealth and influence Alexander has to offer. If we now think that the two worlds differed in only one relevant aspect, wealth, we could derive Diogenes' preference for poverty over wealth. But even though we do not know much about them, we can suspect that Diogenes' other choices could not have been subsumed under such a simple prospect preference. Even that most hardened despiser of material wealth, we suspect, must have seen that wealth and power were desirable for him too—he could have survived without panhandling, he could have bought his freedom, or he could have convinced the elders of Sinope to remove the ban and let him return to his homeland. So had Alexander asked (his immediate reaction is not reported), in slight astonishment, "But don't you want to be rich?" Diogenes' answer, if for once straightforward, would have also been complex. "On the one hand," he would have retorted, "there is a sense in which I want to be rich. But on the other hand look at the world I live in—if I took a significant boon from you, I would be obliged to show my gratitude. Further, my lifestyle would be considered implausible; and people would envy me for my easily achieved wealth. Under these conditions, I do not want to be rich."

With this extra bit of information, we may try to apply the ceteris paribus framework for an analysis of Diogenes' preferences. According to the account I have put into his mouth, Diogenes identifies four aspects of w^u and w^o to be relevant—wealth (r), independence from donors (i), personal credibility (c), and the envy of others (e). Clearly, all these aspects are logically independent. Thus the specification of f in the table 11.1 applies. According to it, Diogenes compares $w_1^u = \{\neg r, \neg i, \neg c, \neg e\}$ with $w_1^o = \{r, \neg i, \neg c, \neg e\}$; $w_2^u = \{\neg r, i, \neg c, \neg e\}$ with $w_2^o = \{r, i, \neg c, \neg e\}$, and so on. Whatever his preferences between those worlds are, and whatever the resulting prospect preferences are, this specification of f does not capture his story at all if it goes: "On the one hand, I want to be rich. But on the other hand, look at the world I live in ..." There, he compares $w_i^u = \{\neg r, i, c, \neg e\}$ with $w_i^o = \{r, \neg i, \neg c, e\}$. According to the ceteris paribus account and the logical independence of the aspects, such a comparison is not admissible, because the worlds are too far apart. So does Diogenes tell us an incoherent story, or is the ceteris paribus approach wrong?

I propose that it is the ceteris paribus approach that is flawed. Diogenes does not employ logical but *causal* possibility when assessing the independence of the worlds' aspects. He envisages a particular way in which he can achieve wealth—through his submission to a donor. As he tells us, he believes in the causal dependence of the other relevant aspects on this genesis of wealth. His wealth would cause the envy of others; his submission to a donor would cause the loss of his independence, which in turn would cause the loss of his credibility. Given the causal dependence Diogenes believes in, worlds that are most similar to w^u except for the realization of wealth are not those the ceteris paribus account suggests. It is causally impossible for Diogenes to be wealthy without being envied; it is equally impossible for him to be wealthy through the benefits of a donor without becoming dependent on him, and hence losing his credibility.

Even though these worlds are logically possible, what matters for a principle of abstraction is *causal* possibility. Logical possibility only forbids what is inconsistent, while causal possibility allows only what can be produced. An agent takes only those p-worlds as possible that are producible according to her causal beliefs. This epistemic notion of causality will restrict the selection function in the following way:

Restriction 1. f picks out only those worlds that are causally compatible with p and $\neg p$, respectively.

But this restriction alone is not sufficient for the right choice of f. The causal structure an agent believes in restricts the worlds she will deem possible; but she will not compare all possible worlds, as some of them are too far removed from her actual situation. Thus, facts believed to be true play a role too.

To stay with the above example, Diogenes might reasonably believe that secretly inheriting from a distant relative causes one to be wealthy without any strings attached. Thus, such a causal story would allow him to introduce into definition 1 the world w^o where he is wealthy, independent, credible, and not envied, due to the secrecy of the inheritance. So it might seem that because of the possibility that this belief opens, Diogenes does not prefer poverty to wealth unconditionally. It seems he only prefers it conditional on other aspects, in this case the absence of any living patron.

This appearance is wrong. Diogenes does not have any wealthy relatives from whom to inherit (or at least, we, as the interpreters of his behavior, do not know of any). To define his prospect preferences, we do not take into account *all* the causally possible worlds that realize the relevant prospects; we only take into account the causal possibilities that can be realized in the world the agent is in.

The above preference expression should therefore be interpreted as taking the relevant causal background conditions to be the same as in the actual world. Of course, not all background conditions can be the same—otherwise no counterfactual world could be constructed that adheres to the causal structure. For Diogenes to imagine a world in which he is wealthy—seen from his actual predicament of poverty—a counter*factual* assumption is necessary; but changing the facts does not mean changing the causal dependency structure. The change of facts, under stable causal dependencies, will require certain causally prior prospects to change as well—somehow, his wealth has to be caused in this possible world. But there are facts in the actual world that offer themselves as ready causes; there are donors offering their support, but there are not any wealthy, distant relatives ready to bequeath estates to Diogenes. Those facts that do not have to be changed in order to accommodate the counterfactual—either because there is no causal link to them at all, or because there are other causes closer to the actual situation—remain as they are in the actual world. Hence,

Restriction 2. f picks out only those worlds that realize p and q but maximally comply with the background conditions pertaining to the actual world.

Under the two restrictions on f for which I argued here, we can indeed say that Diogenes preferred poverty to wealth unconditionally; f identifies the necessary preferences over worlds, and definition 1 determines a prospect preference on that basis. In this sense, definition 1 is a principle of preference abstraction for preferences over mutually exclusive and conjointly exhaustive prospects.

1.2   Mutually Exclusive and Conjointly Nonexhaustive Prospects

Prospect preferences are not only used in the sense that one prefers the realization over the nonrealization of a prospect, as Diogenes prefers poverty over wealth, according to the scheme $p \succeq \neg p$. Preferences also occur in contexts where the two relata do not exhaust the alternatives. For example, over breakfast I prefer reading an English paper to a German one; and I prefer a German to a Russian newspaper. These three types of newspapers certainly do not exhaust the possibilities of breakfast reading, nor do they exhaust my ordering of breakfast readings. However, it is perfectly intelligible to hold preferences between conjointly nonexhaustive prospects; the problem only is that such preferences cannot be represented as cases of the scheme $p \succeq \neg p$.

Conjointly nonexhaustive relata occurring in preference types $p \succeq q$ are not necessarily mutually exclusive. For example, one can meaningfully hold a preference like "I prefer an apartment in New York to a house in

Tuscany," even though it is clearly possible to own an apartment in New York and a house in Tuscany at the same time.[9] However, to express a preference $p \succeq q$ without meaning to express a preference for $p \wedge \neg q$ over $q \wedge \neg p$ is likely to violate Grice's Cooperative Principle (Grice 1989). In particular, if uttered in a situation of choice between either p or q, the conversational contribution made does not satisfy the pragmatic convention of relevance—preferences over relata involving $p \wedge q$ do not help making such a choice.

If uttered in a situation where information about the speaker's evaluations is sought, it does not satisfy the pragmatic convention of informativeness; $p \wedge q \succeq q \wedge p$ is tautological, and thus empirically empty. By conversational implication, then, a preference between mutually nonexclusive relata is interpreted as a preference between the corresponding mutually exclusive relata (Halldén 1957, p. 28). This conventional translation procedure has to be amended for cases where at least one relatum logically implies the other or causally requires the presence of the other. Thus $p \succeq q$ is translated to $p \wedge \neg q \succeq q \wedge \neg p$ only if it is possible that $p \wedge \neg q$ and $q \wedge \neg p$. In cases where it is not, the original relatum remains untranslated (cf. Hansson 2001, pp. 68–70). Thus restriction 1 needs to be reformulated for conjointly nonexhaustive prospects in the following way.

Restriction 3. f picks out only those worlds that are causally compatible with $p \wedge \neg q$ and $q \wedge \neg p$, respectively.[10]

Concerning the actual causal background, a similar restriction holds as for the conjointly exhaustive case. Trapp (1985) gives an example for preferences over different diseases (that are not conjointly exhaustive). A man who prefers contracting cholera to being ill with cancer should not be interpreted as preferring a situation where there is no cure for cholera (e.g., in a country where there are no antibiotics available). The belief in the existence of a cure has significance consequences if one has either cholera or cancer, and hence naturally plays a crucial role in the evaluation of both situations. Thus, the agent prefers cholera to cancer iff he prefers worlds where he has cholera and all the contemporary cures are available, to worlds where he has cancer and all the contemporary cures are available. The restriction is thus reformulated as follows:

Restriction 4. f picks out only those worlds that realize $p \wedge \neg q$ and $q \wedge \neg p$ but maximally comply with those background conditions pertaining to the actual world.

A particularly interesting feature of preferences over conjointly nonexhaustive prospects is that the pairwise comparisons *may* give rise to a preference ordering—but not necessarily. Under particular conditions, the preference pairs $p \succeq q$ and $q \succeq r$ imply the additional preference pair $p \succeq r$. This transitivity property of preferences need not be fulfilled by prospect preferences, even though it is (by assumption) satisfied by the preferences over worlds underlying it. All that needs to be established is that the worlds $w^{p \wedge \neg q}$ (compared in $p \succeq q$ with the worlds $w^{q \wedge \neg p}$) and the worlds $w^{r \wedge \neg q}$ (compared in $q \succeq r$ with the worlds $w^{q \wedge \neg r}$) are not the same as the worlds $w^{p \wedge \neg r}$ and $w^{r \wedge \neg p}$ compared in $p \succeq r$. Thus, if $w^{p \wedge \neg q} \neq w^{p \wedge \neg r}$ and $w^{r \wedge \neg q} \neq w^{r \wedge \neg p}$, it does not follow from $w^{p \wedge \neg q} \geq w^{q \wedge \neg p}$ and $w^{q \wedge \neg r} \geq w^{r \wedge \neg q}$ that $w^{p \wedge \neg q} \geq w^{r \wedge \neg q}$. Hence, by definition 1, it does not follow from $p \succeq q$ and $q \succeq r$ that $p \succeq r$.

1.3   Actions

An action is a particular kind of prospect. Distinguishing actions from other prospects here is important because agents evaluate their own actions, and sometimes those of others, in a different way than they evaluate other prospects. While the evaluation of a prospect takes into account all causal antecedents of that prospect, the evaluation of an action only takes into account the action itself and all its consequences, while disregarding any causal history that led to the action.

Take Diogenes' example again. The only way for him to achieve wealth would have been to submit to a donor, which in turn would have had consequences for his independence and credibility. All in all, he preferred a world without those consequences to a world with them; thus, he preferred poverty to wealth. But if he took those indirect consequences of wealth and poverty into account, shouldn't he cast the net even wider? Should he not also take into account the causes of his own action, and other effects that those causes brought about?

Let us push the Diogenes story one step further. Imagine that his propensity to reject a potential sponsor is based on his contempt for authority. This character trait *causes* Diogenes (he believes) to be so disposed. It also *caused* him (he suspects) to rebel against paternal authority, shaming his father and bringing disgrace to his family—consequences he found utterly undesirable. To have to choose between being rich and being dependent upon Alexander's offer will remind him of his character trait and its consequences. Insofar as the prospect that Diogenes stays poor is realized only in a world in which he rejects Alexander's offer, that world then also brings with it his rebellious character trait, his father's shame, and his family's disgrace.

Should he derive his prospect preferences from a comparison between worlds that honor these causal dependencies? Some claim so: Actions should not be treated differently from other prospects.

[T]o the extent that acts can realistically be identified with propositions, the present notion of preference is active as well as passive: it relates to acts as well as to news items … From this viewpoint, the notion of preference is neutral, regarding the active passive distinction. If the agent is deliberating about performing act A or act B, and if AB is impossible, there is no effective difference between asking whether he prefers A to B as a news item or as an act, for he makes the news. (Jeffrey 1983, p. 84)

On Jeffrey's account, Diogenes takes his rejection of a donor as the news of his character trait and its consequences. Presumably, what Jeffrey means by "he makes the news" is that there is no further causal history to an action that carries news characteristics. But the above example shows that this assumption is not generally true. By observing his own choice, the news that he makes includes information about the cause of his choice—his character trait—and further effects of that cause. If Diogenes evaluated his action just as any other prospect, he would take those effects into account, comparing worlds in which his contempt for authority disposes him to reject his sponsor and shame his father, with worlds in which he had not humiliated his father, accepts Alexander's offer, becomes wealthy, dependent, and loses his credibility. If he preferred the latter to the former, given the causal dependencies, he may indeed have prefer being wealthy to being poor.[11]

I think this model of evaluation is flawed. Neither Diogenes nor any other responsible actor takes into account the causes of their actions, and the effects of these causes, when evaluating their actions. An agent who evaluates a non-action state of the world takes a passive outlook—he takes into account what consequences this state has, and how this state came about, with the other consequences which that cause witnessed. An agent who performs an action exhibits an active outlook—she chooses between various options according to the benefit of their consequences; but she takes the world as it is, disregarding any influences that might have caused her action.

Statements that describe acts are different in kind from other sorts of propositions simply because the actor has the power to make them true. With this power comes a kind of responsibility. An agent must, if rational, do what she can to change things for the better … rational decision makers should choose actions on the basis of their efficacy in bringing about desirable results rather than their auspiciousness as harbingers of these results. Efficacy and auspiciousness often go together, of course, since most actions get to be good or bad news only by causally promoting good or bad things. In cases where causing and indicating come apart, however, the causal decision theorist maintains that it is the causal properties of the act, rather than its pure evidential features, that should serve as the guide to rational conduct. (Joyce 1999, p. 150)

Acts must be considered exogenous. Thus Diogenes should disregard the causes of his choices and their respective effects, when evaluating the prospects of wealth and poverty respectively. Instead, he compares worlds that replace the effects of the cause of his action with what he actually believes happened, irrespective of what action he chose. The principle of abstraction is therefore amended for the case of actions.

Restriction 5. If p and q are actions, f picks out all those worlds that are compatible with $p \wedge \neg q$ and $q \wedge \neg p$, respectively, and their respective causal consequences, while disregarding their causal histories.

The disagreement between the two positions sketched out here remains, however, insofar as prospects often cannot be clearly identified as actions or non-actions. Thus the allies of Jeffrey might be right in insisting that some apparent actions are evaluated as news items. This does not touch on the basis of the argument, and is of no further relevance here. With these amendments added to the specification of f, definition 1 is a principle of abstraction for all prospect preferences.

2   Constructing the Selection Function

The concepts of causal compatibility, maximal compliance with the actual world, and causal history so far have been given only intuitive meaning. This section seeks to specify their meaning more formally, by reference to a formal concept of causal models.

A causal model is defined by Pearl (2000, p. 203) as a triple

$$M = \langle U, V, G \rangle$$

where:

1. U is a set of background variables, determined by factors outside the model.

2. V is a set of endogenous variables, determined by variables of the model—that is, variables in $U \cup V$.

3. G is a set of functions $\{g_1, g_2, \ldots g_n\}$ such that each g_i is a mapping from $U \cup (V \backslash V_i)$ to V_i and such that the entire set G forms a mapping from U to V. In other words, each g_i tells us the value of V_i given the values of all other variables in $U \cup V$, and the entire set G has a unique solution $V(u)$. Symbolically, G is represented by

$$V_i = g_i(V_j, U_i), \quad i = 1, \ldots, n.$$

$U_i \subseteq U$ stands for the unique minimal set of variables in U sufficient to determine V_i on the basis of G.

The variables in Pearl's model are random variables. I take the individual realization of a random variable to be equivalent to a prospect, for example, $p \equiv (V_i = v_i^1)$. Given a particular constellation of background variables, $U_1 = u_1, \ldots, U_n = u_n$, the model has the unique solution $V(u_1, \ldots, u_n)$. Prospects can be directly deduced from this solution: $V(u_1, \ldots, u_n) \vdash p$, where $\vdash$ is the classical inference relation.

  M can be represented as an acyclical directed graph, with the arrows representing the function g. Forked arrows show that g has more than one argument. Figure 11.1 is an illustrative example of such a representation of $M^* = \langle U^*, V^*, G^* \rangle$, with all variables in $U^* = \{U_1, \ldots, U_4\}$ and $V^* = \{V_1, \ldots, V_4\}$ having only two realizations each, and $G^* =$

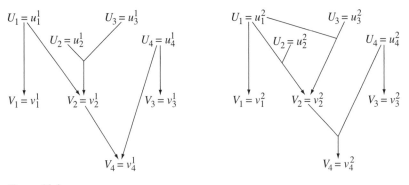

Figure 11.1
An example of a causal graph.

$\{V_1 = g_1(u_1), \ldots, V_4 = g_4(v_2, u_4)\}$. Each realization is equivalent to a proposition or its negation. Let the first realization of a background variable be expressed by $a, b, c \ldots$, that is, $a \equiv (U_i = u_i^1)$, etc.; the realization of a endogenous variable by $p, q, r, \ldots$, that is, $p \equiv (V_i = v_i^1)$, etc.; and the respective second realization by a negation of that proposition, $\neg p \equiv (V_i = v_i^2)$, etc.

Each world w specifies the values for all U_i and for all V_i of every M. Because the functional relationships g_i of M restricts the endogenous V's given the exogenous U's, many worlds are inconsistent with a specific causal model.

Definition 2. A world w is *consistent* with a causal model $M = \langle U, V, G \rangle$ iff there is a set of realizations u^*, such that $U_1 = u_1, \ldots, U_n = u_n$, for which $w \vdash u^*$ and $w \vdash V(u^*)$.

For example, the world $w_1 = \{a, \neg b, c, \neg d, p, q, r, \neg s\}$ is consistent with the model M represented in figure 11.1, while the world $w_2 = \{\neg a, b, \neg c, d, p, q, r, s\}$ is not. Having specified the relations between prospects and worlds on the one hand and the causal model and its variables on the other, we can now define causal compatibility:

Definition 3. w is *causally compatible* with p with respect to M iff there is a causal model $M = \langle U, V, G \rangle$ such that w is consistent with M, and $w \vdash p$.

For example, the world $w_1 = \{a, \neg b, c, \neg d, p, q, r, \neg s\}$ is compatible with p with respect to M. Worlds which are causally compatible with p represent the possible causal histories of p. In such a world there is at least one "chain" that leads from background conditions to p in the following way.

Definition 4. A prospect p is dependent with respect to the background conditions in $U^* \subseteq U$ iff there is a functional chain: $V_1 = g_1(u^*)$, $V_2 = g_2(V_1, u^*), \ldots, V_n = g_n(V_1, \ldots, V_{n-1}, u^*)$ with $g_1, \ldots, g_n \in G$ and p being equivalent to $V_n = g_n(v_1, \ldots, v_{n-1}, u^*)$.

According to M represented in figure 11.1, for example, q is dependent on a and (b, c), while r is dependent on a, (b, c), and d. Now if a prospect p is not realized in the actual world $w^@$, all it takes for p to be realized is that one background condition on which p is dependent is realized. Of course p is realized as well in worlds where more than one background condition on which p is dependent is realized, but in those cases the ensuing worlds are not as similar as possible to the actual world.

Definition 5. A world w^* is maximally similar to the actual world $w^@$ iff for w^* out of the set of all worlds: $\max(\#(w^* \cap w^@))$.

"#" here signifies the cardinality of the intersection of the respective world with the actual world. By maximizing the cardinality of this set, those worlds are chosen which have the highest overlap with the actual world.

Restrictions 1 and 2 (or 3 and 4, respectively) are satisfied if f selects worlds w^p and w^q, which are compatible with p and q with respect to M, respectively, such that both w^p and w^q are most similar to $w^@$ by the above similarity measure. With the concepts discussed in this section, we can therefore specify definition 1:

Definition 1*. $p \Leftrightarrow q \Leftrightarrow w_i^p \geq w_i^q$ for all $\langle w_i^p, w_i^q \rangle$ that are compatible with $p \wedge \neg q$ and $q \wedge \neg p$ with respect to M, respectively, such that both w_i^p, w_i^q are most similar to $w^@$.

Definition 1* yields a preference relation $\succeq$ over propositions with the following properties.

Theorem 1. If the causal model is non-cyclical, $\succeq$ is reflexive.

Proof: For each world w_i compatible with p, there is a realization of the background variables u_i such that the proposition equivalent to $V(u_i) \cup u_i$ is contains in w_i. u can be distinguished into the independent and the dependent background conditions, u^*. If there is only one set u^* for p, the proof is trivial, because there is only one world that is compatible with p. If there is more than one u^*, then the similarity relation ensures that only identical u_i^*'s are paired. Hence, for all $\langle w_i, w_j \rangle \in f(\langle p, q \rangle)$: $w_i = w_j$. Given that $\geq$ is reflexive, the relation $\succeq$ defined thus is equally reflexive.

Theorem 2. If for all prospects $p, q, r \ldots$, all causally possible conjunctions $p \wedge \neg q$, $p \wedge \neg r$ are dependent on the same background variable u^{p^*} (and similarly for $q \wedge \neg p$, $r \wedge \neg q, \ldots$), then a prospect preference ordering over $p, q, r, \ldots$ is transitive.

Proof: Without loss of generality, we take the case where $p \succeq q$ and $q \succeq r$. If all $p \wedge \neg q$, $p \wedge \neg r$ are causally possible, then there are causally compatible worlds such that $p \wedge \neg q \in w^{p \wedge \neg q}$ and $p \wedge \neg r \in w^{p \wedge \neg r}$. If for all p, q, r, $p \wedge \neg q$ and $p \wedge \neg r$ are dependent on the same variable u^{p^*}, then there is at least one world $w^p = w^{p \wedge \neg q} = w^{p \wedge \neg r}$ which is causally compatible with both $p \wedge \neg q$ and $p \wedge \neg r$. If $p \wedge \neg q$ and $p \wedge \neg r$ depend only on u^*, then $w^p = w^{p \wedge \neg q} = w^{p \wedge \neg r}$ is the world causally compatible with $p \wedge \neg q$ and $p \wedge \neg r$

which by definition 5 is most similar to $w^@$ (for the same reasons, mutatis mutandis, $w^q = w^{q \wedge \neg p} = w^{q \wedge \neg r}$ is the world causally compatible with $q \wedge \neg p$ and $q \wedge \neg r$ which is most similar to $w^@$). By definition 1*, and $p \succeq q$ and $q \succeq r$, $w^{p \wedge \neg q} \geq w^{q \wedge \neg p}$ and $w^{q \wedge \neg r} \geq w^{r \wedge \neg q}$. By the argument above, $w^{p \wedge \neg q} = w^{p \wedge \neg r}$ and $w^{q \wedge \neg p} = w^{q \wedge \neg r}$, hence $w^{p \wedge \neg r} \geq w^{q \wedge \neg r}$ and $w^{q \wedge \neg r} \geq w^{r \wedge \neg p}$, and thus by transitivity of $\geq$: $w^{p \wedge \neg r} \geq w^{r \wedge \neg p}$. Then by definition 1*, $p \succeq r$.[12]

It is further noteworthy that $\succeq$ is not complete, even if $\geq$ is. This can easily be seen by the following counterexample. Take a $\langle p, q \rangle$ such that $\langle w_1^p, w_1^q \rangle \in f(\langle p, q \rangle)$ and $\langle w_2^p, w_2^q \rangle \in f(\langle p, q \rangle)$, such that $w_1^p > w_1^q$ and $w_2^q > w_2^p$. Then $\succeq$ is not defined over $\langle p, q \rangle$.

These results are quite weak, but they represent genuine properties of pairwise preferences. The antecedent of theorem 2 is of course often not fulfilled, which explains the manifold existence of intransitive preference comparisons. That preferences are not complete over the set of all prospects should not be surprising at all.

The formal apparatus developed in this section can now be applied to the case of Diogenes, discussed in section 1. Diogenes lives in world where he is without a donor, and therefore poor and not envied, but independent and credible: $w^@ = \{\neg s, \neg r, \neg e, i, c\}$. The causal model M that Diogenes believes in is represented in figure 11.2.

The actual world is thus causally compatible with the prospect of poverty $(\neg r)$ with respect to M, and it is obviously maximally similar to itself. The world $w^o = \{s, r, e, \neg i, \neg c\}$ on the other hand, is compatible with the prospect of wealth (r) with respect to M. Because wealth is dependent on only one background variable in model M, there is no other world compatible with the prospect of wealth with respect to M. Thus even though

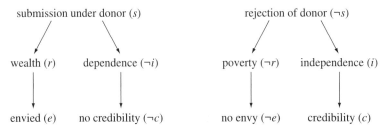

Figure 11.2
Diogenes' causal beliefs.

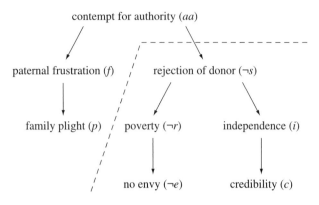

Figure 11.3
Truncating the causes of Diogenes' action.

$\#(w^o \cap w^@) = 0$, w^o is picked by f. By definition 1*, $\neg r \succeq r$ iff $w^@ \geq w^o$. Diogenes' behavior before Alexander, as reported by Diogenes Laertius, does indicate his preference for $w^@$ over w^o; and hence—through his causal beliefs—his preference for poverty over wealth.

But what if the causal model gets extended to include causes of Diogenes' choice between accepting and rejecting the donor? The background intuitions of such an extended model were discussed in section 1.3. In figure 11.3, the corresponding causal model M' is represented.

If definition 1* operated with M' instead of M, the conclusions of the above example would no longer be valid. Diogenes would prefer poverty over wealth if and only if he preferred the world $w^{o\prime} = \{\neg aa, \neg f, \neg p, s, r, e, \neg i, \neg c\}$ over the world $w^{aa} = \{aa, f, p, \neg s, \neg r, \neg e, i, c\}$; which is a completely different condition from preferring w^o to the actual world.

However, restriction 5 tells us to neglect all causal antecedents of a prospect if that prospect is an action. When evaluating non-action prospects, we assumed the truth of a prospect counterfactually and investigated how the causal dependencies and effects of that counterfactual assumption would determine the worlds compatible with that prospect. When evaluating an action, we assume the truth of that action-prospect not counterfactually, but as an intervention. An intervention, in contrast to a counterfactual assumption, does not have a retrospective influence on the past.[13] An intervention is represented as a truncation of the causal graph—

all direct ancestors of the model are removed from a causal model M, the model thus transformed into a truncated model M^T.

Definition 6. A causal model M is transformed into a truncated causal model $M^T = \langle U, V, G \rangle$ by eliminating all $g_i \in G$ which have an action prospect in their range.

The thick dotted line in figure 11.3 shows such a truncation. The function that connects aa with $\neg s$ is eliminated, thus cutting the causal connection between aa and $\neg s$ in M^T. By replacing M in definition 1 with M^T, restriction 5 is always satisfied.

Definition 1**. $p \succeq q \Leftrightarrow w_i^p \geq w_i^q$ for all $\langle w_i^p, w_i^q \rangle$ that are compatible with $p \wedge \neg q$ and $q \wedge \neg p$ with respect to M^T, respectively, such that both w_i^p, w_i^q are most similar to $w^@$.

In cases where M does not include any action prospects, definition 1** is obviously identical with definition 1*. In all other cases, definition 1** still satisfies theorems 1 and 2, as they were proven for all causal models, including truncated ones.

Thus, despite Diogenes' belief in the extended causal model M', definition 1** secures that his preference for poverty over wealth is still derived on the basis of the truncated model M^T, which in this case coincides with the original model M.

3   Conclusion and Remarks

I have offered a principle of abstraction between an agent's preferences over prospects and her preferences over worlds. More specifically, I represented the agent's beliefs as a causal model, and argued with the help of this model which of the agent's preferences over worlds serve as definiens for her preferences over propositions.

I have argued why such a principle of abstraction is necessary for the explanation and prediction of behavior with preferences; however, the model presented here leaves open many important questions. I will finish with two remarks on how to develop the discussion further.

3.1   Possibility or Probability

The criterion of the causal possibility of a world might be too rough a distinction to be viable. Instead, it has been suggested that prospects should be evaluated according to a weighted average of value of those worlds in which they are realized. The weighing can be determined as a probability index, which measures the likelihood of a world occurring given the actual world. Ideally, such a measure combines the criteria of causal possibility and actuality.

A first step was made by Rescher (1967). He constructed a ranking over worlds by assigning to them a numerical index of merit. From this ranking he derived an index over states: The index number of a state $\#(a)$ is the arithmetic mean over the index numbers of all possible worlds in which a is true. These index numbers over states give rise to a semantic definition of preferences over states: a is preferred to b iff $\#(a) > \#(b)$.

Trapp (1985) picked up Rescher's idea; but unlike him, Trapp suggested a probabilistic weighing of the index of possible worlds. Such a weighing can be interpreted as a continuous similarity metric: An agent assigns higher probability to those worlds that he thinks are closer to actuality. Jeffrey gave a similar account. He derived the desirability index over propositions from the desirability index over worlds: "the desirabilities of a proposition is a weighted average of the desirabilities of the cases [worlds] in which it is true, where the weights are proportional to the probabilities of the cases" (Jeffrey 1983, p. 78).

The most pressing problem of these accounts is their uniform treatment of actions and non-action prospects, as discussed in section 1.3. More generally, the probabilistic weighing of the worlds does not necessarily co-incide with the concept of causal compatibility presented here. Causal deci-sion theory has tried to remedy this problem by recasting the probability measure as a specification of objective chances or a measure of counterfac-tual dependency. Instead of trying to import all relevant information into the probability measure, the natural expansion of the account presented here suggests employing a subjective probability measure *conditional* on other relevant causal factors held fixed. The notion of relevant causal fac-tors, of course, needs to be provided independently and prior to the proba-bility measure; a task fulfilled by the causal graph discussed in this paper. The structure needed for a probabilistic weighing of worlds to determine the preferences (expressed as a utility index) over prospects then requires a *Bayesian network* which consists of a causal model and a probability func-tion defined over it, satisfying certain conditional dependencies. To construct a utility function on the basis of Bayesian networks will be the task of a future paper.

3.2 Prospect Preference Aggregation

The model presented here provides a definition of more abstract prospect preferences in terms of world preferences. Once the prospect preferences are specified for a particular agent, the question arises: How are they employed in the explanation of the agent's behavior in novel situations? In the simplest case, the new situation is analyzed into its aspects, and the prospect preferences of the agent may provide us with clues of what the agent will do or why she did what she did. For example, a guest's preference for coffee over brandy at dinnertime is applicable to all new dinner situations. Such an application is easy in cases where the available prospect preferences are unanimous—that is, where all aspects of one situation are either preferred or noncomparable to the aspects of another situation. But what can we say if conflicts arise? For example, our guest may have a preference for nonalcoholic beverages, but also a preference for caffeine-free ones. How can one explain her choice between brandy and coffee with these preferences?

One suggestion for such a case is to employ the framework of ordinal preference aggregation as found in the social choice literature. But instead of using it for questions of how the rational preferences of a group of individuals can be aggregated into a coherent ranking of the group, this strategy proposes "to apply interpersonal economic theory to intrapersonal problems" (Elster 1985, p. 232)—that is, the different prospect preferences are aggregated back into one world preference.

The general results of such an application are that there is no aggregation rule for prospect preferences that satisfies certain minimal constraints and results in a coherent, transitive world-preference order (cf. Steedman and Krause 1986). It does not preclude that in many situations, coherent world-preferences can be aggregated from prospect preferences, or that with the help of external information, the decisiveness of some prospect preferences can be justified.

Again, further discussions of these questions require another paper. With the current state of research in this area, however, there is hope that prospect preferences can, in many cases, be aggregated to coherent world preferences and can thus function in the prediction and explanation of action.

Acknowledgments

I thank Richard Bradley, Joseph Keim Campbell, Nancy Cartwright, Isaac Levi, Daniel M. Hausman, Rainer W. Trapp, Joanne Grüne-Yanoff, and two anonymous referees for helpful comments on earlier drafts of this essay.

Notes

1. Pettit's claim is that property preferences determine world-preferences. The ultimate determining preference is often called value (as does Pettit himself). Disagreement prevails between those who defend value atomism—that value has its origin in a few very abstract aspects of the world (cf. Harman 1967; Quinn 1974)—and those who defend value holism—that value has its origin in the most specific states of the world (cf. von Wright 1963, pp. 29–34; von Wright 1972; Rescher 1967; Trapp 1985; Hansson 2001). Pettit claims that it is a folk psychological platitude that "choosing on the basis of the properties displayed by the alternatives" captures "choosing for a reason." As there is considerable disagreement among philosophers about this claim, I would be cautious granting it folk status.

2. This in effect assumes that all choices are, in Savage's terminology, constant acts (cf. Savage 1972, p. 25). I make no attempt to justify this problematic assumption. For the sake of simplicity, I have excluded all considerations of uncertainty. To elaborate in a probabilistic framework what is discussed here under certainty will be the task of another paper.

3. This account must not be identified with the revealed preference theory known from economics. Revealed preference theory *defines* preferences as consistent choices over options under a given budget. The present account discusses preferences as mental states, which are *indicated by* behavioral evidence. For a detailed discussion of the revealed preference approach, see Grüne 2004.

4. It now becomes clear why the paper is restricted to *certain* prospects. This definition does not work if p or q are gambles over worlds. Take the following example: p and q are gambles such that

p: if dice rolls 6 you receive $100.

q: if dice rolls 4 or 5 you receive $100.

According to the definition, one prefers q to p only if one *both* prefers worlds w^{q*}, in which the dice rolls 4 and you receive $100 to w^p, as well as world w^{p**}, in which the dice rolls 5 and you receive $100 to w^p. Given a fair dice, however, it is plausible to be indifferent between these worlds, even though it is very plausible to prefer q to p.

5. This is the case that comes closest to Pettit's discussion of property desires.

6. I will argue that the third case, preferences over mutually nonexclusive prospects, must be translated into preferences over mutually exclusive ones. A translation procedure will be discussed in section 2.2.

7. This approach was to my knowledge first discussed by von Wright (1972, p. 146). It is also defended by Hansson (2001, pp. 67–94).

8. Diogenes Laertius 1931, p. 38. I use the source as an inspiration, and hasten to add that the following is obviously not intended as a textual analysis.

9. Trapp claimed that "no two relata of a preference relation should be considered to be true in the same possible world," at least in those worlds that are chosen by the selection function (Trapp 1985, p. 301). For a rejection of this view, see Hansson 1989, p. 6.

10. Or, if one of the relata is not causally compatible with any world, f picks out worlds that are compatible with the untranslated relatum.

11. This situation is in many ways similar to the so-called Newcomb's Problems in probabilistic models of decision making.

12. The reverse claim does not hold: one cannot infer from the transitivity of a preference relation over $p, q, r, \ldots$ that all their causally possible conjunctions $p \wedge \neg q$, $p \wedge \neg r$ are dependent on the same background variable u^{p*}. For example, the evaluation of $w^{p \wedge \neg q}$ and $w^{p \wedge \neg r}$ might coincide without the two worlds being identical.

13. For a more extensive discussion of intervention, see Pearl 2000, pp. 85–89; and Spohn 2002, pp. 23–27.

References

Diogenes Laertius. 1931. *Lives, Teachings, and Sayings of Famous Philosophers*. Loeb Classical Library. Cambridge, Mass.: Harvard University Press.

Elster, J. 1985. "Weakness of Will and the Free-Rider Problem." *Economics and Philosophy* 1: 231–265.

Grice, H. 1989. "The William James Lectures." In *Studies in the Way of Words*. Cambridge, Mass. and London: Harvard University Press.

Grüne, T. 2004. "The Problems of Testing Preference Axioms with Revealed Preference Theory." *Analyse & Kritik* 26.2: 382–397.

Halldén, S. 1957. *On the Logic of Better*. Lund: Library of Theoria.

Hansson, S. 2001. *The Structure of Values and Norms*. Cambridge: Cambridge University Press.

Harman, G. 1967. "Towards a Theory of Intrinsic Value." *Journal of Philosophy* 64: 792–804.

Jeffrey, R. 1983. *The Logic of Decision*. Chicago: University of Chicago Press.

Joyce, J. 1999. *The Foundations of Causal Decision Theory*. Cambridge: Cambridge University Press.

Pearl, J. 2000. *Causality: Models, Reasoning, and Inference*. Cambridge: Cambridge University Press.

Pettit, P. 2002. "Decision Theory and Folk Psychology." In *Rules, Reasons, and Norms*. Oxford and New York: Oxford University Press.

Quinn, W. 1974. "Theories of Intrinsic Value." *American Philosophical Quarterly* 11: 123–132.

Rescher, N. 1967. "Semantic Foundations for the Logic of Preference." In *The Logic of Decision and Action*, edited by N. Rescher. Pittsburgh: University of Pittsburgh Press.

Savage, L. 1972. *The Foundations of Statistics*. New York: Dover.

Spohn, W. 2002. "Dependency Equilibria and the Causal Structure of Decision and Game Situations." Unpublished ms., University of Konstanz.

Steedman, I., and U. Krause. 1986. "Goethe's Faust, Arrow's Possibility Theorem, and the Individual Decision Maker." In *The Multiple Self: Studies in Rationality and Social Change*, edited by J. Elster. Cambridge: Cambridge University Press.

Trapp, R. 1985. "Utility Theory and Preference Logic." *Erkenntnis* 22: 301–339.

von Wright, G. 1963. *The Logic of Preference*. Edinburgh: Edinburgh University Press.

von Wright, G. 1972. "The Logic of Preference Reconsidered." *Theory and Decision* 3: 140–169.

12   Decisions, Intentions, Urges, and Free Will: Why Libet Has Not Shown What He Says He Has

Alfred R. Mele

Psychologists Patrick Haggard, Chris Newman, and Elena Magno (1999, p. 291) recently described a 1983 article by physiologist Benjamin Libet and colleagues as "one of the most philosophically challenging papers in modern scientific psychology." A striking thesis of that 1983 article is that "the brain ... 'decides' to initiate or, at the least, prepare to initiate [certain actions] at a time before there is any reportable subjective awareness that such a decision has taken place" (Libet, Gleason, et al. 1983, p. 640; cf. Libet 1985, p. 536).[1] That article and subsequent work on this topic by Libet and various colleagues has attracted a great deal of attention in a variety of fields. I myself have used some of Libet's results to shed light on some philosophical questions about self-control (Mele 1997; 2003, ch. 8). What I found useful were the data, not Libet's interpretation of them. To use his data without misleading my readers, I found it necessary to criticize a certain central element of Libet's interpretation of them that is directly relevant to the thesis I quoted from Libet, Gleason, et al. 1983. In setting the stage for my own use of Libet's data in understanding our prospects for exercising self-control in the face of temptation at roughly the time of action, I argued that they fall well short of justifying his thesis, and I defended an alternative interpretation of them. Part of the problem is that Libet and his colleagues ignore a directly relevant conceptual distinction between deciding and intending, on the one hand, and motivational states like wanting, on the other.

Patrick Haggard, in his contribution to a recent discussion with Libet, says that "conceptual analysis could help" (Haggard and Libet 2001, p. 62). Haggard is referring specifically to conceptual differences between "will (generation of action) and choice (selection of action)" (Haggard and Libet 2001, p. 61). My conceptual focus will be on another pair of phenomena—

wanting and intending. I will also distinguish between intending and deciding, and identify a conceptual connection between them. Drawing partly from Mele 1997, I criticize Libet's defense of his thesis about decisions and extend the criticism to his conclusions about free will.

Conceptual Matters

Because Libet uses such terms as "intention," "decision," "wanting," "wish," and "urge" interchangeably, some conceptual preliminaries are in order in interpreting his work.[2] I start with a distinction between wanting and intending. Its relevance to interpreting Libet's results will become clear in the following section.

Wanting to do something is distinguishable from intending to do it. One can want (or desire, or have an urge) to A without being at all settled on A-ing.[3] Yesterday, I wanted to meet a friend at a 7 o'clock movie and I wanted to join another friend at a 7 o'clock lecture. I knew that I could do either, but not both; I needed to make up my mind about what to do. In forming an intention to go to the movie, I made up my mind to do that. To intend to do something is, at least in part, to be settled (but not necessarily irrevocably) on doing it (Mele 1992, chs. 9 and 10). Wanting to do something is compatible with being unsettled about whether to do it. In normal scenarios, the transition from wanting to A to intending to A is progress toward A-ing (Mele 1992, pp. 72–73, and chs. 9 and 10). For reasons of convenience, one may use the verbs "want" and "desire" interchangeably, and it is natural to treat the noun "urge" as a label for a kind of desire. If wanting and intending have importantly different functional roles in the production of intentional actions, as I and others have argued they do, failing to distinguish intending from wanting can lead to serious errors.[4]

Another relevant distinction for present purposes is between two ways of coming to intend to A. Many philosophers have claimed or argued that to decide to A is to perform a mental action of a certain kind—an action of forming an intention to A.[5] On my view, deciding is a momentary mental action of intention formation, and it resolves uncertainty about what to do (Mele 2003, ch. 9). In saying that deciding is momentary, I mean to distinguish it from, for example, a combination of deliberating and deciding. A student who is speaking loosely may say, "I was up all night deciding to major in English," when what he means is that he was up all night deliberating or fretting about what major to declare and eventually decided to major in English. Deciding to *A*, on my view, is not a process but a momentary mental action of forming an intention to *A*, "form" being understood as an action verb. Not all intentions are formed in this sense, or so I have argued elsewhere. For example, "When I intentionally unlocked my office door this morning, I intended to unlock it. But since I am in the habit of unlocking my door in the morning and conditions ... were normal, nothing called for a *decision* to unlock it" (Mele 1992, p. 231). If I had heard a fight in my office, I might have paused to consider whether to unlock the door or walk away, and I might have decided to unlock it. But given the routine nature of my conduct, there is no need to posit an act of intention formation in this case. My intention to unlock the door may have been acquired without having been actively formed.

It should also be noted that some of our decisions and intentions are for the nonimmediate future, and others are not. I might decide on Tuesday to attend a meeting on Friday, and I might decide now to phone my father now. The intention formed in the former decision is aimed at action three days in the future. (Of course, if I need to prepare for the meeting—or need to write a note on my calendar to remind myself of it—the intention may motivate relevant overt conduct sooner than that.) The intention I form when I decide to phone my father now is about what to do now. I call intentions and decisions of these kinds, respectively, *distal* and *proximal* intentions and decisions (Mele 1992, pp. 143–144, 158). Proximal decisions and intentions also include decisions and intentions to continue doing something that one is doing and decisions and intentions to start *A*-ing (e.g., start running a mile) straightaway.

I claimed that it is risky to ignore functional differences between wanting and intending. It is plausible that effective proximal intentions play roles in the initiation, guidance, and sustaining of intentional actions and that effective proximal desires to *A* help generate proximal intentions to *A* (Mele 1992, chs. 8 and 10). On this view of things, the primary causal contribution such desires make to the production of intentional actions is mediated by associated proximal intentions.[6]

A distinction between *relatively specific* and *relatively unspecific* intentions is also in order. Bob now intends to attend next week's departmental meeting. That is a more specific intention than the intention he had, at the beginning of the academic year, to attend at least a few departmental meetings during the year. He had the latter intention without being settled on any specific meetings to attend. In another illustration, Cathy has agreed to be a subject in an experiment in which subjects are instructed to salute whenever they feel like it on at least forty occasions during a two hour period. When Cathy begins her participation in the experiment she has a relatively unspecific intention to salute many times during the next two hours. At various times during the experiment she has specific proximal intentions to salute.

Libet's Work

This section develops an interpretation of Libet's work that is sensitive to the conceptual points just made. In some of his studies, subjects are instructed to flex their right wrists or the fingers of their right hands whenever they wish. Electrical readings from the scalp—averaged over at least 40 flexings for each subject—show a "negative shift" in "readiness potentials" (RPs) beginning at about 550 milliseconds (msec) before the time at which an electromyogram shows relevant muscular motion to begin (Libet 1985, pp. 529–530).[7] Subjects are also instructed to "recall ... the spatial clock position of a revolving spot at the time of [their] initial awareness" (Libet 1985, p. 529) of something, x, that Libet variously describes as an "intention," "urge," "wanting," "decision," "will," or "wish" to move (see note 2). On the average, "RP onset" preceded what the subjects reported to be the time of their initial awareness of x (time W) by 350 msec. Time W, then, preceded the beginning of muscle motion by about 200 msec.

Diagram 1

-550 msec	-200 msec	0 msec
RP onset	time W	muscle begins to move

(Libet finds independent evidence of a slight error in subjects' recall of the times at which they first become aware of sensations [Libet 1985, pp. 531, 534]. Correcting for that error, time W is -150 msec.)

At what point, if any, does a specific intention to flex arise in Libet's subjects? Again, Libet, Gleason, et al. write that "the brain ... 'decides' to initiate or ... prepare to initiate the act ... before there is any reportable subjective awareness that such a decision has taken place" (1983, p. 640). If we ignore the second disjunct, this quotation (given its context) apparently offers the answer that a specific intention to flex appears on the scene with "RP onset," about 550 msec before relevant muscular motion and about 350 to 400 msec before the agent becomes aware of the intention (see Libet 1985, p. 539); for to decide to initiate an act is to form an intention to initiate it.[8] But are decision and intention the most suitable mental items to associate with RP onset? Again, Libet describes the relevant occurrence of which the agent later becomes aware not only as a "decision" and the onset of an "intention" to move, but also as the onset of an "urge," "wanting," and a "wish" to move. This leaves it open that at −550 msec, rather than acquiring an intention or making a decision of which he is not conscious, the agent instead acquires an *urge* or *desire* of which he is not conscious—and perhaps an urge or desire that is stronger than any competing urge or desire at the time, a *preponderant* urge or desire.

I believe that if Libet himself were to distinguish between intending and wanting (including having an urge) along the lines I sketched, he might find it more credible to associate the readiness potentials with the latter than with the former. To explain why, I turn to another experiment reported in Libet 1985 (and elsewhere).

Libet proposes that "conscious volitional control may operate not to initiate the volitional process but to select and control it, either by permitting or triggering the final motor outcome of the unconsciously initiated process or by vetoing the progression to actual motor activation" (1985, p. 529; cf. 1999, p. 54). "In a veto, the later phase of cerebral motor processing would be blocked, so that actual activation of the motoneurons to the muscles would not occur" (Libet 1985, p. 537). Libet offers two kinds of evidence to support the suggestion about vetoing. One kind is generated by an experiment in which subjects are instructed both to prepare to flex their fingers at a prearranged time (as indicated by a revolving spot on a clock face) and "to veto the developing intention/preparation to act … about 100 to 200 msec before the prearranged clock time" (Libet 1985, p. 538). Subjects receive both instructions at the same time. Libet writes:

a ramplike pre-event potential was still recorded … resembl[ing] the RP of self-initiated acts when preplanning is present.… The form of the "veto" RP differed (in most but not all cases) from those "preset" RPs that were followed by actual movements [in another experiment]; the main negative potential tended to alter in direction (flattening or reversing) at about 150–250 [msec] before the preset time.… This difference suggests that the conscious veto interfered with the final development of

RP processes leading to action.... The preparatory cerebral processes associated with an RP can and do develop even when intended motor action is vetoed at approximately the time that conscious intention would normally appear before a voluntary act. (1985, p. 538)[9]

Keep in mind that the subjects were instructed in advance *not* to flex their fingers, but to prepare to flex them at the prearranged time and to "veto" this. The subjects intentionally complied with the request. They intended from the beginning not to flex their fingers at the appointed time. So what is indicated by the RP? Presumably, not the acquisition or presence of an *intention* to flex; for then, at some point in time, the subjects would have both an intention to flex at the prearranged time and an intention not to flex at that time. And how can a normal agent simultaneously be settled on A-ing at t and settled on not A-ing at t?[10] That is, it is very plausible that Libet is mistaken in describing what is vetoed as "*intended* motor action" (1985, p. 538; my emphasis).

If the RP in the veto scenario is not associated with an intention to flex at the appointed time, with what might it be associated? In the passage I quoted above, from Libet 1985, Libet compares "the 'veto' RP" with:

1. "'preset' RPs that were followed by actual movements";

2. "the RP of self-initiated acts when preplanning is present."

The RP referred to in (1) is produced in experiments in which subjects are instructed to watch the clock and flex when the revolving spot reaches "a pre-set 'clock time'" (Libet et al. 1982, p. 325). "The subject was encouraged to try to make his movement coincide as closely as possible with the arrival of the spot at the pre-set time." The RP referred to in (2) is produced in two kinds of studies:

i. studies in which subjects instructed to flex spontaneously are not regularly encouraged to aim for spontaneity (Libet et al. 1982, pp. 324–326);

ii. studies in which subjects who did receive such encouragement reported that they experienced "some 'pre-planning,'" even if only in "a minority of the 40 self-initiated acts that occurred in the series for that averaged RP" (Libet et al. 1982, p. 328).

"Even when some pre-plannings were recalled and reported, subjects insisted that the more specific urge or intention to actually move did not arise in that pre-planning stage" (ibid., p. 329). Reports of "pre-planning" seem to include reports of thoughts about when to flex and reports of anticipations of flexing (ibid., pp. 328–329). Libet and his coauthors remark that "Subject S. B. described his advance feelings [of pre-planning] as 'pre-tensions' rather than pre-plannings to act" (ibid., p. 329). This subject may have meant that he occasionally experienced tension that he expected to result in flexing.

The RPs referred to in 1 and 2 have a very similar form (Libet et al. 1982, pp. 330, 333–334; Libet 1985, p. 532). RPs with that form are called "type I RPs" (Libet et al. 1982, p. 326). They have significantly earlier onsets than the RPs produced in studies of subjects regularly encouraged to aim for spontaneity who report that they experienced no "pre-planning"—"type II RPs." "The form of the 'veto' RP" is the form of type I RPs until "about 150–250 [msec] before the preset time" (Libet 1985, p. 538). What does the veto group (group V) have in common until that time with the three kinds of subjects who produce type I RPs: those with a pre-set time for flexing (group PS), those who are not regularly encouraged to aim for spontaneity (group N), and those who are regularly encouraged to aim for spontaneity but who report some "pre-planning" (group PP)?

Presumably, subjects in group PS are watching the clock with the intention of flexing at the preset time. But it certainly does not follow from that and the similar RPs in groups N and PP—and V for a time—that members of each of these groups are watching the clock with a similar intention to flex. For one thing, as I have explained, it is very likely that those of group V—subjects instructed in advance to prepare to flex and then veto the preparation—are watching the clock *without* an intention to flex at the targeted time. Given that the members of group V lack this intention, we should look for something that groups V and PS actually have in common that might be signified by the similarity in the RPs until "about 150–250 [msec] before the preset time." One possibility is that members of both groups have *urges* to flex (or to prepare to flex) soon—or undergo brain events that are pretty reliable, relatively proximal causal contributors to such urges—that are associated with an RP and regularly play a role in generating subsequent flexings in the absence of "vetoing."[11] In the case of group V, perhaps a subject's wanting to comply with the instructions—including the instruction to prepare to flex at the appointed time—together with his recognition that the time is approaching produces a growing urge to (prepare to) flex soon, a pretty reliable causal contributor to such an urge, or the motor preparedness typically associated with such an urge. A related possibility is suggested by the observation that "the pattern of brain activity associated with imagining making a movement is very similar to the pattern of activity associated with preparing to make a movement" (Spence and Frith 1999, p. 27). The instructions given to group V would naturally elicit imagining flexing very soon. Finally, the "flattening or reversing" of the RP "at about 150–250 msec before the preset time" might indicate a consequence of the subject's "vetoing" his preparation.

What about groups N and PP? It is possible that they, along with the subjects in groups PS and V, begin acquiring urges to flex at a greater temporal distance from 0 msec than do subjects encouraged to flex spontaneously who report no pre-planning. That difference may be indicated by type I RPs' having significantly earlier onsets than type II RPs. Another possibility is consistent with this. Earlier, I distinguished proximal from distal intentions, and Libet himself recognizes the distinction (see Libet et al. 1982, pp. 329, 334; Libet 1989, pp. 183–184). Presumably, subjects in group PS respond to the instruction to flex at a preset time with an intention to flex at that time. This is a distal intention. As the preset time for flexing draws very near, that intention may become, help produce, or be replaced by a proximal intention to flex, an intention to *flex now*, as one naturally says (see Libet 1989, p. 183; 1999, p. 54; 2004, p. 148). That may happen around the time subjects in group V veto their urge to flex or closer to 0 msec. And it may happen at or around the time subjects in groups N and PP acquire a proximal intention to flex. They may acquire such an intention without having had a distal intention to flex soon: recall that members of group V probably had no distal intention to flex soon and that their RPs are very similar to those of groups N, PP, and PS until "about 150–250 msec before the preset time." All this is consistent with the similarities in RPs in the various groups of subjects, on the assumption that no segment of the RPs before about −150 to −250 msec for subjects in group PS specifically represents subjects' distal intentions to flex at the preset time—as opposed, for example, to something that such intentions have in common with distal urges to flex (or to prepare to flex) at the preset time—even though those intentions are present.

The main difference between type I and type II RPs, in Haggard's words, is that the former have "earlier onsets than" the latter (Haggard and Libet 2001, p. 49). The earlier onsets may be correlated with earlier acquisitions of urges to flex soon—urges that may be brought on, variously, by the instruction to flex at a preset time (group PS), the instruction to prepare to flex at a preset time and to veto that later (group V), unsolicited conscious thoughts about when to flex (groups N and PP), or unsolicited conscious anticipations of flexing (groups N and PP). (Of course, it is possible that some such thoughts and anticipations are instead products, in part, of urges to flex soon.) These urge inciters (or perhaps urge products, in the case of some experiences in groups N and PP) are absent in subjects instructed to flex spontaneously who report no "pre-planning"—at least, if their reports are accurate. If type I RPs indicate urges, or urges together with proximal intentions that emerge later than the urges do, the same may be true of type II RPs. The difference in the two kinds of RP may mainly be a matter of when the urge emerges—that is, how long before 0 msec. Once again, Libet describes in a variety of ways the mental item that is indicated by RPs. Even if "intention" and "decision" (to flex) are not apt choices, "urge" and "wanting" are still in the running.

If "RP onset" in cases of "spontaneous" flexing indicates the emergence of an urge to flex soon, proximal intentions to flex may emerge at some point between RP onset and time W, *at* time W, or *after* time W—at time W the agent may be aware only of an urge that has not yet issued in a proximal intention. Again, Libet writes that "in a veto, the later phase of cerebral motor processing would be blocked, so that actual activation of the motoneurons to the muscles would not occur" (1985, p. 537). Perhaps, in non-veto cases, activation of these motoneurons is the direct result of the acquisition of a proximal intention (cf. Gomes 1999, pp. 68, 72; Mele 1997, pp. 322–324). Libet suggests that this activation event occurs between 10 and 90 msec before the muscle begins moving, and apparently favors an answer in the 10 to 50 msec range (1985, p. 537). Elsewhere, he asserts that the activation event can occur no later than 50 msec before the onset of muscle motion (Libet 2004, pp. 137–138).

Although I will not make much of the following point, it merits mention that urges that may be correlated with RP onset at -550 msec might not be *proximal* urges, strictly speaking. Possibly, they are urges to flex *very soon*, as opposed to urges to flex straightaway. And perhaps they evolve into, or produce, proximal urges. Another possibility is that urges to flex very soon give rise to proximal intentions to flex without first evolving into or producing proximal urges to flex. Some disambiguation is in order. A smoker who is rushing toward a smoking section in an airport with the intention of lighting up as soon as he enters it wants to smoke soon. That want or desire has a specific temporal target—the time at which he enters the smoking section. A smoker walking outside the airport may want to smoke soon without having a specific time in mind. Libet's subjects, like the latter smoker, might at times have urges or desires to flex that lack a specific temporal target. Desires to *A* very soon, or to *A*, beginning very soon, in this sense of "very soon," are *roughly proximal* action-desires.

I have been using a (roughly) proximal urge to flex as an *example* of something that might be indicated by type II RPs beginning around −550 msec. The alternatives I mentioned are (roughly) proximal urges to prepare to flex, brain events that are pretty reliable, relatively proximal causal contributors to such urges or to (roughly) proximal urges to flex, relevant motor preparedness, and imagining flexing very soon. It would be helpful to have a name for this collection of alternatives: I opt for the name *(roughly) proximal urge**. What I dub the *urge* hypothesis* is the hypothesis that one or another of these things is indicated by type II RPs beginning around −550 msec. "Urge" sans asterisk continues to mean "urge"—not "urge*."

Libet's experimental design promotes consciousness of urges and intentions to flex, since his subjects are instructed in advance to be prepared to report on them—or something like them—later, using the clock to pinpoint the time they are first noticed. For my purposes, what is of special interest are the relative times of the emergence of a (roughly) proximal urge* to flex, the emergence of a proximal *intention* to flex, and consciousness of the intention. If RP onset indicates the emergence of proximal, or roughly proximal, urges* to flex, and if acquisitions of corresponding intentions directly activate the motoneurons to the relevant muscles, we have the picture given in diagram 2, of subjects encouraged to flex "spontaneously" who report no "pre-planning"—subjects who produce type II RPs. Possibly, the intention is *consciously* acquired. My point here is simply that this diagram is *consistent* with Libet's data on type II RPs and on time *W*.

Diagram 2

a. −550 msec: proximal or roughly proximal urge* to flex emerges

b. −90 to −50 msec: acquisition of corresponding proximal intention[12]

c. 0 ms: muscle begins to move.[13]

I mentioned that Libet offered a second kind of evidence for "veto control." Subjects instructed to flex "spontaneously" (in non-veto experiments) "reported that during some of the trials a recallable conscious urge to act appeared but was 'aborted' or somehow suppressed before any actual movement occurred; in such cases the subject simply waited for another urge to appear, which, when consummated, constituted the actual event whose RP was recorded" (Libet 1985, p. 538). RPs were not recorded for suppressed urges. But if these urges fit the pattern of the unsuppressed ones in cases of "spontaneous" flexing, they appeared on the scene about 550 msec before the relevant muscles would have moved if the subjects had not "suppressed" the urges, and subjects did not become conscious of them for about another 350 to 400 msec. Notice that it is *urges* that these subjects are said to report and abort or suppress. This coheres with my "urge*" hypothesis about groups V, PS, N, and PP. In group V (the veto group), as I have explained, there is excellent reason to believe that no proximal *intention* to flex is present, and the RPs for this group resembled the type I RPs for these other three groups until "about 150–250 [msec] before the preset time." If it is assumed that these RPs represent the same thing for these four groups until the RPs for group V diverge from the others, these RPs do *not* represent a *proximal intention* to flex before the point of divergence, but they might represent a growing urge to (prepare to) flex or other items in the urge* collection. And if at least until about the time of divergence there is no proximal intention to flex in any of these groups, we would need a special reason to believe that the type II RPs of the spontaneous flexers indicate that proximal intentions to flex emerge in them around −550 msec. In the "Further Testing" section below, I show that there is independent evidence that their proximal intentions emerge much later than this.

Does the brain decide to initiate actions "at a time before there is any reportable subjective awareness that such a decision has taken place" (Libet, Gleason, et al. 1983, p. 640)? Libet and his colleagues certainly have not shown that it does, for their data do not show that any such decision has been made before time W or before the time at which their subjects first are aware of a *decision* or *intention* to flex. Nothing justifies the claim that what a subject becomes aware of at time W is a *decision* to flex that has already been made or an *intention* to flex that has already been acquired, as opposed, for example, to an *urge* to flex that has already arisen. Indeed, the data about vetoing, as I have explained, can reasonably be used to argue that the "urge*" hypothesis about what the RPs indicate is less implausible than the "decision" or "intention" hypothesis. Now, there certainly seems to be a connection between what happens at −550 msec and subsequent muscle motion in cases of "spontaneous" flexing. But it obviously is not a temporally direct connection. Between the former and latter times, subjects apparently form or acquire proximal intentions to flex, in those cases in which they do intentionally flex. And, for all Libet's data show, those intentions may be consciously formed or acquired.

Free Will

When Libet's work is applied to the theoretically subtle and complicated issue of free will, things can quickly get out of hand. The abstract of Haggard and Libet 2001 opens as follows:

> The problem of free will lies at the heart of modern scientific studies of consciousness. An influential series of experiments by Libet has suggested that conscious intentions arise as a result of brain activity. This contrasts with traditional concepts of free will, in which the mind controls the body. (Haggard and Libet 2001, p. 47)

Now, only a certain kind of mind-body dualist would hold that conscious intentions do *not* "arise as a result of brain activity." And such dualist views are rarely advocated in contemporary philosophical publications on free will. Moreover, contemporary philosophers who argue for the existence of free will typically shun substance dualism. If Libet's work is of general interest to philosophers working on free will, the source of the interest must lie elsewhere than the theoretical location specified in this passage.

In a recent article Libet writes, "it is only the final 'act now' process that produces the voluntary *act*. That 'act now' process begins in the brain about 550 msec before the act, and it begins unconsciously" (2001, p. 61).[14] "There is," he says, "an unconscious gap of about 400 msec between the onset of the cerebral process and when the person becomes consciously aware of his/her decision or wish or intention to act" (2001, p. 61). (Incidentally, a page later, he identifies what the agent becomes aware of as "the intention/wish/urge to act" [2001, p. 62].) Libet adds: "If the 'act now' process is initiated unconsciously, then conscious free will is not doing it" (2001, p. 61).

I have already explained that Libet has not shown that a decision to flex is made or an intention to flex acquired at −550 msec. But even if the intention emerges much later, that is compatible with an "act now" process having begun at −550 msec. Regarding processes of many kinds, it is hard to be confident when they begin. Did the process of my baking my frozen pizza begin when I turned my oven on to preheat it; when I opened the door of the preheated oven five minutes later to put the pizza in; when I placed the pizza on the center rack; or at some other time? Theorists can argue about this, but I would prefer not to. One might say that "the 'act now' process" in Libet's spontaneous subjects begins with the formation or acquisition of a proximal intention to flex, much closer to the onset of muscle motion than −550 msec, or that it begins earlier, with the beginning of a process that issues in the intention.[15] I will not argue about that. Suppose we say that "the 'act now' process" begins with the unconscious emergence of a (roughly) proximal urge to (prepare to) flex—or with a pretty reliable, relatively proximal causal contributor to such an urge—at about −550 msec and that the urge plays a significant role in producing a proximal intention to flex many milliseconds later. We can then agree with Libet that, given that the "process is initiated unconsciously ... conscious free will is not doing it"—that is, is not initiating "the 'act now' process." But who would have thought that conscious free will has the job of producing urges (or causal contributors to urges)? In the philosophical literature, free will's primary locus of operation is typically identified as deciding (or choosing), and for all Libet has shown, his subjects make their decisions (or choices) consciously.

Libet asks, "How would the 'conscious self' initiate a voluntary act if, factually, the process to 'act now' is initiated unconsciously?" (2001, p. 62). In this paragraph, I offer an answer. One significant piece of background is that an "'act now' process" that is initiated unconsciously may be aborted by the agent; that apparently is what happens in instances of spontaneous vetoing, if "'act now' processes" start when Libet says they do.[16] Now, processes have parts, and the various parts of a process may have more and less proximal initiators. A process that is initiated by an unconscious urge* may have a subsequent part that is directly initiated by the conscious formation or acquisition of an intention.[17] "The 'conscious self'"—which need not be understood as something mysterious—might more proximally initiate a voluntary act that is less proximally initiated by an unconscious urge*. (Readers who, like me, prefer to use "self" only as an affix may prefer to say that the acquisition or formation of a relevant proximal intention, which intention is consciously acquired or formed, might more proximally

initiate an intentional action that is less proximally initiated by an unconscious urge*.)

Recall that Libet himself says that "conscious volitional control may
operate ... to select and control ['the volitional process'], either by permitting or triggering the final motor outcome of the unconsciously initiated
process or by vetoing the progression to actual motor activation" (1985,
p. 529). "Triggering" is a kind of initiating. In "triggering the final motor
outcome," the acquisition of a proximal intention would be initiating an
action in a more direct way than does the urge* that initiated a process
that issued in the intention. According to one view of things, when proximal action-desires help to initiate overt actions they do so by helping
to produce pertinent proximal intentions, the formation or acquisition of
which directly initiates actions (Mele 1992, pp. 71–77, 143–144, 168–170,
176–177, 190–191).[18] What Libet says about triggering here coheres with
this.

Further Testing

I have argued that the urge* hypothesis about what the type II RPs indicate
in Libet's studies is less implausible than the decision or intention hypothesis. Is there an independent way to test these hypotheses—that is, to
gather evidence about whether it is (roughly) proximal urges* that emerge
around −550 msec in Libet's studies, or instead decisions or intentions?
One line of thought runs as follows:

1. all overt intentional actions are caused by decisions (or intentions);

2. the type II RPs, which emerge around −550 msec, are correlated with
causes of the flexing actions (because they regularly precede the onset of
muscle motion); so

3. these RPs indicate that decisions are made (or intentions acquired) at
−550 msec.

I have shown that this line of thought is unpersuasive. A lot can happen in
a causal process that runs for 550 msec, including a subject's moving from
having an unconscious roughly proximal urge* to flex to consciously deciding to flex "now" or to consciously acquiring a proximal intention to flex.
One can reply that, even so, (3) *might* be true. And, of course, I can run
through my argumentation about the veto and related matters again to

remind the imaginary respondent why (3) is improbable. But what about a test?

If makings of proximal decisions to flex or acquisitions of proximal intentions to flex (or the physical events that realize these things) cause muscle motion, how long does it take them to do that? Does it take about 550 msec? Might reaction time experiments show that 550 msec is too long a time for this? Some caution is in order here. In typical reaction time experiments, subjects have decided in advance to perform an assigned task (A) whenever they detect the relevant signal. When they detect the signal, there is no need for a proximal *decision* to A.[19] (If all decisions are responses to uncertainty about what to do, and subjects are not uncertain about what to do when they detect the signal, there is no place here for proximal decisions to A.)[20] However, it is plausible that after they detect the signal, they acquire an *intention* to A now, a proximal intention. That is, it is plausible that the combination of their conditional intention to A when they detect the signal (or the neural realizer of that intention) and their detection of the signal (or the neural realizer of that detection) produces a proximal intention to A. The acquisition of this intention (or the neural realization of that event) would then initiate the A-ing.[21] And in at least one reaction time experiment (described shortly) that is very similar to Libet's main experiment, the time between the "go" signal and the onset of muscle motion is much shorter than 550 msec. This is evidence that proximal intentions to flex—as opposed to (roughly) proximal urges* to flex—emerge much closer to the time of the onset of muscle motion than 550 msec. There is no reason, in principle, that it should take people any longer to start flexing their wrists when executing a proximal intention to flex in Libet's studies than it takes them to do this when executing such an intention in a reaction time study. More precisely, there is no reason, in principle, that the interval between proximal intention acquisition and the beginning of muscle motion should be significantly different in the two scenarios.[22]

The line of reasoning that I have just sketched depends on the assumption that, in reaction time studies, proximal intentions to A are at work. An alternative possibility is that the combination of subjects' conditional intentions to A when they detect the signal, and their detection of the signal, initiates the A-ing without there being any proximal intention to A. Of course, there is a parallel possibility in the case of Libet's subjects. Perhaps the combination of their conditional intentions to flex when they next feel like it—conscious intentions, presumably—together with relevant feelings (namely, conscious proximal urges to flex) initiates a flexing without there being any proximal intentions to flex. (They may treat their initial consciousness of the urge as a "go" signal, as suggested in Keller and Heckhausen 1990, p. 352.) If that possibility is an actuality, then Libet's thesis is false, of course: there is no intention to flex "now" in his subjects and, therefore, no such intention is produced by the brain before the mind is aware of it.

The reaction time study I mentioned is reported in Haggard and Magno:

Subjects sat at a computer watching a clock hand ... whose rotation period was 2.56 s.... After an unpredictable delay, varying from 2.56 to 8 s, a high-frequency tone ... was played over a loudspeaker. This served as a warning stimulus for the subsequent reaction. 900 [msec] after the warning stimulus onset, a second tone ... was played. [It] served as the go signal. Subjects were instructed to respond as rapidly as possible to the go signal with a right-key press on a computer mouse button. Subjects were instructed not to anticipate the go stimulus and were reprimanded if they responded on catch trials. (Haggard and Magno 1999, p. 103)

"Reaction times were calculated by examining the EMG signal for the onset of the first sustained burst of muscle activity occurring after the go signal" (ibid., p. 104). "Reaction time" here, then, starts *before* any intention to press "now" is acquired: obviously, it takes some time to detect the signal, and if detection of the signal helps to produce a proximal intention, that takes some time too. The mean of the subjects' median reaction times in the control trials was 231 msec (ibid.). If a proximal intention to press was acquired, that happened nearer to the time of muscle motion than 231 msec and, therefore, much nearer than the 550 msec that Libet claims is the time proximal intentions to flex are unconsciously acquired in his studies. Notice, also, how close we are getting to Libet's time W—his subjects' reported time of their initial awareness of something he variously describes as an "intention," "urge," "wanting," "decision," "will," or "wish" to move (−200 to −150 msec). If proximal intentions to flex are acquired in Libet's studies, Haggard and Magno's results make it look like a better bet that they are acquired around time W than that they are acquired around −550 msec.[23] How seriously we should take his subjects' reports of the time of their initial awareness of the urge, intention, or whatever, is a controversial question, and I will say nothing about it here.[24]

Conclusion

In a recent article, after writing that "many of the world's leading neuroscientists have not only accepted our findings and interpretations, but have even enthusiastically praised these achievements and their experimental ingenuity," and naming twenty such people, Libet adds:

It is interesting that most of the negative criticism of our findings and their implications have come from philosophers and others with no significant experience in experimental neuroscience of the brain. (2002, p. 292)

Later in the article, he writes of one of his critics,

As a philosopher Gomes exhibits characteristics often found in philosophers. He seems to think one can offer reinterpretations by making unsupported assumptions, offering speculative data that do not exist and constructing hypotheses that are not even testable. (2002, p. 297)[25]

When I first read the latter passage, I experienced an urge to point out that one does not need any "experience in experimental neuroscience of the brain" to realize that there is a difference between deciding and intending, on the one hand, and wanting—including having an urge—on the other. Also, one who understands Libet's data and the studies that generate them can see that nothing warrants his claim that the RPs at issue are correlated with decisions or intentions rather than with urges strong enough to issue pretty regularly in related intentions and actions, or relatively proximal causes of such urges. Incidentally, as is obvious, I eventually made the transition from having an urge to comment on the quoted remarks to intending to do so.

Even though Libet's data do not show what he says they show, his work is interesting and important. For one thing, the data give us a sense of how much time might elapse between the acquisition of a (roughly) proximal desire to A—even one that is stronger than any competing desire—and an A-ing motivated by that desire. Perhaps, in some cases in which such a desire is at odds with what the agent consciously believes it would be best to do, there is time enough for the agent to reverse the balance of her motivation, thereby deflecting herself away from a course of action that is contrary to her better judgment. If so, Libet's work provides fertile ground for reflection on some issues central to the interrelated topics of weakness of will (akrasia) and self-control (see Mele 1997; 2003, ch. 8). A defining

feature of akratic action, on a traditional conception, is that it is freely performed (Mele 1987, pp. 4–11, 22–30).[26] Libet's data have some bearing on
free will by way of their bearing on the conceivability of situations in
which agents' strongest (roughly) proximal desires are at odds with their
conscious beliefs about what it would be best to do, and both akratic action
and its contrary are real possibilities.

Recall Haggard's assertion that "conceptual analysis could help" (Haggard and Libet 2001, p. 62). This article may be read as a test of his assertion. In my opinion, the result is positive. Attention not only to the data
but also to the concepts in terms of which the data are analyzed makes it
clear that Libet's striking claims about decisions, intentions, and free will
are not justified by his results. That, in certain settings, (roughly) proximal
urges to do things arise unconsciously or issue partly from causes of which
the agent is not conscious—urges on which the agent may or may not subsequently act—is no cause for worry about free will.

Acknowledgments

Versions of this essay were presented at the Munich Philosophical Lecture
Series: On the Nature and Culture of Volition (Max Planck Institute for
Psychological Research, February 2003); the Inland Northwest Philosophy
Conference (May 2003); the North Texas Philosophical Association (April
2005); the Australasian Association of Philosophy (July 2005); the NIH
(August 2005); Syracuse University (November 2005); and at the universities of Miami (March 2003), Manchester (June 2003), Edinburgh (June
2003), Oregon (October 2003), Helsinki (June 2004), Calgary (September
2004), Cincinnati (October 2004), Florida (February 2005), Siena (March
2005), Zurich (April 2005), Birmingham (November 2005), and Oxford
(November 2005). I am grateful to my audiences for productive discussions.

Notes

1. In a later article, Libet writes, "the brain has begun the specific preparatory processes for the voluntary act well before the subject is even aware of any wish or intention to act" (1992, p. 263).

2. Some passages in which two or more of these terms are used interchangeably are
quoted in the following two sections. Libet, Gleason, et al. report that "the subject
was asked to note and later report the time of appearance of his conscious *awareness*

of 'wanting' to perform a given self-initiated movement. The experience was also described as an 'urge' or 'intention' or 'decision' to move, though subjects usually settled for the words 'wanting' or 'urge'" (1983, p. 627).

3. In this article, I adopt the common convention of using *A* as a variable for prospective and actual actions.

4. See Mele 1992, pp. 71–77, 142–146, 166–170, 175–194; cf. Brand 1984, pp. 121–127; Bratman 1987, pp. 18–20; McCann 1986b, pp. 193–194.

5. See, e.g., Frankfurt 1988, pp. 174–176; Kane 1996, p. 24; Kaufman 1966, p. 34; McCann 1986a, pp. 254–255; Mele 1992, p. 156; Mele 2003, ch. 9; Pink 1996, p. 3; and Searle 2001, p. 94.

6. Our desires and intentions, in my view, are realized in physical states and events, and their causes are or are realized in physical states and events. I forego discussion of the metaphysics of mental causation, but see Mele 1992, ch. 2. I leave it open here that although desires and intentions enter into causal explanations of actions, the causal clout is carried, not by them (qua desires and intentions), but by their physical realizers.

7. For background on the generation, analysis, and use of electroencephalograms (EEGs) and "event-related brain potentials," including readiness potentials, see Coles and Rugg 1995.

8. I say "apparently," because an author may wish to distinguish an intention to flex one's wrist from an intention to initiate a flexing of one's wrist. I discuss initiation in the "Free Will" section. For completeness, I observe that if we instead ignore the quotation's first disjunct, it makes a claim about when an intention to *prepare* to flex—or to prepare to initiate a flexing of one's wrist—arises.

9. For a more thorough discussion of the experiment, see Libet et al. 1983, or Libet, Gleason, et al. 1983.

10. I do not wish to exclude the possibility of such settledness in commissurotomy cases.

11. Another is that they have an intention to prepare to flex, if *preparing* is understood in such a way that so intending does not entail intending to flex.

12. Recall that Libet suggests that the activation event occurs between 10 and 90 msec before the onset of muscle motion (1985, p. 537) and later revises the lower limit to 50 msec (2004, pp. 137–138).

13. In an alternative picture, the acquisition of a proximal intention to flex sends a signal that may be regarded as a command to flex one's wrist (or finger), and that signal helps produce finer-grained signals that directly activate the motoneurons to the relevant muscles. This picture moves the time of the acquisition of a proximal

intention further from 0 msec, but it does not move it anywhere near −550 msec. See the "Further Testing" section.

14. When does the *action* begin in all this—that is, the person's flexing his wrist or fingers? This is a conceptual question, of course. How one answers it depends on one's answer to the question, "What is an action?" Libet identifies "the actual time of the voluntary motor act" with the time "indicated by EMG recorded from the appropriate muscle" (1985, p. 532). I favor an alternative position, but there is no need to disagree with Libet about this for the purposes of the present article. Following Brand (1984), Frederick Adams and I have defended the thesis that overt intentional actions begin in the brain, just after the acquisition of a proximal intention; the action is proximally initiated by the acquisition of the intention (Adams and Mele 1992). (One virtue of this view is that it helps in handling certain problems about deviant causal chains; see Mele 2003, ch. 2.) The relevant intention may be understood, in Libet's words, as an intention "to act now" (1989, p. 183; 1999, p. 54), a proximal intention. (Of course, for Libet, as for me, "now" need not mean "this millisecond.") If I form the intention now to start running now, the action that is my running may begin just after the intention is formed, even though the relevant muscular motions do not begin until milliseconds later.

15. A central point of disagreement between Haggard and Libet is usefully understood as a disagreement about when the "'act now' process" begins (see Haggard and Libet 2001; cf. Haggard and Eimer 1999). Haggard apparently views the onset of lateralized response potentials (LRP), which happens "later than RP onset," as the beginning of the process (Haggard and Libet 2001, p. 53; see also Trevena and Miller 2002).

16. Notice that in addition to "vetoing" urges for actions that are not yet in progress, agents can abort attempts, including attempts at relatively temporally "short" actions. When batting, baseball players often successfully halt the motion of their arms while a swing is in progress. Presumably, they acquire or form an intention to stop swinging while they are in the process of executing an intention to swing.

17. Readers who believe that some item or other in the collection designated by "urge*" cannot be unconscious should exclude that item from consideration when they read "unconscious urge*."

18. Those who view the connection as direct take the view that actions begin in the brain. See note 14.

19. It should not be assumed that detecting the signal is a conscious event (see Prinz 2003).

20. In a reaction time study in which subjects are instructed to *A* or *B* when they detect the signal and not to decide in advance which to do, they may decide between *A* and *B* after detecting the signal.

21. Hereafter, the parenthetical clauses should be supplied by the reader. They serve as a reminder of a point made in note 6.

22. Notice that the interval at issue is distinct from intervals between the time of the occurrence of events that cause proximal intentions and the time of intention acquisition.

23. In a study by Day et al. of eight subjects instructed to flex a wrist when they heard a tone, mean reaction time was 125 msec (1989, p. 653). In their study of five subjects instructed to flex both wrists when they hear a tone, mean reaction time was 93 msec (1989, p. 658). The mean reaction times of both groups of subjects—defined as "the interval from auditory tone to onset of the first antagonist EMG burst" (1989, p. 651)—were much shorter than those of Haggard and Magno's subjects. Day et al.'s subjects, unlike Haggard and Magno's (and Libet's), were not watching a clock.

24. For an instructive review of the literature on this, see van de Grind 2002.

25. Incidentally, Gilberto Gomes has informed me that he works in a psychology department.

26. Agents who manifest weakness of will in acting contrary to what they judge best are distinguished, for example, from (actual or hypothetical) addicts who, owing to compulsions, unfreely do something that they judge it best not to do.

References

Adams, F., and A. Mele. 1992. "The Intention/Volition Debate." *Canadian Journal of Philosophy* 22: 323–338.

Brand, M. 1984. *Intending and Acting*. Cambridge, Mass.: MIT Press.

Bratman, M. 1987. *Intention, Plans, and Practical Reason*. Cambridge, Mass.: Harvard University Press.

Coles, M., and M. Rugg. 1995. "Event-Related Brain Potentials: An Introduction." In *Electrophysiology of Mind*, edited by M. Rugg and M. Coles. Oxford: Oxford University Press.

Day, B., J. Rothwell, P. Thompson, A. Maertens de Noordhout, K. Nakashima, K. Shannon, and C. Marsden. 1989. "Delay in the Execution of Voluntary Movement by Electrical or Magnetic Brain Stimulation in Intact Man." *Brain* 112: 649–663.

Frankfurt, H. 1988. *The Importance of What We Care About*. Cambridge: Cambridge University Press.

Gomes, G. 1999. "Volition and the Readiness Potential." *Journal of Consciousness Studies* 6: 59–76.

Haggard, P., and M. Eimer. 1999. "On the Relation between Brain Potentials and the Awareness of Voluntary Movements." *Experimental Brain Research* 126: 128–133.

Haggard, P., and B. Libet. 2001. "Conscious Intention and Brain Activity." *Journal of Consciousness Studies* 8: 47–63.

Haggard, P., and E. Magno. 1999. "Localising Awareness of Action with Transcranial Magnetic Stimulation." *Experimental Brain Research* 127: 102–107.

Haggard, P., C. Newman, and E. Magno. 1999. "On the Perceived Time of Voluntary Actions." *British Journal of Psychology* 90: 291–303.

Kane, R. 1996. *The Significance of Free Will*. New York: Oxford University Press.

Kaufman, A. 1966. "Practical Decision." *Mind* 75: 25–44.

Keller, I., and H. Heckhausen. 1990. "Readiness Potentials Preceding Spontaneous Motor Acts: Voluntary vs. Involuntary Control." *Electroencephalography and Clinical Neurophysiology* 76: 351–361.

Libet, B. 1985. "Unconscious Cerebral Initiative and the Role of Conscious Will in Voluntary Action." *Behavioral and Brain Sciences* 8: 529–566.

Libet, B. 1989. "The Timing of a Subjective Experience." *Behavioral and Brain Sciences* 12: 183–184.

Libet, B. 1992. "The Neural Time-Factor in Perception, Volition, and Free Will." *Revue de métaphysique et de morale* 2: 255–272.

Libet, B. 1999. "Do We Have Free Will?" *Journal of Consciousness Studies* 6: 47–57.

Libet, B. 2001. "Consciousness, Free Action, and the Brain." *Journal of Consciousness Studies* 8: 59–65.

Libet, B. 2002. "The Timing of Mental Events: Libet's Experimental Findings and Their Implications." *Consciousness and Cognition* 11: 291–299.

Libet, B. 2004. *Mind Time*. Cambridge, Mass.: Harvard University Press.

Libet, B., C. Gleason, E. Wright, and D. Pearl. 1983. "Time of Unconscious Intention to Act in Relation to Onset of Cerebral Activity (Readiness-Potential)." *Brain* 106: 623–642.

Libet, B., E. Wright, and A. Curtis. 1983. "Preparation- or Intention-to-Act, in Relation to Pre-Event Potentials Recorded at the Vertex." *Electroencephalography and Clinical Neurophysiology* 56: 367–372.

Libet, B., E. Wright, and C. Gleason. 1982. "Readiness Potentials Preceding Unrestricted 'Spontaneous' vs. Pre-Planned Voluntary Acts." *Electroencephalography and Clinical Neurophysiology* 54: 322–335.

McCann, H. 1986a. "Intrinsic Intentionality." *Theory and Decision* 20: 247–273.

McCann, H. 1986b. "Rationality and the Range of Intention." *Midwest Studies in Philosophy* 10: 191–211.

Mele, A. 1987. *Irrationality*. New York: Oxford University Press.

Mele, A. 1992. *Springs of Action: Understanding Intentional Behavior*. New York: Oxford University Press.

Mele, A. 1997. "Strength of Motivation and Being in Control: Learning from Libet." *American Philosophical Quarterly* 34: 319–333.

Mele, A. 2003. *Motivation and Agency*. New York: Oxford University Press.

Pink, T. 1996. *The Psychology of Freedom*. Cambridge: Cambridge University Press.

Prinz, W. 2003. "How Do We Know about Our Own Actions?" In *Voluntary Action*, edited by S. Maasen, W. Prinz, and G. Roth. Oxford: Oxford University Press.

Searle, J. 2001. *Rationality in Action*. Cambridge, Mass.: MIT Press.

Spence, S., and C. Frith. 1999. "Towards a Functional Anatomy of Volition." *Journal of Consciousness Studies* 6: 11–29.

Trevena, J., and J. Miller. 2002. "Cortical Movement Preparation Before and After a Conscious Decision to Move." *Consciousness and Cognition* 11: 162–190.

van de Grind, W. 2002. "Physical, Neural, and Mental Timing." *Consciousness and Cognition* 11: 241–264.

13 Constitutive Overdetermination

L. A. Paul

Our best philosophical and scientific pictures of the world organize material objects into a hierarchy of levels or layers—microparticles at the bottom, molecules, cells, and persons at higher layers. Are objects at higher layers identical to the sums of objects at lower layers that constitute them? (Note that this question is different from the question of whether *composition*—as opposed to *constitution*—is identity.) As I will define the positions, *reductionists* are monists who claim that constitution is identity and *nonreductionists* are pluralists who deny it.

Paul Oppenheim and Hilary Putnam (1958) present the classic characterization of the layered world model, arguing that the world has multiple layers of objects ordered by the mereological relation of spatiotemporal part to whole.[1] In Oppenheim and Putnam's reductionist model, sums of lower layer objects are identical to objects at higher layers and objects at higher layers are exhaustively (i.e., without remainder) decomposable into parts that are objects at lower layers.

Jaegwon Kim describes how the model of the natural world is stratified into hierarchical layers via mereological compositionality:

The Cartesian model of a bifurcated world has been replaced by that of a layered world, a hierarchically stratified structure of "levels" or "orders" of entities and their characteristic properties. It is generally thought that there is a bottom level, one consisting of whatever microphysics is going to tell us are the most basic physical particles out of which all matter is composed (electrons, neutrons, quarks, or whatever). (1993, p. 337; see also Kim 2002, pp. 3–4)

As Kim notes, the layered world was proposed as a substitute for Cartesian dualism, according to which there were mental *substances* that were ontologically independent of physical substances; the layered world model rejects mental substances and organizes the physical domain into layers.

Oppenheim and Putnam categorize and present the objects belonging to different layers this way (Boyd 1991, p. 409):

6. social groups

5. (multicellular) living things

4. cells

3. molecules

2. atoms

1. elementary particles

Any whole that is exhaustively decomposable into parts belonging to layer L is counted as also belonging to L, so objects at each layer include all objects at higher layers. According to Oppenheim and Putnam, different layers correspond to different ways we can mereologically carve objects, but there is no ontological increase or decrease as we move between layers. This suggests that we can model their ontology O of what there *is*, as opposed to how to *carve* what there is, as nonlayered:

O = particles / atoms / molecules / cells / (multicellular) living things / social groups.

Contemporary reductionists are unlikely to accept all the details of the Oppenheim-Putnam model. For example, they might hold that there are additional layers, that the ordering might not always be linear, and that it is unclear where some objects belong in the hierarchy. However, they will embrace its defining characteristics of ontological minimalism and of modeling the world in terms of a hierarchy of objects ordered by exhaustive spatiotemporal mereological composition where sums of lower layer objects *are* the higher layer objects they constitute.

Now, a model of the world as layered can be independent of reductionism: nonreductionists can accept layers even if they deny the reduction of objects at higher layers to sums of objects at lower ones. Why deny the reduction? Because the properties of higher layer (constituted) objects seem to be different from the properties of their lower layer (constituting) sums of objects, and by the Principle of the Indiscernibility of Identicals, things with different properties cannot be identical. The thought is that, for example, statues are valuable, sums of particles of bronze are not; persons are handsome, sums of cells are not (Fine 2003); protein molecules have their carbon atoms accidentally, but sums of atoms that include carbon atoms have their carbon atoms essentially (e.g., Wiggins 2001; Lowe 1998).[2] Ultimately, nonreductionists mean something ontologically substantial when they use the term 'layer', while reductionists do not.

Thus, nonreductionists make ontological distinctions where reductionists do not. We have the object that is the sum of cells and other matter, and the object that is the person—the nonreductionist holds that these differ (for they differ in their properties) whereas the reductionist identifies them.[3] When the nonreductionist rejects the claim that the sum of the lower layer objects is identical to the higher layer object, she holds that the sum constitutes but is not identical to the higher layer object. Moreover, according to the nonreductionist, in cases when the sum constitutes the higher layer object, it will not share all of its parts with the higher layer object. The sum of cells and other matter constitutes the person, and so the sum and the person share their microparticles and hence some of their parts. But they do not share *all* of their parts—for example, the head of the person is not identical to the head-shaped sum of cells and other material, since their properties differ.[4] The nonreductionist should thus distinguish between constitution and composition: *composition* is the familiar mereological fusion relation of parts to whole and is analogous to (or is) identity, while constitution requires a separate explication and is neither identity nor analogous to it.[5] (This distinction raises several interesting and delicate issues; see my manuscript "The Ontology of Objects" for a discussion of the matter.)

Rejecting the identification of higher layer objects with their constituting sums of lower layer objects implies that there are robust ontological differences between objects and their constituting sums. This means that, according to the nonreductionist, *in addition* to having a person, we have a sum of cells, a sum of atoms, a sum of particles, and so on. All of these entities (somehow) occupy the same region of spacetime and involve the same matter. When this nonreductionist stance is combined with a picture of the world as layered, we end up with objects in higher order layers that are irreducible to objects in lower order layers. This suggests that nonreductionists model their *ontology* as layered. For the nonreductionist, particles and molecules and so on, belong to lower layers, but *contra* the Oppenheim-Putnam interpretation, there are ontological differences as we move up layers (there is an increase in the number of objects in the world as each layer is added).

Why would nonreductionists accept a version—albeit a modified version—of the reductionists' layered model? First, perhaps, because having layers of some sort in the world seems to be a fairly natural world view: early versions of a (nonmereologically) layered model were proposed by emergentists, whose views bear an affinity to the nonreductionists' views.[6] Second, having a layered world model allows us to represent relationships between the smaller and larger objects referred to by theories of natural and social science in a way that is consistent with contemporary philosophical work on supervenience and related topics. Third, and perhaps most important, if the model is rejected, it is unclear what to put in its place. Recall the context in which the layered world model was adopted—it was seen as the antidote to substance dualism. If the layered world model is rejected, it seems we must revert to a mysterious Cartesian-like picture—with the unwelcome twist that there are now many material substances (one for each former layer). It is surely incorrect to hold that nonreductionism about objects related by constitution implies some sort of substance pluralism. (Compare the thought that nonreductionism in mind implies substance dualism.)

But for the nonreductionist who accepts the layered world, trouble comes quickly. Assume that the nonreductionist can adequately motivate her view and can explain enough about the constitution relation for us to understand how sums are numerically distinct from what they constitute and how sums and higher layer objects share their matter and spatiotemporal region without sharing all their parts.[7] Even if all this is accomplished, the nonreductionist still faces the problem of symmetric causal overdetermination.[8] (The substance pluralist would also face the problem of symmetric causal overdetermination, so rejecting the layered world model in favor of substance pluralism won't help.)

Those familiar with the debate over mental causation will recognize that the problem is the sort of problem that arises for nonreductionists about the mind (except that here the focus is on objects rather than properties). When philosophers of mind hold that mental properties are not identical to or reducible to physical properties, they need to explain the causal efficacy of mental properties given the sufficiency of physical properties for our actions, thoughts, beliefs, and so on; similarly, nonreductionists about layers need to explain the causal efficacy of objects that are constituted by sums of smaller objects. (Philosophers of mind sometimes argue that the overdetermination problem for nonreductionists about the mind arises in the context of the *exclusion thesis*: if an event c, together with associated background conditions and laws, is entirely sufficient for an event e, then no additional event c^* is a cause of e. Although the exclusion thesis is trying to capture a compelling intuition about the way causation works, the thesis itself is not particularly plausible, since some sorts of overdetermination—such as the case where the three golf balls shatter a window, or perhaps cases involving overdetermination between parts and a whole—are surely possible.)[9]

Imagine that I hit a tennis ball and it bounces off my racquet at a speed of 100 miles per hour. What causes this effect? Well, *I* do. (I am eliding the difference between object causation and event causation here.)[10] But even though I cause the bouncing of the tennis ball, I am constituted by a sum of cells and other matter, and this sum causes the bouncing as well. In fact, according to the nonreductionist, there are *many* different objects causing the bouncing. Just for starters, I, the sum of elementary particles that constitutes the sum of atoms, the sum of atoms that constitutes the sum of molecules, the sum of molecules that constitutes my cells and other matter, and the sum of cells and other matter that constitutes me, all cause the bouncing. How can we explain this? The ball didn't bounce off my racquet at 500 miles per hour, and yet the action of each of the five objects causes a bouncing of 100 miles per hour. (Strictly speaking, multiple effects are overdetermined, since the sum of molecules that constitutes the tennis ball moves at 100 miles per hour, as does the sum of particles that constitutes the tennis ball, and so on; but I ignore this complication for simplicity's sake.) The same worry arises when I write a book: what causes the book to be written? Do I, the sum of my cells and other matter, the sum of my fundamental particles, and so on, all cause the writing of the book? The point here, of course, is that it seems as though nonreductionism generates massive amounts of symmetric causal overdetermination, which I shall call "constitutive overdetermination."

In contemporary discussions of causation, standard cases of symmetric causal overdetermination are defined (roughly) as cases involving multiple distinct causes of an effect where the causation is neither joint, additive, nor preemptive (and it is assumed the overdetermining causes do not cause each other). Common examples involve cases where three bullets simultaneously enter a victim's heart, or three golf balls simultaneously shatter a window. Each cause makes exactly the same causal contribution as the other causes to the effect (so the causal overdetermination is *symmetric*); each cause without the others is sufficient for the effect; and for each cause the causal process from cause to effect is not interrupted.

Many of those who contribute to the literature on philosophical theories of causation think that symmetric causal overdetermination is problematic but peripheral.[11] There are several reasons for this. First, such cases are supposed to be rare or nonexistent in the actual world. Second, it is supposed that even if cases of overdetermination do exist, most of them are artifacts of the coarse or robust individuation of effects. If so, effects can be individuated more finely so as to remove the overdetermination: for example, in the case where three golf balls shatter a window, one can hold that the shattering is a slightly different effect when there are three golf balls as opposed to one or two. This makes the overdetermination in the golf ball case disappear, turning the case into a case of joint causation that was misidentified under a too-robust individuation of the shattering. Third, since our commonsense intuitions are vague as to how to understand symmetric overdetermination in the context of a reductive analysis of causation, some hold that true cases of symmetric overdetermination should be treated as spoils to the victor; that is, if better understood, more central cases are solved by an analysis, whatever verdict given by this analysis on symmetric overdeterminers should simply be accepted.[12] Finally, there is a special sort of overdetermination that may result (if composition is not identity but merely analogous to identity) such that the collection of objects that compose c and the whole that is c overdetermine e. The thought here is that it is unclear how concerned we should be about this sort of overdetermination or whether we should even balk at accepting it. The reason for a laid-back approach is that compositionality—the special mereological relationship of "almost identity" between things and the whole they compose—is so intimate that this sort of overdetermination is not metaphysically troubling.[13]

But none of this will help the nonreductionist. First, the sort of overdetermination implied by her view would not be rare—it would be the norm. Practically every instance of the sort of garden-variety causation involved in our commonsense, scientific, or philosophical claims would be overdetermined! Second, merely individuating effects more finely will not solve the problem, since the effects in question will not be any different if there is no overdetermination. The bouncing of the tennis ball is not changed by the fact that both I and my constitutive sum of cells hit the tennis ball; the bouncing would be unchanged if, for example, I cause the bouncing but my sum of cells somehow does not. Third, the "spoils to the victor" solution is only plausible (if it is plausible at all, which I doubt) in a context where we are performing a conceptual analysis and the troublesome cases are not the central sort of case handled by the analysis. As we have seen, the nonreductionist's view makes symmetric overdetermination *the most* central and common sort of causation around. Finally, the nonreductionist denies that constitution is merely composition, that is, she denies that when the sum of lower layer objects constitutes the higher layer object that this is just the relation of the sum composing the higher layer object. Indeed, the nonreductionist denies that the sum and the object it constitutes share their larger spatiotemporal parts, so the constitution relation cannot be the composition relation. Since constitution is not composition, the claim that overdetermination is not problematic in the special case of compositionality will not help the nonreductionist. Result: the nonreductionist cannot ignore the problem of constitutive overdetermination.

Of course, the nonreductionist could respond by giving up her views and granting that objects are identical to their constituting sums. If objects are identical to their constituting sums then the problem with overdetermination that the nonreductionist faces is avoided. But there are other options that the nonreductionist might prefer to consider.

One option is to be an eliminativist about objects at all higher layers. (The nonreductionist is unlikely to find this option attractive, but may feel pushed towards it given her view that should objects like statues and persons exist, they must differ from their constituting sums.) Outright eliminativism is clearly more radical than reductionism: instead of holding that objects at higher layers exist but are identical to sums of objects at lower layers, objects at higher layers are *eliminated* in favor of objects at lower layers.[14] The usual assumption, if this is done, is that the privileged layer is that of microphysics, following Oppenheim and Putnam. (See Schaffer 2003a for a discussion of privileged layers.)

The eliminativist argues for the elimination of higher layer objects by claiming that all or most objects do not compose sums. Because there are no sums of objects, there are no higher layer objects that they constitute, so there is no constitutive overdetermination. For thoroughgoing eliminativists, nothing except fundamental particles, or fields, or whatever is most fundamental exists. I take eliminativism to be an interesting non-starter, since eliminating proteins, rocks, and stars must be a position of last resort. Surely it is more acceptable to have widespread constitutive overdetermination—or even epiphenomenalism—than to accept that such higher layer objects do not exist. Eliminativism suffers from more than just radical implausibility: if there exists an infinitely descending series of layers, such that for every elimination we allow, another beckons, then we never end up with any fundamental existents. We eliminate endlessly.[15]

There are two more options for the nonreductionist to consider—some sort of widespread causal supervenience, or true symmetric overdetermination. Consider the first option: what if the sort of widespread symmetric causal overdetermination we seem to see is not true symmetric overdetermination after all? Instead of true overdetermination, there are multiple layers of causal relations, where the causal relations at higher layers nonreductively supervene on causal relations at lower layers. In this picture, there is no overdetermination because causal processes initiated by higher layer objects only cause higher layer effects and lower layer objects only cause lower layer effects.

I think such a picture has some nice intuitive appeal but is ultimately a nonstarter. Do we really think there are all these different layers of causation? As with symmetric overdetermination, this view seems to produce a lot more causation in the world than we ever knew about or wanted. Not only do we have microphysical causation, but we have numerically different processes of chemical causation, individual causation, artifact causation, mental causation, and so on. This is unattractive. But there is a more serious problem in the offing.

The way I described the problem with overdetermination and a layered world may make you think that the right way to view the problem is to hold that things caused other things on the same layer; that is, persons cause things like bouncings of tennis balls at their layer, while sums of cells cause things at theirs. But in fact, the problem with overdetermination is not layer specific—causation seems to cross layers. As Kim (1998, pp. 42–43) puts it, when you take an aspirin to relieve a headache, intuitively, you also causally intervene in the brain process upon which the headache supervenes.

Similarly, we have strong intuitions that it is possible for a person to causally intervene at the layer of fundamental particles and for a society to causally intervene at the layer of individuals. If I remove a carbon atom from a carboxyl group, then I cause a change in a protein *and* in the sum of atoms that constitute it, and this cannot be explained away by suggesting that I am only causing something at a higher layer which supervenes on my sum of atoms causing a change in another sum of atoms. It seems importantly right to say that I am causing a change in the protein, *and* that *I* (not just my sum of atoms) am also causing a change in the sum of atoms that constitutes the protein. If so, then the claim that causation is layer specific is ad hoc and implausible. (Jonathan Schaffer, in conversation, suggests two other reasons why skepticism about causation between layers is unwarranted. First, if the universe were created by a Big Bang, then if there were no causation between levels we would lack original causes for objects at other levels, such as mental objects. Second, we would need an explanation for the robust regularities we find between levels.)

It may seem that we have reached our final option—accept constitutive overdetermination and defend it as unproblematic or at least inevitable. Once we understand how sums of lower layer objects constitute objects at higher layers, we grant that widespread symmetric overdetermination exists after all, and explain its being widespread by means of the constitutive tie between sums of objects and what they constitute. After all, when we have the sum, we have the higher order object it constitutes, and both are treated equally under the laws. So why be surprised that we have multiple causes? But accepting this option comes at a heavy cost. To see this, we must investigate the phenomenon in more depth. Constitutive overdetermination is stranger than at first it might appear.

The best way to think of cases of symmetric overdetermination is in terms of multiple causal processes: for each overdetermining cause, there is an uninterrupted process from cause to effect such that each process runs to completion. According to this account, *modulo* irrelevant interaction effects, the intrinsic character of each causal process is the same as if there were only one process: none of the overdetermining processes is changed by the addition or removal of another overdetermining process (Hall and Paul forthcoming, § 3).[16]

There is an alternative way to understand symmetric overdetermination. Instead of each cause individually bringing about the effect, all the objects we have been calling "causes" are conjoined to bring about the effect, even while none of these objects taken individually causes the effect. Only the objects taken together can be said to be the cause of the effect. For example, instead of saying that each of the three golf balls is a cause of the shattering of the window, none of the individual golf balls is a cause of the window's shattering—while the sum of all three golf balls is. As Schaffer (2003b) points out, if none of these objects alone counts as a cause of the effect, it is hard to see how all of them together can count as a cause. Nothing more is added! (For an in-depth discussion of other problems with this sort of approach, see Hall and Paul forthcoming.)

So the more plausible way of thinking about symmetric overdetermination adopts the first approach—think of it in terms of multiple causal processes, each running uninterrupted from overdetermining cause to effect. (To require that a causal process exists from each cause to the effect in cases of overdetermination rules out the possibility of conflating overdetermining causes with epiphenomena.) But although this picture is an improvement over the view that overdetermining causes are conjoined, significant conceptual problems remain.

The trouble with symmetric overdetermination in general, and by extension with constitutive overdetermination, is that it is mysterious how each cause could really be a *full* cause of the effect; it is hard to understand how exactly having multiple complete causes of an effect is supposed to *work*. There is something deeply puzzling about true overdetermination, as opposed to preemption and the like. For in true overdetermination, *multiple competing causal processes run all the way to completion*, where each cause is a *complete* cause of the effect that acts independently of the other overdetermining causes C (i.e., setting aside irrelevant interaction effects, the overdeterminer does not cause jointly with any of C and is not caused by any of C). Somehow, multiple causes are subsumed by the same laws and multiple processes run all the way to completion, each bringing about the effect independently of the other causes bringing about the very same effect.

To bring out the intuitive difficulty we have with this picture, consider the difference between symmetrically overdetermined effects and jointly caused effects. An effect is jointly caused if multiple causes combine to produce it. For example, Billy and Suzy each spray some paint on a wall. Billy's paint is red and Suzy's is blue, and the resulting graffiti has red parts and blue parts (and perhaps some purple parts). We can see how each cause is contributing to bringing about the effect, and it is easy to understand the causal contribution of each cause because if any of the causes of the effect were missing, the effect would not have occurred just as it did (if Suzy hadn't sprayed her paint, the graffiti would have been red). True symmetric overdetermination does not exhibit this characteristic: each cause does enough to do all the (relevant) causal work that is actually done, so if one or more of the overdetermining causes were removed, the effect would occur just as it did when caused by all the overdeterminers.

The graffiti example illustrates how we have a deep understanding of how joint causation works, since each cause makes a clearly defined (and clearly limited) contribution to the production of the effect. But since this model does not extend to true symmetric overdetermination, how are we to understand this sort of causation? Remember, each overdeterminer generates an uninterrupted causal process running to completion from cause to effect. If each cause brings about a process that generates the effect all by itself, why aren't there multiple instances of the very same (type of) effect, one created by each overdetermining cause? (If we treat causation in terms of properties, we can ask why there aren't multiple instances of the same properties.) We seem to have too much causation to go around.

Note that the situation is not merely one where we have many *possible* causes, or overdetermination of mere sufficiency for each effect. If the nonreductionist's picture correctly describes the actual world and is consistent with our best physical theories, there is a transfer of energy, momentum, or some other conserved quantity from *each* overdetermining cause to the effect, and each of these transfers brings about the entire effect. (Describing the case as a transfer of a conserved quantity is a way of saying that in the actual world there is an uninterrupted causal process from each cause to the effect.) Return to our example of the tennis ball. According to the laws, when I hit the tennis ball, I transfer an amount of momentum, p, to the ball. But also according to the laws, when the sum of particles that constitutes me hits the tennis ball, *it* transfers an amount of momentum p to the ball. This brings a central problem to the fore—the problem of additivity of conserved quantities. For example, under the laws, momentum is additive; when there are two transfers of momentum p the total transfer is $2p$. But the tennis ball only exhibits an increase of magnitude p, not $2p$![17]

Perhaps the nonreductionist will hold that in cases of overdetermination transfers of conserved physical quantities are not additive. But in order to accept this claim, reductionists will want to know *why* and, more importantly, *how* this failure to be additive could be the case. Note that it isn't enough just to claim that some sort of special relationship between the overdetermining causes prevents additivity. As long as there are multiple independent causal processes overdetermining the effect, there will be multiple transfers of conserved quantities to the effect, so additivity constraints seem to apply. (Perhaps in cases of compositionality the special relationship of proper part to whole eliminates the problem of additivity because strictly speaking it eliminates the overdetermination. The whole causes the effect in virtue of the proper part causing the effect; the whole only initiates a causal process in virtue of its proper part initiating that process.)[18]

A more general problem with overdetermination (more general because it applies to accounts of causation in nomically different worlds in addition to accounts of this-worldly causation) concerns our implicit intuitions about the intrinsicness of the causal relation. Consider a structure S of events consisting of an event E together with all of its causes back to some earlier time. Intuitively, it seems right to say that the causal characteristics of S will be fixed solely by its intrinsic character together with the governing laws. But now add some extrinsic detail D to the picture (D is external to S), such as an additional, overdetermining cause of E. By hypothesis, adding D does not affect the (relevant) causal character of S: everything that was a cause of E before the addition of D is a cause afterwards, and E occurs exactly as it would have occurred. But then we can put the worry about symmetric overdetermination this way: what causal contribution is D making to the production of E, and how does it make it? Simply replying that D is sufficient to cause E does not explain how D makes its causal contribution to the production of E, it merely reiterates that D *is* a cause of E. How can it be the case that the causal facts about E can be changed without changing the intrinsic causal character of S? (The causal facts are changed because E is now overdetermined.) The worry is that symmetric overdetermination seems to violate the natural intuition that the complete causal character of S is fixed solely by its intrinsic character plus the laws.[19]

These considerations help to bring out the fact that, no matter how we try to gloss the way it is supposed to work, true symmetric causal overdetermination is *strange*. It is a real mystery how symmetric overdetermination can be understood on a deep level, and how we are to fit this sort of causation into our more general picture of how causes bring about effects. Since it is reasonable to assume that every macroscopic object is constituted by sums of particles, we can now see that the problem for the nonreductionist amounts to a problem with explaining just about every instance of macroscopic causation in the world. If constitutive overdetermination is supposed to occur almost everywhere in the actual world (since almost everything actual is constituted by or constitutes something else), then we lack a decent understanding of the way causation works in almost every actual-world case. To simply bite the bullet and accept constitutive overdetermination is to accept that actual causation is fundamentally mysterious in a hitherto unrecognized way.

This problem extends past the worry that we have made ordinary causation mysterious, since it also creates trouble for analyses of causation. Extant analyses of causation do not adequately explain symmetric overdetermination even if they give the right answer, namely, that each overdeterminer counts as a cause. If overdetermination cannot be set aside as peripheral, the task of developing an analysis of ordinary causation is made significantly harder. Since an acceptable analysis of ordinary causation is needed for *fully* informative treatments of many central topics in philosophy—free will, action, decision theory, reference, perception, and laws of nature, for example—worsening the prospects for an acceptable analysis of ordinary causation means worsening the prospects for complete versions of these theories as well.

Note that I am happy to grant that symmetric overdetermination is metaphysically possible, and perhaps even actual. The claim is not that symmetric overdetermination is metaphysically incoherent, nor that we have no reason to believe in overdetermining entities. (See Sider 2003 for a critical discussion of such claims.) Rather, the point is that constitutive overdetermination (and perhaps other sorts of true symmetric overdetermination) should be thought to be mysterious and problematic, and if a philosophical theory implies this sort of overdetermination, it implies widespread mystery. Accepting that a few localized instances of causation are mysterious is unpleasant. Accepting that almost all instances of ordinary causation are mysterious is unacceptable.

If there is no better option, then perhaps accepting that the world has constitutive overdetermination is the best option nonreductionists have. I used to think it *was* the best option—I thought that constitutive overdetermination, while extremely problematic, was simply a feature of the world that nonreductionists had to accept. After all, at least it didn't make objects epiphenomenal or causally inefficacious (e.g., by holding that higher or lower order objects are continuously preempted by lower order objects).[20] But it *is not* the best option.

To see this, we need to trace our chain of reasoning back to an early assumption we made about the nature of the world. How did the problem arise in the first place? It arose when nonreductionists combined the thesis that objects are not identical with their constituting sums, with a model of the world as layered. If material objects are numerically distinct from the sums of material objects that constitute them, without additional guidance to their ontology this suggests that they are somehow stacked on top of their constituting sums within the same space-like extra-dense layers of cake like some sort of weird Escher building. While the view is not quite substance pluralism (since the nonreductionists' layers are not ontologically independent), it is awfully close. Rejecting the identity claim made by the reductionist without explaining how to reinterpret the model of the layered world leads to this situation.

The idea that nonreductionists must endorse a "stacking" or "dense" interpretation of the layered model is the source of objections to nonreductionism that complain that if a statue is not identical to the sum of its bronze particles, "why don't the two together weigh twice as much?" (Lewis 1986a, p. 252). Since contemporary nonreductionists should deny that higher layer objects share the spatiotemporal parts of their constituting sums of lower layer objects because of differences in their properties— for example, differences between properties of the larger spatiotemporal parts of a person and properties of the sums of particles that constitute those parts—the need to make sense of how the world is layered becomes even more pressing. We need additional guidance as to the nature of the constitution relation if we are to avoid deep ontological quagmires.

I suspect some version of this mysterious picture of extra-dense layers has been subtly attributed to nonreductionists by many philosophers, especially by reductionists. And the trouble with this (aside from the conceptual difficulties surrounding such a picture), as we have seen, is that if multiple distinct objects related by constitution are each causally sufficient for the effect in question, then it seems that we must admit massive amounts of constitutive overdetermination.

Nonreductionists need to produce a clear account of how the layered world model works according to their views—an account that does not

imply widespread overdetermination and does not endorse epiphenomenalism, substance dualism, or some sort of emergentism. Below, I sketch an
account of the ontology of constitution that provides a working understanding of the relation of constitution and thus a working interpretation
of the layered world model. By providing an outline of how objects can
overlap when they are related by constitution, I outline an interpretation
of the model of the world that points nonreductionists away from constitutive overdetermination. (For a more developed account of this ontological
approach and of overlap between coincident objects, see Paul 2002, 2006,
and my manuscript "The Ontology of Objects.")

The first step is to characterize the fundamental ontology of the objects
of the world. Instead of thinking of objects in primarily spatiotemporal
mereological terms, think of them in terms of their properties. Objects are
sums of properties, so they have properties as parts.[21] According to this account of the objects of the world, objects like persons are fusions that include property instances such as *having mass m* and *having shape s*, and so
forth, as are the sums that constitute them.

When sum *A* constitutes higher layer object *B*, *A* and *B* overlap with
respect to many of their property instances: they literally share such
instances as overlapped parts, especially those that we can dub *material*
instances like *having mass m* or *having shape s*. If we do not assume that
objects are individuated by their matter or region, we can see that we can
have numerically distinct objects that differ with respect to some of the
property instances (such as *de re* modal property instances) they include
even if they share their material and place. The idea is that objects related by constitution can share material property instances such as *having
mass m* or *including particle p*, even if they do not share *all* of their property instances.[22]

For example, the person and the sum of cells that constitutes him overlap with respect to many of their material instances, but they do not overlap with respect to all their property instances, even if they share their
matter and spatiotemporal region. The person includes the property instance of *being handsome* while the sum of his cells does not, and the sum
of his cells includes the property instance of *having n cells essentially* while
he does not. Likewise, a protein and the sum of microparticles that constitutes it share some, but not all, of their property instances. The protein
includes the property instance of *having mass m*, and the sum of particles

also includes *having mass m*. But the protein includes the property instance of *having particle p accidentally*, while the sum of microparticles includes an instance of *having particle p essentially*. These objects differ in the property instances they include, and hence they are absolutely, or numerically, different even while they spatiotemporally and materially overlap. When objects only partially qualitatively overlap, the objects share only some (qualitative) property instances and in this sense are only "partly" identical.

The nonreductionist now has the basic tools to construct a (partial) working interpretation of the model of the layered world. The layers are organized into a hierarchy governed by the relations of constitution and composition such that sums of objects at lower layers constitute objects at higher layers—sums of particles constitute atoms, sums of atoms constitute molecules, and so on.[23] When objects constitute other objects, they are partly identical in that they partly overlap by sharing many of their property instances. This last point is of essential importance: the objects overlap with respect to some of their property *instances*; if the person and his constituting sum of cells overlap with respect to property instance *P*, then they *share* the very same property instance. Since the property instances had by constituting and constituted objects are literally shared, the nonreductionists' interpretation shows how the world is not extra-dense with respect to shared property instances in a constitutional hierarchy—any more than a shared office wall is twice as dense because it is part of two different offices.

Now that we have a nonreductionist interpretation of objects related by constitution, we can assess the overall picture for the possibility of constitutive overdetermination. First, we need to say a bit more about the way causation is supposed to work in the world. There are two features of any successful reductive account of causation that will be important for our solution. For *c* to cause *e*, *c* must lawfully entail *e*, given the background conditions and the laws. In other words, some sort of nomological sufficiency is required for causation, at least for the cases I am concentrating on. Also, causation involves property instances—either as constituents of events and objects, or as causes and effects in their own right.

In Paul 2000, I argue that it is best to take property instances as the causal relata. But even if you insist that events or objects must be the causal relata, property instances must play a central role. Events or objects are causal actors only in virtue of their property instances, for property instances (or exemplifications, etc.)[24] are what are subsumed by laws. Ideally, for nomic subsumption of cause and effect, for event c with property p and event e with property q, c lawfully entails e iff c's exemplification of p is subsumed by the antecedent of the right law or laws that entail a consequent subsuming e's exemplification of q.

Why does this matter? I want to draw attention to the role of property instances in causation because I think it is essential to see that when we say an object or event is a cause of an effect, we usually mean that the object or event is a cause in virtue of some of its distinguishing properties being involved in the requisite nomic subsumption. Not all of its properties must be involved, but enough of the *important* ones need to be involved in order to say that c caused e. This means either that property instances are causes and effects, or that objects and events are causes and effects in virtue of exemplifying certain properties.

Either we need to take property instances as causes and effects, or we need to be clear about what properties of an event or object are causing what. Imagine a sphere that is spinning while being heated. The spinning is a cause of the sphere's motion. The heating is a cause of the sphere's high temperature. As it turns out, the hot, spinning sphere touches a flag, which flutters and then bursts into flame. The hot, spinning sphere is a cause of the fire, but the breeze it created also caused the flag to flutter. If we say that the sphere causes the fire and causes the fluttering, we must be careful to say that the sphere causes the fire in virtue of its temperature properties, while it causes the fluttering in virtue of its motion properties.

The role of property instances in causation is relevant to whether constitutive overdetermination is implied by the nonreductionist view. Under the model of the world that the nonreductionist proposes, the way the world is arranged involves a number of numerically different but literally overlapping objects (and events that include these objects as constituents) that share their material, their spatiotemporal region, and in general many of their nonmodal property instances. In the relevant cases, the objects *share* many, if not all of, their nonmodal properties, and they do this by sharing *instances* of these properties. In particular, they share many of their material nonmodal property instances; instances of properties of having particular colors, weights, masses, shapes, temperatures, and so forth. Such nonmodal property instances typically figure in laws of nature and are involved in causing many of the effects we observe. For example, when I weigh my cat on the bathroom scale, the scale reads 8 pounds. My cat exemplifies (includes) the property of *weighing 8 pounds*, and this property is part of a lawfully sufficient condition for the scale's reading 8 pounds. So, my cat's standing on the scale is a cause of the scale's reading 8 pounds, in virtue of her having the property instance of *weighing 8 pounds*.[25]

Now, of course, the sum of cells that constitutes my cat also exemplifies (includes) the property of *weighing 8 pounds*, as does the sum of molecules that constitutes the sum of cells. But do we have constitutive overdetermination of the reading on the scale? No, because my cat and her sums *share* the causally efficacious property instance of *weighing 8 pounds*. My cat and her sums are numerically distinct objects that are not entirely distinct— and a common part of the objects, the property instance of *weighing 8 pounds*, is what does the causing. Only *one* causal process is initiated here, since only one property instance is subsumed by the (relevant) laws. Since a part of the shared portion of these entities is what is causally relevant we can say that the cat and the sum of cells, the sum of molecules, and so on, each caused the reading on the scale but there is no overdetermination.

Likewise for the protein and its sum of particles, and other objects in the hierarchy of constitution. It was only when we thought of the different objects as somehow stacked or piled up in some way with duplicated property instances or parts that we seemed to get constitutive overdetermination. Of course, not all of the property instances of the objects or events we are considering will be causally relevant: modal property instances, and perhaps some other property instances may not be causing anything in some cases. But we do not need *every* property instance of an event or an object to be causally efficacious in order to say that the event or object was a cause—just the important ones. In the cases of putative constitutive overdetermination, we need the property instances that figure in the relevant laws of nature to be the causes, not *de re* property instances of being essentially such and such or relational property instances such as *being an art object*. The important property instances are the ones that we thought all along were doing the causing—we thought all along that it was my cat's property of *weighing 8 pounds* that was responsible for the reading on the scale.

If we thought that it was the cat's *being accidentally 8 pounds* that caused the reading on the scale, then we wouldn't have worried that the reading was overdetermined in the first place, since the property instance of *being accidentally 8 pounds is not* shared by the cat and the sum of her cells. But we don't think the cat's being *accidentally* 8 pounds, as opposed to her being 8 pounds *simpliciter*, is a cause of the reading. Whether she is *accidentally* 8 pounds or whether she is *essentially* 8 pounds has nothing to do with my causal judgment—only whether she *is* 8 pounds.[26] Likewise for my cat's property of *being gorgeous*: my cat is gorgeous but the sums that constitute her are not, and so anything caused by her gorgeousness (the *oohs* and *aahs* of my dinner party guests upon beholding her, for example) is not overdetermined.

The same goes for the causal action of a protein: let us say that a few of the empirical properties of a protein cause a scientist to get an interesting result using NMR or IR spectroscopy. Of course, the sum of fundamental particles that composes the protein also includes these properties. It is the shared property instances of the protein and its sum—for example, the property of *including particle p*—that cause the spectroscopic readings. What *does not* cause the readings is the protein's property of *accidentally including particle p*. Nor does the sum's property of *essentially including particle p* affect the readings: these properties simply are not causally relevant to the effect in question, and they are not shared by the objects. (Some might even claim that *de re* modal properties are never causally active. Then all the shared properties of the objects could be the causally relevant properties, and we would not have to worry about excluded properties in our causal story. Questions arise about how we know about such properties if they are causally inactive—the same questions we might have about how we know about numbers, abstract objects, and so on.)

We need to consider one final worry. Have we simply dodged the overdetermination bullet by talking about objects when the real problem lies with the properties of objects? Can the reductionist move the debate from relations between objects to relations between properties, and argue, for example, that the properties of *being a sum of particles* and *being a protein* overdetermine the spectroscopic readings? Presumably, the justification for such a move would involve the claim that the nonreductionist must hold that property instances at different layers are just as irreducible as objects at different layers, and since property instances are the real causes and effects, we need to pay special attention to them when investigating possible overdetermination.

Fortunately for the nonreductionist, shifting the terms of the debate to properties merely shifts the terms of the solution to properties. First, recognize that there are many more predicates than properties and property instances, but allow that there may be a property instance of *being protein P* if this property instance is really just a conjunction or fusion of ontologically more fundamental property instances. Consider protein *Pro*, constituted by sum of molecules *Mol*. The nonreductionist should hold that the property instance of *being protein Pro* is a complex property instance that is really just a conjunction of many more fundamental property instances such as *having shape s, having mass m, having n molecules accidentally*, and so on. Now consider the property instance of *being sum Mol*: it is a complex property instance that is just a conjunction of many more fundamental property instances such as *having shape s, having mass m, having n molecules essentially*, and so on. Just as *Pro* and *Mol* partly overlap or share their property instances, the property instance of *being Pro* and the property instance of *being Mol* share some of their conjuncts. (Further, as a conjunctive property instance such as *being Pro* is just the fusion of the conjuncts, likewise the property instance of *being Mol*.) And just as with the solution in terms of objects—it is the shared (instances of) conjuncts that are responsible for the problematic cases of putative constitutive overdetermination.

This should be no surprise when we consider our ontology of objects: to say that an object has the property instance of *being protein Pro* is to say that there is an object that is protein *Pro*, and to say that an object has the property instance of *being sum Mol* is to say there is an object that is the sum *Mol*.[27] Since *Mol* constitutes *Pro*, *Mol* and *Pro* partly overlap and thus both can count as non-overdetermining causes of effects. For the same reasons and in the same way, the property instance of *being Mol* constitutes the property instance of *being Pro*, and so both property instances can count as non-overdetermining causes of effects. (The move parallels the debate in philosophy of mind over mental causation, and the neo-Kripkean nonreductionist about the mental can defend a similar solution there: mental property instances include conjuncts such as *being accidentally embodied*, and physical property instances include conjuncts such as *being essentially embodied*, but they overlap with respect to many of their material conjuncts.) The often-raised objection about a mental entity causing an effect "in virtue of being mental" fails here for the same reason that a parallel objection about my hitting the tennis ball "in virtue of being me" fails. In each case, a nontrivial proper part is the cause (some of my material instances, some of the mental entity's material instances) and this is sufficient for me and for the mental entity to be causes.

Whether we focus on objects or properties, once we realize that it is the involvement of certain property instances that determine whether one thing causes another, and that in the cases of constitutive overdetermination we have considered, the causally important or relevant property instances are shared, we can see why causal responsibility is shared, not overdetermined. When I, my constitutive sum of cells, constitutive sum of molecules, and so on, hit the tennis ball, a *shared* part (a shared property instance) causes the tennis ball to bounce off my racquet at 100 miles per hour. The problem of constitutive overdetermination is merely an artifact of a flawed interpretation of the layered model of the world.

Acknowledgments

I am particularly grateful to Jonathan Schaffer for comments and discussion. I would also like to thank audiences at the 2003 Inland Northwest Philosophy Conference on Explanation and Causation, and the 2003 Annual Conference of the Australasian Association of Philosophy.

Notes

1. The original Oppenheim-Putnam program was characterized in terms of reductions involving nomic equivalence and the construction of bridge laws between terms of theories of objects in different layers, and does not explicitly address issues concerning constitution. For the purposes of this argument I characterize reductionism more directly, in terms of an identity claim about objects. Debates about reduction of objects intersect with debates about the reduction of properties, especially in philosophy of mind and philosophy of science. Whether "layer," "level," or "order" is used to discuss the Oppenheim-Putnam model varies from author to author. I have chosen "layer," but I don't think much turns on the nomenclature.

2. Proteins are constructed from amino acids joined by peptide bonds, and most amino acids include carboxyl groups (OH–C = O, or –COOH).

3. Most reductionists will also argue for redescriptions of the sum and the higher order object such that there is no difference in properties after all (e.g., Lewis 1986a). I don't hold out much hope for these strategies; see Fine 2003 and Paul 2006 for discussion.

4. I defend this point in detail in Paul 2006.

5. Some contemporary reductionists will hold that mereological composition is identity, so that there really is just one ontological layer; whereas other reductionists will hold that mereological composition is merely analogous to identity, but such that wholes are "nothing over and above" their parts. It is unclear to me how the latter sort of reductionist will represent the layered world.

6. Kim (2002, p. 7) suggests that work by emergentists like C. Lloyd Morgan is the origin of the layered approach.

7. Defenders of nonreductionism who try to address these issues include Lowe (1998), Wiggins (2001), and Paul (2006). Rea (1997) gives an excellent survey of the early debate.

8. Kim (1984, 1998), Baker (1995), and Merricks (2001) discuss the problem of symmetric overdetermination for other nonreductionist views. Baker and Kim are important representative examples of those who focus on issues involving the reduction of the mental to the physical. Merricks is concerned about overdetermination in cases where parts compose wholes.

9. I am assuming that epiphenomenalism is not an option.

10. There are related worries about overdetermination due to the nonidentity of objects and events. Sider (2003) rightly notes that this sort of overdetermination deserves more attention. The solution I propose at the end of this paper can also be used to resolve worries in cases where objects partly constitute events; I address the issue in more detail in my manuscript, "The Ontology of Objects."

11. There are exceptions; see Schaffer 2003b and Hall and Paul forthcoming.

12. See, for example, Lewis 1986b, p. 194.

13. Merricks (2001, 2003) argues that this sort of overdetermination is troubling; Sider (2003) argues that it is not. A discussion of this issue will take us too far afield; in any case, this sort of overdetermination is faced by reductionists and nonreductionists alike.

14. Van Inwagen (1990) and Merricks (2001) are recent defenders of a partly eliminativist position. Cian Dorr (2002) defends a thoroughgoing eliminativism. A different kind of skeptic might argue for eliminativism from the bottom up, claiming that, for example, rocks exist but the particles that supposedly compose them do not.

15. Block (1990, 2003), Schaffer (2003a), Sider (1993), and Sosa (1999) all point out this problem for the eliminativist.

16. I am helping myself to an intuitive notion of a causal process here.

17. There is a parallel problem with effects, since each overdetermining cause overdetermines many effects (all those related in the constitutional hierarchy). My hitting the tennis ball, my constitutive sum of cells hitting the tennis ball, and my

constitutive sum of particles hitting the tennis ball, etc., each overdetermines the bouncing of the tennis ball at 100 mph. But each object overdetermining the bouncing of the tennis ball also overdetermines the bouncing of the tennis ball's constitutive sum of molecules at 100 mph and the bouncing of the tennis ball's constitutive sum of particles at 100 mph, etc. Under the laws, my hitting the tennis ball only imparts momentum p, but somehow, many (otherwise causally unrelated) entities receive an increase of p from the hit—the tennis ball, its constitutive sum of molecules, its constitutive sum of particles, etc. For ease of exposition I have ignored this complexity. (Note: don't think that the solution to the problem of additivity is solved by the complexity of the overdetermination. If anything the problem is worsened, since if there is causal overdetermination, each object—myself, and each of my constitutive sums—somehow imparts momentum p to each of many objects— the tennis ball and each of its constitutive sums. If there were a one-to-one mapping of transfer of momentum—for example, if there were no causation across layers— there would be no problem of additivity, but only because there would be no overdetermination. I've already shown above that rejecting causation across layers is unacceptable.)

18. If there is true symmetric overdetermination in cases of compositionality, such that the thing that is a proper part initiates a causal process sufficient for the effect, and the whole initiates another causal process sufficient for the effect, the problem of additivity might return. To explain why there is still no additivity problem, perhaps one could argue that the non-additivity of conserved quantities of parts and wholes is implicit in the laws or at least the practice of science. In other words, the claim is that in the special case where parts compose wholes, science implies that the conserved quantities are not additive after all. If such a view is to be made plausible, an explicit account of how science can be thought to imply non-additivity needs to be provided. (I am indebted to Timothy Williamson and Terry Horgan for discussion of this point.)

19. This perspective was first defended in Hall 2004, and is further developed in Hall and Paul forthcoming, section 3.

20. If there can be infinitely descending preempted chains this creates interesting problems for a counterfactual analysis of causation; see Lewis's postscript to "Causation" in Lewis 1986b, for a discussion.

21. I introduce and develop this approach in Paul 2002 and Paul 2006. Since spatiotemporal parts are not shared but spatiotemporal regions are, spatiotemporal parts are individuated by more than the regions they occupy. This follows from ordinary nonreductionist reasoning about property differences between the parts of spatiotemporally coinciding objects.

22. Defenders of constitution need to explain why *de re* modal and other property differences do not supervene on shared matter and location; see Paul 2006.

23. Reductionists who hold that composition is not strictly identity will agree with the nonreductionist that composition and constitution are different relations. The complete interpretation of the layered world model for this sort of reductionist and for the nonreductionist will be complex. For starters, both will need to say more about how composition and constitution together define the overall hierarchy of objects. On the nonreductionist view I am outlining here, particles compose sums of particles, but only partly compose atoms: particles compose sums of particles, sums of particles constitute atoms; atoms compose sums of atoms, sums of atoms constitute molecules; and so on. See my manuscript "The Ontology of Objects" for more discussion.

24. Property instances are located properties. Rather than assume a particular account of properties, I will speak interchangeably of properties had by events or objects, properties exemplified by events or objects, and property instances. What matters for my purposes here is that the property is located or exemplified at a location, not whether the property is a trope or an instance of a universal. If a property is had by an object or event then the property is located, because objects and events are located.

25. A different sort of worry involves the possibility of not having enough joint causation. What if two materially distinct particles (particles that do not share their matter and are not related by constitution or composition), each including the property of *having charge c*, jointly cause effect *e*? How can this be possible if the particles share the causally relevant property? In response we must remember that it is property *instances*—not properties—that are causes. If there are two materially distinct particles, they include numerically distinct property *instances* of *having charge c* even if they both have the property of *having charge c* (suppose the instances can be individuated even if the particles have the same location). Each instance initiates a causal process, so *e* is jointly caused. I discuss the different ways to individuate objects with the same properties in "The Ontology of Objects." (I am indebted to Adam Elga for raising the worry about not having enough causation.)

26. So for these reasons we do not fall victim to the epiphenomenalism objection to Davidson's treatment of mental causation—the important causal properties of our higher layer objects are not epiphenomenal.

27. The claim here is that certain sorts of claims about properties function as veiled identity claims. For example, to say that I have the property of *being Laurie* is just to say that I *am* Laurie. If I am identical to a fusion of properties *LP*, then the property of *being Laurie* is just that fusion of properties *LP*.

References

Baker, L. 1995. "Metaphysics and Mental Causation." In *Mental Causation*, edited by J. Heil and A. Mele. New York: Oxford University Press.

Block, N. 1990. "Can the Mind Change the World?" In *Meaning and Method*, edited by G. Boolos. Cambridge: Cambridge University Press.

Block, N. 1997. "Anti-Reductionism Slaps Back." *Mind, Causation, World: Philosophical Perspectives* 11: 107–133.

Block, N. 2003. "Do Causal Powers Drain Away?" *Philosophy and Phenomenological Research* 67: 110–127.

Boyd, R., P. Gasper, and J. Trout, eds. 1991. *The Philosophy of Science*. Cambridge, Mass.: MIT Press.

Dorr, C. 2002. "The Simplicity of Everything." Ph.D. dissertation, Princeton University.

Fine, K. 2003. "The Non-Identity of a Material Thing and Its Matter." *Mind* 112: 195–234.

Hall, N. 2004. "Two Concepts of Causation." In *Causation and Counterfactuals*, edited by J. Collins, N. Hall, and L. Paul. Cambridge, Mass.: MIT Press.

Hall, N., and L. Paul. Forthcoming. *Causation and Its Counterexamples: A User's Guide*. Oxford: Oxford University Press.

Kim, J. 1984. "Epiphenomenal and Supervenient Causation." In *Midwest Studies in Philosophy*, vol. 9, edited by P. French, T. Uehling, and H. Wettstein. Minneapolis: University of Minnesota Press.

Kim, J. 1993. "The Nonreductivist's Troubles with Mental Causation." In J. Kim, *Supervenience and Mind: Selected Philosophical Essays*. Cambridge: Cambridge University Press.

Kim, J. 1998. *Mind in a Physical World*. Cambridge, Mass.: MIT Press.

Kim, J. 2002. "The Layered Model: Metaphysical Considerations." *Philosophical Explorations* 5: 2–20.

Lewis, D. 1986a. *On the Plurality of Worlds*. Oxford: Blackwell Publishers.

Lewis, D. 1986b. *Philosophical Papers II*. New York: Oxford University Press.

Lowe, E. 1998. *The Possibility of Metaphysics: Substance, Identity, and Time*. Oxford: Clarendon Press.

Merricks, T. 2001. *Objects and Persons*. Oxford: Oxford University Press.

Merricks, T. 2003. "Replies." *Philosophy and Phenomenological Research* 67: 727–744.

Oppenheim, P., and H. Putnam. 1958. "Unity of Science as a Working Hypothesis." In *Minnesota Studies in the Philosophy of Science: Volume II*, edited by H. Feigl, M. Scriven, and G. Maxwell. Minneapolis: University of Minnesota Press. Reprinted in Boyd 1991.

Paul, L. 2000. "Aspect Causation." *Journal of Philosophy* 97: 235–256.

Paul, L. 2002. "Logical Parts." *Noûs* 36: 578–596.

Paul, L. 2006. "Coincidence as Overlap." *Noûs* 40: 623–659.

Paul, L. "The Ontology of Objects." Unpublished manuscript.

Rea, M. 1997. *Material Constitution: A Reader.* Lanham, Md.: Rowman and Littlefield.

Schaffer, J. 2003a. "Is There a Fundamental Level?" *Noûs* 37: 498–517.

Schaffer, J. 2003b. "Overdetermining Causes." *Philosophical Studies* 114: 23–45.

Sosa, E. 1999. "Existential Relativity." In *Midwest Studies in Philosophy*, vol. 23, edited by P. French and H. Wettstein. Boston: Blackwell Publishers.

Sider, T. 1993. "Van Inwagen and the Possibility of Gunk." *Analysis* 53: 285–289.

Sider, T. 2003. "What's So Bad about Overdetermination?" *Philosophy and Phenomenological Research* 67: 719–726.

van Inwagen, P. 1990. *Material Beings.* Ithaca: Cornell University Press.

Wiggins, D. 2001. *Sameness and Substance Renewed.* Cambridge: Cambridge University Press.

14 *Ex nihilo nihil fit*: Arguments New and Old for the Principle of Sufficient Reason

Alexander Pruss

Introduction

"Ex nihilo nihil fit," goes the classic adage: nothing comes from nothing. Parmenides used the Principle of Sufficient Reason to argue that there is no such thing as change: if there were change, why should it happen when it happens, rather than earlier or later? "Nothing happens in vain, but everything for a reason and under necessitation," claimed Leucippus. Saint Thomas insisted in *De Ente et Essentia*: "Everything, then, which is such that its act of existing is other than its nature must needs have its act of existing from something else" (Aquinas 1949, chapter 4). Leibniz (1991, section 32) considered the principle that everything that is the case, has a reason why it is so and not otherwise to be one of the two central principles of philosophy, the other being the principle of contradiction.

All these claims are closely related and have significant intuitive appeal. Each claim insists that an existent or occurrent thing has an explanation. The ordinary person accepts the claim—it is taken for granted that airplane crashes have causes. Some of the claims, like the *ex nihilo nihil fit* adage, limit themselves to saying that for certain kinds of things, such as those that come into existence, there are explanations, or at least that they cannot come from nothing. Others, like the claims of Leucippus and Leibniz, are fully general and state the Principle of Sufficient Reason (PSR), that every true proposition has an explanation for why it is true.

All the particular claims I have cited are special cases of the PSR. It is difficult to see what intuitions could be given to support any one of these particular claims without supporting the full PSR. There is little reason to think, for instance, that a contingent being has any less need for an explanation of its existence if it has existed longer—indeed if it has always existed—than if it has existed for a finite time (see Pruss 1998). Thus, I will take it that intuitive support lent to any of the versions of the PSR transfers, at least to some degree, to other versions. I will, however, for convenience distinguish two versions. First, there is the Causal Principle which says that a contingent event has a cause. Second, there is what I will simply refer to as the Principle of Sufficient Reason, which I will henceforth take to be the claim that every *contingent* true proposition has an explanation. I will not be concerned with explanations of necessary true propositions, because at this point we do not know enough about how the concept of explanation applies in fields like mathematics that deal with necessary propositions. Aristotle thought to explain a mathematical proposition by showing how it follows from the objective axioms, but the problem here is the possibility of multiple axiomatizations. One can include the parallel postulate as an axiom and derive the Pythagorean theorem, or one can do things the other way around, and the notion of objective axiomhood is thus in peril. Mathematicians *do* tend to think that some proofs more clearly show why a theorem holds than others. But it is not clear that this is an *objective* notion of explanation rather than a subjective notion of "increasing understanding," and the PSR deals in an objective notion of explanation. I will, thus, *deem* necessary propositions to be self-explanatory. Finally, note that the PSR and the Causal Principle present themselves as conceptual truths, even when they are applied to contingent claims.

The illustrious philosophical history of the PSR notwithstanding, the PSR is widely denied in analytic philosophy circles. One reason for this denial is the feeling, I believe justified (see Pruss 1998; Gale and Pruss 1999), that the PSR implies the existence of a supernatural cause of the universe. This is not a very good argument against the PSR, unless one has independent reason to believe that the kind of supernatural being whose existence the PSR implies does not exist. Note, for instance, that the problem of evil is irrelevant here, unless one could produce a successful argument that a supernatural cause of the universe would be a morally good person. There is also an argument against the PSR based on quantum mechanics—which depends specifically on the interpretations being indeterministic, an assumption that can be questioned—and an argument that van Inwagen formulated against the coherence of the PSR, which I will discuss in detail.

On the other hand, most people who accept the PSR or its variants accept it simply because they take it to be *self-evident*. I will argue that the defender of the PSR need not limit herself to claims of self-evidence. I will sketch three arguments for the PSR and the Causal Principle—an argument from predictability of things in the world; a technical modal argument based on the nature of causality; and an argument based on the nature of modality.

Throughout, I will understand explanation to be a relation between propositions such that: that q explains p entails, in turn, that both q and p are true. If one wishes to deal with false propositions, one can introduce the notion of *putative* explanation where q putatively explains p provided that, were both p and q to hold, q would explain p.

The van Inwagen Objection

Take the Big Contingent Conjunctive Fact (BCCF) which is the conjunction of all contingent true propositions.[1] This is itself a contingent proposition. By the PSR, it must have an explanation. This explanation is a true proposition. This proposition is then either contingent or necessary. If it is contingent, then this explanation will itself be a part of the BCCF—remember that the BCCF contains *all* contingent true propositions, and hence it also contains the explanation of the BCCF. But if this explanation both explains the BCCF and is contained in the BCCF, then it explains, inter alia, itself. But no contingent proposition can explain itself. Thus, the explanation of the BCCF must be necessary. But an explanation has to entail that which it explains—the explanandum must follow logically from the explanans. Otherwise, how does the explanation do any explaining? Thus, the explanation of the BCCF entails the BCCF. But anything that logically follows from a necessary proposition is itself a necessary proposition. Thus, if the explanation of the BCCF is a necessary proposition, so is the BCCF. But the BCCF is contingent. To put it differently, if the explanation of the BCCF were a necessary proposition, then it would be equally logically compatible with the BCCF's holding as with the BCCF's not holding.

This I will call the "van Inwagen objection" (van Inwagen 1983, pp. 202–204), though it was in effect posed earlier by James Ross (1969, pp. 295–304) and William Rowe (1975). As I have formulated it, it has two controversial premises: (1) no contingent proposition can explain itself, a claim that appears akin to the fact that nothing can cause itself; and (2) no necessary proposition can explain a contingent proposition.

The challenge, then, is: how could the BCCF be explained? If the PSR is true, the explanation will have to be through a necessary proposition or a contingent one. In fact, either horn of the dilemma can be embraced by the defender of the PSR.

First, take the necessity horn. The argument against this relies on the claim that if q explains p then q entails p. But we know this is not always so. Consider an explanation that cites a law of nature that merely holds all other things being equal, ceteris paribus. Many, and perhaps all laws of nature are like that. Thus, the law of gravity says that two massive objects accelerate toward each other—but only ceteris paribus, since there might be, say, electric repulsion between them. Take then an explanation of why the planets move in elliptical orbits in terms of the law of gravitation and the initial positions and velocities of the planets. The law of gravitation and the proposition reporting the initial planetary positions and velocities do not *entail* that the planets move in elliptical orbits, since the law and the initial conditions are logically compatible with there being some other operative force that makes the planets not take elliptical orbits. Thus, we have here a case where the explanation does not entail the explained proposition. But it is still fine explanation. One might, of course, argue that it is insufficient as an explanation; but in that case it may well be that *all* the scientific explanations we have ever given are insufficient, and one may have thus severed the concept of explanation from too many of its paradigm cases.

We can also give an ad hominem argument against the claim that if q explains p then q entails p, an argument directed at someone who denies not just the necessity of the PSR but that of the Causal Principle as well. Here is an explanation of why a dog did not bark: "None of the possible causes of the dog's barking occurred." This is a perfectly good explanation, and one that we would ordinarily accept. But unless a Causal Principle is necessarily true (and the opponent of the PSR is apt to deny the necessity of the CP as well), that none of the possible causes of barking have occurred does not entail that the dog did not bark—it might have barked causelessly, after all. Hence, at least the opponent of the necessity of the Causal Principle should admit that the explanans need not entail the explanandum if such explanations of negative facts are allowed, as they surely should be.

What kind of an explanation of the BCCF could be given on the necessity horn of the dilemma? Simplifying, so as to leave out some issues involving human free will, it might be something like this: it is necessarily true both that there is a supernatural being and that this supernatural being freely (in the libertarian sense) decided what to create while appreciating such-and-such values. (Which values? We may not be in a position to know. Perhaps the Leibnizian answer of a balance between orderliness and diversity could be part of the story, though.) True, this does not entail that this being created this world rather than another, since the explanandum is compatible with the supernatural being's simultaneously appreciating other values that tell in favor of creating a different world. But perhaps even though it does not entail that this world exists, it *explains* it.

Here is one reason to think this explains it: when one has cited the *cause* of an event and said what there is to be said about this cause's state prior to its exercise of causal power, one *has* explained the event. Finding the cause of something is a *paradigmatic* way of explaining it—cases of causation are the primary source for our concept of explanation. On this story, a supernatural being is the cause of the BCCF's being true. Hence once one has stated the necessary facts about the supernatural being—namely the facts prior to his free choice to create, including the fact that, necessarily, he freely chooses what to create; it not being necessary, of course, that he chooses to create *this* cosmos, but only that he freely chooses to create some cosmos or other, mayhap an empty one—one has explained the explanandum. Since the story has not been shown to be impossible, van Inwagen's argument is unsuccessful.

Admittedly, this explanation does not give a logically *sufficient condition* for the explanandum to hold. That a necessarily existing supernatural freely chose to create, and so on, is not a sufficient condition for the BCCF since it does not entail the BCCF. But we need not read the words "Sufficient Reason" in the "Principle of Sufficient Reason" as implying a sufficient *condition*. We can read the PSR, rather, as a principle of *sufficient explanation*. And once one has cited a cause, one *has* given a sufficient explanation.

What about the contingency horn of the dilemma? Here is a contingent self-explanatory proposition that, if true, might count as explaining why the BCCF is true. A necessarily existent supernatural being freely brought it about that the BCCF is true. Or perhaps we might expand this to: a necessarily existent supernatural being freely brought it about, for the sake of reason *R*, that the BCCF is true. This proposition is a sufficient explanation of itself: there ought to be no more puzzlement about why someone freely chose something for a reason R, once one understands that this person freely chose it for R. We accept this as an explanation-ender in ordinary discourse. The sense in which it is a sufficient explanation of itself is that once one understood and accepted the proposition, one would no longer have any mystery about why it is true—and explanation is sought and given, after all, precisely to remove mystery.

Finally, let me offer an argument that someone who accepts the possibility of libertarian free will *must* reject the van Inwagen argument. Since van Inwagen is a libertarian, he too must reject his own argument. To make this more than an ad hominem, I would need to argue for the possibility of libertarian free will, for which, of course, there is no space here.

Libertarian free will is nondeterministic. From the condition of the mind of the agent prior to the choice, one cannot deduce what choice will be made. This has given rise to the *randomness* objection to libertarianism: libertarian-free choices are not really caused by the person, but are merely *random* blips, like some think quantum events are. We would not account a person free if acts of will occurred *randomly* in her mind or brain.

The libertarian is, of course, committed to a denial of the randomness objection. In whatever way she manages to do so, she *must* reject the claim that libertarian-free actions are random. She might, for instance, insist that they are not random because they are caused by agent-causation. Now suppose that a libertarian allowed that in the case of a libertarian-free choice between options A and B, where in fact A was chosen, there is no sufficient explanation of why A was chosen. Such a libertarian, I submit, has succumbed to the randomness objection. If there is no explanation for why option A was chosen, then that A was chosen is a brute, unexplained, uncaused fact—a *random* fact. Thus, the libertarian cannot allow that there is no explanation of why A was chosen.

Look at this from another direction. Suppose someone is externally determined to choose A instead of B, so that the explanation of why A was chosen was that some external puppet master has caused the agent to choose A rather than B. In that case, there would indeed be an explanation for why A was chosen rather than B—namely, the causal efficacy of the puppet master. The libertarian will insist that in that case, there is no free will. Now take this situation and *subtract* the puppet master, without adding anything. We get a situation where there is no explanation for the choice of A rather than of B; we get a genuine case of randomness, or at least of a mere brute fact, having replaced the puppet master by nothing at all. And this mere removal of the puppet master does nothing to give freedom to the agent. Libertarian freedom is not supposed to be something purely negative—the lack of a puppet master—but something positive, like self-determination. To go from the choice determined by the puppet master to a genuine libertarian-free choice, we cannot merely delete the explanation of the action in terms of the puppet master—we must *add* something to the situation. It is plausible that what needs to be done is to substitute the free agent and/or her free will for the puppet master: the action must be explained in terms of the agent now, instead of in terms of something external. The basic intuition of a libertarian is that determinism places the ultimate point of decision outside the agent, in the environment that has formed the agent. This external determinism, to produce freedom, must not only be removed, but must be replaced by something within the agent.

Thus, the libertarian *must* hold that there is an explanation for why one rather than another choice was freely made; otherwise, the randomness objection to libertarianism succeeds. This forces the libertarian to say, either: (1) that a description of a mind in a state that is equally compatible with either of two actions, A or B, can in fact be used to explain why A was in fact freely chosen—a denial of the thesis that the explanans entails the explanandum; or (2) that the claim that action A was freely chosen, or perhaps freely chosen for reason R, is "almost" a self-explanatory claim, despite its contingency, with the only thing unexplained being why the agent existed and was free (and aware of R, if we take the "freely chosen for reason R" option). If the agent were a being that necessarily existed freely and omnisciently, nothing would be left unexplained.

It might, however, turn out that the van Inwagen objection is quite insoluble if the explanation of the BCCF does not involve the free choice of a necessarily existent supernatural agent, though I am not defending this claim in this paper. If this turns out so, then the van Inwagen objection turns into a cosmological argument for the existence of a supernatural being, along the lines in Gale and Pruss 1999.

Predictability

The following argument goes back to the ancient Greeks. The Causal Principle is plainly true in the case of ordinary, medium-sized objects: if I leave a brick somewhere, then that brick will remain there, barring a cause to the contrary. It will not pop out of existence for no reason at all. Bracketing the question of the infinitesimal (quantum stuff) and the immense (the origins of the universe), the Causal Principle is surely true on an everyday level.

But *why* is it true? I would like to suggest that the best explanation for the truth of the Causal Principle on an everyday level just might be that the Causal Principle is a necessary conceptual truth. What I am doing in this argument is not a question-begging invocation of the PSR, but simply an instance of inference to best explanation.

Suppose the Causal Principle is not a necessary truth. Why then do we not see violations of it all around us? One might say that violations of it are *unlikely*. But does it make any sense to talk of the likelihood or unlikelihood of a causeless, unexplainable contingent event? One can argue that such events would not be happening under the sway of the laws of nature or as a result of the causal efficacy of entities with fixed statistical dispositional properties, since then nomic explanations—at least statistical ones—could be given. But then it is unclear how one could assign objective probabilities to such events. And on a purely intuitive level, were the Causal Principle not a necessary truth, violations of it would seem subjectively quite likely. After all, for any one possible world in which the Causal Principle holds for midsized objects there is an innumerable array of possible worlds which are just like the given world, except that bricks or other objects appear in droves out of nowhere for no reason at all; and even if there is no difference in cardinality between the class of worlds where the Causal Principle holds for midsized objects and that where it does not, the latter class is more diverse and intuitively more probable.

The natural response is that the applicability of the Causal Principle to medium-sized phenomena is a consequence of the laws of nature. But whether this can be so depends on general considerations about laws of nature. Some, such as Nancy Cartwright, think that *all* laws of nature hold merely ceteris paribus. Laws describe, even when all conjoined, what must happen *in the absence of external influence*. The observational consequences of the laws are thus never *entailed* by the laws. But if so, then it is not clear how laws of themselves can make the Causal Principle true. How can they fail to be powerful enough to prohibit external influence, while being powerful enough to prohibit causeless events? Even the abstract conjunction of *all* of our ceteris-paribus laws of nature will be logically compatible with a macroscopic material object's suddenly acquiring, *due to an external influ-*

ence, some completely new property—since the actual conjunction of all of our ceteris-paribus laws is logically compatible with some non-actual ceteris-paribus law being added—a property as different from its former properties as charge is from mass. But why wouldn't these laws then be equally compatible with the object's acquiring that new property *causelessly*? The only answer I am aware of is that there is a metaphysical Causal Principle that prohibits such acquisitions.

For a related argument, note that if one takes the laws of nature to be, even when taken all together, ceteris paribus, then the Causal Principle may be needed to allow any scientific predictions to be made from these laws. For to make a prediction we need to say what the relevant laws influencing a given experimental setup will be, and then assume that in the given context, the predicted outcome will be affected only by these relevant laws. But unless the Causal Principle is in play, not only need the scientist rule out the possibility that some other law of nature or nomic event will relevantly affect the outcome, but she must rule out the possibility that some causeless event will affect it.

If one further takes an Aristotelian view that laws of nature are dependent on interactions between substances with certain essences, then the need for the Causal Principle as a metaphysically necessary truth becomes particularly clear. Consider, for instance, the law of conservation of mass-energy. Given an Aristotelian view of laws of nature, if the essences and causal powers of interacting substances have appropriate properties, one might derive the claim that of nomic necessity mass-energy is conserved in the interactions between *existing* substances. But without the Causal Principle, one cannot conclude that it is nomically necessary that *new* particles do not come into existence ex nihilo, completely independently of the powers of existing substances.

An Argument Based on Causality and Counterfactuals

If my striking the match caused the match to light, then, roughly, were I not to have struck the match, the match would not be afire. This illustrates the principle that if *A* caused *B*, then *B* would not have occurred had *A* not occurred. But this is not quite right—for it might be that had *A* not occurred, *some other* potential cause of *B* would have occurred. Perhaps there was someone standing behind me with a lighter, and she would have lit the match had I not struck it.

But there still seems to be something right about the counterfactual condition—were the cause not to have occurred, the effect would not have occurred—even if we have difficulty in formulating it precisely. Moreover, this condition does not say simply that the effect would be impossible without the cause; that would beg the question against many opponents of the Causal Principle, opponents who insist with Hume that events that ordinarily have causes need not have had them.[2] But even they should accept the weaker claim that, *were* the causes not to have occurred, the effects *would* not have occurred.

The following formulation gets around the counterexamples: since the match's coming on fire had a cause, then were it the case that no event causing the match to light occurred, the match would not have come on fire. In every possible world where the match's coming on fire has a cause, it is true that, were no event causing the match to light to have occurred, the match would not have come on fire.

I am now going to argue based on the above that there *necessarily* is a cause for the match's lighting up—that there are no possible worlds at which the match lights up causelessly. For suppose we are at such a possible world, and can actually truthfully say, "The match causelessly caught on fire." We admit, however, that it is logically possible that the match's lighting up had a cause. Consider now what would have been the case had the match's lighting up had a cause. Had the match's lighting up had a cause, then it would have been the case that had there been no cause for the match's lighting up, then the match would not have lit up. Let L be the event of the match's being lit or coming on fire. Let "$\rightarrow$" indicate a counterfactual conditional. Then:

(*)   (L has a cause) $\rightarrow$ (there is no cause of $L \rightarrow \sim L$).

Moreover, in fact it is actually true that L occurs and L has no cause.

But now we have a problem. Here is a plausible story about how to make sense of counterfactuals. To evaluate a counterfactual that were p to hold q would hold, we look at a class of *relevant* worlds where p holds, and check whether q holds at all of them. If it does, then all is well—were p to hold, q would hold. What counts as the class of relevant worlds is not at all obvious. Stalnaker proposed we just limit ourselves to the most similar world at which p holds, but we have counterexamples to that. However something like this possible-worlds picture of how we evaluate counterfactuals is pretty close to our ordinary language use of counterfactuals, though the difficulty is in the details, in figuring out which worlds count as relevant relative to ours and relative to an antecedent *p*.

Here then is one intuition about which worlds are relevant. Suppose in the actual world we have not-*p*, and we look at all the worlds relevant to a counterfactual with antecedent *p*. And suppose in *those* worlds, we look for worlds relevant to a counterfactual with antecedent not-*p*. The intuition is that the actual world will always be included in the latter class. Suppose I won the lottery. Could I say that, were I not to have played in the lottery then it would have been true that had I played, I would have lost? Certainly not. If *w* is some world relevant to the antecedent that I did not play in the lottery, then from the point of view of *w*, the actual world will be relevant to the antecedent that I *did* play in the lottery. But in the actual world, I win. Thus, at *w* it is not true to say that in all relevant worlds where I play in the lottery, I lose. Hence, at *w* it is false that were I to play I would lose. Thus it is not the case that, were I not to have played in the lottery, then it would have been true that had I played I would have lost. If *p* is true, then were not-*p* to hold, it would be the case that were *p* to have held, things might have been just as they actually are.

We can summarize the above in symbols. If *q* and *p* are true, then we have $\sim p \rightarrow \sim(p \rightarrow \sim q)$. Or even more weakly:

(**) $\sim(\sim p \rightarrow (p \rightarrow \sim q))$.

If *p* and *q* are true, then it is not the case that were *p* to have failed, then were *p* to have held, *q* would have failed.

But now take our previous conclusion (*). Let *p* be the proposition that *L* has no cause, and let *q* be the proposition that *L* occurs. Then, this previous conclusion of ours is precisely the negation of principle (**). Hence, we have contradicted ourselves. Thus, our assumption that the match's coming on fire had no cause leads to a contradiction.

The argument I have given shows more generally the following. If *E* is an event that *could* have a cause, then in fact *E* necessarily has a cause: in every world in which *E* occurs, it has a cause. Thus, a match's having come afire always has a cause, since it plainly always *can* have a cause. If one adds the plausible assumption that every contingent non-self-explanatory event *could* have a cause, we conclude that every such event *does* have a cause. Thus, we get a version of the Causal Principle that nothing comes about without cause.

Let us expand on the central point in the argument. A reader uninterested in the more technical discussion that follows can skip to the next section. My argument needs something like the following claim:

(1) $(q \ \& \ p \ \& \ M{\sim}p) \supset ({\sim}p \rightarrow (p \ \Diamond{\rightarrow} \ q))$,

where the "might conditional" $p \ \Diamond{\rightarrow} \ q$ is defined as ${\sim}(p \rightarrow {\sim}q)$. (Proposition (**) is formally a little weaker, but the intuitions behind (**) are the same as those behind the stronger (1).) If we actually have both p and q holding and then move to a relevantly similar world w in which p does not hold in order to evaluate a counterfactual with antecedent p, the events of the actual world are going to be relevant for the evaluation of counterfactuals at w. Hence, if we ask in w what would happen were p to hold, we need to say that q might happen since q in fact happens in the actual world.

Consider how (1) plays out in some paradigmatic cases. Suppose, say, p says that Jones freely chose to set fire to a barn and q says that Jones was arrested. Then, were Jones not to have set fire to the barn, it would certainly have been true that were he to have set fire to the barn, he at least *might* have been arrested. In the case where p reports the occurrence or nonoccurrence of some punctual event in time, we can think of the space of possibilities as a branching structure. Were p not to have occurred, we would have gone on a different branch from the one we had in fact gone on. But were we to have gone on that branch, it would have been true that were p to have occurred, things *might* have gone just as they have *actually* gone. The fact that things *have* gone a certain way witnesses to the relevant possibility of them going this way. In this sense, (1) is a counterfactual analogue to the Brouwer axiom of modal logic (if p, then necessarily possibly p).

The first difficulty with (1) is that it cannot be a conceptual truth on Lewis's semantics for counterfactuals. According to David Lewis, $p \rightarrow q$ is true if and only if either p is necessarily false, or there is a $p\&q$-world closer to the actual world than any $p\&{\sim}q$-world, where by an r-world I mean simply a world where r holds.

Write Aw for a proposition true at w and only at w. We might take Aw to be the BCCF of w, or we might take Aw to be the proposition that w is actual. Let $q = Aw_0$, where w_0 is the actual world. Let w_1 be any other world, and let $p = {\sim}Aw_1$. Then, $q \ \& \ p \ \& \ M{\sim}p$ holds. Consider the consequent of (1). This says that there is a $\sim p$-world w at which $p \diamondsuit\!\!\rightarrow q$ and which is closer than any $\sim p$-world at which $\sim(p \diamondsuit\!\!\rightarrow q)$. In fact, there is only one $\sim p$-world, namely w_1. Thus, the consequent of (1) says simply that $p \diamondsuit\!\!\rightarrow q$ holds at w_1. Now, $p \diamondsuit\!\!\rightarrow q$ is equivalent to $\sim(p \rightarrow \sim q)$. The proposition $p \rightarrow \sim q$ holds at w_1 if and only if there is a $p\&\sim q$-world which is closer to w_1 than any $p\&q$-world is. Now, there is only one $p\&q$-world, namely w_0, and a $p\&\sim q$-world is just a world different from w_0 and w_1. Thus, $p \rightarrow \sim q$ holds at w_1 if and only if there is a world different from w_0 and w_1 that is closer to w_1 than w_0 is. Thus, $\sim(p \rightarrow \sim q)$ holds if and only if the closest world to w_1 is w_0.

What we have shown is that if (1) holds in general, then for any world w_1 other than the actual world w_0, the closest world to w_1 is w_0. But this is most unlikely. Moreover, (1) is presented as a conceptual truth. If it is such, then the above argument should work in all possible worlds. Denote by $C(w)$ the closest world to w (other than w of course), if there is such a world. We have shown that $C(w_1) = w_0$ for every w_1 other than w_0. Since the argument relies only on alleged conceptual truths, if it holds for w_0 it holds for all worlds. Thus, for any world w and any other world w_1 we have $C(w_1) = w$. Let w_0, w_1, and w_2 be any three distinct worlds. Then, $C(w_1) = w_0$ by putting w_0 for w and $C(w_1) = w_2$ by putting w_2 for w. Thus, $w_0 = w_2$, and so w_0 and w_2 are both distinct and identical, which is absurd. Hence, the assumption that (1) is a conceptual truth leads to absurdity on Lewis's semantics.

However, all we need (1) for is the special case where q reports an event and p reports the nonexistence of an event under a certain description (namely, under the description of being a cause of the event reported by q), and it might well be that in those cases (1) could still hold on Lewis semantics. The above counterexample was generated using very special propositions—the proposition q was taken to be true at exactly one world and the proposition p was taken to be false at exactly one world. Ordinary language counterfactuals do not deal with such special propositions, and hence it might be that the intuitions supporting (1) do not require us to make (1) hold for these propositions, and hence these intuitions are not refuted in the relevant case by the counterexample.

This, however, is shaky footing. One might perhaps more reasonably take (1) to entail a refutation of Lewis's semantics. In any case, Lewis's semantics are known to be flawed, and one flaw comes out precisely when the semantics are applied to propositions like the ones in the above counterexample. To see this flaw, suppose that w_0 is the actual world, and we have an infinite sequence of worlds $w_1, w_2, w_3, \ldots$ such that w_{n+1} is closer to the actual world than w_n is. For instance, these worlds could be just like the actual world except in the level of the background radiation in the universe, with this level approaching closer and closer to the actual level as n goes to infinity. Let p be the infinite disjunction of the Aw_n for $n > 0$. Fix any $n > 0$. On Lewis's semantics we then have: $p \to \sim Aw_n$. For w_{n+1} is a $p\&\sim Aw_n$-world which is closer than any $p\&Aw_n$-world, since there is only one $p\&Aw_n$-world, namely w_n, and w_{n+1} is closer than it. This implies that it is true for every disjunct of p that, were p true, that disjunct would be false! But surely there has to be some disjunct of p such that were p true, that disjunct at least *might* be true.

Like the counterexample to (1), this counterexample deals with propositions specified as true at a small set of worlds—in the case of p here an infinite set, but still only countably infinite and hence much "smaller" than the collection of possible worlds which is not only not countably infinite, but not even a set (Pruss 2001). This shows that there is something wrong with Lewis's semantics, either in general or in handling such propositions.

To see even more clearly (though making use of a slightly stronger assumption about closeness series) that there is a commonality between a problem with Lewis's semantics and the Lewisian counterexample to (1), suppose the following principle of density: for any non-actual world w, there is a non-actual world w^* closer to the actual world than w is. This should at least be an epistemic possibility—our semantics for counterfactuals should not rule it out. Let w_0 be the actual world and put $p = \sim Aw_0$. Then, by the principle of density, on Lewis's semantics, there is no possible world w such that were p true, w might be actual, that is, such that $p \diamondsuit\!\!\to Aw$. For suppose that we are given a w. First, note that it is hopeless to start with the case where w is w_0 since p and Aw_0 are logically incompatible. Next, observe that we in fact have $p \to \sim Aw$. For let w^* be any world closer than w. Then, w^* is a $p\&\sim Aw$-world which is closer than any $p\&Aw$-world, there being only one of the latter—namely, w. Thus, we do not have $p \diamondsuit\!\!\to Aw$.

But surely if p is possible, then there is *some* world which is such that it might be actual were p to hold. Lewis's semantics fails because of its incompatibility with this claim on the above, not implausible principle of density, which should not be ruled out of court by a semantics of possible worlds. Note, further, that the failure here is precisely a failure in the case of a might-conditional $p \diamondsuit\!\!\rightarrow q$ with p of the form $\sim\!Aw_1$ and q of the form Aw_2, which is precisely the kind of might-conditional that appeared in the analysis of the above apparent counterexample to (1). Lewis's semantics makes too few might-conditionals of this sort true, and it is precisely through failing to make a might-conditional of this sort true that it gave a counterexample to (1).

Thus, rather than having run my argument within Lewisian possible-worlds semantics, it was run on an intuitive understanding of counterfactuals, which intuitions do support (1). It would be nice to have a complete satisfactory semantics for counterfactuals. Lewisian semantics are sometimes indeed helpful—they are an appropriate model in many cases; but as we have seen, they do not always work. Other forms of semantics meet with other difficulties. We may, at least for now, be stuck with a more intuitive approach.

David Manley (2002) has come up with the following apparent counterexample to (1), which I modify slightly. Suppose our soccer team wins twenty to zero: then it is true that the team won overwhelmingly in the actual world w_0. What would have happened had our team not won? Presumably the score would have been rather different, say twenty to twenty, or zero to five, or something like that. Suppose the score is one of these—that we are in a possible world w_1 where our team had lost. Then it is *not* true that, were our team to have won it would have won overwhelmingly. If our team in fact failed to win, as at w_1, then worlds where the team wins *overwhelmingly* are much more distant from our world than are worlds where it wins by a bit. Thus, it is true at w_1 to say that were our team to have won, it would have won by a tiny amount. Putting this together we conclude that, were our team not to have won, then were it to have won it would have won by a tiny amount. But this is incompatible with (1), which claims that were our team not to have won, then were it to have won, it *might* have won overwhelmingly.

Unfortunately, this account also relies on David Lewis's semantics, and again does so in a context in which Lewis's semantics *fail*. For by the above reasoning, if we are in a world where our team has not won, then we should say that were it to have won it would have won by exactly one point. But this need not be true: were our team to have gotten ahead by a point at some point in the game, then perhaps the other team would have become disheartened and lost by more than a point. We can even more clearly see the problem in the Lewisian reasoning if we substitute a game very much like soccer except that its scores can take on any real value. Perhaps instead of a flat one point for a goal, one gets a real-valued additive score depending how close to the middle of a goal one hits. Then, by the above reasoning, were our team not to have won, it would be true that were it to have won, it would have won by no more than 1/10 of a point. Worlds where one wins by no more than 1/10 of a point are closer than worlds where one wins by more than that. But this reasoning is perfectly general, and the "1/10" can be replaced by any positive number, no matter how tiny. But this is absurd. It is absurd to suppose that were our team not to have won, it would be true that were it to have won, it would have won by no more than 10^{-1000} points.[3]

Modality

We make modal claims like, "I could have failed to make it to this talk." If we are to be realists about such claims, we need to say what makes these claims true. What is it that makes unicorns possible while round squares and water-that-is-not-H_2O are impossible? What is it that makes it necessary that $2 + 2 = 4$, while it is merely contingent that horses exist?

It is tempting to say that this is a merely a matter of logic. What makes something impossible is that it entails a contradiction in a logically regimented manner, and what makes it possible is that it does not. Something then is necessary if and only if its negation is impossible, that is, if and only if it can be derived from the axioms. Unfortunately, then, everything depends on what rules of inference and what axioms one allows in the derivations. The axioms are all automatically going to come out necessary from such an account. But what makes one proposition fitter than another for being an axiom? Is this not our original question about what makes propositions possible or necessary, in a slightly different guise? One might try to solve this problem by listing as axioms all *definitional* truths, such as that a bachelor is a never married marriageable man. But this will not do because it will not cast the net of necessity widely enough to include Kripkean facts (such as that it is necessary that water be H_2O), and may not even include such facts as that it is impossible for it to be both true that A

causes B and that B causes A. To cast the net of necessity widely enough on the logical-derivation view, we would need to include enough necessary truths, such as that water is H_2O or that causation is noncircular, among the axioms. But then the account would fail to answer why these truths are necessary—they would simply become necessary by fiat.

David Lewis (1986) proposed that what makes a proposition possible is that it is actually true—not of our world, but of some other concrete existing physical universe. This led to serious paradoxes, which I will not address here. Robert M. Adams (1974) and Alvin Plantinga (1974), on the other hand, grounded possibilities and necessities in a Platonic realm of abstracta. What makes the proposition that a unicorn exists a possible proposition is that this proposition—an abstract entity existing in the Platonic realm—has the abstract property of possibility. Unfortunately, this leaves it a mystery why facts about the Platonic realm or other worlds are coordinated with facts about our physical world. Why are facts about propositions (such as that some proposition is impossible) relevant to figuring what concretely exists in the world? How is the concrete fact that a driver had the concrete *power* to kill me while I was crossing the road last year coordinated with the fact about the Platonic realm that the proposition that I never completed this paper has the Platonic property of possibility?

The long and short of it is that it is not easy to find a satisfactory account of what makes some propositions possible and others not. But what I just said gives a hint, as explored in recent work by Penelope Mackie (1998) and Ullin Place (1997), as well as in Pruss 2002. It is easy to say what makes it possible that I not write this paper. There are many things that make it possible, each sufficient on its own: a driver could have brought it about; the pilot of an airplane I flew on could have brought it about; I could have brought it about myself. This leads to an Aristotelian account of possibility: a non-actual event is possible, providing some substance or substances could have initiated a causal chain leading up to it.

This account is attractive. But it does imply that the PSR is necessarily true. For suppose that the PSR is in fact false. Let p be a contingent true proposition, then, which has no explanation. Let q be the proposition that p holds and has no explanation. Since p is contingently true, so is q. Thus, there is a possible world w at which q is false. Let us transport ourselves to that world. In that world, the proposition q is false, but it is still going to be *possible*. (This uses the Brouwer axiom which is weaker than S5. Actually, the Aristotelian account of possibility can be shown to entail S5, so this assumption is not problematic.[4]) So, we are now in a world where q—the proposition that p holds and has no explanation—is possible but false. By the Aristotelian account, then, there exists something which could initiate a chain of causes leading up to q's being true. But were it to do that, then the chain of causes would also *explain* q. But one of the conjuncts in q was the proposition that p has no explanation, and the other conjunct was p. If one has explained q, then one has explained p. But then q is false. However, the chain of causes was supposed to lead up to q's being true. Thus, the chain of causes would lead to q's being true *and* to q's being false, which is absurd.

Hence the assumption that the proposition q is true leads to absurdity. Thus, it is impossible that p be true and lack an explanation. Thus, a contingent proposition, if true, must have an explanation.

Acknowledgments

I would like to thank Richard Gale, David Manley, Nicholas Rescher, Richard Sisca, Thomas Sullivan, and Linda Wetzel for discussions related to various parts of this project. The research was supported by an NEH Summer Stipend and a Georgetown University Summer Stipend.

Notes

1. We may wish to remove repetitions, delete necessary conjuncts, and so on. For a discussion of some of the technical issues here see Gale and Pruss 2002.

2. For an argument for the PSR based on the assumption that causes are necessary conditions, see Sullivan 1994.

3. This is similar to the coat thief example cited in Edgington 1995.

4. The Brouwer axiom holds on the assumption that if A initiates one chain C_1 of events and is capable of initiating another chain, C_2, then were it to have exercised this capability for initiating C_2, it would still *have been* capable of initiating the chain C_1. It is important that what the powers of an item (state of affairs or substance) at t are and have been, the actualization of which powers grounds various possibilities, should not itself depend on which of these powers are actualized. For then the powers would not be prior to the actualization. An argument for S4 can also be given, though we do not need it for this paper, and of course S4 together with the Brouwer axiom yields S5.

References

Adams, R. 1974. "Theories of Actuality." *Noûs* 8: 211–231.

Aquinas, T. 1949. *On Being and Essence*. Translated by A. Maurer. Toronto: Pontifical Institute of Mediaeval Studies.

Edgington, D. 1995. "On Conditionals." *Mind* 104: 235–329.

Gale, R. 1976. *Negation and Non-Being*. Oxford: Blackwell.

Gale, R., ed. 2002. *Blackwell Guide to Metaphysics*. Oxford: Blackwell.

Gale, R., and A. Pruss. 1999. "A New Cosmological Argument." *Religious Studies* 35: 461–476.

Gale, R., and A. Pruss. 2002. "A Response to Oppy and to Davey and Clifton." *Religious Studies* 38: 89–99.

Leibniz, G. W. 1991. *G. W. Leibniz's Monadology*. Translated by N. Rescher. Pittsburgh: University of Pittsburgh Press.

Lewis, D. 1986. *On the Plurality of Worlds*. Oxford and New York: Basil Blackwell.

Mackie, P. 1998. "Identity, Time, and Necessity." *Proceedings of the Aristotelian Society* 98: 59–78.

Manley, D. 2002. Commentator on Alexander R. Pruss, *"Ex nihilo nihil fit."* Society for Catholic Analytical Philosophy Meeting, November 2002.

Place, U. 1997. "*'De re'* Modality without Possible Worlds." *Acta Analytica* 12: 129–143.

Plantinga, A. 1974. *The Nature of Necessity*. Oxford and New York: Oxford University Press.

Pruss, A. 1998. "The Hume-Edwards Principle and the Cosmological Argument." *International Journal for Philosophy of Religion* 43: 149–165.

Pruss, A. 2001. "The Cardinality Objection to David Lewis's Modal Realism." *Philosophical Studies* 104: 167–176.

Pruss, A. 2002. "The Actual and the Possible." In *Blackwell Guide to Metaphysics*, edited by R. Gale. Oxford: Blackwell.

Ross, J. 1969. *Philosophical Theology*. Indianapolis: Bobbs-Merrill.

Rowe, W. 1975. *The Cosmological Argument*. Princeton: Princeton University Press.

Sullivan, T. 1994. "On the Alleged Causeless Beginning of the Universe: A Reply to Quentin Smith." *Dialogue* 33: 325–335.

van Inwagen, P. 1983. *An Essay on Free Will*. Oxford: Oxford University Press.

Index

Absences, 15–19, 51
Actions, 157, 166, 227–229, 296–297
  goal-directed, ch. 8 *passim*
Adaptability, 35
Agent, 119, 158–165, 296–297
Aggregation, 64
  preference, 237
Antirealism, 172, 177
Aquinas, 40, 41, 291
Aristotle, 40, 41, 119, 292, 299, 307–308
Artificial intelligence, 26
Associationism, 1–2, 12, 16, 19, 20, 22, 24, 25, 29

Bayes' theorem, 179, 181, 183
Bayesian network, 14, 236, 237
Belief revision, 174
Ben-Menahem, Y., 177–179
Bias, 2, 173–177
Boolean network, ch. 3 *passim*
Brownian motion, 182
"Brute fact" account, 144–145

Cartwright, N., 207–208, 298
Causal
  assumptions, 21, 23–25
  asymmetry, ch. 1 *passim*, 192
  attribution, 25
  claims (*see* Claims, causal)
  compatibility, 224, 226, 229, 231–233
  decision theory, 210–213, 236

dependence, 81, 225, 228
direction, 9–11
entailment, 114
explanation, 2, 124–125, 128–129
graph, 76–79, 88–89, 234
history, 229
independence, 221
inference, 1, 26, 51
influence, 4, 12, 29, 110–116
judgment, 24, 25, 44, 62, 65
learning, 2
model, 76, ch. 10 *passim*, 229–235
overdetermination (*see*
  Overdetermination, causal)
power (*see* Power, causal)
principle, 292–294, 297–301
processes, 129, 180
properties, 44
relations, 1, 3, 9, 21–23, 29, 30, 43, 69, 120, 124, 128–130, 191, 197, 219
strength, 11, 25, 26, 28
structure, 72–76, 80–84, 88–89, 224
sufficiency, 110–111, 113–116
supervenience, 272–273
support model, 21–23
Causation
  actual, ch. 3 *passim*
  correlation, distinct from, 108–111
  deterministic, 33, 36, 37, 62, 296–297
  indeterministic, non-, 292, 296

Causation (cont.)
Mackie's theory of, ch. 5 *passim*
potential, ch. 3 *passim*
probabilistic, 192, 212
production model of, 120–125, 129–130
regularity model of, 128–130
Cause
conjunctive, 1, 15, 16, 25
definition, 1
occasional, ch. 6 *passim*
physical, 33, 35, 119
possible, 211, 294
producing, 98–99
secondary, 120, 125
simple, 1, 15, 25
Ceiling effect, 13, 14
Ceteris paribus conditions, 37, 294, 298–299
Chancy events, 136–142, 145–147, 149, 152
Cheng, P., 62, 65
Chi-square test, 2, 11, 14, 16, 20, 21
Choice, 217, 219, 228, 295–297
Claims, causal
counterfactual accounts, 93–97
difference-making accounts, ch. 5 *passim*
INUS account, ch. 5 *passim*
Mackie's account, ch. 5 *passim*
role in understanding, 111–112
Clamping, 57–59
Cognitive dis-ease, 133, 137, 142
Coherence, 25–29, 180
Completeness, 45
Complexity, 20
Computations, ch. 2 *passim*
Computers, 35
Concrete realizers, 98, 109
Conditioning, 2
Confirmation, Bayesian account, 173
Conservatism, 180, 182
Constant conjunction, 128–129

Constitution/composition distinction, 265, 267
Cooperative principle (Grice), 226
Counterfactuals, 77–79, 84–87, ch. 10 *passim*, 128, 221, 224, 225, 234, 299–306
might-conditionals, 302, 305
Cross-product ratio, 2, 16

Davidson, D., 155, 157, 158, 159
Dawkins, R., 159–165
Day, T., 177–180, 182
Decisions, 241–245, 249, 251–258
distal, 243
proximal, 243, 255
δP model, 2, 3, 10–12, 14, 16, 20–24
Descartes, R., 120, 122
Desire(s), 242–243, 245, 250, 254, 257–258
proximal, 243, 250, 254, 257–258
Diogenes Laertius, 222–225, 227, 228, 233–235, 239
Douven, I., 177, 186
Dutch book, 172–174, 180, 181, 185–187

Eliminativism, 271–272
Emergentism, 268, 279
Epidemiology, 26
Error, 33
Events, 49–50, 53, 58, 62, 71–72, 85–88, 124, 126–130, 296, 298, 300, 302
Exclusion thesis, 269
Experiment, 51–53, 57, 59–62, 202, 204–205, 212–213, 299
Explanation(s)
brute fact, 144–148,150
conspiracy, 135–136, 140–142, 144, 146–147, 150–151
contrastive, 138–140, 142–148, 151–152
covering-law, 135
deductive, 138–140, 144–145, 151–152

deterministic, 138
historical, 43, 291–298, 307–308
Humean, 134–136, 144–149, 151–152
inductive, 137–138, 140, 142, 144
statistical mechanics, 136–137, 140–141, 143–148, 150
surprise-reducing, 133–135, 140–142, 144, 151
teleological, ch. 8 *passim*
understanding-conveying, ch. 7 *passim*
Explanationism, ch. 9 *passim*
Explanatoriness, 171, 172, 175, 178, 187
Explanatory
deductivism, ch 5. *passim*
parity, thesis of, 139
presupposition, 142
relevance, 137–138, 142–143

Freedom, 34

Goals, ch. 8 *passim*
Griffiths, T., 21–24
Group effects, 64

Hall, N., 80, 85, 88
Halpern, J., 45, 50–51, 88
Harman, G., 178–180, 182
Hausman, D., 192, 194, 197, 199, 207, 214n3
Heckman, J., 191, 193, 200, 202–208, 212, 214n8, 215n11
Hitchcock, C., 51, 74, 78, 139–140, 142–144
Hoover, K., 196, 197
Howson, C., 180, 187
Hume, D., 121, 127, 129–130, 134, 300

Impossibility, 295, 300, 306–307
Inference
ampliative, 175
to the best explanation, 171–173, 178, 179, 182–186, 298

Intention(s), 44, 157, 166, ch. 12 *passim*
distal, 243, 248
proximal, 243–244, 248–256
specific, 243–245
unspecific, 243–245
Intentional states, 159, 163, 164, 165
Interventions, 52–53, 59–60, 62, 123–124, 234
INUS account, ch. 5 *passim*
Invariance, principle of, 13

James, W., 40
Jeffrey, R., 228, 229

Kant, I., 34, 127–128, 130
Kim, J., 265, 272
Kincaid, H., 177–180, 182

Lagnado, D., 65
Laws of nature, 26, 43, 119–120, 124–130, 201, 203, 207, 294, 298–299
Layered world model, 265–268, 271–273, 278–280, 283, 285
Leibniz, G., 123–128, 130, 291, 295
LeRoy, S., 191, 197–202, 206, 215n5
Lewis, D., 44, 50, 69–70, 72, 75–76, 80, 85, 87, 193, 203, 302–307
Libet, B., ch. 12 *passim*

Mackie, J., ch. 5 *passim*
Malebranche, N., ch. 6 *passim*
Markov processes, 36
Maximal compliance, 225, 226, 229
McDermott, M., 75–76
Mele, A., ch. 8 *passim*
Methodological behaviorism, 218

Necker cube, 13, 15
Neural systems, ch. 4 *passim*
Neuron diagrams, ch. 3 *passim*, ch. 4 *passim*
"No confounding" condition, 6, 12, 26–28

Noisy gate, 3, 6, 24, 61–62
Non-contrastivity, thesis of, 139–140, 152
Non-identity of reasons, thesis of, 140
Nonredundancy, spurious, 112–115
Norms, 37–39

Occasionalism, ch. 6 *passim*
Okasha, S., 179, 180, 182
Oppenheim, P., 266–269
Oppenheim-Putnam model, 266
Overdetermination, causal, 72, 75, 84, 85–88
  constitutive, ch. 13 *passim*
  symmetric, 104–107, 268–277

Parameter estimation, 21–24
Parents, 44–45
Parity, explanatory, 139–144, 152
Pearl, J., 28, 45, 50–51, 88, 191, 192, 194–195, 202–203, 205, 207, 229
Possibility
  branching, 302
  causal, 223, 224, 232, 235, 236
  epistemic, 304
  logical, 81, 221–224, 300
Possible worlds, 77, 124, 199, 298, 300, 303–306
Power, causal, 1, 3, 4–7, 11, 26, 28, 29, 62, 120, 295, 299
  generative, 4, 12, 13, 25–27
  model, 21, 22
  preventive, 3, 5–7, 12, 13, 25
  theory, 3, 11, 25
Preemption, cases of, 93–107, 115–116
  early, 99–102
  late, 102–104
Preference(s), ch. 11 *passim*
Preference approach
  absolute, 220, 221
  ceteris paribus, 221–223
Preference attribution, principle of, 218–220, 224, 229, 235

Prevention, 43
Probabilistic contrast model, 3, 11
Programs, 38
Prospects, 218–220, 222, 225, 227, 237
Putnam, H., 266–269

Quantum mechanics, 36, 292, 296

Rationality, 172, 181
Realism
  causal, 204, 207
  modal, 306
  scientific, 172, 173, 177, 181
  teleological, 155, 156, 168, 169
Reductionism vs. nonreductionism, ch. 13 *passim*
Relativity, 36
Rescher, N., 236, 308
Rescorla, R., 2, 3
Responsibility, 43

Salmon, W., 128–129
Simplicity, 127–128, 178, 180, 182
  principle of, 158
Sinai billiards, 36, 37
Sloman, S., 65
Strevens, M., 140–142, 144–147
Structure learning, 21–24
Sufficient reason, principle of, 83, 126, ch. 14 *passim*
Superimposition, principle of, 16–19

Teleological
  explanation, ch. 8 *passim*
  interpretation, 162, 163
  realism, 155, 156, 168, 169
Teleology, epistemology of, 157, 158–165, 167, 169
Tenenbaum, J., 21–24
Transitivity, causal, 51, 58, 63, 74–76, 78, 192
Trapp, R., 226, 236

Urbach, P., 180, 187
Urge, 242, 244–253, 256–258
 distal, 248
 proximal, 249–250, 253, 256, 258
Urge*, 250–251, 253–255
 hypothesis, 250–251
 proximal, 250
Utility function, 159–162

van Fraassen, B., ch. 9 *passim*
van Inwagen, P., 292–293, 295–297
Variables
 intervening, 59–60
 policy, 60
von Neumann, J., 33, 38, 39

Wagner, A., 2, 3
Wanting, 241–245, 247, 249–250, 256–
 257
Woodward, J., 194, 207, 214n3
Will
 free, 40, 252–254, 295–297
 God's, ch. 6 *passim*
 theory of the, 40, 121–122, 296